"Why Study for a Future We Won't Have?"

OMPLICATED

CONVERSATION

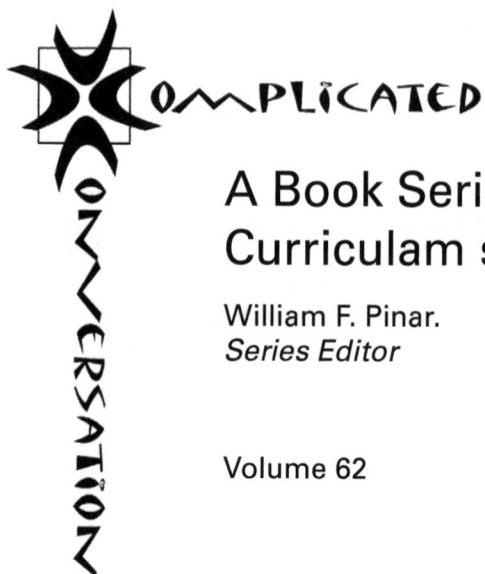

A Book Series of Curriculam studies

William F. Pinar.
Series Editor

Volume 62

David W. Jardine

"Why Study for A Future We Won't Have?"

Commiserations and Encouragement for Ecologically Sorrowful Times

PETER LANG

New York - Berlin - Bruxelles - Chennai - Lausanne - Oxford

Library of Congress Cataloging-in-Publication Data

Names: Jardine, David William, author.
Title: "Why study for a future we won't have?" : Commiserations and encouragement for ecologically sorrowful times / David W. Jardine.
Description: 1. | New York : Peter Lang, [2024] | Series: Complicated conversation, 1534-2816 ; volume 62 | Includes bibliographical references.
Identifiers: LCCN 2024013354 (print) | LCCN 2024013355 (ebook) | ISBN 9781636678115 (paperback ; alk. paper) | ISBN 9781636678108 (hardback ; alk. paper) | ISBN 9781636678085 (pdf) | ISBN 9781636678092 (epub)
Subjects: LCSH: Education—Environmental aspects. | Hermeneutics. | Traditional ecological knowledge.
Classification: LCC LB1027 .J298 2024 (print) | LCC LB1027 (ebook) | DDC 304.2071—dc23/eng/20240606
LC record available at https://lccn.loc.gov/2024013354
LC ebook record available at https://lccn.loc.gov/2024013355
DOI 10.3726/b21773

Bibliographic information published by the Deutsche Nationalbibliothek.
The German National Library lists this publication in the German National Bibliography; detailed bibliographic data is available on the Internet at http://dnb.d-nb.de.

Cover design by Peter Lang Group AG

ISSN 1534-2816 (print)
ISBN 9781636678115 (paperback)
ISBN 9781636678108 (hardback)
ISBN 9781636678085 (ebook)
ISBN 9781636678092 (epub)
DOI 10.3726/b21773

CONTENTS

ACKNOWLEDGMENTS

I am grateful to the following publishers and journals for their support over the years, and wish to acknowledge the sources of previously published chapters in this collection:

CHAPTER THREE
Jardine, D. (2023). An upwell near Father's Day and some thoughts on embodied reflexivity. *Qualitative Inquiry.* Special Issue: *Embodied Reflexivity Through the Arts* (E. Lyle, J.Y. Ryu, & C. Snowber, Eds.). https://doi.org/10.1177/10778004231176090

CHAPTER FOUR
Jardine, D. (2018). To know the world, we have to love it. In C. Leggo & E. Hasebe-Lud (Eds). *Canadian curriculum studies: A Métissage of inspiration/imagination/interconnection* (pp. 224–225). Canadian Scholars' Press.

CHAPTER FIVE
Originally published as: Jardine, D. (2017). "In the noontime sun in summer": Abundance reconsidered. *Journal of School and Society.* Special Issue: *How Can Neo-Liberal Ideologies Be Resisted?* 4(2), 4–14. http://www.johndeweysociety.org/the-journal-of-school-and society/files/2018/01/Vol4_No2_2.pdf

CHAPTER SIX

Jardine, D. (2020). "Owning up to being an animal": On the ecological virtues of composure. In H. Bai & D. Chang (Eds.). (2020). *A Book of Ecological Virtues: Living Well in the Anthropocene* (pp. 201–212). University of Regina Press.

CHAPTER SEVEN

Jardine, D. (2016). The more intense the practice, the more intense the demons. *Journal of Applied Hermeneutics*. http://jah.journalhosting.ucalgary.ca/jah/index.php/jah/article/view/136/pdf

CHAPTER EIGHT

Jardine, D. (2017). Thoughts on the return of yesterday's war. *Journal of Applied Hermeneutics*. http://jah.journalhosting.ucalgary.ca/jah/index.php/jah/article/view/141/pdf5tfcuuujj

CHAPTER NINE

Jardine, D. (2017). "A hubris hiding from its nemesis": Why does the affirmation of diversity tend towards the proliferation of multiple identities, and to what consequence? In E. Lyle (Ed.), *At the intersection of selves and subject: Exploring the curricular landscape of identity* (pp. 9–18). Brill/Sense Publishers

CHAPTER TEN

Jardine, D. (2022). Guest editorial: Beet juice. *Journal of Applied Hermeneutics*. https://journalhosting.ucalgary.ca/index.php/jah/article/view/74349. https://doi.org/10.11575/jah.v2022i

CHAPTER THIRTEEN

Jardine, D. (2018). We arrive, as it were, too late. In E. Lyle (Ed.), *Fostering a relational pedagogy: Self study as transformative praxis* (pp. 10–19). Brill Sense.

CHAPTER FOURTEEN

Jardine, D. (2015). How to love black snow. Introduction to M. Derby (2015). *Towards a critical eco-hermeneutic approach to education: Place, being, relation* (pp. xv–xxiii). Peter Lang Publishing.

CHAPTER FIFTEEN

Jardine, D. (2020). "It will startle you": Thoughts on a pedagogical conspiracy of birds. *Canadian Journal of Environmental Education*, 23(3). Open Issue (Online First). https://cjee.lakeheadu.ca/article/view/1505/908

CHAPTER SEVENTEEN
Jardine, D. (2019). "The … readiness … to be 'all ears.' " In M. Quinn (Ed.), *Complexifying curriculum studies: Essays on the generative and generous gifts of William E. Doll Jr.* (pp. 73–79). Routledge.

CHAPTER EIGHTEEN
Jardine, D. (2021). It might just be Ravens writing in mid-air. *Journal of Curriculum Theorizing, 36*(1), 1–9.

CHAPTER TWENTY
Jardine, D. (2018). Asleep in my sunshine chair. *Journal of Applied Hermeneutics.* https://doi.org/10.11575/jah.v0i0.53335

CHAPTER TWENTY-ONE
Jardine, D. (2015). Quickening, patience, suffering. In D. Jardine, G. McCaffrey, & C. Gilham, C. (Eds.), *On the pedagogy of suffering: Hermeneutic and Buddhist meditations* (pp. 109–121). Peter Lang Publishers.

CHAPTER TWENTY-TWO
Jardine, D. (2021). Tears run down Heaven's gaunt face. *Philosophy of Mathematics Education, 37.* https://socialsciences.exeter.ac.uk/education/research/centres/stem/publications/pmej/

CHAPTER TWENTY-THREE
Originally published as: Jardine, D. (2020). Shadowcast: Reflections from quarantine. *Journal of Applied Hermeneutics, 2020,* 1–5. https://doi.org/10.11575/jah.vi0.70918

CHAPTER TWENTY-FIVE
Jardine, D. (2021). Two arced fishes and a Raven's eye: Thoughts on selfies, pandemics, and a door, ajar. Special issue of the *Journal of School and Society,* "Education on the other side of the pandemic: A call to parents, teachers, elders, and other community leaders," 7(2), 4–18.

CHAPTER TWENTY-SEVEN
Jardine, D. (2018). Sunflowers, coyote, and five red hens. *Journal of Applied Hermeneutics.* https://doi.org/10.11575/jah.v0i0.53327

CHAPTER TWENTY-EIGHT
Jardine, D. (2020). Things reveal themselves passing away. In M. Bussey & C. Mozzini-Alister (Eds), *A phenomenology of grace: The body, embodiment, and transformative futures* (pp. 123–135). Palgrave.

CHAPTER THIRTY-ONE

Jardine, D. (2018). To be dying under their wings is a weird miracle. *Journal of Applied Hermeneutics*. https://doi.org/10.11575/jah.v0i0.58417

CHAPTER THIRTY-FOUR

Jardine, D. (2023). On temporarily regaining a measure of well-being. *Journal of Applied Hermeneutics*. https://doi.org/10.11575/jah.v2023i2 023.77349

CHAPTER THIRTY-FIVE

Jardine, D. (2023). An early childhood education. *Journal of Curriculum and Pedagogy*. https://doi.org/10.1080/15505170.2023.2191355

CHAPTER THIRTY-SEVEN

Jardine, D. (2023). "To lend ourselves to its life": Some nearby thoughts on early literacy and other early matters. *Journal of Educational Thought*, *56*(1), 13–26.

CHAPTER THIRTY-NINE

Jardine, D. (2022). From the town by a spring. *Holistic Education Review*, *2*(1), 1–13. https://her.journals.publicknowledgeproject.org/index.php/her/issue/view/140

CHAPTER FORTY

Jardine, D. (2015). Nobody understood why I should be grieving. In D. Jardine, G. McCaffrey, & C. Gilham, C. (Eds), *On the pedagogy of suffering: Hermeneutic and Buddhist meditations* (pp. 157–166). Peter Lang Publishers.

CHAPTER FORTY-TWO

Jardine, D. (2018). It's February. It won't last. *Journal of Applied Hermeneutics*. Online https://doi.org/10.11575/jah.v0i0.53332

All other chapters are published here for the first time.

CHAPTER ONE

Introduction: "Why Study for a Future We Won't Have?"

Triggered now, firm thrust and smooth unfolding,
fell swoop and talon strike.
A mere moment swept away, devoured.
Echoed perhaps in a ripple of air,
or brief shrug of robust bough.

—JUDSON INNES, FROM "TIME" (2016A, P. 117)

Outing a Trick as Old as the Hills

This book is a collection of new and previously published essays about education, schools, study, and their interweaves with our ecological circumstances and with the long, often deeply buried, mixed and contested ancestries of thought and action that we drag along in our living, often without quite realizing it.

My work, both in writing and in the day-to-day work in schools with teachers and students, has been focused on exploring how much contemporary teaching, learning and curriculum are, however unwittingly or unwillingly, complicit in our "ecologically sorrowful times." Schooling, broadly put, is fashioned after what turned out to be an ecologically disastrous form of fragmentation that despoils the living disciplines of knowledge with which schools have been entrusted. It also despoils the grace notes of teaching and learning itself by degrading the living fields in which teaching and learning might occur. Degrading the affection and deep pleasures of coming to know. This great analogy—between the degradation of ecological interrelatedness and the degradation of the interrelatedness of knowledge and experience and study—forms one core of this book.

The other core is this. My own work, over decades, has been directly focused on how "ecopedagogy"—a rethinking of theory and practice regarding teaching, learning and curriculum—offers, I believe, a hale, viable, sustaining, and rigorous alternative to these inherited complicities. I have seen it working—vibrantly, joyously, with tough and good work for and from all concerned—in school classrooms, in teachers' writings and discussions, in students' ventures, and in the work of us "university" folks.

It is not easy, but arranging and orchestrating a whole and hale classroom is never easy *no matter what way you do it*. Tugging against an often simply unknown undertow of worn-out ideas, images and practices simply make trying to shift away from these legacies all the tougher. It makes for cynicism: why study at all?

The good news is, there are myriad sources to draw from, myriad examples to try out, to emulate, in this long-standing orbit of, I have found, hopeful, relieving and generous work. There is nothing "new" about this move toward an ecologically viable understanding of teaching, learning, and curriculum. In my own case, I've been "at it" for nearly 35 years, and I am utterly surrounded and supported by a vast body of good, solid work, far beyond the scope of my own voice.

This book is simply a small breath of threads, of course, because the breadth and variety of sane, vivid classroom work and the philosophies that underwrite it goes beyond any one voice. This be but one set of paths and trails to follow, full of hints and side trails, each side trail with its own kin and relations (see Latremouille et al. [2024] and all its cited offshoots and bloodlines; see also Seidel and Jardine [2016], which is full of writing by practicing teachers and school administrators about such matters).

The sorrowfulness of our current ecological circumstances is undeniable, as is the uprising of often well-warranted anxieties, feelings of powerlessness, of being trapped or overwhelmed. I'm currently editing my way through this writing you are reading while news of Yellowknife, N.W.T. and Kelowna, B.C remain headlined, as news of the tropical storm heading to California is yet to be in full herald. And the fact that these references are utterly out of date is, somehow, somehow, part of the fix we're in.

There's smoke in the air where I live in the Eastern Slopes of the Rocky Mountains, 53 degrees N., 4200' or there abouts. At one point, the dogs stood inside in the doorway looking out, staying in. Animal bodies wise to the warn. The air quality index here in Bragg Creek topped 215 (https://www.accuweather.com/en/ca/bragg-creek/t0l/air-quality-index/2289595). It is now down to 27.

Why sit here writing? Why be *relieved* by this clearer air? This clearer head? Short answer: I have two grandchildren living 10 km away. I must do any work I am able to do. I write. We all must find that locale of our own agency. And, let me say it outright. I must do it no matter its outcome, no matter its future. What else might I do instead?

My own weep and wail are not going to last.

There is something else mixed in here that is also seems far more pronounced—nebulous, hazy scatter shots of often deliberate deceptions and distractions that are preyed upon so easily, that, in often deeply buried ways, *profit at our often-hidden expense.* They are mixed, too, with a myriad of promises that take an old, familiar shape. If you wail, I alone can fix it. Sound familiar?

Try to read this as a sort of ancient echo of an ancient bait-and-switch: "What you're seeing and what you're reading is not what's happening" (Trump, 2018), coupled with claims of being redeemed, finding justice and retribution by whomever is making that promise (D. Smith, 2023), that same source being one who must *maintain* our anxiety *and* seem to remedy it in one deft gesture.

That it is difficult to carefully consider *this maneuver itself* without getting caught up in all the barking surrounding who exactly said it in this case—that is also part of our troubles. It is a marketing maneuver bent on suckering anyone who can't snap out of its well-shaped and well-designed spell. We—I—get sucked in, mesmerized, angry, and thereby disabled. The disabling, of course, is part of the trick. This trick is as old as the hills, as old as our animal-body susceptibility to falling for it. It is simply uninformed and harmful to believe that this is something new or that it is a trick only "they" use or "they" fall for, even though its current drastic-ness is undeniable. That very "us and them" is *itself* manipulated to the profit of some and the agony of the earth and our earthly being.

Yet another trick as old as the hills. And I cannot let myself forget that the grievances preyed upon themselves are real, so the untangling and uprooting of the trick means that *the root troubles remain*. This last move should, of course, be one of the greatest concerns. It is not just tricks all the way down.

It is an old wisdom to remember that the present is *always* on the edge of portend, of looming. And being wrapped up in its temptings can elicit a "naive self-esteem of the present moment" (Gadamer, 1989, p. xxii) where my own so-called "gut reaction" can take over, blindly or otherwise. To stop. To consider. To come to know with great intimacy and detail. These things can get scared off in the stampedes of immediacy.

Even the Ravens who've come for years are a bit a-skitter and askew.

Thus be our current tangle. The environment heats our air and our imaginations, news seems fake, fakery seems promising, electronic inundation pelts from all directions, geared to cultivating wanting more and more, faster and faster:

> One becomes kind of world-weary. You go through a stage where you just look at this world and think it's crazy! "I'm living in a madhouse! Society is nuts!" And you think "No! Not this again! Don't they ever learn? Do we have to go through this again?" If you attach to world-weariness, you attach to just another thing. (Sumedho, 2010, p. 95)

Schools and those who populate them are both *suffering under* an ecologically disastrous inheritance, *and* they are often unwittingly *perpetuating* and *perpetrating* that very disaster. And this, I suggest, has seeped deeply into the very logic used to understand the living disciplines entrusted to school, how to handle them, how to teach and learn them. It has seeped so deeply that it has fallen out of view, this inherited logic, and it is *this* that must be interrupted. It is *this* to which a more ecologically sane theory and practice of teaching and learning and curriculum must set itself. As you'll see in the chapters that follow, research and theory itself is part of the culpability, here, and finding new ways to study must themselves find interrelatedness, intergenerationality, sustainability, place, interrelatedness, aliveness in the very act of studying well itself.

There is no doubt at all that the glib, standard story of [ever-accelerating] reality, is full of powers and potentialities, interests and persuasions, histories, interests, and profitability, lies, deep truths, insights, stupidities, and on and on. There is little doubt at all that what is needed is something like a "hermeneutics of suspicion" (Gadamer, 1984) aimed at carefully and in great detail, untangling us from these blinder-binds. And this, as long experience has shown, must be done over and over and over again. It is relentless work, to remain alert and on the vibrating edge of suspect and resolve, worry and relief, somnambulance and insight. Again, an old story in which we can take heart. The tough task we face is nothing new, and we have companions— ready and able bodies of flesh and work and friendship, writing and conversation, birds called and foxes trotted.

But, of course, again, here is what has also happened, that questioning our circumstances has itself become easily marginalizable as "conspiracy theorizing," itself often unwittingly manipulated by the very potentialities and powers that want to remain profiting from the surface stories.

There is, it seems, no time to sit, to think, to carefully consider, to commiserate and to encourage. Yet here I am, keyboard to hand, and you, book browsing or leafing through or sat down for a long feast of words. It is heartbreaking to be old enough to have experienced this in a very long arc of time, this acceleration I first experienced in so many schools so long ago, about the cast of mathematics education in schools (Jardine, 1990a), about curriculum integration (1990b), about the relentless pursuit of more and more writing in the early grades (Jardine &

Rinehart, 1993; Jardine, 1994), the frazzled mood of classroom activities (Jardine, 1996).

Right at the point of weariness, here comes, lasery-eyed from the camera's insistence on flashing, late afternoon, August 31, 2023:

> It is not so much that this bear is an "other" (Shepard, 1996), but that it is a relative, that is most deeply transformative and alarming to my ecological somnambulance and forgetfulness. It is not just that I might come awake and start to remember these deep, Earthy relations. It is also that, even if I don't, they all still bear witness to my life. Relations. Who would have thought? Coming across *one of us* that I had forgotten. Coming, therefore, across myself as also one of us. Such a funny thing to be surprised about again. In the face of this Great Alert Being, I, again, become one of us. Great Alert Being, this bear. Great Teacher. His and my meaty bodies both of the same "flesh of the [Earth]" (Abram, 1996, pp. 66–67), rapt in silent conversations (p. 49). Where, my god, have I been? (Jardine, 1997, p. 124)

FIGURE 1. GREAT ALERT BEING

Of course, my spine uprighted taking that picture. Of course. I was being studied, no doubt.

What a strange and sad and sorry mess. And yet here comes an email the day before the picture:

> ... this is what it is like to encounter prophets. We went wading in rivers and got caught in the most horrific terrifying thunderstorm and hiked for over 30 minutes in ankle deep mud and hail and water shaking with cold after sheltering and shivering in totally a not safe place where another human joined us and had just seen a bear. We sat in tall grass (like the deer!) in a little piece of aspen grove, where we could just see the tips of each other's heads. (Jackie Seidel, personal communication)

It is difficult, I know, to not read some of the language in this book and the sources it cites as sheer exaggeration. But there is a deep seam of artful philosophizing requisite of it. Like this: bears, every fall and spring. Migratory: "every repetition is as ... original" (Gadamer, 1989, p. 122) and new as that great alert being above. *At the very same time,* every repetition makes every repetition seem richer and fuller. Each bear sighting is perfectly and only and exquisitely *itself* and "it has its being only in becoming and return" (p. 123). What does this mean, for heaven's sake? That last year's bear ambles shift up and rise and get remembered, just like last year's garden bespeaks this year's. Just like one grandson makes the two-year-old now an older brother. "To be present" to this "means to participate" (p. 124) in an "increase in being" (p. 140) because, of course, I've *become* a grandparent of two, just like that. And everything old murmurs and creaks and rises up in witness. This is what ecological insight looks like. This is what hermeneutics offers as a theory of human understanding and experience.

Every that age-old citation from 1997, alongside that new email just arrived, add themselves to the complex ecosystem of experience, knowledge, remembering, recounting, relating, and weaving. I must say, though, that some days those old papers read like antiquated headstones, weathered, mossy, and a bit unreadable. Of course, attaching myself to *that* is being tricked all over again. That murmurs of graveyard walks which can have their own insights under the moss-gatherings and dates and hints and sorrows. That bear seems like a death-omen and a prophet all at once.

However, here I am, two grandsons in hand. My own narrow abilities can't budge many of the tangles twisted up here—economic, market-driven, gender-tilted, racial, Indigenous, political, media-aroused, colonial, power-laden, deceitful, malicious, or simply dull-minded. I must remember that the good-hearted, well-intended, beautifully expressed, lovely things, are themselves tangles, too. This betangledness is the heart of ecological work, of hermeneutics, of teaching and learning at its ripest and most ready.

We all find ourselves meagre in these times, but, well, again, *here we are*. Luckily, this area of work is broad and deep and strong and teeming and on hand. What is contained here is—of course—just one fabric fold of threads.

"It's Here, Eh?"

Dozens of Calgarians gathered on the steps of City Hall to demand government action on climate change Friday afternoon. Similar climate strikes in more than 130 countries around the world took place under the Fridays for Future banner, calling on politicians and industry leaders to do more to stop global warming. "I don't believe that the people who don't believe in climate change have any logic," said Day Kloetzel, one of the students at the rally. "Climate change is real. There's lots of evidence already. I'm here because I want people to think the truth," she added. Kloetzel was surrounded by other students who hoisted handmade signs with messages like, "Why Study for A Future We Won't Have?" (CBC News, 2019)

And what comes to my mind right away?

> But what to do, what to do?
> The geese say only, "study"
> ROBERT BLY (2008)

"Everything points to some other thing. Nothing comes forward just in the one meaning that is offered to us" (Gadamer, 2007e, p. 131). Damn geese. I tracked an overhead gaggling pair just yesterday at my grandsons' house. Spellbound under an arc of sight and sound overhead, itself rich enough to last a lifetime. The two-year-old, in imitation—one of the great human arts—touched his ear with a finger when he heard. Not just "I hear something" but also a gesture for me to "listen":

> Genuine literacy is most creatively a discursive activity that does not rest with a pedagogic literalness that puts language at the service of the will. Reading the world, inscribing and being profoundly inscribed by it, has to do more with deep attunement or hearing and involves a kind of obedience to life's deepest resonances (< Fr. *Obeir*, "to obey"; > L. *ob audire*, "to hear from"). (Smith, 2020b, p. 158)

The maps of migratory lines are things of great beauty and knowledge. Reminding me—get back to that manuscript and figure out what to do about it. These geese are near to migration lines. This book, too, is a long stretch. That bear, winter coming, is migrating uphill, not south.

Such is my own lot. I write. I do what geese tell me to do. Well, some of the time. Meanwhile bears migrate uphill, so to speak. Whether these lines be their futures, though, I don't know. They will migrate. Or not be. I will cease. Breaths will curve. Such be futures.

"Why Study for A Future We Won't Have?" I expect that this title phrase gave you a start. I did me, for sure. I knew I had to hold it close and live with it long before I knew what I might have to face to do that. It straightened me up a bit.

I'm playing amid peas and carrots in the garden, these days, with my two-year-old grandson and watching the warm squirms of his young brother, under 2 weeks old in my bent arm, my shirt pulled up and over to block the orangish smoke-sun. I wrote the word "currently" beside each age and each age aged by the time I got back to the writing. *This is not off topic.* We move into a future one way or the other, and *that* is the futurity that needs study, repeated, open-hearted. Picking peas to shuck and freeze for the winter sure to come, even though this summer's weather trembles that future, trembles our dreaming, trembles my eyes sore from smoke.

Red and itchy. Looking for places to settle.

Part of what follows in this book are chapters that rose up out of lingering around this new life in, and under, and amid these "ecologically sorrowful times." These babes in arms and in hand make that main title all the more necessary to face, full on as much as I possibly can, in ways that I can, I always hope, help out and be a bit useful. I have to protect myself, too, measure my own measure, and not just end up spent at a breach I cannot attend. There's a chapter on the guilt and necessity of loving this time with the vibrant "aliveness" of two wee ones in the face of screaming news, chapters on how "aliveness" and "inter-generationality" are key and core to what study must study.

I've even ventured to say that it is not clear, with my grandsons nearby, exactly *who* is giving or receiving an early childhood education right now. Feeling meagre again, happy armfuls and river water rushes—ah, of course:

> Lean, thin, emaciated" (of persons or animals), from Old French *megre, maigre* "thin" (12c.), from Latin *macrum* (nominative *macer*) "lean, thin" (source of Spanish, Portuguese, and Italian *magro*), from PIE root *mak- "long, thin." Compare emaciate. (*Online Etymological Dictionary* [hereafter OED], under "meager, adj.")

I know it might seem frilly and foolish, but our mixed and shared languages hide secrets were living in and living out as much as does the pea garden's yields. Language, too, is an overwhelming *ecological plenitude and mystery*, if you treat it the right way, full of lodged memories, and long-forgotten pathways, especially now, up against arising tongues and tales long suppressed or marginalized—of birds, of tongues, of voices, of owl-swoops, outside the euro-orbit that can read back into this orbit something hale, healing one hopes.

Meanwhile, an old friend, Chris Gilham from Saint Francis Xavier University in Nova Scotia has been visiting family in Medicine Hat, here in Alberta. I sent him an early draft of this book's proposal and we commiserated over the drastic, foreboding flooding back home in Nova Scotia.

And with a single, singularly Canadian phrase, he summed:

> "It's here, eh?"

Yes. It's here. And here we are sat square in the midst. Educators, parents, grandparents, two-footeds anxious over the smoky air, dogs hesitating at the doorway, bear, head down ass up headfirst into compost, just like me reading Tsong-Kha-Pa all over again, digesting, filling my belly, nourished. Scholars, writers, readers, teachers, learners, those with handmade signs on the steps of City Hall. All squaring off with that title, that "why," Chris' both utterly clear and also nebulous "it" that's "here" in specific and palpable ways, as well as in a brand-new and age-old blur and murmur of blood-curdles.

"Sorrow" is rooted etymologically in the idea of "care," but this only if it does not paralyze me. It is one of the deep roots of hermeneutic insight—care, German *Sorge* as in the nature of our being human (its source in the contemporary hermeneutic tradition is Martin Heidegger's *Being and Time* [1926/1962]). To maintain myself in this wee slipstream of insight and light, I must, over and over and over again (this is part of our lot,) refract my study away from its Medusa-like spells. We are not just bound. Stories of Medusa can *free us* just a tiny little bit so that we can clear our heads, talk with each other, parse what we're hearing, relieve some of that which we were just flailing in. This, of course, is why there are *stories* of Medusa that let us get nearby enough to learn. Studying, properly allowed, can provide us companions that let the immediacies of my own experience work itself *out into a world of companionship*.

In what follows, *this* is a key to how I hope this book will be read. It is how it was written. It is why much of what follows details the work of *hermeneutics*, not only as a way of studying teaching, learning, curriculum schools and so on in sane, rigors, interrelated and interdependent ways, but how hermeneutics itself a deeply ecopedagogical "philosophy" of how thinking and experiencing work, how we get stuck in traditions, how we might enliven those which portend life, how livable relations between the young and the old, the new and the established might work, what the dangers are, where suspicion might lie and how, of course, suspicion can itself devolve away from its alerting function into one more dead end about fake confidences in fakeries.

To maintain myself in this wee slipstream of insight and (however dim the) light, I must think again, write anew, gather up the loved ones nearby, over and over and over again remember, commiserate, find that old Don Domanski poem and read it out loud, let my voice quiver over the words and the breaths between them. This "over and over" is itself part of our lot, not a failure to be efficient and effective enough. This is part of what our work requires. We are not building a new speedway Utopia, because, as the phrase betrays, that is "no place, fast." We are not expecting something that will last forever, because forever is not an especially Earthly pursuit. In fact, that sort of hallucination born of fear and trepidation is only one of the circumstances that brought us here to this sharp brink.

Those of us who are teachers and students know about how here, mid-August writing this, there is a portend of new arrivals coming soon. We realize that working things out again, and again, is not the error of our ways but its profound strength and resilience, one we learn precisely from our ecological circumstances, one we'd better learn by paying good attention to these new arrivals. We be finite *no matter how enlivened our work*; this is the reason for some chapters below—they aren't meant to be "morbid" but, instead, enlivening of our actual lot, making its Earthly fabrics real and palpable and full of encouragement, commiseration, and the poetics and fresh airs that can swirl up around us, even in the middle of the acrid smell this summer.

The new and the established. The young and the old. The coming and the going: Like my two grandsons, we can experience, experiment, commiserate, share, laugh, cry over a bumped forehead and cuddle wet and hot for a hug. We can love birdsongs and seek out the conditions of their arrivals and the ways of maintaining both them and our attention to them. We can share this affection over their swoops, study aerodynamics and migration patterns. This by itself won't "save the world," but what would you have us do? Nothing "by itself" will do that. It does increase the prospect that my actions will become more considered, more delicate, more adoring. Cleaving near it would make schooling more in line with the ecological bloodlines that are oozing all around us, to study this, deeply careful, well, over and over, here, there, *every single curriculum topic can be treated this way*, as a living field worthy of careful attention, and that acts of teaching and learning can re-gain some of their gracefulness and toughness and love.

Some of this fanciful sounding parade has been a long-standing-one in my own odd wander through these matters as a scholar, parent, teacher, student, grandfather, companion, writer, co-author, friend, fellow-being—and this last of air and Ravens, too, nearby Elbow River waters, old memories of cicadas of my young (ref), and even the cougar that killed one of our dogs years ago. This:

"Keeping ourselves open" and "keeping the world open" (Eliade, 1968, p. 139) are the same thing. As we become experienced, having cleaved with affection and made ourselves "roomier," the world's roominess can be experienced. (Jardine et al., 2008, p. 53; cited in Jardine, 2016a, p. 81)

The first glimmer in my own writing about the intermixes of matters philosophical/ecological/pedagogical was 35 years ago as of this writing (Jardine, 1988a). It would take a while for me to insinuate these insights into my work with students, student-teachers, and teachers in schools and then on into graduate classes, co-writing, and so on. It would take me a long time to learn from teachers and students whose vibrant and hale work came to blend into my own philosophizing, how my writing became enthused by the examples manifest day to day in the early days working with Patricia Clifford and Sharon Friesen in their classrooms, and the writing we would then do (Clifford et al., 2008; Friesen & Jardine, 2009, 2010; Jardine et al., 2006a, b, 2008; see especially Clifford & Friesen, 1993, written before I had arrived with student-teachers in hand):

This was the insistence of Pat and Sharon: "We want a theory for *this*"—what was going on in their classroom—was what they insisted. The reason for this is that they knew something enticing and rigorous and vital was going on, but they had had enough of professors trotting in an asking to set up some sort of research project or telling them about theories that did not begin with and stick with witnessing what was actually going on in their classroom. (Jardine, in press-b)

All this, then extended over countless classrooms, came to color how I thought of curriculum, how interrelatedness and interdependence and living relations figures in the voices and work of teachers and students alike, how ancient I took "becoming a teacher" to be, how able

I slowly became able to understand how vital, how *pleasurable* it was to remain a student. Right here, right now, writing, loving the passages of word, their lilts, their stops and starts.

Their startlings. One thing one does in this sort of work is honor one's ancestors, name them, cite them, repeat the citations as a way of remembering, recalling. So when Indigenous voices rise up, re-recalling of the breaths and voices that led me here, to writing this very line, murmur and stark, like the river's low water this summer, shallows voicing louder than usual (Jardine, 2014a), reminders of unmarked graves.

The attest of this book is both well-considered and naïve and it is based on working with hundreds of folks involved in education, inside and outside of schools. If we allow the beauty of our earthy being to become a teacher, education becomes beautiful, a relief, an open space. It does not solve every problem. It does not cure every ill. But study, properly done, can be our shared locale of commiseration and encouragement, and—I'll whisper it—hope.

There's another wee secret here. This ecopedagogical work is deeply pleasurable right in the midst of all its limitations. It makes the geometries of tree-shadows exhilarating, bewildering, and attractive. It is playfulness is dead serious. Playing around, here, is not fooling around in order to simply seem fooling and fooled. We've already got plenty of that.

However, Hans-Georg Gadamer links this nebulous sense etymologically to the German word for "play" (*Spiel*): as sense that "something is going on, [*im Spiele ist*], something is happening [*sich abspielt*]" (Gadamer, 1989, p. 104).

And having all these brackets and dates and pages numbers is *part of this inter-play*. Just like the V-ed bear, it draws me in an it plays me out. Read them like trail markers to other fields:

> There is, in play [in interpretive understanding and exploration (see Gadamer, 1989, pp. 101–164) for an exploration of how "play" serves as a model for human understanding], an experience of "detachment" from the compelling necessity of the "standard story of reality" (Fish, 1980), a story whose standardness compels us to see it, not as a possibility in which we have found ourselves, but as simply necessary, simply "the way things are," and, therefore, simply and obviously the measure of other provinces. Hence the "paramount" character of everyday life (Schutz and Luckmann, 1967), the

power of the notion of "literal meaning" (Fish, 1980), the binding character of tradition (Gadamer, 1989), the tranquillizing character of what "they" say. (Heidegger, 1962; Jardine, 1988b, p. 30)

I understand. I'm old and susceptible to all the woes that come with it. But that block citation above *was written in 1988*, 35 years ago. My son was 5. It was written up against the dominant, hard-shell certainties of how schools must work, hard-shell certainties that are still at work, as petulant and as frightened as ever. I've seen these ecopedagogical reliefs come and go, from school to school, from grade to grade. I've seen how commonplace it is for schools to not only retrench but act as if nothing ever happened. Thus be the character of "dominance" that has also come to dominate and re-dominate the sort of interpretive work I have pursue. We all know about the dead-weight we repeatedly confront.

Here is the terrible omen, though. That standard story has become one of anxiety and the bought and sold promises of its cure. But we have all become quite spellbound by these circumstances, and, of course, they bind us, frighten us. The animal-body retreats under threat. The retreat increases the fear. The fear causes retreat or, as we are witnessing all around us, violent human actions and violent environmental currents. A reminder recited:

What benefit? What seductive or intimidating bonus? What social or political advantage? Do they want to cause fear? Do they want to cause pleasure? To whom and how? Do they want to terrify? To make one sing? To blackmail? To lure into a going-one-better in enjoyment? Is this contradictory? With a view to what interests, to *what ends* do they wish to come with these inflamed proclamations? (Jacques Derrida, cited in Foster, 2018, p. 41)

"What Is Not Understood Cannot Be Healed"

Staying with the trouble is a way of remaining truly present to our experiences and interpretations, "not as a vanishing pivot between awful or Edenic pasts and apocalyptic or salvific futures, but as mortal creatures entwined in myriad unfinished configurations of places, times, matters, meanings" (Haraway, 2016, p. 1). These ways of writing are an attempt to take up Donna Haraway's critical and creative challenge to make kin in lines of inventive connection as a practice of learning to live and die well with each other in a thick present. Our task is to make trouble, to stir up potent responses to devastating events, as well as to settle troubled waters and rebuild quiet places. The standard academic language that has me so well-schooled is rooted in the history of economic exchange; it is a language governed by laws easily bent "in order that treaties might be broken, and wounded beyond healing." (Hogan, 1995, p. 45; Jodi Latremouille, in Latremouille et al., 2024, p. 46)

> [Watch carefully. Baby blues—two grandsons borne, blue-eyed, since first writing almost all of this. What do you imagine it is like for me to read the very words that I myself wrote *now*? Or that Jodi casts up into the air? *That* is the phenomenon that ecopedagogy points to—ongoing, transforming interrelatedness.
> Flower to bee.
> To honey.
> TRANSUBSTANTIATION. *ALIVENESS*.]

Plants to compost to bear to plants:

FIGURE 2. HEAD DOWN ASS UP

"Living and dying with each other in the thick present." Together. Gathered. The thickets of contemporary education that have been inherited and whose inheritance has calcified into (a false belief that it is simply) "the real world" is in no way just "the way things are." Things turned out this way. Things shifted and can shift.

New things can be learned, faced. New effacements of old certainties can arise. "The laws easily bent," can bow and bow. Unearthings can happen. Even unmarked graves and stuffed toys tethered to fenceposts, and all the griefs and joys that come from their cleanse and cleanse again, can become spoken, even just a little bit.

Many of us involved in, broadly speaking, "ecopedagogy" (there are, of course, myriad names roiling inside those quotation marks) have gained wonderful proximities to peoples and places and languages and ideas out beyond Western strangulations. You'll see it in Jodi's citation above and through the book of which it is a part. Part of these ventures have involved for me returning to my own philosophical and cultural bloodlines, looking for signs of life, for lingers hidden buried in my own language, ideas and imagination. As with any tradition, it is not simply Edenic or Salvific although its lean is hard, but vital to bear. I've given some detailed attention to is colonial leanings in this regard elsewhere (Jardine, 2008a, 2012a, c, 2013).

It is not an easy task to rebuild in quiet places. It never seems enough, but that, too is a lesson unearthed in the chapters that follow, that the endpoint of study is not now being done with coming to know. It is always and inevitably still coming.

Like this. Out of the dear blue Alberta sky (sight unseen lately), another old friend perused an early proposal for this book and sent me back what is a hard-to-trace "old saying" in Western medicine: *Ignoti nulla est curatio morbi*. Please excuse my clumsy translation of this as "What is not understood cannot be healed."

What schools have found themselves living in the middle of has become stuck and moribund and now, dangerous, and unlivable. Allow me a very quick example (elaborated below in many places). Think about commonplace complaints that students seem, "these days," to "lack initiative." Here is a very brief statement by a person *whose work came to underwrite the structure of contemporary schooling*:

In our scheme we do not ask for the initiative of our men. We do not want any initiative. All we want of them is to obey the orders we give them, do what we say, and do it quickly. (Fredrick Winslow Taylor, 1906; cited in Kanigel, 2005, p. 169)

When I first read this, I had never heard of the author of this statement, me, the academic who had been writing, teaching and studying in a Faculty of Education for, at time I found it, about 25 years. I had never heard his name mentioned, *not once* in all those years.

This little statement from 1906 hit hard, and put into stark, *legible* relief the foolish tragedy of blaming students for repeatedly asking "tell me what to do and I'll do it" in the bowels of an institution *unwittingly premised and designed around precisely those chilling words in that citation from above.*

Deep breath first. We all have to forgive ourselves for not knowing this and *then* do the work necessary to know it well, because that will loosen its bind on us and will allow us a shared space of commiseration about our profession, our work, our students. Just imagine letting one's students see that citation. Hah. Letting my student-teachers, who themselves have all been well-schooled, see it, read it, let it inform their walks through the school hallways of their practicum classes. And, of course, as happens with this sort of work, you get used to the curative pleasures of introducing folks to the relatives:

David G. Smith's [2020a, p. 98] chilling statement of a commonplace in which we are all variously implicated: "Tell me exactly what it is you want in this assignment."

There is not an endpoint to this venture. One slowly becomes accustomed to this "yet-to-be-decided" (Gadamer, 1989, p. 119) character of our living, becomes accustomed to what living takes and gives. Study and conversation and learning and teaching can help with this give and take when it becomes knotted up. It can become vibrant, alluring, however-little or however-much healing in fact. My own work with student-teachers, teachers and administrators in countless school practicums, in graduate courses, as co-writers and friends, and across all schools grade levels, in all curriculum areas, up through undergraduate classes, MA courses, Ph.D. work and supervision—I've seen it, the tough work of stepping away from studying for a future we won't have and stepping toward words, ideas, practices, images, commiserations, explorations that have hale in them, the very lessons that the earth offers of itself in all directions all at once.

I've seen it work. I've seen beautiful, healing work. Patience. Composure. Just imagine this in these tough times and the hysterias swirling around us like storms bearing Valkyries—loud, frightening, sword-bearing daughters of the Earth and the Gods, winged-horses. Music used—of course!—in the movie *Apocalypse Now*.

A headshake. An affectionate voice. A dear colleague of mine heard from her supervisor, a mutual friend, a simple piece of advice ... the door is open, we are here:

> I'm recalling Carl's advice to Jackie that I heard about years ago, re: all the smothering crap of graduate work—just turn away. It can harm you if you don't step out into the wild. You'll end up with a critical-theory induced crone's hunch that is built from thinking you can undo *samsara* single-handedly with just one more thing, just one more thing.
>
> (David Jardine, from Latremouille et al., 2024, p. 129)

And a poem writ to Carl from the same text, a section called "A Death in the Family":

Daresay February 26th, 2019, 7:03AM.
Still, no word. Still. No word.

> *A Poem Found Near Sea Level (for Carl)*
> The word still
> Is enough.
>
> ... speaking of this "still,"
> ... this "and yet,"
> ... this "persisting,"
> ... this "quieting,"
> ... this secret source of pirated spirits deep in the woods,
> all giggled together, distilled into words at sea level.
>
> (David Jardine, from Latremouille et al., 2024, p. 182)

Carl Leggo died on March 7, 2019. He be buried, marked. I'll just mention a collection of mostly practicing schoolteachers' and administrators' writing: Seidel, J., & Jardine, D. (Eds.). (2016). *The ecological heart of teaching: Radical tales of refuge and renewal for classrooms and communities.* This is certainly a wee bit self-aggrandizing, but it is also how this work works—opening doors, letting aching bodies pass by, letting children's voices erupt out of the Earth, sharing, sending names, expressing your griefs and joys, hints, readings, examples. I've seen it work with very young children (discussing the Latin origins of the word "monster" in kindergarten), and with old hands in schools.

I've seen it *heal* students, teachers, and even the lives of living disciplines of knowledge entrusted to school. The open-air-ness of this sort of work—it has helped me, it has helped them, maintain composure and camaraderie and bristling encouragements.

Would that I'd learned more from all this earlier, but, well, that lament is always true. My grandsons are nearby and safe and patient with me.

I pull back into this: https://www.youtube.com/watch?v=T8oK Ex1-J1w&ab_channel=TonyCello and let the breath catch me all over again, here, luxuriating as the lux gets smoky all over again. Music that's been a steadfast companion since I was around 20 years old.

Variations on a Theme by Thomas Tallis.

I just sent the URL to David Smith, whose voice you'll hear again and again as you read:

Always gives me chills and weeping. Cuts right into my bone marrow.

David has given me so many ways to think and speak and writing in ways better than I ever knew. That, too, is part of how this work works.

Talk back and forth of the possible wee boy's name "Tallis," Welsh, means "shining brow." Nope. No name yet.

Go Slow, Ever Vulnerable

It is a lousy joke, but the slow food movement is not a matter of cooking fast food slowly. What is sketched out in what follows has an indigenous sense of how the time and tempo of Earthly things and our care for and about them must guide us in our teaching and learning of those very matters. Under the regimes we've inherited, *time itself* and our lived experience of it got viciously rendered into ever-accelerating machinations. Slowly down, thought of from inside that accelerated vortex, seems *at the very least* opulent, more often simply insane to even suggest. If there be no Earthliness, no sense of a living topography, to hold attention and reward it in those holds, all we can do is "hurry up," like the obedient worker on an assembly line.

This insight into time and our lives inside it, is a deeply hermeneutic one (Gadamer, 1970, 1989; Heidegger, 1962; Jardine, 2008, 2016a, b; Ross, 2006; Ross & Jardine, 2009). Carefully and lovingly attending to things.

> This can't be hurried. Learn all you can about where you are, make common cause with that place, and then, resign yourself, become patient enough to work with it over a long time. This is the dreadful position that young people are in and I think of them, and I say that the situation you're in now is going to call for a lot of patience, and to be patient in an emergency is a terrible trial. The important thing to do is to learn all you can about where you are, to make common cause with that place, and then, resigning yourself, become patient enough to work with it over a long time. And then, what you do is increase the possibility that you'll make a good example. And what we're looking for in this is good examples. (Berry, with Moyers, 2013)

"What is not understood cannot be healed." A wound that is ignored festers. A wound that is not admitted will grow as monstrous (Latin, *monere*, to show, to teach) as it needs "to show, to teach" (Latin, *monere*) until, well, City Hall signs finally catch an eye, letting it sit alongside the children's stuffed toys bound to fenceposts nearby as marks of unmarked graves. Loving the utterly luxurious and opulent ability to hold my grandchildren, my family, nearby and safe, for now. Facing the small guilts that arise out of this rare calm. To face dying and living. Looking for awakes.

It means to become, finally, ever vulnerable. Why? Ever vulnerable is, one way or the other, *what we most deeply are.*

There will be a future one way or the other. We can gather and weave and unweave. We can help each other not be blinded by the panic-vortexes that want to sweep us away. That is no future.

Instead, as naïve as it may be called, we can cultivate an "ecological pedagogy of joy" (Latremouille et al., 2024). I can increase the possibility, no matter how unlikely, that I might make a good example, here and there, now and again. David Smith, again, in an email on August 26, 2023:

> No healing without understanding" or, positively, "With understanding comes healing." A good parable for hermeneutics, no? If our work doesn't contribute to human healing somehow, it's off target somehow, the real meaning of "sin" > Greek, *hamartia*, lit. "missing the target."

And me writing back, feeling feeble. Aliveness is not a giddy, ecopoetic dream (although there is a deep, often silent *pleasure* to be had, not just walking among wind-trees, but walking through geometries and grammars and periodic tables). It means venturing exactly toward the open wound that living always is:

> … then, it becomes an issue of what exactly is the wound, as well, who has insight into what the wound might be. "Why study for a future we won't have?" is so full of myriad wounds. Including us being alive to read it after all our years of friendship and affection.

It means, at the same time, gathering my wits about me and not being simply spent at these breaches, knowing full well that doing enough can only mean doing what I can, what I'm able to do. Take to the steps if you have the energy and desire. Wail at the fires. Love those who help. Comfort and encourage.

So, here's to falling ever so deeply in love again, and again with *exactly those locates of suffering*, despite everything, with no spite. Writing is all that's left me, and the hold of a warm child, eyes of family, rivers, Ravens, peas.

"Wounded beyond healing." Still:

> *That spark in a synapse somewhere …*
> *saying* look, you have time, even yet
> To come to love this too. (Lee, 1998, p. 109)

CHAPTER TWO

"Sacrificing Their Futures to Protect Ours"

FIGURE 3. FALL DRIVEWAY DREAM

We've sacrificed our children on the altar of Covid.

> Camilla Tominey, Associate Editor, *The Telegram*, June 25, 2021. https://www.telegraph.co.uk/news/2021/06/25/sacrificed-children-altar-covid/

Did we really sacrifice our children on the altar of Covid extremism?

> Harry de Quetteville, *The Telegram*, June 19, 2022
> https://www.telegraph.co.uk/news/2022/06/19/did-really-sacrifice-children-altar-covid-extremism/

Sorting out what's what, thinking it through carefully, being vigilant and alert, thoughtful, discerning, commiserating but encouraging, is an endless knife-edge parade. It can be a parade of clowns so easily. And every word in these sentences is itself currently up for debate and worry and argument and sometimes vitriol, sometimes simply silence, mistrust, and withdrawal.

We're battered between extremes. Even that photograph above can be a false flag of some sort, a sort of sucker-punch set up, trying to evoke what? Nostalgia? Deep feelings?

Aww.

The child facing away, reaching a bend in the road, nearly to be out of sight.

It is so easy to get swept away in these ecologically sorrowful times. As easy as it has always been perhaps.

Then this, too. There are long-standing tales about the sacrifice of the child, the sacrifice of new life, of innocence, etc., at this altar or that. That God stayed Abraham's hand at the last minute and left him having to live his long life knowing what he would have done. Killed his child. This act from a God who then let his own son be killed instead. And tells me I must love Him and his boy for doing so, or I will be sacrificed.

We've all lived through or nearby thoughts and images of protecting ourselves and our children. But then this comment from an old friend when we were discussing COVID and its terrains back in July 2020:

Children are virtually immune here, with a few tragic exceptions. The rationale for keeping schools closed is that they could act as carriers and infect adults, but not going to school is going to create a crippled generation of youth, emotionally, physically in some cases, and intellectually. Children need more engagement than parents can typically provide in today's world. Just wanted to push on the notion. When I started reading your piece, I actually leap to the idea that the "sacrifice of children stuff' meant what I think we are doing: sacrificing their futures to protect ours."

One of the agonizing consequences of study is that surface flutters of news items and passing images and words take on a resonance that is difficult to avoid and easy to just give in to. This is the double-edge. Paying careful attention, but then trying to be attentive at the same time to the often-deliberately-distorting lures that come with attention-getting. Even the large statement that forms the main title of this book is susceptible, here, as is the title of this chapter. How to think about those titles and their stings and winces and not just wince—and this in a way that might do some good, whatever that might now mean.

These tells and words and images are often simply incendiary, and their incendiariness is enhanced by responses to them that leave them untold, unspoken. They betray something that is thematic in what follows, cited here only to be recited below:

> I'm reminded, too, of Ivan Illich's terribly acute idea of "apocalyptic randiness: 'I have an even more horrible example to tell you! Let's imagine an even worse situation!' " (Illich, with Cayley, 1992, p. 127).
>
> Edward Said calls this "vocabulary of giantism and apocalypse" (2001, p. 4). Chuck Bowers calls it a "Titanic mind-set" (2008, p. 11).
>
> This tale is as old as the hills, how the monster feeds on fear and grows in proportion to the (unwittingly) loving attention that the fearful give it.
>
> Pausing over writing this, I'm thinking, am I in love with my panic? Does it make me feel alive and useful and "connected?"

Here's the trick, however, about being tricked into this randiness. Hermeneutics itself is premised, in part, upon *exactly something of this trick*: "because he is pointing to something, he has to exaggerate, whether he likes it or not ... to leave out and to heighten" (Gadamer, 1989, p. 113). Students new to hermeneutics always think, at first, that they get to be Hermes, the trickster. The tough lesson is that I am subjected to the trick more often than not, pulled up short from my own sleepiness, exhaustion or weakness, and that this keeps happening, over and over and over again.

The question here, writing this, becomes: what is the purpose of such heightening in what I go on to write? To arouse? To frighten? To alert, to warn, to teach to heed—like the roots of the word "monster"?

It is no coincidence that hermeneutics is premised on a measure of "suspicion" (Gadamer, 1984) about what is taken for granted in everyday life, but it is also important to note that we are now into a swirl where *suspicion itself is becoming suspect*. I'll even venture to say that the goal of "study" is *well-practiced suspicion* that remains alert to its own vulnerability and to the myriad seekings and hidings of this world of ours.

What to do, then? How to resist simply falling for what we have unwittingly inherited and try to think our way through it, untangle it, without simply becoming simply unraveled altogether and at every turn.

Here is a simple example under the title of this chapter. Maintaining the status quo of schooling by sacrificing our children to its ways? See how easy this is? The child that has trouble with schooling and its ways becomes an easy goat to scape. This child becomes sacrificed to its shapes and forms. That child is banished to the special needs class. Hah! Check this, almost too easy to find:

> In the Bible, a **scapegoat** is one of a pair of kid **goats** that is released into the wilderness, taking with it all sins and impurities, while the other is sacrificed. (https://en.wikipedia.org/wiki/Scapegoat).

See how easy this is, how mixed and myriad and, in fact, wonderfully complex and enduring and messy? What is the suspicion *for*, that brings up all this muck? On behalf of what? Wouldn't it be wonderful if there was some external measure that could, without effort or error, relieve us, here, of this situation?

Joni Mitchell gave me a hint, recently:

> You can make it like Van Gogh's paintings, which are exaggerated to make the emotional experience of these landscapes realer for the deadened. It's not

really that blue, the sky, and the stars aren't *really* that big. But you're not seeing them. So in a way it is to get you to see the truth.

> The Joni Mitchell Interview: A CBC Music Exclusive. An
> interview with Jian Ghomeshi. Published June 11, 2013
> at: http://www.youtube.com/watch?v=pEJuiZN3jI.

The art of learning to become well-practiced in doing this delves into
the underbellies of our living is utterly full of the dangers of sleepiness
and elitism, all at the same time. There is a chapter below, for example,
on "getting back to normal." And schools, with the hidden inheritances
they often unwittingly inhabit, are quite adept at marginalizing and
trivializing and excluding that which might interrupt them—the uprising "child." Familiar, too, is displacing students who can't "keep up"
on the scales of grades and expectations to "alternate" classes or, in the
end, to simply "dropping out" if they can't concede to the sacrifice.

This an old story. *And* what is newly arriving can sometimes be stupid, petulant, and naive. *And* what is old can be deadly in its assurances
and fixities. Yep.

And then there is the luxury of the artist to pretend to the art of
"awakening." Hah.

And, of course, deserts and the wandering of them have long been
identified as locales from which wisdom might come, places from
which one might return renewed and refreshed—but often then suspicious of the "normal" to which one returns.

Such unwindings as these have provided me with little reliefs, with
locales of commiseration and encouragement and the illuminating, in a
soft light, of pathways that might bring some hale and breath. They also
provide deep confirmations, that my woes and my joys have a warrants
and companionships and articulations beyond my own skin. I also have
the commiseration of mountains, of a safe life of relative well-being. I've
also had a long life of having the luxury of stepping away from the
frays toward open air.

They also provide the warning that constitutes, it seems, being
alive at all. Learn to be alert. Learn about how tricky that is. Take up
Derrida's question of "Who profits?" from my learning, from my distraction, from my fears and insecurities? From me trying to write about

this here? And rest assured that the exact citation for this idea will occur in what follows and that that path and its warrants will be out in the open as much as I can manage it. A meagre form of assurance, of course, from someone well-endowed in precisely the "education" that seems to have no future.

So here we are. "No learned or mastered technique can save us from the task of deliberation and decision" (Gadamer, 1983, p. 113)

A wee nibble to end, for now. These things will be cited again as you read on, recurring path-markers, memorial recitations:

> Under such false assurances, education becomes akin to a sometimes overt, but more often subtle war on the very possibility of unanticipated "uprising." Free spaces and those who cultivate them become suspect. Natality becomes experienced as a perennial insurgent threat to security that must be planned for and secured against. Education becomes cast as akin to a counterinsurgent war on terror—a perpetual war (Postel & Drury, 2003), given the perpetuity of the world's mortality [and the perpetuity of children arriving, arriving, arriving]. After all, a war against our response ("terror") to the very existence of uprising is, of necessity, perpetual. It is also profoundly Thantic—a long for the end of this roil, for finality, fixity, death. (Jardine, 2012a, p. 5)

> Pedagogy left in peace ... sets out an image of education, not as the pacified outcome of a bureaucratic system, but as a perennial, personal and intimate task ... always and inevitably needing to be taken up here, now, once again and anew—the perennial raising anew of the question of what is worth our while in this limited life, what possibilities might help us go on together. There is thus a terrible intimacy to a pedagogy left in peace. It is, after all, my life, the only life I will have, that is being or failing to be shaped, and thus, too, for every student and teacher. "It is everyone's task," for the lives of teachers and students will be shaped one way or the other. Education's only prospect is that we might have some hand, some however-small say in the setting right of the world and the shape of our learning to live therein.
>
> We might. (Jardine, 2012a, p. 6)

I would say, now, here, in this book, *we do have such a hand, however small.* The small hands of my grandson up that driveway.

We're planting tomato seeds indoors in about a week or so.

Planting for a future that we might have.

Sacrificing the seeds for the next plants whose fruits we will eat and whose seeds we will gather for the year after that.

And whose inedible parts will go into the compost.

In which deer sometimes stand.

And Ravens.

And bears.

And off to the septic tank's run-offs.

And so on.

CHAPTER THREE

Meanwhile Saints Graze on the Begonias[1]

A delve down into a long-standing legacy of schools and education. This chapter details the work of Fredrick Winslow Taylor and the efficiency movement and the effects that this had on the shape of study, the shape of schools. It is a long, drawn-out tale. If you're a teacher, or a student, slowly, something will start to be very familiar.

1 An early, much briefer version of this chapter was published as Jardine (2017). The reason for the name-change was in honor of a recently deceased teacher of mine who I never met, yet met and met over words. See Seidel et al. (2014, pp. 100–118). See the Elegy at the end of the chapter for more information.

Preamble

FIGURE 4. ECLIPSED

In the process of writing this chapter a several years ago, I decided, a bit ironically, I suppose, to take a break and get a bit of sun during the eclipse: August 21, 2017, around 11:30 a.m., MDT, and me, 52 degrees north in the Rocky Mountain foothills, west and south of Calgary, Alberta, Canada.

And then I just happened to notice these shadows on the deck cast through a leafy lilac bush.

My camera doesn't quite do this justice, but the bush's overlapping leaves made countless, overlapping pinhole-camera images betraying arcs of the moon's shadow in what appears to be a three-dimensional image.

It is a simple example of the happenstance exuberance of things— and it fell right in line with what I was trying to write. It is exhilarating to think about how much is folded into the curves of this image, and how freely and freshly available it was.

Treating this image not as an isolated thing but as a gateway into worlds of relations takes patience and practice. "Without the readiness of the person who is receiving and assimilating the text to be 'all ears,' no ... text [or thing or image] will speak" (Gadamer, 2007a, p. 189). Such readiness, too, is a practice that must be practiced if we are to become practiced in it. When such a photo first appears, it seems like a tough nut to crack. But stepping toward it, showing it to others, asking around, enjoying it, expressing one's dear amazement, thinking and writing about it can slowly, slowly unfurl. It will respond to careful, affectionate attention. It will blossom and come to a glow. You'll find this idea repeated as you read.

And, of course, as soon as one's attention moves to another topic, another locale, another curriculum thread, you have to start all over again. You get used to it, this recurrence. You can get more deft at it, slowly, painfully slowly sometimes. But what increases is the odd comfort of knowing that the relations are *there*, and they'll be there when you get there. As if patiently waiting, like a Raven on the deck railing finally letting me see its rictal bristles after decades of attention and devotion. Utterly beautiful humiliation is always right around the corner, again and again.

I think, too, about how very easy this would have been to miss.

Teachers already know something of this when listening carefully to students, this student and the enlivening difference they sometimes bring, the insight, the tough enriching of my own study and bearing.

It is how to read the sky with some acuity, how to decode the whiffs of smoke in the air this whole summer.

Becoming thus practiced takes the patience and fellowship of others reading my own experiences of things back to me in ways that go beyond my own ability and experience. It takes work. It takes study. Curriculum in abundance, like teaching and learning itself, is a rigorous practice.

And part of its practice requires parsing our way, again and again, through those often-unspoken forces that mitigate against its pursuit. It seems too slow to some, too inefficient and too, well, "touchy-feely" instead of hard-nosed and efficient. Many schools and school curricula have been framed in light of these semblances.

But if you think, only for a moment, about the knowledge and careful work needed to take good care of those deck photos and to come to understand what is happening in them, these claims, however broadly and easily and unquestioningly assumed, show themselves to be utterly ridiculous. Pitiable, even.

And I must add one little secret, here. The utter, delicious, *pleasure* to be had in carefully working in the presence of such intriguing matters acts as a counterbalance to the often-dour countenance of the efficient regimes of what's sometimes touted as "the real world of schools."

Part One: "Regimes of Scarcity"

In educational circles, "regimes of scarcity" (Illich, with Cayley, 1992, p. 119) have promoted [the belief] that things *are* simple and monitor-able and manageable. Abundance and diversity become drained out of the topics [being taught] and become signs, rather, of the pathological variety of "learning styles" we each bring with us to the classroom. We are suggesting something different—that the topics entrusted to schools *are* abundant and, therefore, suggestions of multiplicity and diversity are not opulent educational *options*. Rather, the [diverse and multiple] ways of traversing a place that students bring to the classroom *is precisely what [abundant, multiple and diverse] things require if they are to be "adequately" understood in their abundance.* (Jardine et al., 2006a, p. 88; Italics are mine)

It has been over ten years since my colleagues, and I glanced upon the idea of curriculum in abundance. This image of abundance struck a chord with practicing teachers, but the chord it struck was not one of Romantic hopes and sloppy dreams.

Rather, teachers, then and since, have spoken of the ubiquitous experience of scarcity, of time and materials and energy and knowledge itself always on the verge of running out, causing a mood of embattlement and the need to be, as a consequence, hunkered down, barricaded, doling out teaching and learning in a zero-sum game of competition, exchanges of piece-work for marks, and an ever-accelerating pursuit of an ever-receding promise, leading to exhaustion, frustration, and, in some schools, an unfulfilling culture of complaint.

Under regimes of threat—not enough time, high-stakes tests, competition for spots in further education, and so on—vibrant, rich and exploratory attention is hard to maintain. Without practice, it atrophies, and such atrophy makes exploratory attention increasingly unpracticed, thus increasing a sense of scarcity and threat, thus tying tighter the knot.

The tragedy comes when, once atrophied, one is resignedly glad of threat-induced procedures, rubrics, manageable routines and assessment tools, since pedagogical experience, in students and teachers alike, has not been able to be well cultivated in such circumstances.

Harry Braverman (1998) called this process "deskilling" and showed how it forms a deliberate and strategic part of the maintenance of efficiency in industrial production. It makes workers easily replaceable and compliant, because they are only asked to follow a few simple rules that anyone could follow. They no longer need any cultivated craft or skill or practical experience.

Hence the echoes we hear in David G. Smith's chilling statement of a commonplace in which we are all variously implicated, echoed here once again: "Tell me exactly what it is you want in this assignment" (D.G. Smith, 2020a, p. 98). Even more chilling is how this echoes a June 4th, 1906 lecture by Fredrick Winslow Taylor, the "father" of what came to be known as the efficiency movement. Taylor was, in a sense, hired to make American schools more efficient by replicating his work in industrial assembly: "In our scheme we do not ask for the initiative of our men. We do not want any initiative. All we want of them is to obey the orders we give them, do what we say, and do it quickly" (cited in Kanigel, 2005, p. 169). Like two Ravens coming back to the feeder and looking me in the eye all over again, these cites.

Given Taylor's words about the "scheme" he insinuated into the organization of schooling, blaming "kids these days" for lack of initiative—while at once living out the legacies of efficiency in how schools are structured—is, frankly, a tragic form of cultural amnesia.

Part Two: "So Permeates the Soil"

Educational rituals reflected, reinforced, and actually created belief in the value of learning pursued under conditions of scarcity (Illich, with Cayley p. 165).

Part of the hard work of understanding curriculum in abundance is having to repeatedly unravel this long legacy of fragmentation and scarcity that comes down to us from the efficiency movement.

The efficiency movement of industrial assembly (Taylor, 1903, 1911) became codified into how curriculum topics were broken down into separate bits and pieces and sequenced in the content and procedures and testing of their reassembly and how, therefore, anything that could not be thus codified—tarrying, for example, over a deck shadow and consider how arcs and circles create a seeming three-dimensionality— was marginalized or eradicated as a threat to efficiency itself.

Rich, thoughtful and rigorous explorations become cast as "frills" which we'll get to later, if we have time. And, it seems inevitably, there is never time for such things. This should already seem vaguely familiar to most teachers in most school. The regnant regime of efficiency has the power to marginal anything that might interrupt it. But not only this. It gets to *name it* ("frills") in light of its own desires in a way that maintains its marginality. Such marginalization and naming have the power to exhaust any energies that might interrupt that power.

Now there is nothing wrong with efficiency per se, but there is something amiss regarding its hidden dominance, especially insofar as it invades living fields of thought, living disciplines of knowledge, and renders them into fragments that *seem to*—this emphasis is important— bear no inner affinity to each other, each ready for separate, sequenced and standardized assembly:

We hear in this the future prospects of F.W. Taylor's efficiency movement which codified this fragmenting logic into both the substance (separate bits and pieces) and the standardized method or means of industrial assembly (F.W. Taylor sought "one best way" [see Kanigel, 2005] of any assembly, and required its identical application by any worker) which then was adopted, almost holus bolus, by educators at the beginning of the 20th century.

Education then starts to take on the character of industrial assembly. From Ellwood P. Cubberley, Dean of the School of Education at Stanford, from his book *Public School Administration* (1922) originally published in 1916:

> In time it will be possible for any school system to maintain a continuous survey of all of the different phases of its work, through tests made by its corps of efficiency experts, and to detect weak points in its work almost as soon as they appear. Every manufacturing establishment that turns out a standard product or series of products of any kind maintains a force of efficiency experts to study methods of procedures and to measure and test the output of its works. Such men ... [also] train the workmen to produce a larger and a better output. Our schools are, in a sense, factories in which the raw products (children) are to be shaped and fashioned into products to meet the various demands of life. The specifications for manufacturing come from the demands of twentieth-century civilization, and it is the business of the school to build its pupils according to the specifications laid down. This demands good tools, specialized machinery, continuous measurement of production to see if it is according to specifications, [and] the elimination of waste in manufacture. (Cited in R. Callahan, 1964, p. 97; Jardine, 2012c, p. 86)

With each particular curricular fragment, we experience lack, scarcity, and "not enough," and this propels the subsequent urgency to "get through" the curriculum. And, once locked into this dominant regime, the urgency created and maintained by this regime—can only be satisfied by further fragmentation and standardization. Taylor suggested that it helps keep workers and, hence, teachers and students on their toes. And, just in case this sounds like ancient history, consider this:

> Alan Greenspan [5-term chairman of the Board of Governors of the U.S. Federal Reserve System, August 1987-January 2006] testified to Congress, explaining [that] the basis for the success of the economy he was running .... He explained that it was based on was growing worker insecurity. Growing worker insecurity. Meaning, if workers are beaten down enough and intimidated enough, so that they can no longer ask for decent wages and decent benefits, then it creates a healthy economy by some measure. (Chomsky, 2017)

This regime of efficiency/insecurity leads, inevitably, to failed, market-driven promises of sure-fire "teaching methods," with no experience needed for success, just compliant obedience. Just do what it says to do, and everytrhing will be fine. And if it is not fine, *you can rest assured that it is your fault,* because the system of efficient production is tried, tested and true, so to speak. You can rest assured that inefficient workers—inefficient students *and* inefficient teachers—are part of the waste that needs elimination.

Addition, we are told, has nothing to do with subtraction. It is taught first because it comes before subtraction in the curriculum guide—in a developmentally determined and standardized sequence of "assembling" what passes, in this regime, as "mathematical knowledge." This way of thinking, I suggest, is a mathematical disaster, and a pedagogical and ecological one as well. Relations severed in all directions.

Part of the work in which I have engaged with teachers is precisely sorting through and studying this legacy—its hold on how the work of teaching and learning is imagined and practiced. We read, for example, Raymond Callahan's now-classic text, *America, Education and the Cult of Efficiency* (1964) and dozens of other sources that elaborate what has happened to education. To us and our students and to the knowledge entrusted to us in schools. All under this regime.

"Taylor's thinking so permeates the soil of modern life we no longer realize it's there" (Kanigel, 2005 p. 7). Hence the gasps of recognition (my own included) and that weird moment of realizing that what seemed to be just "the way things are" in the world of schools is in fact nothing of the sort. We are not dealing with "the real world" under "regimes of scarcity." Rather, we are dealing with how the world of schools happened to have turned out—once it is fashioned after the model of efficient industrial assembly, with the control, surveillance, acquiescence and obedience it requires.

To understand curriculum in abundance, a weird sort of spell must be broken.

A cautionary note, however. Breaking free of the spell of efficiency leads to an experiential onrush of the great abundance of the world. But it also leads me to experience my own poverty regarding my knowledge of what, now, to do in the face of this reality. Where do I start? Who should I talk with and about what? How much is enough? How might I talk about my own developing teaching practice in ways that are strong and well-grounded and well-informed?

Breaking this spell causes its own sort of momentary panic. But there is good news, here, too. I don't have to try to gobble up and amass as much experience and knowledge as possible—as quickly as possible. I recall telling a group of student-teachers that when you glance at a globe and see the Tropic of Cancer and Tropic of Capricorn lines around it, you don't have to worry. When you are ready and able, the knowledge that unfolds from attention to those lines is right there, patiently waiting for you—of constellations, of maps and mapmakers, of the tilt in the Earth's pole, of seasons, of the tropics (Latin *tropos*, "turning"), of the Sun (Latin *Sol*) stopping (Latin *stasis*) its lowering, turning, and starting to rise at Winter solstice (Latin *Sol-stasis*).

Right there on that globe, just in those two lines, sits such a wealth of history, science, language, names, dates, places, seasons, sailing, that no lifetime could outrun it, so no longer running slowly, sometimes agonizingly and repeatedly, becomes understood to be the best thing to do. In schools (and, more and more, outside of schools) such advice seems slightly naive, even insane. It is why, even with this simple example, if you are going to try something like this with your own students, it is important to orchestrate things so that you and they can start to sense the profound and giddy yield of such careful attention, that it is not lolling around but meticulous and intense. It is not the all-too-familiar acceleration of "the multiphrenic intensities and sensations of the surface of the images" (Usher & Edwards, 1994, p. 11) but a deepening and a slowing. It is a matter of *becoming studious* in how we let ourselves experience the world. "We can entrust ourselves to what we are investigating to guide us safely in the quest" (Gadamer, 1989, p. 378). We can glance at deck shadows and know that there is great abundance there, ready for our attention and devotion.

But again, caveats. As a teacher, I need to become practiced in this sort of work, in this sort of risky knowing. Otherwise, I will have no practiced skill at attending to the uprisings of students' questions and how to help cultivate and sustain them. Part of this, daresay of course, includes being able to heed how students' questions can often by the very source of my own learning more about the ways of the topic under consideration.

Paradoxically, my openness to hear what is happening is not an empty-headed acceptance but is itself something *cultivated*. Sometimes *unknowingly* cultivated. Here is an example that, I expect, readers will recognize something of.

In large, Grade 1–4 classroom, Pat Clifford, Sharon Friesen and I were enjoying Pat's reading of a version of Beowulf to the students, and how Beowulf came to the throne of the King of Denmark and asked whether the monster he was to confront had weapons.

The answer was "No." And Beowulf chose right then to lay down his own weapons. One student in the class, Grade Three, shouted out "That's nuts!" and many murmurs of agreement spread over the 70 students gathered in the spell of the story.

A Grade Two student piped up: "He'll be stronger if he doesn't have his weapons." Thus shot old and familiar quick glances between Pat and Sharon and myself. We knew without doubt that *something really interesting just happened* even though we didn't quite know what. The class uproar about this Grade Two student's contention was rippling. We knew we had to stop, that something was going on, something was at play in this talk of weapons and strength, something age-old and contentious and beautiful and worth some time whiling over, parsing, exploring.

Thus, there is a profoundly aesthetic face to curriculum in abundance, the experience of being struck by something, being drawn in by some thing or image or idea or utterance. More on this later. Because, again, the pullback is always close at hand:

> As one student was coloring in a map of Canada in his [Grade Four] classroom for the purpose of understanding the [country's] borders, another has found an on-line site where a then-contemporary dispute between Denmark and Canada over the sovereignty of Han Island is being described and discussed. Sad to say, since Han Island wasn't "in the curriculum" (as the teacher put it), the coloring continued. [What arises is] an all too familiar pull back into old forms and old ways, either as a cynical response to efforts at reform, or as a retrenchment after the promises of reform are broken, or as a reactionary response to how new proposals leave behind traditional values and ways. This is very often accompanied by an equally familiar move wherein old practices and their familiar outcomes are understood to be more "basic" and therefore in need of being done first: once you color in the map

and memorize the names of the provinces, *then*, if we have time, you can look at that website. (Friesen & Jardine, 2009, p. 7)

And one more caveat for now that needs to be said with the full weight of its contentiousness. If we, as a class, do not select a topic that is *worthy of careful, sustained attention and exploration*, or if we disassemble a worthwhile topic into worthless bits where all that is needed is assembly, not affection and involvement, attention and devotion will be quickly spent, quickly repelled.

How do you know if a topic is thus worthy? As a function of *the very same practice*. I'll let this paradox sit for now. It is not a mistake. It is what happens when you fall in love with a new type of music, or you come to slow down in a place and Ravens come nearby and draw you in, or a young child suggests that strength and weaponry have a stranger relation that you might have thought. You get drawn in before you might come to know why or how or whether the venture was worth it. (Hence, below, a chapter title, "We Arrive, As It Were, Too Late").

Outside of the rushes of schools, you give yourself up to it and try to learn what is being asked of you and see if the love affair lasts and strengthens. Sometimes it works. Sometimes it peters out. Sometimes I'm not up to the task. Sometimes I misjudge the object of my affection. But this is not as strange as it seems. It is profoundly ordinary. It is what we humans do when we are drawn to something that catches our attention and we start to lend our lives to its presence.

So, the lovely question of a student-teacher in that Beowulf classroom. "How did you know that that was a good place to stop?" Well, how *did* we know? And *what* did we know? And what did we venture without especially knowing full in advance what might happen next? It becomes clear how the regnant regimes of efficiency are utterly unnerved by this sort of thing.

Part Three: "Our Work Perishes Quickly"

Perhaps it is only when we focus our minds on our machines that time seems short. Time is always running out for machines. They shorten our work by

> simplifying it and speeding it up, but our work perishes quickly. (Berry, 1983, p. 76)

Since no shortened and simplified fragment of industrial assembly requires much attention, this leads to a cascade of hurry and panic over bits and pieces—no one of which requires any careful attention. This then leads to grasping for regimes of management to secure one-self against precisely the rush that is produced and sustained by such regimes.

This phenomenon is palpable in many schools, and in much of contemporary living beyond those walls—not just speed but *acceleration*. There is a great irony here that entangles us, our emotions, our attention, our livelihoods, in the most intimate of ways.

Regimes of scarcity, fragmentation and efficiency produce precisely the sense of time running out that they seem to be designed to ameliorate. Time running out is precisely yet another way in which efficiency induces a sense of scarcity, and thereby an unquestioning obedience and compliance from those under its sway.

Part Four: Monsters in Abundance

"Time is [not] always running out" (Jardine, 2013; see Jardine, 2016c). The real work of teaching and learning does not perish quickly. In fact:

> Time is a bringer of gifts. These gifts may be welcomed and cared for. To some extent they may be expected. They cannot in the usual sense be made. Only in the short term of industrial accounting can they be thought simply earnable. Over the real length of human time, to be earned they must be deserved. (Berry, 1983, p. 77)

Years ago, I was speaking in the school hallway with a kindergarten teacher about monsters, that most delicious of topics for us all. She asked me to come in and talk to her students about it. I sat with him and the children and tossed around ideas of what you think of when you hear the word: scary, big, hairy, green, under the bed, in that story Papa tells, trolls, bridges, bears in the woods, darkness, being chased, my little brother, run, help, grr!

I diligently wrote all this down on the paper beside me and then told the children that this word, "monster," comes from an old Latin term, *monere*, which means "to warn, to show, to teach."

This, too, was scribed on the paper behind me.

After we all had a laugh looking over at their teacher, "the monster," we talked about the fact that monsters aren't just there to scare you in a story. They are trying to tell you something, or tell someone in the story something.

Who sees the monster? When do they see the monster? Where does it live? What does the monster want? I asked them to have another look at books they had mentioned and think about what the monsters are up to.

I also suggested that they write down the word, *monere*, and take it home and tell their parents that they are learning Latin in kindergarten. We laughed and laughed at the thought. In the weeks and months that followed, I stopped in, saw myriad books, and heard countless tales of heeding, of showing, of teaching.

Six years later. Same school.

A young boy came up to me in the hallway holding the latest *Harry Potter* volume in his hands.

"You're the monsters guy, right?"

He flipped the book open.

"I want to show you something. Look at this."

Our work perishes quickly only if it remains in separate fragments in which no future tug of past memory can be experienced. Isolated fragments need no such tug. They reject it. Curriculum in abundance works to help us see through this situation, to see how any seeming fragment is, in fact, a fragment *of* something and is, therefore, *always already full of relations and kin, full of stored, shared, and contested memory and stories, rife with appearances and re-appearances in our lives and living.*

And it is reliably and consistently thus *even if we don't have time.* Even if we don't know what might be there for the finding. This now-Grade-Six boy's stop in the hallway was unexpected and yet totally otherwise. Noticing and ongoing border dispute is as simple a thing as can be—there, borders, this is a real thing, a real dispute, here, now. Time is the bringer of gifts once untethered from the rush. Imagine the—unintended?—message to that student who went back to coloring the map of Canada. And, don't forget to imagine the pedagogical grief that has been visited upon that teacher as well. Just doing their job, I suppose. When we start unpacking these matters, we can feel some affinity for those suffering under these unspoken regimes.

Just a little aside, then. I always advised teachers and student-teachers in such situations to not directly approach a colleague with debates about teaching methods or the like. The best thing, very often, was to simply show them some of the work students were doing and, often, leave it at that if need be. Imagine an email back from the Danish embassy about the Han Island matter? Or, I recall a detailed response from a graduate student in Manitoba doing paleontological work—he sent a Grade Two class copies of maps of his digs and several photos. The students, meanwhile, learned specifics about how to compose a good letter (a curriculum mandate all on its own, but *the world of thoughtful, careful communication* is asking that it be good, not just "school"), and had days and days of mapping out his maps that he sent.

Something about this is so simple, and the things that students produce can often carry the day to the next question. Beautiful things draw our attention in spite of ourselves, sometimes.

Many teachers have voiced an immediate recognition of something like abundance in moments of their day-to-day work with students: when a question or conversation takes flight, when an exploration yields to careful attention and blossoms open into unforeseen territories, when a text or a geometrical figure suddenly gives up its secrets and opens up and out and beyond our immediate ken and asks us to search, to study, to be patient and rigorous and attentive.

When deck shadows suddenly stand there, beckoning me to be all ears and eyes and photos and stilled breath.

Given this experience of interdependence, interrelatedness, and abundance, teaching and learning are no longer rushed matters of industrial assembly, but more akin to an ecological acts of recognizing the "places" (Greek *topos*) we inhabit. How they work, what they ask of us, what holds them together, who we might consult to deepen our knowledge, who has worked this place before our arrival, and what our work we might therefore be in for if we are to take good and proper care of these curriculum "topics" (Greek *topos*):

> Coming to know a living field of work and its gatherings [is thus linked] to the transformation of the one coming to know into someone who "know[s] one's way around" (Gadamer, 1989, p. 260): "this means that one knows one's way around *in it*" (p. 260), in the gatherings of and in the dependently co-arising gathering presence of mind regarding, a living field of work. (Jardine, 2016d, p. 250)

This is an ancient and always-brand-new experience enjoyed and enjoined far beyond the confines of school. Careful and affectionate attention does not exhaust the topographies of human experience scantly sketched in curriculum guides. On the contrary, well treated:

> [The world] compels over and over, and the better one knows it, the *more* compelling it is. There comes a moment when something is *there*, something one should not forget and cannot forget. This is not a matter of mastering an area of study. (Gadamer, 2007c, p. 115)

What this insight can accomplish is the dropping of the pretense that if we just work hard and fast enough, we can eat up the whole world such that there will be no more need for affection, no more need for exploration and venture. We know this isn't true of being human. We know that our skilled knowledge of the world is not a simple conquering and subduing, but is, instead, as much a subservience as it is a mastery—best, then, to just let this binary go. It is a more delicate, ecopedagogical matter of coming to know our way around a living place that helps sustain our knowing and keeps it vibrant and true, coming to know a deep interdependence that needs rigorous nurturing and care.

In fact, in describing this phenomenon, Hans-Georg Gadamer links this nebulous sense etymologically to the German word for "play" (*Spiel*): as sense that "something is going on, [*im Spiele ist*], something is happening [*sich abspielt*]" (Gadamer, 1989, p. 104).

Part Five: And Pythagoras' Ghost

> When the idea of scarcity insinuates itself into how we imagine the curriculum topics entrusted to teachers and students in schools, those topics become necessarily bounded in ways that make it possible to control, predict, assess, and monitor their production distribution, consumption, dispensation and accumulation. This is how a scarce resource appears in a market economy. Pythagorean Theorem, for example, becomes stripped of its abundance of unmonitorable and uncontrollable relations, possibilities and unguarded appearances. It becomes reduced to its manageable and monitorable surface features. Under this regime, to understand Pythagorean Theorem means to memorize its formula and to be able to correctly apply it to mathematics problems on demand in an examination. Understanding thus becomes equated with "possession" and "dissemination." Under the assumption of scarcity, curriculum topics must be broken down and doled out in carefully monitored, zero-sum exchanges. Such curricular fragments become thus identified, as we have previously explored [see Jardine et al., 2008, originally published in 2003], with "the basics" in education. (Jardine et al., 2006b, p. 4)

I think of how intensely patient were Patricia Clifford and Sharon Friesen's long and winding classes on the surroundings—the "topography"—of the Pythagorean Theorem. Full of images and words and ghosts and relations, diagrams and circles and angles and perpendiculars and angle bisections (see Friesen & Jardine, 2009, p. 149–175). Full, too, of tree-shadows, now, in the winter sun, longer than they were last summer.

And a slightly astonished 12-year-old boy facing south on the playground, toes at the end of the long shadow, blurting: "But Pythagoras says that something is still *the same*." Half a wide-eyed declaration, half a question (Jardine et al., 2006b, p. 3).

This is why Sharon and Pat and I took on a sort of rescue mission of the idea of "the basics" in education (Jardine et al., 2008). We knew from decades of practice that fragments are not basic but are, rather, arcane and abstract outcomes of incredibly elaborate and invasive *interventions into living fields of interdependent relations,* tearing apart any memory of their belonging together, their inherent relatedness. And then, in a great act of forgetting what we have done, these fragments are said to come somehow "before" and to be more basic than the living field from which they have been fragmented in the first place.

What comes first, what is basic, is our human draw toward such kinships, such relatedness, wherein my own interest—Latin *inter*, "in the middle," plus *esse*, "of things"—is not only a testament to, but part of that very relatedness. Such "interest" is something that most teachers secretly know but have little recourse to express, that "something awakens our interest–*that* is really what comes first" (Gadamer, 2001, p. 50).

In this sort of awakening to the abundant interrelatedness of things, the Pythagorean Theorem (or those deck shadows, or adding, or subtracting):

> No longer has the character of an object that stands over and against us. We are no longer able to approach this like an object of knowledge, grasping, measuring and controlling. Rather than meeting us in our world, it is much more a world into which we ourselves are drawn, so long as it is not placed into the object-world of producing and marketing. (Gadamer, 1994, pp. 191–192)

Each seemingly separate thing or seeming fragment "possesses its own worldliness" (p. 192) and to teach it, to learn it, is to come to know this worldliness. Again, this echoes how each fragment has its own ecosystems of relations that rise up with it, given classroom inquiry a sense of en-fieldedness and to give teaching a whiff of being a field guide.

It is to quite literally replace it back into all its relations that were, in reality, hidden there all along.

Part Six: School

> Young people want to know if, under the cool and calm of efficient teaching and excellent time-on-task ratios, life itself has a chance, or whether the surface is all there is. (D.G. Smith, 2020c, p. 405)

Abundance points to a long-forgotten cluster of etymological origins of the word "school"—from the Greek *skhole* and the Latin *schola*, meaning both "leisure" and "a holding back, a keeping clear" (OED). The great arts of teaching and learning are to be conducted, in part, away from the day-to-day fray of immediate, impinging, hurrying concerns, anxieties, distractions, renderings, wall-building, and threats that are not indigenous to the workings of the topics being explored.

In such leisure and holding back, it is possible to notice and to confirm how good—how mathematically rich and mathematically abundant—is that 12-year-old boy's questioning declaration over a lengthening tree shadow that has somehow also remained the same. Yes, Pythagoras is flourishing right here underfoot, right here in the arc of seasons and sun and shadows, and right by your toes at the end of that shadow. It becomes palpable. Beautiful. Even. Even this mathematical Theorem is not just an isolated and memorizable fragment but also a memorable and befitting reminder of a living field of relations in isolation from which it would not properly be what it is:

> Thus, getting to return to something worthwhile has its own attraction that then teaches us about the worth of this kind of returning. The tough work is to be drawn into that compelling and *not* reifying what then arrives but rather making it more compelling and drawing others into this experience of dependent co-arising and gathering. This is what is *there*, something that beckons attention and continuance. Good, worthwhile work creates a desire for good, worthwhile work and impatience with trivial things that are not only not worthwhile but that ravage and atrophy and betray our keenness for worthwhile things. As Chris Dawson (1998, p. xxvi) notes in his "Translator's Introduction" to Hans-Georg Gadamer's *Praise of Theory*, this links to the hermeneutic interest in old Greek ideas of "the beautiful": "any beautiful thing has a radiant elegance about it which … points beyond itself and drives us to look for further elegant unities in other things." Again, then, whiling over a good story teaches something more than the tale being told. It "attracts the longing of love to it. [It] disposes people in its favor immediately" (Gadamer, 1989, p. 481) and it disposes us to seek out and surround ourselves with such things. It disposes us to clear out the junk we have surrounded ourselves with and the junking of our lives that such junk induces. It teaches us—teachers and student alike—something about the worth of whiling and what it requires of us and what happens when we strive to surround ourselves and fill our lives with things worthy of, quite literally, spending our lives on. (Jardine, 2016d, p. 252)

There is no hurry here, no time running out, no scarcity, and no lack. It does not need to be doled out, surveilled, and monitored. It has its own indigenous relatedness and rigorousness, its own orderliness, its own tale to tell. It is not used up by our attention. It does not become scarce but precisely the opposite. The more we learn of it, the more we know of the inexhaustibility of its relations and kin, and this sense of being inevitably "outplayed" is part of the deep pleasure of such work. Just for a moment, my own anxieties, wrapped up as they are in the distractions and rush of "producing and marketing," can let go, out into the leisurely time of this rich place which, of itself, does the work of holding back and keeping clear.

In the school-as-*schola*, the living field of knowledge being investigated can flourish of its own accord. I have called this elsewhere a "pedagogy left in peace" (Jardine, 2012a; see also Illich, with Cayley, 1992, p. 16).

Part Seven: From Little Panics to Terror

Animals under various forms of threat—the continuous presence of predators, lack of adequate food, drought, and the like—tend to play less and less. They tend, quite naturally, to revert to those kinds of activities that will aid them in gaining comparative control over their environment, activities that involve little or no risk. (Jardine, 1992a, p. 121)

People whose governing habit is the relinquishment of power, competence and responsibility, and whose characteristic suffering is the anxiety of futility, make excellent spenders. They are the ideal consumers. By inducing in them little panics of boredom, powerlessness, mortality, paranoia, they can be made to buy virtually anything that is "attractively packaged." (Berry, 1986, p. 24).

We have been schooled in these governing habits. We have become habituated. The promise of efficiency and its consequent cultivation of a sense of lack, of scarcity, and the need for obedience, dovetails easily with the never-fully-fulfilled-promise of market logic. It also cultivates an insatiable sense of needing *more*.

Early in the twentieth century, once efficiency movements in industry reached a certain threshold of increased production, the desire to consume more and more quickly became subject to equally hidden and systematic psychological manipulation, using the same easily induced sense of lack, scarcity, and panic, threat and never-quite-fulfilled promises of relief (see Leach, 1994). If we cannot produce any more efficiently, the only way to increase profits is to increase people's desire to consume.

So, then, this, from Kevin O'Leary. O'Leary, once a candidate for leadership of the Conservative Party of Canada, was affiliated with *The Learning Company,* currently owned by Houghton Mifflin Harcourt, one of North America's largest providers of packaged educational products, "learn to read" series, and educational video games such as *Carmen Sandiego* and *Reader Rabbit:*

> I'm all for children, but I want to make a buck. I *am* Carmen Sandiego. I *am* Reader Rabbit. People will do anything for their children to help them in math and reading scores. I made a fortune just servicing that market. I love the terror in a mother's heart when she sees her child fall behind in reading. I made a fortune from that. (O'Leary, 2012)

I encourage practicing teachers and parents to read it carefully and with an open heart, because something vaguely suspected is finally being said clearly, unequivocally, and out loud, and for that we should be oddly grateful. If we can untangle it, there may be a livable future. Ignore schooled study. Study *this.*

Part Eight: From Terror to Perpetual War

"Given ... abundance, scarcity must be a function of boundaries" (Hyde, 1983, p. 23). And we've all heard quite enough about wall-building lately, and the suppressed psychopathologies it hides so well.

The insistence on well-wrought boundaries and the building of walls is a function of feeling invaded, vulnerable, and under threat. It is also a function of the hoarding by those in power of what is of value and the subsequent manipulation of scarcity and threat as a means to deflect attention away from the realities of such manipulative functioning. Thus, maintaining those regimes of power and profit.

"I made a fortune from that."

We have seen a lot of this recently. How easy it is to induce and manipulate, especially if we remain immersed in the roiling distortions and distractions of attention, unable to hold back or keep clear (*schola*) enough to think through what is being perpetrated and to what end, and to whose benefit.

"I love the terror in a mother's heart." And a great means of inducing such terrors is to deliberately keep those terrorized in the dark about the hidden mechanisms that are actually at work, like monsters in the dark under the bed.

"I love the poorly educated" (Donald Trump, in Associated Press, 2016a; Quartz Staff, 2016).

This suggests why the issue of curriculum in abundance is perhaps far more relevant than it was, now 15+ years ago.

A great inversion has occurred, where a reliable means of relieving this sense of embattlement, of breaking its spell, of holding back and keeping clear our knee-jerk panics and anxieties—the school as *schola*—is now often identified as one of the *causes* of embattlement.

This inversion works like this. Regimes of scarcity are regimes of threat. And, in light of the retractions and subsequent xenophobic suspicions produced and sustained by threat-consciousness, any suggestion of abundance feels like a breach, a border-violation, a counter-threat, an uprising:

> Education becomes akin to a sometimes overt, but more often subtle war on the very possibility of unanticipated "uprising." Natality itself becomes experienced as a perennial insurgent threat to security that must be planned for and secured against. Education becomes cast as akin to a counterinsurgent war on terror. (Jardine, 2012a, p, 5)

Those who suggest abundance, show affection for it, and demonstrate a desire to live one's life in its sway, become suspect:

> Trying to act on the belief (inside or outside of schools) that the matters at hand need more intellectual subtlety than purged and clarified

exaggerations-under-threat allow, starts to appear as an act of betrayal or sedition. Believing that there is more complexity to the story ... is to be branded a conspiracy theorist. Wanting to know something more than the simplistic, threat-induced clarities ... is [considered] egregious. *Knowledge and its pursuit become experienced as a threat to security.* (Jardine et al., 2012, pp. 31–32)

It becomes clearer and clearer how those who might want to cultivate rich, engrossing, beautiful, difficult work in schools have a tough row to hoe:

Ironically, schooling itself became subjected to a profound form of "anti-intellectualism" (R. Callahan, 1964, p. 8). "What [Taylor] really wanted working men to be [and what is wanted from students and teachers when these matters are transferred to schooling] [is] focused, uncomplicated and compliant" (Boyle, 2006). Couple this with how many teacher-education programs become geared towards such uncomplicated, assembly-line delivery of fragments of knowledge and we end up with teachers who, despite their voiced desires to participate in [rich abundant, intellectually sound] conversations, have not cultivated in themselves the ability to make sound judgments about the intellectual quality of such conversations. (Friesen & Jardine, 2010, pp. 15–16)

We have, it seems, been had, and we need look no further than Kevin O'Leary to get a beginning sense of who benefits from this situation. It is not enough to shut the door, hunker down and work with one's students. From F.W. Taylor:

Every day, year in and year out, each man should ask himself over and over again, two questions," said Taylor in his standard lecture. "First, 'What is the name of the man I am now working for?' And having answered this definitely then 'What does this man want me to do, right now?' Not, 'What ought I to do in the interests of the company I am working for?' Not, 'What are the duties of the position I am filling? Not, 'What did I agree to do when I came here?' Not, 'What should I do for my own best interest?' but plainly and simply, 'What does this man want me to do?' " (Cited in Boyle, 2006)

Danish border disputes? What does this man want me to do? Deck shadows? Sorry, time is running out. Accelerated and exhausted teachers and students. All the better to maintain orderliness and efficiency.

Curriculum in abundance gives us a glimpse that *this is not "the real world."* It is just how the world happens to have turned out, and this for reasons that can be unwound, questioned, revealing alternatives that can arise. The students who ask for exactly what to do on an assignment just might be more acute in reading their circumstances than those reprimanding them for lack of initiative.

There is no doubt at all that acceleration and exhaustion are, of course, intimately and immediately experienced and the *deliberately* paralyzing power of such intimacy is not to be trivialized. We all variously and repeatedly feel, as a Welsh great-uncle once expressed it "up against the coal face." Efficiency, once embraced with almost salvational glee—even marriage breakdown was attributed to lack of efficiency in popular magazines of the time (R. Callahan, 1964). This is part of its current abiding power and spell and discovering these threads of inheritance can begin to go some small way at breaking its spell and forgiving ourselves for feeling so very trapped sometimes:

> As a result of F.W. Taylor's re-imagining of industrial production, industrial efficiency, production and profit increased dramatically. Moreover, this image of efficiency and its promise took over the public imagination and swept through all facets of then-contemporary life, from mayor's offices to hospitals to how housewives should organize their kitchens and their housework schedules and on and on (for more detail on these matters see Taylor, 1903, 1911, Kanigel, 2005, Dufour & Eaker, 1998, Callahan, R., 1964, Gatto, 2003, 2006, Wrege & Greenwood, 1991, Friesen & Jardine, 2009, to name but a few available sources). Dozens of articles in popular magazines and scholarly journals were written and poured over, along with recurrent declamatory newspaper articles about the inefficiencies of this or that facet of then-contemporary life. "What about efficiency?" became a polemical, even moral clarion call in all quarters of North American consciousness: "Taylor's thinking so permeates the soil of modern life we no longer realize it's there. It has become, as Edward Eyre Hunt, an aide to future President Herbert Hoover, could grandly declaim in 1924, 'part of our moral inheritance.'" (Jardine, 2016c, pp. 186–187; Kanigel, 2005, p. 7)

This might explain some of the occasional moral affrontery that can arise in some school settings when one suggests pursuing some rich and vibrant line of thought, or online debate about Denmark and Canada, or tree-shadows and Pythagoras.

I'll only note in passing that Robert McNamara, United States Secretary of Defense from 1961–1968, was one of the "Whiz-Kids" that instituted modern efficiency regimes into the Ford Motor Company in the mid-1940s and later brought efficiency and flow-charts to his "management" of the Vietnam War. As with shop workers in Taylor's factories, and as with teachers in a Taylorian school setting, McNamara was not interested in the initiative or knowledge of members of the military in the field (Leiby, 1991).

But, despite all that let's be clear, here. *There is nothing wrong with efficiency per se. Sometimes* it is the very thing that is needed in a certain situation. But *that* insight requires loosening oneself from its pervasive grip and coming to understanding that efficiency is *possible*, not *necessary* at every turn, sometimes *called for*, sometimes not. It is the distended *dominance of efficiency* that is the issue, and that it tends to be a voracious beast that preys on disease and exhaustion while creating them in the same gesture, becoming, in hidden ways, both cause and cure. It

Abundance. Joyful, tough work. Unwinding the ties that bind us is also part of the task of a curriculum in abundance.

And, too, sometimes, simply turning away from the regimes of deliberate, panic-inducing distraction is the best I can do. And there is no sense pretending. "Once curriculum is experienced in abundance, sometimes continuing to live in some schools becomes unbearable" (Jardine, 2006, p. xxvi).

Part Nine: Elephants and "A Terrible Trial"

As with any new way of imagining education, the regime of scarcity had the effect, initially, of giving rise to a certain level of productivity in educational circles. Early in the 20th century, it was productive to imagine education along the lines of an industrial assembly line, where tasks were portioned out, outcomes could be easily measured, and troubles could be easily identified and fixed. However, we believe that this way of imagining education has reached what Illich identified as the point of "counterproductivity" (Illich, with Cayley, 1992, p. 110). There is a certain point where any system operating under the regime of scarcity begins to aggravate and, in fact, *create* the troubles for which it was meant to be the solution. He demonstrates that in the field of medicine, for example, we are now experiencing how hospitals are the breeding grounds of "superbugs." In transportation, he presents a startling fact: the faster that air travel becomes, the *more* time we spend traveling this way. Moreover, "up to a certain speed and density automobiles may expand mobility, but beyond this threshold society becomes their prisoner" (Cayley, in Illich, with Cayley, 1992, p. 15) and we spend more and more time caught immobile in our cars. The more we accelerate, the more we experience "time consuming acceleration" (Illich, 2000, p. 31). (Jardine et al., 2006b p. 6)

What ever shall we do, then?

We don't need new buzzwords, checklists, acronyms, and yet another sleek packaged curriculum resource. "We need to let the words stand like single malt whiskey or aged cheddar, instead of always seeking the fast-food remedy" (Carl Leggo, 2006, p. 78; cited in Latremouille et al., 2024, p. 182)

We ought to be like elephants in the noontime sun in summer, when they are tormented by heat and thirst and catch sight of a cool lake. They throw themselves into the water with the greatest pleasure and without a moment's hesitation. In just the same way, for the sake of ourselves and others, we should give ourselves joyfully to the practice. (Pelden, 2007, p. 255)

I felt compelled to leave in this scene of elephants plunging into cool water as a way to counterbalance a bit of the dourness that is being discussed here. The work of studying the world in its abundance is full of great and difficult and repeated joys—of discovery, of reliable and time-tested insight, full of ancestral wisdoms and foibles, books and books of tough work, full of stings and little reliefs, breakthroughs and wonders and, too, failures and commiserations and starting all over again. It can provide long, solid, rigorous, multifarious, scholarly ancestries to ideas of dependent co-arising, interdependence, and abundance.

This is not New Age froth or emotionally fraught, "liberal" touchy-feely-ness, or do-whatever-you-want-ness. It is the old and reliable warrant of thinking carefully and well, of scholarly work, of evidence, of good and practicable examples, attentiveness, and so on. And this is sometimes simpler than it might seem. I recall having a complex conversation over recess with a student-teacher regarding the ins and outs of multiplying by fractions and how hard it is to articulate, and by the time we noticed, the students in this Grade Five class had returned and were sitting quietly behind us, leaning forward a bit into a mid-conversation.

The student-teacher asked me, "what should I do now?" The answer was weirdly simple.

We should not now do something *else*.

"Let's tell them about the conversation we were just having and see what happens." Entrusting ourselves.

So there we were, the chalkboard full of scrawls and examples and things crossed out, standing up, facing fresh faces just in from the cold, stood up into the hard, joyous work of seeking wisdom about this matter, together in its safe and reliable company.

And, make no mistake, we need Tsong-Kha-Pa's advice from Tibet, 1406: "You can't get anywhere without [also] reading a yak's load of books" (Tsong-kha-pa, 2004, p. 219).

A yak-load of *the right books*. I could spend pages and pages right now with lists and lists of work being done, right now, in real schools, venturing this sort of abundant, difficult work, giving vivid examples of successes, trials, failures, and breakthroughs. And there is an equally abundant set of scholarly sources, too, waiting, rife and ready, to support this work and show its tough, scholarly ancestries.

I'll just mention here, for now, that I had the great good fortune of ending the formal part of my career co-teaching, with Jackie Seidel, at the University of Calgary, two clusters of graduate courses that explored the matters mentioned here. These involved talking together, reading together, taking and passing notes back and forth, writing, publishing, conference presentations, retreats, eating together, laughing, with children born and parents dying in the meanwhile, gathering and re-gathering. Since those courses ended, of us have continued weekly meetings of refuge and comfort in its deepest sense—cultivating "common strength" against the forces of fret and distraction. Jackie and I published a book together (2014), and then another collection arose out of our classes full of chapters written by the classroom teachers/ graduate students (2016). When surrounded in the frays of schooling and trying to just get by, reminders are important, commiseration is vital. Just seeing each other's faces was sometimes enough to invoke a whispered, "oh, yes, right."

I end with part of an interview with Wendell Berry, conducted by Bill Moyers. It was one of the many "texts" that we carefully "read" and "re-read" in our gatherings. Many of us, myself included, looked at the video over and over again, furiously typing out passages to hold nearby and read to friends and colleagues.

Advice, here, from Wendell Berry, about impending ecological troubles, but equally a heartfelt message to teachers and students in schools about the portend of curriculum in abundance:

> This can't be hurried; this is the dreadful situation that young people are in. The situation you're in is a situation that is going to call for a lot of patience, and to be patient in an emergency is a terrible trial. The important thing to do is to learn all you can about where you are, to make common cause with that place, and then, resigning yourself, become patient enough to work with it over a long time. And then, what you do is increase the possibility that you'll make a good example. And what we're looking for in this is good examples. (Berry, with Moyers, 2013)

I would only re-emphasize again that this work needs the company of others—the long and mixed ancestries of thinking and writing and those close by who will sit and argue and think and give examples and commiserate. Ways from our elders, the fresh company of the youngest of children and newest of students, and the affectionate vigor of colleagues. Those who will treat my slim patience and other failings with some patience, and let me do the same with them, over this common work.

I ask for the same from the bustling moose that just barged through last night, or from that whiff of stale smoke from the California and Oregon fires, all this and more that serve as reminders, as gateways, into our abundant and dependent co-arising.

An Unexpected Elegy

One of the required texts that Jackie Seidel and I used in our graduate courses, full as they were with lovely classroom teachers, parents and administrators trying to find refuge and good companionship in the face of the blurs of school, was Canadian poet Don Domanski's *All Our Wonder Unavenged*. It was strange, at first, to run into such a book as an education text, but he slowly took his seat as one of our teachers, alongside Maxine Greene, Cynthia Chambers, David G. Smith, Michael Derby, Ted Aoki and many, many others. In fact, in a chapter that appeared in both of the collections that Jackie and I put together was a piece written by us and 16 of the students in our class called "Echolocations" (Seidel, Jardine, et al., 2014, pp. 91–110; 2016, 100–118). In this co-written piece, we were given permission to cite in full one of Don Domanski's poems from *All Our Wonder Unavenged* (2010) called "Disposing of a Broken Clock" (p. 67).

As I was, now a few years back, trying to finish up this chapter, sad word arrives via an email from Jackie Seidel, that Canadian poet Don Domanski died on September 9, 2020.

Jackie, Friday, September 11, 2020, 12:27
My heart is so, so sad.

And Jackie pasted in a Twitter posting from his publisher, Brick Books in which these words of Domanski's fell about:

I try to follow Meister Eckhart's advice
Do exactly what you would do if you felt
most secure sometimes it takes
sometimes it doesn't meanwhile saints
graze on the begonias meanwhile
ravens go to the edges of the earth
and return with our hearts in their beaks.

This is from a piece entitled "In the Dream of Yellow Birches" (Domanski, 2010, p. 121) again from *All Our Wonder Unavenged*.

I can hardly bear the, what? Coincidence that his words now bear to what I've been trying to write? No. This is no mere coincidence. He was one of my teachers and it feels now that that was more than I could have imagined. I feel like a thief.

Just read those words.

David, Friday, September 11, 2020, 12:42

Oh my, just a wee youngster—actually, just four months older than me ... sigh. He seemed frail, etc., even a few years back. But still, still, here comes the Raven back from the edge with my heart.

Jackie, Friday, September 11, 2020, 12:27
Looks like his wife died this year too. Goodbye to our dear teachers and mentors. Well, he embraced death and renewal and kinship and lineage, so all is well.

Here's a quote from him, perfect for this time:

The "everyday: is the grand act of the human imagination. Nothing that we have constructed comes near to it in terms of sheer inventiveness. There is no "everyday," no "normal" day. We all pretend there is. We all add to the myth. It's an act of pretense which helps us survive, to feel there's ground under our feet, when we know full well that beneath that ground there is an eternity of stars and galaxies, a great unknown which, on one of these normal days will swallow us whole. (Domanski, 2002, p. 249)

This interview, called "The Wisdom of Falling," too, was also one of our required texts.

... meanwhile saints
graze on the begonias

Meanwhile ...

David, Friday, September 11, 2020, 12:49
I found the reference. Now others can trace this thread and it won't be lost. Yes. Teachers dying is a strange thing. Much love. In tears.
d

Jackie, Friday, September 11, 2020, 1:05
Yes. Tears. Heartbreaking ... he was one of my best teachers of my life.

> I remove the mainspring which shivers once
> in my palm and then is still.
> (From Don Domanski, 2010, p. 67, "Disposing of a Broken
> Clock")

CHAPTER FOUR

A Fragment from 2009, Just Before I'd First Read Fredrick Winslow Taylor

A brief email sent to my university co-teacher of a graduate class held at a local high school and populated with teachers from that school. We were discussing the logics that dominant how our work—theirs and ours at the university—are sometimes hidden forces that can override what we try to do. Of course, they are often in place to try to ensure the curbing of bad practice, but we commiserated over how the effect is often placing strictures on interesting, venturous work. This is also a really interesting example of how coming upon an ancestor like F.W. Taylor can help open up and clarify and elaborate the intimate, day-to-day troubles of teachers in schools and what they are experiencing. Studying Fredrick Taylor is not a matter of become more informed about him alone, but become able to be more informed about intimate experiences of schooling via such study.

I think I want to appeal to the staff's love of their disciplines as a way to respond to the student's talk of boredom, etc. Even if some don't love their disciplines, it can't be argued against easily. No one would argue that loving the discipline you teach makes anything worse. Some teachers have told me that they loved their discipline until they had to teach it.

The only thing it makes worse is tolerating the weird presumptions and structures of "schooling." Differently put, how could my work in my classes be more like the hard, real work and intellectual enthusiasm of the discipline I love?

Teachers get exhausted and cynical, and students get bored when a well-known and well-loved discipline gets lost in the structures of "schooling."

What, as teachers, we've all experienced: that the structure of schooling "trumps" the structure of the discipline being taught in school. The structure of the discipline has to "concede" to the requirements of schooling—sequencing, assessment, and on and on. One thing that is commonly conceded is the coherence, questioning, and exploratory nature of the discipline in favor of that disciplines "findings" (facts, theorems, dates, names, events, etc.) in favor of what suits, for example, a large high school department's need to keep everyone on board and at the same pace.

"Structure of the discipline": It is a living, ongoing stream of work. It has a history, cliques, sub-disciplines, offshoots, practices, offshoots, project for which it is especially fit, ancestors who've explored this discipline and left worthwhile traces—ideas, images, formulae, procedures, findings, discoveries, controversies, collaborations, ways of questioning and on and on. *And,* all of this disciplinary work is occurring *right now* in the world. Right now, a buried Anglo-Saxon treasure has just been found, with sword-hilts encrusted with garnets. I keep remembering Pat and Sharon working with that paleontologist graduate student, on-site in northern Manitoba, getting send sketches, photos, maps for their Grades 1–4 kids (see Clifford & Friesen, 1993; Clifford et al., 2008; Jardine et al., 2008).

With the structure of schooling trumping this structure of the disciplines, you get cut off from the exploratory adventurousness of your discipline, cut off from those in the world practicing that discipline, and cut off from thinking about the world in light of that discipline. You get a school setting where no one wants to talk about quadratics or Hamlet anymore. Ask yourself: are your colleagues in your school *literature* colleagues? Do you have discussions in your mathematics departments about *mathematics?* Many teachers that I've spoken to have answered "no" to these questions. Your students also get cut off this way. And the discipline itself gets atrophied—the structure of schooling is so powerful that discipline structure cannot defend itself against and it submits to it, cleaning out all the ideas, images, formulae, procedures, findings, discoveries, collaborations, controversies, and ways of questioning.

Then, when the shape and requirements and demands and forms of assessment of student (and teacher) school success in a curriculum area get untethered from the shape and requirements and demands and forms of assessment that are part of the intellectual discipline for which a curriculum is being developed, things fall apart.

Well, I said: "No one would argue that loving the discipline you teach makes anything worse."

False. It can make school teaching unbearable under its dominance over that love and affection.

CHAPTER FIVE

Sometimes It Takes, Sometimes It Doesn't

I try to follow Meister Eckhart's advice
*Do exactly what you would do if you felt
most secure* sometimes it takes
sometimes it doesn't meanwhile saints
Graze on the begonias meanwhile
Ravens go to the edge of the earth
And return with our hearts in their beaks.

Don Domanski, from "In the Dream of Yellow Birches," from the book *All Our Wonders Unavenged* (Domanski, 2010, p. 121). A colleague and I used Domanski's book as a required text in a cluster of graduate courses in Education populated by practicing teachers and school administrators. Parents, brothers and sisters, friends, Ravens nearby as a matter of course.

We were asked if we needed permission to teach the courses the way we did. That question itself became a lovely spot of thinking, grazing, going to the edge and returning.

We collected their writings together (see Seidel & Jardine, 2016a). Here a glance, the image of the space between being the locale of the work we all did:

> In the coulee a pocket of darkness.
> Marbled pairs of reflected light,
> briefly glow, then shimmer and fade out.
> Alone now, they wind through tangles, relentless,
> and re-emerge into one.
> Call up to the creators; we are here, we are here.
>
> What of those who occupy the spaces in between,
> and linger along the precipice.
> Outlines given vague shape by the fleeting;
> ephemeral and haunting.
> Await the familiar, an echo emerging from below.

(Judson Innes, from "A Pocket of Darkness"; cited in full in Seidel & Jardine, 2016, p. 110)

Things arise in teaching, in learning, in bearing the lofts of wings, in dealing with a troubled student or one who as walled up and become schooled. These things are difficult to face, difficult to work through. *Accepting* that *this* is not a mistake on my part or yours, but is in *the nature of the living world* is important. *This* doesn't need to be fixed. *This is precisely the open path.* This is true, also, of all of the living disciplines we are asked to teach in schools—they are difficult, they challenge, provoke, disturb, and as more of us than their schooled versions allow.

Schools falsely make us believe that these sufferings—the allures and troubles of literary history, or of national hopes and desires, or chemical bonds or right angles, or social justice and it waxings and wanings, or ecological uprisings that are haunting us all and asking for attention—*can be fixed.* Thus an old reminder originally from 1406:

You must accept [suffering] when [it] arise[s] because:

(1) if you do not do this, in addition to the basic suffering, you have the suffering of worry that is produced by your own thoughts, and then the suffering becomes very difficult for you to bear.

(2) if you accept the suffering, you let the basic suffering be and do not stop it, but you never have the suffering of worry that creates discontentment when you focus on the basic suffering; and

(3) since you are using a method to bring even basic sufferings into the path, you greatly lessen your suffering, so you can bear it. Therefore, it is very crucial that you generate the patience that accepts suffering. (Tsong-kha-pa, 2004, pp. 172–173)

"Why study for a future we won't have?" is not asking for a fixed future that we will have. It is asking for a future that is open and livable out from under the false promises of fixity. Remedying our current ecological troubles is making possible and effective and sustainable the tough work that will take. This is not just a matter of adding "environmental studies" to an array of moribund other courses that do not course. Part of this remedy is treating the living fields of knowledge entrusted to teachers and students in schools as *living fields*, with all the attention and devotion that that requires.

CHAPTER SIX

An Upwell Near Father's Day

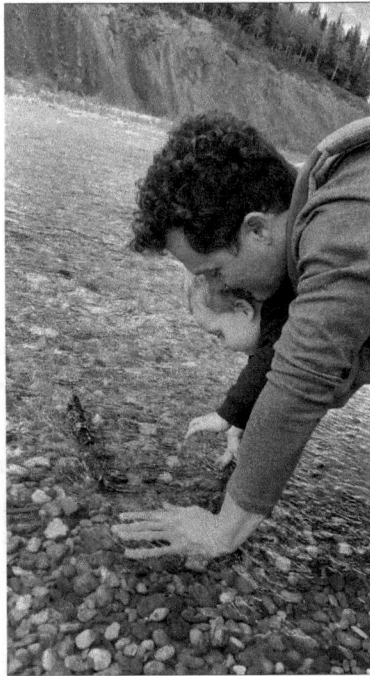

FIGURE 5. FATHER. SON. RIVER
Photo: E. Jardine, used with permission.

Let me introduce you to the waters
You knew well and know
Still. Still waters running. Water, wells and flows.

Bent over ancient actions, father son. Water. Touched and touching.
These two so near to me and my own
Little-boy-asthma love of air, of water.
These two arc an old act of rippling grace notes.
Under fingers and palms and reach
The water sings.
Under freshed air.
And pleasure.

Hit by the cold glacial melt.
Astounded. *Ex-tonare*—"to thunder out"
(*Online Etymological Dictionary*, accessed 2022,
under "astound,"
this reference to be read like a
very old part of the very same family tree).

—Ahh, cold! Laugh! Stand up!
Laugh.

Inquiry, in this simple sort of work, sniffs out "songlines" (Chatwin, 1988) that are already well-strung well before we arrive—multiple, contested, ambiguous, intermingling, buried, remembered, forgotten—wounding sometimes, sometimes healing.

A photo sometimes, but only sometimes, becomes a singular plectrum up against sometimes taunt, sometimes slackened, strings, "interweaving and criss-crossing" (Wittgenstein, 1968, p. 32). And I cite these things here, in the midst of this moment so intimate, because they give voice, in the lineages of my raising and writing and study, to "kinship" (p. 36) and "family resemblance" (p. 33), instead of the older philosophical habits of sharp-edged, clear, unambiguous *is* or *is not* (Jardine, 1990c).

As you'll see, too, things get tumultuously self-referential and reminiscent, having not only been turned a grandfather, but having them all move close by.

An echo up off the water surface:

The bewildering abundance and recognizable resemblances of the world and its creatures, irresolvable to either of the extreme simplifications of identity or difference—Jean Piaget [1965, p. 6] noted Henri Bergson's early 20th century "surprise at the disappearance of the problem of 'kinds' ... in favor of the problem of 'laws.'" Hans-Georg Gadamer's thoughts (1989, p. 114) on "versimilitude"—"likeness." Not surprisingly, there is a "kind-ness" [here] at the heart ... (Jardine, 2012b, p. 224)

Looking for kindness. Again:

... that anciently perceived likeness between all creatures and the earth of which they are made. (Berry, 1983, p. 76)

A look-see into how I carry kinship and affection for more than those two over the river, who have helped me sing over my nearer-by loves. They start a quiet gathering around that photo's heartstrings.

Adumbrations. And Jodi whispering to me and to him and to his, a little, remembered help-quell, "hush, *child* ..." (Latremouille, 2014, p. 31). I want to get the page exact so that the trail has a small mark for you, reading. For me, remembering and honoring.

And the dark arcs over Elbow River water. A single photograph can sometimes make rise up great nightmares of water, of plastic vortexes and swirls, of guilt.

Of sorrow over my son and grandson's hands feeling the still-fresh.

North Atlantic Right Whales disappearing right there not-so-very-hid in the Hymnal singsongs of a nearby river:

eubalaena glacialis
oh sorrow
only with you do we matter. (Seidel, 2016a p. 111)

Pang:

Any beautiful thing has a radiant elegance about it which ... points beyond itself and drives us to look for further elegant unities in other things. (C. Dawson, 1998, p. xxvi)

It's beauty, its ugly reminder, that a beautiful thing "attract the longing of love to it. [It] disposes people in its favor immediately. The beautiful ... has its own radiance" (Gadamer, 1989, p. 481). This ghastly ecological countenance welled up in that boy's eyes bent over hidden joy-sorrow. His boy's too.

Stop. Gathering. Take a breath. This is how this work works. A simple picture, a deeply intimate portrait, but then come cluster the things I've read or written myself, the voices I've heard and recall, the stories, the dreams and nightmares, both. The ones that come to mind in the water chill hit of son and grandson in the river nearby. Ecological reminders of how art works, how beauty works:

> Only beauty can save the planet. Even the strongest combination of guilty feelings, economic reasoning, and scientific evidence are not enough to turn the tide so that our planet's life may continue. Nevertheless, if you love something, you want it to stay around and stay close, and keep radiantly well. And it is precisely beauty that makes you fall in love. [It] gives you the feeling that what is here is to be treasured and not misused or harmed, and certainly not to be regarded in terms of functional usefulness or economic return, for such is to look at the world as a slave or a whore. (Hillman, 2006a, p. 182)

My own age wells up, my own measure of summers left to me, this, too, a familial matter full of far too many stories to count—personal commiserations, poems of poise and laceration, scholarly mediations and tear and tear beckons over what I know full well, that this summer is far more likely my last than any summer has been.

In these "ecologically sorrowful times" (Jardine, 2015a, p. xv), what, pray, am I waiting for? I'm waiting for this: "Where you are is a place to practice" (Tsong-kha-pa, 2004, p. 191). And especially, for the tough, ongoing work of inquiry that helps keep me out of the mire of self-indulgence, keeps me seeking links through written breath in traces of ancestors, wisdoms and cautions, into the arts of the image and the arts of writing. My work is deeply biased in favor of maintaining a glimpse of dependent co-arising, despite is howls of emptiness and finitude:

> Oh, emptiness, tell me about your nature
> Maybe I've been getting you wrong. (Lenker, 2020)

"Texts are instructions for practice" (Tsong-kha-pa, 2000, p. 52). Well, they can be if you watch for this. Some texts lean toward this description originally from 1406. Shun those other texts that prattle and skitter and distract. Seek out what instructs on stilling, on beauty. Learn to read this way, to read for this. My work is deeply cut on this bias of things, of these boys, this water, being my own flesh, as is the echo of the water off the far cliff, my ear whorls being proof enough.

So, the quality of this sort of inquiry: to take rest and comfort and pleasure in this eco-ecstatic feel of being outlived, outdone, outstripped, where the play outplays the player (Gadamer, 1989, p. 106) over and over again. This be a strange freedom, a strange affection.

To be disposed in its favor. A wee, old example from a Grade One class, where they were busy over lines of letters, pencils over-gripped, and that hot, wet spot on your middle finger where the pencil can rub. I had them stop for a moment and asked why they were having such a tough time. One child said "Because we're in Grade One." And I said "It is also because it is a hard thing to do, a hard thing to get good at." They were relieved to hear this, that the work of hand and pencil and line was a difficult thing.

I showed them the callous on my own finger. And then, editing this chapter, that little event, which I had told to many student-teachers and teachers over decades, went "pssst ..."

Such episodes can see so small but can then suddenly "break forth" (Gadamer, 1989, p. 458)—you see, I had to mull at first, to watch them a bit, to think of so many decades ago, of the hot red spot I knew well, the grip. I had to get it to break forth a bit myself and *then* try saying it out loud, and *then* noticing them getting back to work with a bit more ease over the difficulties they face. Shaping and forming.

Something awakens me, catches my eye or ear or skin, and *then* the question of what befits this something can follow—an old Aristotelean *mensuratio ad rem, in the measure of the thing*. This is why Gadamer (1989) railed in such detail against "the subjectivization of aesthetics" (pp. 42–100) that he had inherited, because it short-circuits the experience of being summoned and drawn out and thrown into question, for example, that photograph possessed. It short-circuits how his hermeneutics places aesthetics at the heart of *any* venture bent on coming to understand:

> Does one have to choose one's own standpoint and firmly hold to it? No, one must seek out the point from which "it" best comes forth! The point is not one's own standpoint. One makes oneself a laughingstock if in front of the artwork [in front of the river, the Raven] one says what one otherwise could [have already said], that one is [...] standing at one's own standpoint. If an artwork exercises its fascination, everything that has to do with one's own meaning and own opining seems to disappear. (Gadamer, 2007a, p. 214)

Thus, a hidden second point:

> When we say about the artwork that to be an artwork "it" must come forth, then I think one would do better to compare it to nature, which lets the flower come forth. The work of art is precisely not a product that is finished when the artist's work in it is done. (p. 214)

Regarding the work itself, then, this very writing (to use this nearby example that, if you happen to be still reading) is clearly and obviously not done when the writer's work is done. What you are reading, just like that photograph, just like that song of Adrianne Lenker's cited above, *is not done with me* and thus, *it* is necessarily likewise *undone*, unfinished and open and susceptible to being read and re-read, open to being ignored, adored, scorned, dismissed, forgotten, found useful or trite. This sort of inquiry and writing deliberately attempts to keep this live wire open and vulnerable, *because that is what it is*—open and vulnerable—this father, grandfather, rivers, memory, entwining, love, sorrow, song, ancient new things:

> To use the hermeneutic adage, the world has become open to interpretation to *exactly* the extent that I am open to the interpretability of the world. And here is the great, seemingly paradoxical situation: "keeping ourselves open" and "keeping the world open" (Eliade, 1968, p. 139) are the same thing. As we become experienced, having cleaved with affection and made ourselves "roomier," the world's roominess can be experienced. (Jardine et al., 2008, p. 53 as cited in Jardine, 2016a, p. 81)

> My heart is broken,
>   Open. (Fields, 1990)

Don't worry about running into repeated citations as we go along. My repertoire is limited, as is the case with repertoires. Let them re-murmur. Like this—the grips of handwriting as a place to settle together, staying with the troubles that are real and part of the real work.

Thus, I am right at the center of this in practicing my own vulnerability to the interpretability of the world—what Buddhism would call my ability to experience the lines of dependent co-arising (*pratitya-samutpada*) bristling around the simplest of things—but this center is not subjective in character. I myself get exploded outward into these lines of dependence and inquiry becomes following these trails as my blood trails behind. When it works, *I myself* "break forth as if from a center" (Gadamer, 1989, p. 458). I can't contain myself! That's when I know it is working. That is when I know that I have to get to work and not just sail with abandon.

And if this starts to sound like easy, *off the cuff*, dimwitted, overly emotional ecological babbling, go read those passages in *Truth and Method* (1989) or *The Great Treatise* (2000) for all they are worth, for all they ask of you, and trace the dozens of penstroke colors of reading them and rereading. This sort of work can have a lovely (or vaguely nauseating) poetic face full of lilts and swoops and the great challenge of remembering and echoing.

Watch out, though. A phrase just tossed out above has more teeth than expected, has more depth than I have the life to fully follow. Outplayed in this lovely, gentle pitch, hot potato now in your lap:

> It is necessary that a man should dwell with solicitude on, and cleave with affection to, the things which he wishes to remember. (Thomas Aquinas, paraphrasing the *Ad Herennium*; cited in Yates, 1974, p. 75)

Might you happen to be Catholic? Watch what happens, because this reminds me of Thomas King's (2003, p. 61) lovely pitch that I remember with affection:

> Take [this] story, for instance. Do with it what you will. Tell it to friends. Turn it into a television movie. Forget it. But don't say in the years to come that you would have lived your life differently if only you had heard this story. You've heard it now.

See why I might want to have not forgotten it? Then this:

> If one's sight is clear and if one stays on and works well, one's love gradually responses to the place as it really is, and one's visions gradually imagine possibilities that are really in it. Vision, possibility, work, and life—all have changed by mutual correction. (Berry, 1983, p. 70)

And this:

> To know the world, we have to love it. (Berry, [w. Moyers], 2013, n.p.)

And I'm deliberately stringing these citations out this way because I don't want to simply give you referential information that you can store. This sort of inquiry is bent on *affecting* those who come upon it, stimulating a sense of *energeia* rattling along these lines of song, multiple, interweaving and crisscrossing. Asking something of me as a reader. Talking directly *to me*—so, to a student-teacher, let yourself love the weird terrains of multiplying by fractions and what it takes to treat it well, this topography, this *topic* in the curriculum guide. If you treat it the right way, the topic will guide you, as will myriad voices—mine, your teacher's, your students, other good writing about this topic. *These* are the voices to seek out. Over and over again. And all over again when you start thinking of the next topic to be taught and learned.

This is another not-so-secret about this work. To do full justice to all this is a goal I have to give up. However, I am obligated, as a scholar and an inquirer into the quality of our shared and contested ancestries, to get the page number correct, to open readers to Yates' extraordinary book and how Aquinas seems to nestle there, that tree, that species of winged flight that give me comfort, make me recite about you, reading: "Cultivate love for those who have gathered" (Tsong-kha-pa, 2000, p. 64). Pathways. Sidetrails. Cultivate love for a grandfathers' heart grown warm, grown cold. One has to learn to pick one's way and fail at it, too—this, too, eventually left in the hands of readers, in the hands of a future that is not especially certain or clear.

And with this sense of openheartedness, it makes better sense why Gadamer uses the language of play in stepping beyond subjectivization, to recover something of the commonplace aesthetic stirring: at the heart of coming to try to understand anything, work of art or otherwise, we sense that "something is [already] going on, (*im Spiele ist*), something is happening (*sich abspielt*)" (Gadamer, 1989, p. 104). We are called out (of the skin of our selves, our *interior experiences*), not just to play, but to find ourselves *played, elaborated, changed* by what I experience in this way.

Grandson rapt by the hose shower garden sun giggling. And him walk out there and eat the first peas right from the pods, that, too, an old story. We make sure to toss the pods in the compost afterward, part of the Spiel. When it works the works artfulness works on me as much as I on it:

> [It] is an *Ereignis*—an event that "appropriates us" into itself. It jolts us, it knocks us over, and sets up a world of its own, into which we are drawn, as it were. (Gadamer, 2001, p. 71)

And, just to push Gadamer's provocation the whole way, I find a delicious passage like this one, one that I adore but don't yet quite adequately understand. It his abrupt portrait of the "the intimacy with which the work of art touches us":

> Disclosed in a joyous and frightening shock … it … says to us "You must change your life!" (Gadamer, 2007a, p. 131)

And yet, here we bend and stand.
Riverbent waterplay, breathing all around,
Its and his and his and now mine and
Now words, the moist of your very own eye
tripping over this very work to make a giggly stream that
Might stop
You
Too.

This, then, another clue in inquiring in this manner. Not every photograph, not every tree, not every moment, and there is no method for making this happen, making something rise up and open up and flint and tear at my experience:

> I invoke the concept of *energeia* here [regarding "what truth, *aletheia*, or unconcealment, really means"], which has a special value. With this new

conceptual word Aristotle was able to think a motion ... something like life itself, like being aware, seeing, or thinking. All of these he called "pure *energeia*" (Gadamer, 2007a, p. 213)

Energeia. Energy. And how my knees are buckling a bit reading this because of how much energy comes near one's first birthday, how much loving exhaustion and sweet sleep deprivation and shared commiseration over such matters. Ordinary. Like life itself, like water bubbled up, still welling after decades.

In an alternate translation, Sheila Ross (2006) renders part of this passage of Gadamer's as "something like aliveness itself" (p. 108). And how this aliveness now includes boys and their boys and a river and Aristotle, musing. Statics and lightning hits and night-terror awakenings of an old man jolted over a baby's living and dying.

Dead ordinary, all this. Stories of it are everywhere, the sky full of birds and singings. I write. Cultivating love best I can. Betraying myself in the process in ways I can't even imagine alone. Composing this in order to compose myself in its presence. Yet another old Tsong-kha-pa idea:

"I compose this in order to condition my own mind" (Tsong-kha-pa, 2000, p. 111)

Settling down to take care of it settles me in its presence. And—surprise!—it seems that it is something already knew long before I read him:

There is something about such gathering that is deeply personal, deeply formative, deeply pedagogical. As I slowly gathered something of this place, it became clear that I was also somehow "gathering myself." And as I gathered something of the compositions of this place, I, too, had to become composed in and by such gathering. And, with the help of cicadas, I did not simply remember this place. Of necessity, I remembered, too, something of what has become of me. A birding lesson: I *become* someone through what I know. (Jardine, 1998a, p. 95; see Jardine, 2016b)

The fact that I forgot this seems to be part of this work as well, remembering and forgetting—Gadamer suggests that this is how one's self is composed and re-composed. In doing this work, one slowly becomes caught up in the quickening re-quickening of the world. It does something to you, this.

This, then, another clue: this sort of work links directly to a sort of whiling or "tarrying time" (Ross, 2006, p. 108; see Jardine, 2008a; Ross & Jardine, 2009)—time-taking over experiencing, sitting waiting, studying, over words and reading and writing and re-writing. As one would do with a work of art, an old photo, an old song. You don't just gobble it up and be done with it. You return. The multitude of the one's gobbled up disappear from view.

Practice has helped me learn that the ones that beckon returning are the ones worthwhile. And this means that *it* takes *its* time, "beyond my wanting and doing" (Gadamer, 1989, p. xxvii), over and over again. Me rereading Gadamer, Tsong-kha-pa, my own writing, even, here, in the face of these boys' arrival. Rereading in ways I could not have done, would not have done, had this not happened. We all know, too, that the better the book, the better the art, the more likely is returning. That likelihood is one of the nests of our affection for it.

That is why this got summoned:

> Cold bites.
> Elbow River.
> Vague memory of an old book (Jardine, 2000),
> an old photo
> taken
> under
> the tough old sun,
> of this father,
> young boy circa 1992

FIGURE 6. UNDER THE TOUGH OLD STARS

(there, in the midst of things
his whole family listening). (Wallace, 1987, p. 11)

Of course the water is part of this family well of midst, as is Bronwen's long-gone breath. She's sung in my ear 33 years and counting:

to find it
here, where it seems impossible
that one life even matters. (Wallace, 1987, p. 112)

It matters.
But stop it. Stop.

I myself tossed shards of broken glass into this water memory. My boy and his and his lovely come back home. I can't just revel.

So, then, this, too, for every father, every mother bereft of such returns, every child buried unmarked, writ right here on this unceded land and water whose name I do not know:

... 215 unmarked graves near a former residential school near Kamloops, British Columbia (Paperny, 2021), reported on May 28, 2021, ...

... 182 unmarked graves of children discovered near Cranbrook, British Columbia
(Migdal, 2021), reported on June 20, 2021, ...

... 751 unmarked graves on the Cowessess First Nation in Saskatchewan (Eneas, 2021), reported on June 25, 2021, ...

And these, now, of course, are already out of date [but leave the urls there even if they have disappeared ... that, too, is a hint of something nearby]. Years and years ago, in a reference I can no longer trace, Canadian author Robertson Davies said something like this, that becoming educated means becomes haunted by more ghosts. This, of course, is good news and bad news. Composing oneself is always haunting. Stuffed toys are lined up along the Tsuut'ina Nation fence nearby. Thought and Memory. "Everything is teaching you. Isn't this so? Can you just get up and walk away so easily now?" (Chah, 2004, p. 5) (—I read this, now, just like driving by those fences every day in eagerness to see my family nearby, living on Tsuut'ina land).

Bloody, meagre start, how that river now clouds red, now clouds tears spent and tears in fabrics. I have to beg forgiveness for enjoying this newly arrived photo oh so much, given recent events, breaking forth in every direction, Kamloops, Uvalde, of children not returning and me so exhilarated over Elbow River photos and returns:

And I have to let myself enjoy *this more than I might have ever imagined*, given those very same recent events. This and writing are all I've got, a meagre, little, quiet witness, useless, inadequate in a surround where there is no adequacy. (Jardine, 2021a, b)

I'm gonna shine out in the wild kindness
And hold the world to its word. (David Berman, 1998)

Crouched in the
same river always the

same river twice.
Cradled right here, waters he knew well and knows.
Welled up.
Still.
Hold the world do its word!
Pick a pea!

I'll have cause to sing these songs again before we're done:

All we can do is try to speak it, try to say it, try to save it. Look, we say, this land is where your mother lived and where your daughter will live. This is your sister's country. You lived there as a child, boy or girl, you lived there. Have you forgotten? All the children are wild. You lived in the wild country.

(Ursula Le Guin, 1989, p. 47, from "Women/wildness")

On this planet every sigh creates a morphic resonance
somewhere in the dark corners of light
… in that shadow rising out of light
the mind's shadow   its brevity   its silent grace
its faint edges dispersing and gathering in again
unsure of where to settle down for the night.

Don Domanski (2021, p. 18), from Homeworld

CHAPTER SEVEN

To Know the World, We Have to Love It

If one's sight is clear and if one stays on and works well, one's love gradually responses to the place as it really is, and one's visions gradually imagine possibilities that are really in it. Vision, possibility, work, and life—all have changed by mutual correction. (Berry, 1983, p. 70; I understand. Same gaggle from a few pages back. Still lovely)

Below the ecological crisis lies a deeper crisis of love. For love to return to the world, beauty must ... return, else we love the world only as a moral duty. (Hillman, 2006b, p. 175)

I don't know of any topic in any curriculum guide that is not worthy of love, devotion, and study. I've never seen any topography, treated with affection, that cannot become an open and rich and living field of good work, good questions, shared and contested ancestral voices, and thrilling, often humiliating and painful and worthwhile discoveries and lessons. Loved, such places begin to glow and shed their light on us.

They become light, buoyant. Places to settle for the night, full of morphic resonances. This old piece of writing now staggers to stand in the face of "Why study?" That question condemns the deadliness that schooling has come to represent. It partly means that we need to give up studying *at all*. It also means that we have to give up studying *this* and now need to study *that*. I'm offering a foolish third thing: we need to *study properly*, that is, in a way proper to the topics, the topographies, we are studying, a way that does not tear them to pieces but instead comes to carefully align with the interrelatedness of those living fields themselves. Study itself must be ecological *no matter what the topic*, if our sorrowful times are to be felt and dealt and ameliorated.

"Sometimes it is necessary to reteach a thing its loveliness" (Kinnell, 2002, n.p.). This is our central task as teachers, not just with students but also with all the knowledge entrusted to us in schools. *All of it.* Well-meant one-off courses on the environment as a sub-division of "science education"—well, this might be better than nothing, but there is a deep current here as well that needs a skinny dip.

Sometimes we have to re-teach seemingly moribund topics what their loveliness is, where they belong, how they fit, where they are properly placed. Sometimes we have to show them their family relations that they have forgotten, that curriculum guide designers have often severed or hidden or never knew in the first place. Sometimes we must do the tough work of remembering how coming to know the world can be lovely, even when what we come to know is tough news to take.

Sometimes we must out-work students who have, many of them, become moribund by school and by causes and conditions far beyond the school's walls. It is hard work to embody and demonstrate and be adamant about the pleasurable prospect of the worlds of study, of thinking, of creating, writing, reading, and the great measures of things.

And not only this:

> The fragmentation and scattershot acceleration that has come to define much of North American life and even more of our children's school-lives seems more and more like a bizarre hoax. On darker days, it seems that it is purposefully wrought in order to induce the terrifying belief that acceleration and an increased (and increasingly mindless) consumption of pretty fragments will save us. It seems, on darker days, that our children are being prepared to become unthinking consumers of purposefully less and less satisfying junk [and that there is no other satisfaction to be had in coming

to know the world]. It seems, on darker days, that we, as teachers, have swallowed wholesale our role in ensuring this preparation. It seems like Sharon [Friesen] and Pat [Clifford] were right, years ago, when they said that we can't do to children what we haven't already done to ourselves, and that their infantalization and dumbing down is premised on our own. This is the great pedagogical trauma of anti-intellectualism that is passed off in many schools of education as "No Child Left Behind," "accountability," and "the real world." We should be ashamed of ourselves, even if our complicity is a result of simple neglect. We have been *had*. (Jardine, 2008b, pp. 223–224)

Even if our complicity is the result of simply not knowing any better—well, I'll recite this again and again until it takes:

Take [this] story [merely hinted at in these few pages], for instance. Do with it what you will. Tell it to friends. Turn it into a television movie. Forget it. But don't say in the years to come that you would have lived your life differently if only you had heard this story. You've heard it now. (King, 2003, p. 61)

To the extent that I surround myself with junk, my life lives up to this surrounding. My life becomes becoming of my surroundings.

Okay, stop. Forget the guilt. Forget the "I didn't know." Forget the "I don't have time." Forget the "I don't care" and risk, for just a moment, the prospect that you have been schooled into not caring, schooled into feeling like time is always short, schooled.

It's fine. Welcome to the club! We've all been had. Come have a look and listen. "To reteach a thing its loveliness": this is our perennial task *with ourselves*, because, again, we can't open this space in students if we don't open this space in our own hearts and voices. And, frankly, the odds are against us in this venture. But look at these words. You've got companions against these odds, people to gather with, things to read, pleasures to share. Your colleagues in this work might not be those immediately on hand, but they are out there to be found and they are multiple. Here we are.

We stand before all those young children, older children, fellow adults, me, here, in front of you as a writer, as examples of how life can turn out. We are this for both our friends and enemies. Before and the in the witness and summons of each other, along with snow and Ravens, along with right-angled triangles and false click-bait distractions. Here we are. And coming to realize what this asks of me, well, again, murmured again, trials, terrible:

> This can't be hurried; this is the dreadful situation that young people are in, and I think of them and I say, well, the situation you're in is a situation that is going to call for a lot of patience, and to be patient in an emergency is a terrible trial. (Berry [with Moyers], 2013).

This quote from a then-83-year-old—this be what, its second recitation in this book?—showed me that I was the kid, and this was my trial, too. This is my perennial task with myself, this tough, rigorous, scholarly, thoughtful, painful, meticulous work and the utter pleasures it can bring. (Hush. This is a secret that is right out in the open). And, as a teacher, as a writer, the other task for me is to sing these songs about what I've found out, tell tales of its real pain and pleasure, tales of the companionship to be had with the Earth, with its slithers and angles and, this morning, minus 36C, its Ravens hoping for a bit of dog kibble, frosted heads, tilting. The female ate a bit. Stopped. Disappeared. Came back with her mate. It would take the rest of my life and more than that to come to adequately know even about this, these birds, this place, seasons, cold fronts, ice fog, and little seedlings already in the bay window facing south.

Coming to know the world can be—must be—an affectionate act of consideration and of letting go of the rushes that distract and distort. And this, of course, takes practice. And we have no reason to assume otherwise that it will be a long, constant haul, one I'm still worrying over and love more now than ever.

But again, here we are, and there is comfort in that, and, as the etymology betrays, common strength.

In times of embattlement (real or imagined, induced and manipulated or circumstantial, or inevitable), I tend to panic, and panic belies patience which is so easy to frighten off, like a startled bird. And once patience is surrounding by anxiety and rush, affection starts to faulter, love seems to need more time than I've got. And again, we are surrounded with feigned and faked and manipulated reasons to panic, marketing tricks, media traps, and false promises.

Cultivating love and affection for the ways and runs and paths of things (Latin *currere*) is a terrible trial, and that trial is called study. It is the sweet suffering that underwrites scholarship, in students and teachers alike. It is our locale of commiseration. We are being asked, as teachers, as scholars and writers and readers, to not join in the fray of spellbinding, distracting, afflictions-arousing, manipulated, real and imagined urgencies.

We don't need urgent and panicky cures for urgency and panic. Urgency changes landscapes and locales into bordered territories; it changes places into battlegrounds where love and studious affection have no chance. Where love and studious affection seem silly.

In this world, then, our lot, our work, our lives, might seem simply foolish and luxuriant in the face of the world "realities." Be ready, talking and thinking and acting like this, for the ridicule that will surely come from a fraught and frightened world. It is part of the terrible trial.

Know full well that you are not alone in such deeply practical pursuit of readiness and patience.

Listen, again: "To know the world we have to love it" (Berry [with Moyers] 2013). See? You've got Wendell Berry on your side already, and him, of course, with all his limitedness and foibles and the like. Of course.

Again, "To know the world we have to love it." If I can? When I'm able? Later in my career once I'm certified, or have tenure? Should the circumstances allow? If I have the time? The funding? The permission? The right school? The right kids? The right medications?

No. Love is not an outcome of the right circumstances but a cause of the right circumstances.

CHAPTER EIGHT

"High Stakes": On the Trail of a Red Herring

Yet another graduate class email note sent out on May 25, 2011. This class was populated mostly by high school and elementary school teachers and administrators, and was co-taught at a local high school. It was a follow-up on threads of conversations had over the mix of what we were reading together and what was being experienced, day-to-day, in their classrooms.

> The idiomatic sense of "red herring" has, until very recently, been thought to originate from a supposed technique of training young scent hounds. There are variations of the story, but according to one version, the pungent red herring would be dragged along a trail until a puppy learned to follow the scent. Later, when the dog was being trained to follow the faint odour of a fox or a badger, the trainer would drag a red herring (whose strong scent confuses the animal) perpendicular to the animal's trail to confuse the dog. The dog would eventually learn to follow the original scent rather than the stronger scent. An alternate etymology points to escaping convicts who would use the pungent fish to throw off hounds in pursuit.
>
> (*Wikipedia* under "red herring")

Say it out loud: it is easier to do good work in elementary schools because there is less at stake.

There. I said it. And heard it said repeatedly, by teachers, by student-teachers, by students themselves.

This "there is more at stake" (in this grade, in that grade) argument in favor of bad pedagogy is a red herring, putting us off the scent. So that we end up fighting with each other about comparative pressures, and comparative freedoms. We're being duped here, side-tracked by a strong scent. Things are in danger of staying the same if we follow this scent.

Something escapes again with this red herring. If I were a tiny bit more paranoid, I might suspect that this line of argument, this "story"— "you can do interesting stuff in elementary school because the stakes are not as high"—has been planted *on purpose* to divert our attention and to maintain a perceived level of feeling powerless, thereby leaving the "system" uninterrupted. To quote F.W. Taylor at length:

> It would seem almost unnecessary to dwell upon the desirability of standardizing, not only all of the tools, appliances and implements throughout the works and office, but also the methods to be used in the multitude of small operations which are repeated day after day. There are many good managers of the old school, however, who feel that this standardization is not only unnecessary but that it is undesirable, their principal reason being that it is better to allow each workman to develop his individuality by choosing the particular implements and methods which suit him best. And there is considerable weight in this contention when the scheme of management is to allow each workman to do the work as he pleases and hold him responsible for results. Unfortunately, in ninety-nine out of a hundred such cases only the first part of this plan is carried out. The workman chooses his own methods and implements, but is not held in any strict sense accountable unless the quality of the work is so poor or the quantity turned out is so small as to almost amount to a scandal. In the type of management advocated by the writer, this complete standardization of all details and methods is not only desirable but absolutely indispensable as a preliminary to specifying the time in which each operation shall be done, and then insisting that it shall be done within the time allowed. Neglecting to take the time and trouble to thoroughly standardize all of such methods and details is one of the chief causes for setbacks and failure in introducing this system. (From Frederick Winslow Taylor, 1903)

Don't believe for a moment that elementary school teachers are necessarily immune to *any of this*.

Just a quick aside, here. We have to remember that what it means to
be "held responsible for the results" *already means*, in Taylor's system,
"held responsible only and always for the efficiency of the achievement
of the results." One is not acting responsibly if one deviates from, questions, expands upon, explores, questions, elaborates, and spends time
with these pre-determined results. All that—how it is done, what is
done, the material used, the rules to be followed, the order of those
rules, the specification of time allotted—must be in fixed in advance of
the arrival of the "workers" (teachers or students or administrators—
remember that "managers" under Taylor's system are themselves prey
to the system itself, shaped by it, distorted and silenced by it [see Cowley
below]).

And, from Taylor's *Principles of Scientific Management* (1911):

> In the past the man has been first; in the future the system must be first. (p. 2)

On my less paranoid days, I understand how large "systems" like
schooling tend to propagate ways of speaking, ways of "telling the real
story about what's happening." This is the "ghost echo" that we have to
identify more carefully, because it is a story produced in closed system.
After declaring that "the man" used to be first but now "the system"
is first, Taylor goes on to write that "this in no sense implies that great
men are not needed. On the contrary, the first object of any good system must be that of developing first-class men; and under systematic
management the best man rises to the top more certainly and more
rapidly than ever before." (p. 2). Remember, though, that "greatness"
and "first-class" here mean those who can maintain the system and its
efficiencies. Remember that the purpose of the suggestion box in such
settings is to take suggestions that, over time, eliminate the need for
further suggests—this is the moment where the system becomes first,
and "the man" is simply either fitting into it or ejected out of it (teachers and students alike). This is the same "closed circle" echo found in
The Fraser Institute's Annual Report Card on Alberta Schools: "If teachers
were following the provincial curriculum by definition they would be

teaching to the test. If they're not teaching to the test, then they're not doing their job." Once this loop closes, the dominance of this form of thinking then projects upon any dissent the character of being irresponsible, being "unaccountable." Hence another red herring diverts. Inquiry looks like letting kids do whatever they want and to hell with the curriculum, let's just be free and arty and "creative."

There is a whole stream of literature, broadly under the title of "critical pedagogy" that tries to articulate this oppressive, side-tracking, silencing, deliberately intimidating, enclosed and self-referential structure. As with F.W. Taylor's assembly line, such "regimes" (as Michel Foucault calls them) propagate stories that induce sleepiness and dull-mindedness, compliance and so on. Remember that passage from Neil Stephenson's novel *Anathem* that Sharon and I cited in the "Fielding Knowledge" paper of ours:

> We end this meditation with a passage from Neal Stephenson's *Anathem* (2008, p. 414). It sets a fabled scene of fiction that is far more true to "the real world of schools" than those schools' claims of reality:
>> Thousands of years ago, the work that people did had been broken down into jobs that were the same every day, in organizations where people were interchangeable parts. Al of the story had been bled out of their lives. That was how it had to be; it was how you got a productive economy. If … employees came home at day's end with interesting stories to tell, it meant that something had gone wrong. The Powers That Be would not suffer others to be in stories of their own unless they were fake stories that had to be made up to motivate them.
>> (Friesen & Jardine, 2009, p. 155)

"The Powers that Be would not suffer others to be in stories of their own unless they were fake stories means to motivate them." Even though as teachers we all experience intimately the terrible, divisive pressures of our profession, these are diversions and if we fall into them too deeply, they will exhaust us. They will exhaust us because, as Michel Foucault and others have demonstrated, *they are designed to exhaust us*:

> Many models of curriculum design seem to produce knowledge and skills that are disconnected rather than organized into coherent wholes. The National Research Council (1990, p. 4) notes that "To the Romans, a curriculum was a

rutted course that guided the path of two-wheeled chariots. Vast numbers of learning objectives, each associated with pedagogical strategies, serve as mile posts along the trail mapped by texts from kindergarten to twelfth grade." (Bransford, Brown, &Cocking, 2000, 138). An alternative to a "rutted path" curriculum is one of "learning the landscape" (Greeno, 1991-tellingly for us, Greeno's paper is on numeracy). In this metaphor, learning is analogous to learning to live in an environment: learning your way around, learning what resources are available, and learning how to use those resources in conducting your activities productively and enjoyably (Greeno, 1991, p. 175). Knowing where one is in a landscape requires a network of connections that link one's present location to the larger space. Traditional curricula often fail to help students "learn their way around" a discipline. (Bransford et al., 2000, p. 139; Friesen & Jardine, p. 155)

How could something we experience so intimately and personally actually be a Red Herring? Because its realities are not personal but inscribed into the ways of schools themselves in such a way as to *hide from view* and let us think we have a "personal" problem or weakness.

However, under threat (exams coming, kids can't read, multiculturalism, IPPs, increased accountability and surveillance structures, increasing class sizes, removal of support systems and so on), there is a base and sane instinct to revert to "the tried and true" and this is exactly what dismal efficiency-movement-based pedagogy promises. In exchange for your dismal state, the dismal state of your students and your unwanted-but-required dismal treatment of the living disciplines of the world, we'll provide security against threat; we will provide a "cover story" wherein, as long as you do what you are told, you will not be responsible for what happens next. Large systems bent on their own continuance will then, in a brilliant and often unconscious act of project, make me feel as if this is all for my own good and for the good of students (and not simply for the good of the uninterrupted perpetuation of the system itself). Large systems make us believe that if our attendance rates are very low, there is a problem with the kids themselves—they "lack initiative" and this projection leaves undisturbed and unarticulated how we are working in a system which, according to Taylor, do[es] *not want initiative.*

So here comes the smell of the Red Herring. Even those most telling representatives of this systematized regime, Provincial Examinations, are not served well by aiming simply at the perpetuation of this regime. The same is true of those little color-coded developmentally sequence readers that stalk Grade One classrooms: they are bent on manufacturing literacy and end up tearing apart the very living fabrics of language and story telling that they are meant to "teach." When a parent comes to the Kindergarten door and says that it is important for their child to learn to read and spell, etc., *this* is not debatable. Yes, of course it is, but a parent's (or our) panic over such matters must not be allowed to lead to the hunker-down threat reaction that reverts to a pedagogy premised on breakdown and subsequent regimes of industrial assembly. When a student says that his or her performance on a Provincial Examination is important, *this* is not debatable. But we have to resist the panic-reaction that leads to a pedagogy premised on breakdown and subsequent regimes of industrial assembly ("teaching to the test"). All this, as is clear from the language enveloping it, is a pedagogy based on something akin to war consciousness. It is not an accident that High School teachers often called their site of work "the trenches." [see the chapter below entitled "Owning up to being an animal"]

It is our job to unwind this self-perpetuating and circular logic that has us spellbound and sometimes feeling overwhelmed and helpless. Check out the October 2010 issue of *Teacher Librarian*, Sharon Friesen's study entitled "Uncomfortable Bedfellows: Discipline-based Inquiry and Standardized Examinations" that demonstrates that performance on standardized provincial examinations *goes up* when teachers stop teaching—to-the-test and instead pursue engaging inquiries with students in their classrooms. Performance on standardized examinations *goes up* when we stop feeling threatened by the insistent parent of a Kindergarten student *and* by the "this is make-it-or-break-it time for Grade 12 students' whole future life!" The difference between these two is irrelevant. The battles set up between these two is irrelevant. The battles that are set up are themselves F.W. Taylor-like diversions meant to induce panic, complacency, meant to divide in order to conquer dissent and keep the "system" the way it is. The inheritance of breakdown that comes down from F.W. Taylor and that has infested the very structure of schooling is also mean to break us down. Under threat, we retract into the seeming securities of worksheets that teach to the test and into heated battles about the wrong things. Even if our sole goal is to increase performance on standardized system examinations, Taylor is wrong: teaching "to" the test, teaching "to" the system, fails to achieve its own goal of improving performance on such tests. "Teaching to the test" increases a sense of disengagement and lack of initiative ("we do not want initiative from our men" Taylor quote).

In that *Teacher Librarian* document, there is a link to the rubric that was used to assess the character of classroom inquiry as criteria for the study. (Otherwise, to find this, go to: galileo.org).

Look back at the WDYDIST document [Friesen, 2009]. Attendance goes up with engagement; completion rates are affected positively with engagement. Teachers are less managers and more *teachers* who know their way around a living field of knowledge. So, students are "happier" (an old religious adage, the young are attracted to wisdom—David G. Smith at U. of A. has written about this extensively; he also wrote a paper years ago entitled "Children and the Gods of War" [Smith, D.G., 2020c]—see above re: "the trenches"); teachers are able to be re-involved in the disciplines of the world and inviting the young into these living worlds and feel, in however-small a way, less like managers or traffic cops (or, as William Pinar put it, "deliverers of other peoples mail"); the disciplines themselves are treated better and are understood and taken up in ways that heeds the health and well-being of those disciplines.

And marks go up on the Provincial exams.

And Kindergarten kids begin to learn to read for reasons other than "improving my reading skills" (as one Grade Two kid said in response to the question, "Why do you read?" The literature supports this, the Ministry of Education supports this, the curriculum documents support this, scholarship supports this, WNCP [Friesen & Jardine, 2010] supports this).

And yet somehow we live in a profession where it is legitimate to say unchallenged: "I'd love to do more interesting work, but we've got exams coming."

Whatever the stakes, and *whatever* the grade, and *whatever may be* the swirl of echoes we feel day to day in our work, *whatever* the pressures, better things happen (to kids, to teachers and to the integrities of knowledge itself) when students and teachers are engaged in authentically coming to know their way around some living field of the world. Instead of being supported by the false promise of a system unwittingly bent on maintaining the threat just enough to keep us and our students obedient, we can become supported by something far more reliable and trustworthy: the world and its ways.

So, all this ended with my co-teacher and I arguing vehemently. I'm going to give a scattershot of my own spittings and so on. I'm doing this to make the underbelly visible for what then takes time to write about and compose myself over:

> *I think we have to stay focus[sed] on our mutual desire for good pedagogy and let that desire, slowly and over time, shed light on the similarities and differences of our circumstances and help erode some of them and confirm others. Pitting each other in a situation of who has it worse—well, I know of no way to get out of that ditch once we're in it, especially if we start the class on this footing.*

> *I do know that class sizes are different, schedules are different, content is different. I do know this. This came up last night. I know that long-standing habits are harder to break. This was brought up explicitly last night. They are starting to think about this, but it is just starting.*

> *I never said that there is no difference in causes and conditions and threats and pressures between K and 12. This came up last night but is also just starting.*

> *I think elementary schools are more amenable to inquiry, but I don't believe it is because there is less at stake, nor do I believe that the pressures of High School exempt high school teachers from issues of good pedagogy under the rubric of "high stakes therefore can't do it." Not all elementary schools are thus amenable, either. So even under more theoretically amenable circumstances, inquiry doesn't necessarily emerge.*

> *I don't think Grade 12 teachers are stupid or cowardly. They are living in what is often pedagogically degraded and disempowered and strangulated circumstances. That any of these people decided to take these classes at all is already smart and brave and I don't believe that we are ignoring the realities of their lives or trivializing their circumstances.*

> *I never said that the things that condition inquiry are simply in teachers' hands or minds. I was quite explicit about institutional and cultural demands that put us all under threat in different ways. I said that instead of starting out by fighting with each other over these things (and, I've found, that is precisely what will happen if we begin*

there), supporting each other over pursuing good pedagogy and what that might be and then helping each other unwind and decode and, if possible, sidestep our circumstances is a better idea. Otherwise we exhausting ourselves in a fight that is, however real and painful, an institutional set-up. This means, for me, that the elementary school teachers also need to understand something of their amenable circumstances (in some elementary schools) and be more forgiving of and articulate about the circumstances of High School. This, I believe, will come with time.

I never said in what I wrote that it isn't harder in Grade 12. It's often awful. And [this high school's] circumstances are especially awful. That is why we having this class here and not elsewhere.

E.g. we started talking in class last night about the class marks/provincial exam marks "spread" issue. This is the first time some of the H.S. teachers have had an opportunity to say anything or hear anything about any of this out loud at all in a circumstance where they can be supported in thinking this through and becoming more delicate and detailed with it and with how to respond to goofy and incompetent administrative demands. In a place where it isn't just complaining and gossip but true and untangleable, and where alternate ways in real schools are already available to be studied as well. And the elementary school teachers need to hear that this is what happens to so many of their students so they can think through their own circumstances with more delicacy and generosity and insight.

CHAPTER NINE

A Pedagogical Journal Entry from 2010 on a Persistent Analogy

This writing is nearly 15 years old. I've since I've retired from my job but not my work. Since, two grandsons nearby. Since, ecological matters loom and over-loom, distractions have accelerated. Here I sit, 2023, finding reading this again both fond and feeble. Too much and not enough. But then, as with analogies, placing these vivid streams of imagination, thought and study alongside each other, trying to let them be answerable to each other, has allowed me to loosen the enclosedness of each, and let each mingle with the other, let each elaborate, expand and enrich the other.

A small look at the writings from several chapters below shows that each of these three threads would read the list of "all three contain ..." in their own way, and yet, they also, as per the spontaneity of our human ways, lend each other, not identical ideas, but instead, an ear to family resemblances. Here, cite from a passage many pages below:

To understand an analogy, I must:

> ... run [] up and down the known *range* of cases to which the analogy applies, by actually calling up the spectrum of *different* exemplifications and then *catch [] the point.* (Norris-Clarke, 1976, p. 67)

That work of "the spontaneous and inventive seeking out of similari-ties" (Gadamer, 1989, p. 432) is what hermeneutics names as the "basis of the life of language" (p. 432). *Here* is where the counterpoint of "objec-tivity" resides:

> It requires a special effort of memory to recall that, alongside the scien-tific ideal of unambiguous designation, th[is spontaneous and inventive seeking out of family resemblances constitutes the] life of language itself [and] continues unchanged. (Gadamer, 1989, pp. 433–434)

> The topic must be allowed to "to expand to its full analogous breadth of illu-minative meaning." (Norris-Clarke, 1976, p. 72)

...

In retrospect and perhaps as befits passing 60 years old, my work can be read as the working out, on multiple fronts, of a Great Analogy between hermeneutics, Buddhism and ecology.

All three contain critiques of the erroneous belief that things have separate self-existence.

All three point to a way of experiencing, articulating, and under-standing the dependent co-arising of things.

All three speak in variegated ways of the en-fielded family resem-blance or kinships of things.

All three contain images of ancestral lines and great, embodied, shared and contested inheritances.

All three speak of an aesthetic experience that involves suffering, undergoing, and the refuge of a type of letting go in which a fright-ened ego barricaded inside its own self affirmations and wantings and doings ends up played *out* into the abundant embrace of things.

All three speak of the need of certain practices and paths to be taken for such experiences to be cared for, cultivated.

All three speak of taking refuge with those who seek this way, and of avoiding the exhausting distractions of those things we've set up in error.

All three speak of compassion and love for beings caught in these webs of illusory permanence and the desiring grasps that such webs induce.

All three speak of impermanence and finitude and the deeply experienceable earthliness of our common lot.

And all three speak of the agonizing joy that comes from coming to know about and become practiced in practicing such matters.

All three, then, and in the end, speak of passing such matters along to the young. All three are pedagogical.

CHAPTER TEN

"Owning up to Being an Animal": On the Ecological Virtues of Composure

Preamble

My suggestion, here, of composure, of composition, of writing as an ecological virtue is not offered as an indiscriminate, universal aspiration. It is not necessary, only possible, workable. Sometimes we must find ourselves on the steps of City Hall.

But composure has been a worthwhile pursuit for me and others, however successful or not, however fleeting and momentary sometimes. I get blind. I get encased. I easily get riled for the profit of others. Humiliated. The very declaration of universal aspirations is, in its own way, part of how we got into this eco-critical fix we're in.

Sometimes it takes. Sometimes it doesn't.

My aspirations are not universal. Breath, even when its short and hot, is always *someone's*. I own up. Every suggestion of ecological virtue is, at the same time, a wee plea for forgiveness. My capacity, like anyone's, is limited:

When we find ourselves in dangerous situations in which there are abundant stimulants for the afflictions, we should cultivate the antidotes to them with a

> proportionate intensity and we should stand up to them in a thousand ways. It is said that the best practitioners use as the path the very object that gives rise to the afflictions. Average practitioners apply the antidotes and hold their ground. Practitioners of a more basic capacity must abandon such objects and retreat. (Tsong-Kha-Pa, 2000, p. 111)

I'm often unable to stand up in a thousand ways. Sometimes I must abandon and retreat and do what I then am able. When I do, I write. Proportionate intensity might seem like a good aspiration, but not if I'm not up to it in proper proportion. I'll just get spend, worn out.

In the end, "I compose this in order to condition my own mind" (Tsong-Kha-Pa, 2000, p. 49) and then battle with trying to live up to things I can write about that are more ecologically virtuously than I can currently consistently live. Thus, too, Tsong-kha-pa's great reminder: "Practice those things that you can practice now. Do not use your own incapacity as a reason to repudiate what you cannot engage in" (Tsong-Kha-Pa, 2000, p. 49).

Writing, composition, composure, is a small, specific medicine, but not for all ills or all occasions, not for all hands and hearts. And, after all, we've all gathered here in this book to compose ourselves and compose something about the composition ecological virtues. We somehow all agree, however slightly and silently, that to think and rethink such matters, and to write and re-write—might itself be, in some small way, ecologically virtuous.

"To The Sensible Terrain"

The main title of this chapter comes from David Abram's beautiful book *Becoming animal: An earthly cosmology*:

> Owning up to being an animal, a creature of earth. Tuning our animal senses to the sensible terrain: blending our skin with the rain-rippled surface of rivers, mingling our ears with the thunder and the thrumming of frogs, and our eyes with the molten sky. Feeling the polyrhythmic pulse of this place—this huge windswept body of water and stone. This vexed being in whose flesh

we're entangled. Becoming earth. Becoming animal. Becoming, in this manner, fully human. This book is about becoming a two-legged animal, entirely
a part of the animate world whose life swells within and unfolds all around
us. (Abram, 2011, p. 3)

These words are so alluring. I have these green dreams, sometimes nightmares (Jardine, 2023a). To be drawn into this blending. To
deeply feel these pulses. To claim this entirety—the woozy, penumbral
eco-greening of spiny nerve endings: being *of* the earth, embraced and
embracing. And to claim thus the common strength of it, the comfort of
this cuddle and ache and bite, its thrumming and mine. Yes.

I have these green dreams of rain-ripple and mingle, of pulse and
swell. Their pleasures are undeniable.

But what good are they? What is their virtue? Would that I could
stay poised down in this embrace, forgetful of such questions, walking
and breathing under this last foot of dark, solstice snow, and nothing
besides. I know full well, from painful and repeated experience, that
this is a long, hard practice, gaining this poise. Some threads of ecological talk suggest that we let our strange humanity give way to the
yield of this earthward practice, and that this is the path to ecological
virtuousness.

Some suggest being animal, becoming animal. The skysmoke has
the dogs back up in the doorway.

This passage from David Abram doesn't quite say that. It suggests
owning up. It also suggests this *in writing, beautiful* writing carefully
composed.

This composure can be part, I suggest, of such owning up, and it
is a way to offer up oneself to the commiseration and encouragement
of others. Declarations, manifestos, urgent missives and wailings of
grief, too, are needed in this owning up. But so, too, is the art of composure and composition: "Giraffes and tigers have splendid coats. We
have splendid speech" (Hillman, 2008, p. 164) providing we cleave with
calm, composed care to our earthly composition. Providing we practice
and become accustomed to it never quite feeling like enough.

Fall from Memory

Even though it might be possible to, as goes the saying, make a virtue of necessity, something is not virtuous if it is inevitable. However dire our current circumstances might be, action in response is not necessary. In fact, the virtue of something virtuous is that it has no necessity to it. It must be chosen, "actualized." And, of course, chosen and chosen again and again.

Owning up is needed only if it is possible to forget, to deny, to ignore, to lie, to be lied to and drawn into that lie, to withdraw and turn away, to repress, to be misled, or to misconstrue. As Abram's words indicate, our earthly, animate remains can fall from memory. Our earthly mingling can be left uncultivated, unnoticed, even disparaged as sin or contamination or goofy, unrealistic, liberal tree-hugging. Or just emotional or personal. Our skin's feel of its earthly fabric, left unblended and untended, can also atrophy. And yet, all the while, our earthly being and that of our relations thrums along at its own pace, regardless of our regard of it, regardless of owning up or not, affected by our actions even if we deny those effects and lose our affection.

This is why ecological virtue is not what we've done, what we do, or what we will do, but what we *ought* to do, *even if we don't*. (Meanwhile, I've got another sentence ringing in my ears regarding this belched "ought," from James Hillman [2006a, p. 175]): "Below the ecological crisis lies a deeper crisis of love. For love to return to the world, beauty must … return, else we love the world only as a moral duty."

This is part of owning up, this particular thread of my animal earthliness. Distraction and affliction and forgetfulness are always nearby, as near as the rain-thunders hereabouts, nearer, often. If I am animal, a creature of the earth, then this, too, is part of that creatureliness. I can, I have, I continue, to become busy, distracted, forgetful, fearful of thunder, linking the polyrhythmic pulse to night-startles of death, of suffering. Night starts of grandsons' harms imagined more vivid that awake.

And, because of the perpetuity of human suffering, it is easy to be drawn, in response, into marshals of "perpetual war" (Postel & Drury, 2003) against our earthly, animal, living circumstances. We can retract and begin to act as if our dens of retreat can become impervious to choke in the air and flint and blood and memory in the water, forgetting altogether how our unmeasured, panicky actions are themselves not just the *effects* of feeling threatened but are, in fact, part of the *cause* of that very choke and flint. Worse yet, the worse the air and water, the worse can be the threat-based retraction that cues of our large, prehensile brain to build larger and larger gripped buttresses against the threat with little or no notice of how what we build can have a hand in causing the threat we then build against.

If we are creatures of the earth, this is part of our peculiarly human locale in the variegated array of animal fleshes. We lean toward the arising of a war against threat itself. It is perhaps no coincidence that our current ecological circumstances and the "war on terror" have co-arisen.

Owning up means, in part, owning up to how we have been perennially driven by this panic, this fear, how we've become repeatedly caught in a loop, where panic breeds panic, where threat breeds monstrous responses that then threaten us, as so many current ecological warnings are foretelling.

There is no sense trying to think about our circumstances, to think about what might constitute ecological virtue, from *inside* this self-perpetuating loop.

To own up to this, we need to compose ourselves.

Flinching Panic

Owning up to being animal means owning up to the impermanence and perennial, repeated suffering of the world, human and non-human, and learning to not flinch, to not panic at this prospect, as if we could outrun it with our cleverness. As if outrunning is sane and virtuous and not simply exhausting and distracting. We cannot outrun our being animal with coal production, nor with ecological resistances to such production. Differently put, ecological resistance, as much as coal production, must own up to being an animal, to being a creature of earth, and therefore a creature bound to suffering and impermanence *no matter what we do or say or realize or fight for.* Realizing and responding to *this* with composure and grace is the great task of ecological awareness, what distinguishes it, and what makes David Abram's words far more burdensome and beautiful than a nice walk in the woods. Ecological resistance and action must think with terrible composure and not fall prey to flinching panic.

We need to compose ourselves in the face of this insight learn to face it. I need to learn, again and again, of the earthly composition of breath and its coupling with the composition of those birds swooped at the feeder, with that young dog killed a few years back by the cougar and the sorrows that still arise, with this aging pinch of old skin on the back of my hands, and the brisk of a coming Chinook as the sun lows, mooing near the horizon, solstice and the hoped-for coming return of light. To learn, again and again, of the frail winning of my own composure.

How is this earth-fabric composed and how am I composed of it? Who speaks of it? What stories tell of it? To compose myself, I surround myself with composers who can read my life back to me from out beyond my own distraction and frailty. I read David Abram, for example, or:

> sunlight bright on pine boughs   saints asleep in the Great Bear
> the Great Bear asleep in the North Mountain   everything waiting
> for the next words to be spoken something to stir water and gravel
> to braid soil and light a few phrases left over
> from the creation of the world and its sparrow's heart.
>   (Don Domanski, 2013, p. 9, from "Madonna of the Dijaphonous Life")

Or Michael Derby:

> Now little riverbed stones impress upon my bare feet the aggregate intelligence of form and fit, particular trees stand tall in my memory as pedagogically significant, the cheap yellow paint on my pencil peels and reveals flesh—what kind of mushrooms are these? From somewhere deep within the inquiry, beneath the words—how is it possible!— a world approaches.
> (2015, p. 2)

So, I walk and breathe (this, frankly, is tough enough by itself, to not become distracted in such practices), but I, like Abram and Domanski and Derby, also practice writing, composition, as a way to face the fix we're in, this imperiled fix of walking, of breathing, of seeing Great Ursula bristling in the minuses of updraught air chills at night:

> Seeing the frailty of your life through seeing the breath is the meditation on the recollection of death. Just realizing this fact—that if the breath goes in but does not go out again, or goes out but does not come in again, your life is over—is enough to change the mind. It will startle you into being aware. (Chah, 2001, p. 44)

My grandson barefoot on gravel roads without a wince, just like my own feet once loved so well. Another one just an armful of warm and notice.

But why, then, compose? Why struggle with the written word, here, now? Why burden you as a reader with reading such words? Why isn't noticing the ice crystals in intimate display overhead and feeling the animal shivers in response enough?

Because, over the past 35 years, I've walked hallways of schools that are breathless and have no repose. I've too often felt the pulse— of teachers, of students, of my own—quicken in panic over threats of accountability, surveillance-driven rushes, with affection lost for what is learned, for these living fields of work we have inherited. Writing well of these matters can let our affection for these living fields grow. It can help make memory last.

Let me own up: it can, it *might*, outlive me.

I write anyway.

Leisure

In writing, we have a way to own up to part of our animality—we compose about our composition, and some texts work as instructions on how and why to remain under the bristle of stars, even when entering a school's enclosure:

> "Texts are instructions for [the] practice" (Tsong-kha-pa, 2000, p. 52) of precisely paying more intimate and proper attention to the resounding. Don't worry. Study, properly practiced, will not ruin the *aesthesis* of ecological reveries, only their limited and limiting naiveties. (This is re-cited below)

Such well-composed works can thus help me remain composed as much as me trying to compose my own words and the lovely art of mingling these together. They remind me that schools can be locales of teachers and students composing their lives and learning of the composition of things, their incantational grammar:

> The aim of such meditations is the cultivation of the intimacy and immediacy of the experience of everyday life. Not only is "wherever you are ... a place of practice" (Tsong-kha-pa, 2004, p. 191). Tsong-kha-pa also insists [that] ... the purpose and object of study is precisely the deepening of practice itself. After all, "why would you determine one thing by means of study and reflection, and then, when you go to practice, practice something else?" (2000, p. 52). [Composure, composition, is] meant, in the end, to make us more susceptible to the beautiful abundance of things as we walk around in the world. (Jardine, 2016f, p. 304)

To cultivate this work of insight into our composition, our composure, the knife-edge fray of the world that would draw us into simply reacting to its impingement must be held at bay. School, scholar: from the Latin *schola* meaning, in part, "to hold back, to keep clear" (Online Etymological Dictionary, under "school, n."). It also, ironically, means "leisure." Returning school to its Latinate roots of composure—composing myself in the face of coming to know of the composition of things—has been, in my own work, an ecological matter.

In the end, a weird obligation is placed upon the composure of scholarship, to not waste this "leisure time" squandering one's breath while others' breaths are robbed in thin air. Thus, the particular ecological composure of scholarship itself requires its own tough, unflinching scrutiny. It is, in its own way, opulent, luxurious, and privileged, and it had better, therefore, earn its keep:

> Why would I waste ... such a good life? When I act as though it were insignificant, I am deceiving myself. What could be more foolish than this? Just this once I am free from continuously trekking the many narrow cliff-paths of leisure-less conditions, the miserable realms. If I waste this freedom and return to those conditions, it would be similar to losing my mind. (Tsong-Kha-Pa, 2000, pp. 121–122)

It is difficult to find ways to share what I can of the relief from suffering that composure can bring, the ways it can clarify action, identify hidden conditions and causes and antecedents that have blocked insight, reveal unspoken or forgotten or suppressed histories and aspirations. Writing. Study. These both rely on and give rise to composure and thus, like any practices worthy of the name, they require practice to become practiced in.

Their dreadful absence from most schooling is part of why this book threads and streams.

A "Dreadful Position"

Owning up to our "being an animal" is thus, in part, *owning up to the weakness of that animality* and how it can distort our vision as much as clarify it, depending on how well we have learned to not be just drawn into its grieves and panics and startles and starts.

Too much ecological talk asks us to grieve and panic and startle and start. Like this: "alarms," "rapid deterioration," "egregious effects," "darkening shadows," "starkest warnings," "severely and irreversibly compromised," "unprecedented peril" (these are just some of the phrases used in the book proposal for this text). We can all add to this list with great (un)ease. Time is running out. Hurry. Point of no return. Poison. Degradation. Loss. Endangered. Extreme. Drought. Fires. Too late. Too late. Point of no return. Now. Please. Act. Stop. Help.

Every word becomes Capitalized. Then every letter.

Then bolded.

Then bigger in pitch and font and full of ever-multiplying exclamation points. And the email warnings arrive faster, ever-faster, ever-faster, ever-faster, every-single-one-now-marked-**URGENT!**, their sheer and utter frequency—no, *acceleration*—outpacing the possibility of careful attention.

Without being able, somehow, to compose ourselves, we don't suffer simply disappearing ice and bees. We also suffer the environs of our own discomposure over such disappearance. Without composure, we're imperiled twice—first by our circumstances and second by the animal-spittle startle-responses. Our circumstances impend suffering, and our fretful, heated, alarming language *about* those circumstances simply impend the impending of it:

> You must accept [suffering] when [it] arise[s] because (1) if you do not do this, in addition to the basic suffering, you have the suffering of worry that is produced by your own thoughts, and then the suffering becomes very difficult for you to bear; (2) if you accept the suffering, you let the basic suffering be and do not stop it, but you never have the suffering of worry that creates discontentment when you focus on the basic suffering; and (3) since you are using a method to bring even basic sufferings into the path, you greatly lessen your suffering, so you can bear it. Therefore, it is very crucial that you generate the patience that accepts suffering. (Tsong-Kha-Pa, 2000, pp. 172–173)

Bringing our ecological suffering into the path of insight, composure and clarity is how we own up to being an animal, to being *this sort of animal*. And, even though everything around us conspires to tell us that time is running out (you know the words by now. Sing along):

> *This can't be hurried.* Learn all you can about where you are, make common cause with that place, and then, resign yourself, become patient enough to work with it over a long time. And then, what you do is increase the possibility that you'll make a good example. And what we're looking for in this is good examples. (Berry with Moyers, 2013, emphasis mine)

I understand. Here I am, old enough to have the end clearly and constantly in sight, suggesting something terribly difficult to those who will likely suffer longer and more than I:

> This is the dreadful position that young people are in and I think of them, and I say that the situation you're in now is going to call for a lot of patience, and to be patient in an emergency is a terrible trial. (Berry with Moyers, 2013)

Again, this terrible trial is part of the deeply human lot of owning up to being an animal. We must wrench ecological virtue from the grip of our own woes, our own suffering and not fall prey to the modern sins of acquiescence, complacency, distraction, terror, or denial that define far too much educational theory and practice, caught as it too often in the hurry.

There Is No Monster

Here's a nightmare that haunts me too often: that both those protecting the earth and those despoiling it can be caught in analogous loops of discomposure, each pitted against the other, one monstrous prospect summoning up its equally monstrous opposite, meeting in kind over night terrors, each feeding the other, *needing* the other, unwittingly sustaining the other in order to sustain itself. There is no virtue to be had in maintaining ourselves in this particular dance of hubris and nemesis, and the long arguments over which is which. This is such an old story in human history, of one rising up to meet the other in kind, each convinced that they are sheer and utter opposites.

I'm reminded both of Friedrich Nietzsche's (1975, p. 346) characterization of how human will deliberately seeks out that which resists it in order to increase its own feeling of agency and efficacy.

I'm reminded, too, of Ivan Illich's terribly acute idea of "apocalyptic randiness: 'I have an even more horrible example to tell you! Let's imagine an even worse situation!'" (Illich, with Cayley, 1992, p. 127).

Edward Said calls this "vocabulary of giantism and apocalypse" (2001, p. 4). Chuck Bowers calls it a "Titanic mind-set" (2008, p. 11).

This tale is as old as the hills, how the monster feeds on fear and grows in proportion to the (unwittingly) loving attention that the fearful give it.

Pausing over writing this, I'm thinking, am I in love with my panic? Does it make me feel alive and useful and "connected?"

So, what can I do to ensure that the monster won't get me, then? *Realize that there is no monster.* There is only the task, the choice, the possibilities, the work in front of me. "Save The Earth" makes it hard to save the earth beneath my feet. Just like "Literacy Skills" (too easily spoken in some schools with agonizing worry and aghast-ness) distracts from the real ecopedagogical choices to be made, now, with these young children in this classroom, them with their joys and woes, and me with mine, gathering together to huddle over this story, this conversation, "this and this." For pedagogical practice to be composed, it must not think globally and act locally, but must *think locally*, because it is always and only over the particularities of our lives that we live. The choice of what is best to do is small, intimate, here, nearby. Beware the monstrous shouts of Literacy Skills and Accountability and Surveillance and Time is Running Out. Bloated capitalizations can easily overwhelm and make seem ridiculously meagre this small, intimately ecologically virtuous classroom event.

This is why, when speaking to teachers in schools, I often ask: "Who profits from our panic?" I've taken to repeatedly quoting from an interview with Kevin O'Leary, a former CEO of an online publishing company that makes various reading materials for use in schools with children: "I love the terror in a mother's heart when she sees her child fall behind in reading. I made a fortune from servicing that market" (O'Leary, 2012).

In order to maintain my composure in the fray of schools, I must understand with as much precision as possible, that composure is surrounded by regimes bent on *deliberately* disrupting it and *profiting from that disruption*. And I must come to understand these regimes in enough detail to measure up to their arrival so I can decode them and unravel them when they loom up in monstrous display. This is the calm predatory animal eye of scholarship. I compose myself in their presence, I name them, I cite, with great scholarly care, I summon the strength and wisdom of my companions and ancestors to the best of my ability. I cultivate this ability. I practice. I write, again and again, so that I and others might learn how to spot, how to evade, how to not fall prey to such deliberately induced terror.

CHAPTER ELEVEN

The More Intense the Practice, the More Intense the Demons

FIGURE 7. "HAPPY AS THE GRASS WAS GREEN"

A treated enlargement of my grandson's painting,
used with his parent's permission.

The title I gave this painting comes from Dylan Thomas' "Fern Hill" (1971, p, 195):

Now as I was young and easy under the apple boughs
About the lilting house and happy as the grass was green.

Fern Hill was a place of summer holidays for Dylan Thomas. Written when he was 30 years old, 1944. First read by me the summer I was turning 15, 1965. It was terribly perfect for that strange nostalgia that a friend and I loved to suffer, about childhood already seeming so very long lost. About even last summer, its songs and times, dramatically, tragically lost forever except in sad reveries, reading "Fern Hill" and other of Thomas' works.

It is becoming something else, this painting, well-worthy of Hermann Rorschach (1884–1922), a blot to place my nightmares of the utter fragility of air.

A strange, heartbeat intimacy of smiles and warm bodies dashed by sword-wielding. Oh, sorrow that comes from such close happiness.

...

The main title of this chapter has served me as a warning for those interested in hermeneutic work, myself, of course, included. It is from Patrul Rinpoche (1808–1887) in his book *The Words of My Perfect Teacher* (Patrul, 1998, p. 189) and it summons something of the intimate dangers of carefully studying and becoming familiar with the slipstreams of our lives, both those that live in us, and that we, wittingly or otherwise, live within.

There are reasons for these dangers. Hermeneutic begins by "giv[ing] up a special idea of foundation in principle" (Gadamer, 1984, p. 323), that is, giving up the standard Western- philosophical escape mechanism that allows our studying to [seem to] have, or at least hope for, solid, final, fixed grounding and therefore to gain confidence and stability by referencing some external, permanent, verity, or verities. Hermeneutics leaves us "in between," in an orbit of *unheimlichkeit*

(Heidegger, 1926/1962, p. 233) an "un-homelike-ness" in which we must give up such hopes. It is the same spot wherein we realize our animal-bodied-ness *and* the necessity of keeping our human wits about us, and these in a proper measure never fully gained.

This, by itself, is vertiginous enough, because it means that hermeneutic study is inevitably haunted by the ghosts of doubt, affliction, exhaustion, fear, and failing, but also wonder, speculation, imagination, dreaming, love, all these dumb or insightful or both.

One must become accustomed to sensing that one's efforts are not enough, that one just might be nothing more than an imposter in this work, work whose imposture is bound to be found out by someone who will trumpet foundational assurances about the topic I may have found so hermeneutically fleeting. Or that someone might find out that I am nowhere as singing and assured as is my writing. It is where I venture to find a richer field that my living, and then, perhaps, come back to myself with my heart in my beak.

Two things, here. First, get used to it. Second, you have myriad companions in this work, other homeless wanderers. They can't remedy this situation, but they can commiserate and console and clarify this common lot. They can help you study this mess you're in and not just suffer it. Seek them out. These can be fellow students, scholars present or long-dead, families and friends that are fellow to these ways. Books. This or that swash of paint. Hold your suffering in common. Compassion.

"This is why we read. This is why we write" (Jardine, 2014c).

Even the crack of wood split for winter or the next pull of air, well attended, can help. "Everything is teaching you. Isn't this so?" (Chah, 2005, p. 5).

But there is another layer here which, in part, bespeaks the proximity of hermeneutics to a phenomenological origin, but which also sharply cuts its cleave both to it and from it (see http://www.dabhand.org/WordStudies/Cleave.htm for more details on this lovely dual-inverse meaning of cleaving). Hermeneutic meditations are a bit like this:

Understand "meditation" as it is explained in Dharmamitra's Clear Words Commentary (Prasphuta-pada): "Meditating" is making the mind take on the state or condition of the object of meditation. (Tsong-kha-pa, 2000, p. 111)

This bespeaks a whiff of an old Aristotelian notion of *mensuratio ad rem*, that is, that our study must "remain something adapted to the object" (Gadamer, 1989, p. 261) and not, instead, something forced to adapt to our methodology, or to the research granting agencies ideas of how to write up a legitimate proposal, or "to the wishes, prejudices, or promptings of the powerful" (Gadamer, 1989, p. 261), or to my own hidden or overt pathologies and desires. In this studied and practiced movement to take on the state or condition of the object, it can happen that the object starts to yield up depths and characteristics heretofore unnoticed or occluded. So, the first blush is that the topic we are exploring starts, shall we say, to "break forth" (p. 458) with angular, often suppressed, often pointed bloodlines of implication, contestation, and meaning. Such yielding up means that the topic I am investigating starts running down variegated paths whose turns up ahead make me lose sight of what to do, where to go.

"We must entrust ourselves to what we are investigating to guide us safely in the quest" (Gadamer, 1960/1989, p. 378). But don't be fooled, here, because being fooled and frightened will happen. We must entrust ourselves even when and even though what we are investigating might unleash demons in us that need to be faced for us to proceed. When Gadamer speaks of *Bildung* (1989, pp. 9–18), of cultivation and become hale and robust in a complex civil society, of becoming someone through the study one engages in, he's not simply talking about going to art galleries and other "cultivated," elitist pleasantries. He is talking about facing the mess of one's life in our interactions with the world, letting the world in, learning as much as we can, consulting the threads we inherited with good-heartedness and mild suspicion, and letting out our familial, inherited, secret demons to see whether they can live in the light of day:

> If you are frightened, wondering whether there is a demon in a strange cave at night, your fear is not dispelled until you light a lamp and carefully investigate whether it is there. (Tsong-kha-pa, 2002, p. 334)

As the object breaks forth, so, too, do I get heretofore secrets secreted, confidences betrayed, mistakes, gaps, omissions. I find that my life has been fashioned and inhabited "beyond my wanting and doing"

(Gadamer, 1960/1989, p. xviii), and, over and over again, needs a good talking-to.

Want to hear that phrase again? We arrive, these new voices arrive, as it were, too late, over and over again.

It is quite disturbing to find out that I may have been living a life that is far more unintentionally duplicitous than I hoped or imagined. I think back, over decades years of work, to how many times those, myself included, who feel Hermes rushing nearby and find that that rush unleashes hidden afflictions (e.g., Jardine, 2016g). The yielding up of the topic has a tendency to cascade back on my own meditations, beckoning the arousing of my own lived experience and my own deep, perhaps unexamined, complicities in and to these depths. Hermeneutics thus dually cleaves to phenomenology: this is about my own lived experience as a writer, as a scholar and teacher and student, and the complicities and stubborn blind spots of the life I've come to live. But, in such cleavage, I realize that my own lived experience might reveal another level of blockage for which phenomenological descriptions of immediate experience falls bereft: false consciousness.

In speaking with a graduate student about his work, his responses to my queries and his emergent accusations set off in me a roiling resistance and measured and unmeasured response. My immediate, lived experience became an outcome of feeling threatened and a withdrawal into self-protection (and then, unfortunately [but luckily briefly] lashing responses from within this coiled mess). We can follow Freud, here, or Jung, or Tsong-kha-pa, or both Paul Ricouer and Gadamer (1984) regarding the hermeneutics of suspicion, in witnessing that lived experience is often a gloss for deeply hidden afflictions whose spells need "break[ing] open" (Gadamer, 1989, p. 362).

"Neither the knower nor the known is 'present-at-hand'" (Gadamer, 1989, p. 261) just lying there in the open fully clear and exposed and ready to simply recite what it knows. Rather I, and the topics I encounter, are always and already ensnarled in the world, duplicitous and hidden, not just present, entangled, not just self- existent. Supposed and however-deeply-felt phenomenological immediacy is revealed as profoundly mediated, profoundly dependently co-arising, profoundly in need, therefore, not of surface description or "telling my story," but diagnosis. Not just "seeing" but "seeing through," and seeking cure and, one always hopes, comfort in that cure, commonly held strength.

"Insight is more than the knowledge of this or that situation. It always involves an escape from something that had deceived us and held us captive" (Gadamer, 1989, p. 356). "Breaking the spell" can sounds so trite, but as often happens in those children's stories of spells cast and broken, the next gesture can be traumatic: Oh dear, what have I done? What have I been doing, saying, and thinking? I didn't mean it! Honest!

Thus, the poverty of the *mens auctoris*. There is no method here to help those new to such work to avoid this conundrum. "From it no one can be exempt" (Gadamer, 1989, p. 362), and the only recourse is practice, and that practice must always be done by me, by you, for only there does the locale of hermeneutics really emerge. When Gadamer states that, in this work, "we become ... closer to the real givenness, and we are more aware of the reciprocity between our conceptual efforts and the concrete in life experience," this reciprocity is not a general or universal procedure, but is what is cleverly and tortuously translated in Martin Heidegger's Being and Time (1962, p. 68, H42) as involving "in each case mineness [*Jemeinigkeit*]." No one can become practiced in my stead.

So, be careful and take good note of the swirls of commiseration and encouragement that surround you working, and realize that there are good reasons for many lineages of study to say that you must find a good teacher, a practiced teacher. You can hear hundreds of them howling in what you've been reading, the ones I found, the ones that happened to find me. There is a good reason for thinking of the practice of writing as part of the practice of research itself. Play can outplay the players. You can be outrun, overrun, and such "experience[s] ... [are] not something anyone can be spared" (Gadamer, 1989, p. 356). Gadamer does say that "understanding ... means that one recognizes that the other person could be right in what he or she says or actually wants to say" (Gadamer, 2007c, p. 117). However, part of the deceptively alluring face of hermeneutic work can be the false hope that it just might be my turn to be the one who could be right. *Maybe* I can finally tell my story and be heard uninterrupted.

Sorry to disappoint, but that is not how this work works. However, it may be why some hermeneutic ventures (including some of my own) can end with emotional fraught failure, having just aroused and incited fears of one's demons without breaking them open enough to catch the light.

CHAPTER TWELVE

Thoughts on the Return
of Yesterday's War

This chapter and many that follow show how the contestations in which we are all living are also embroiled right into the fabric of often heated discussions about the nature of study itself, of the shapes and forms of "research methodologies" and their warrants. I've proposed throughout this book that hermeneutics is not just a research methodology that is especially fit to study pedagogical matters because it does not recoil from the ambiguities and ongoing-ness that is a necessary part of teaching and learning. It is also because hermeneutics itself is pedagogical. That is, it is about teaching and learning from its topics of interest and linking old and new, hidden and overt, intended and unintended. Being a student of a topic, and a teacher of a topic. It is not "about" tradition, but about the encounter with traditions. It is about the encounter of the young and the old, the new and the established, the ancestral and the contemporary and how each elaborates the other. However much schools may be organized this way, genuine, living study is about encountering and then, in the company and commiseration of others, working through what we've inherited, casting things off, finding good reasons, heartening, life-affirming reasons to keep certain things, to speak certain ways, to rid ourselves of things, to embrace and remember certain things.

> Who wants yesterday's papers?
> Nobody in the world.
>
> MICK JAGGER AND KEITH RICHARDS (1966)
> FROM "YESTERDAY'S PAPERS."

One Characteristic of a Dominant Culture

One characteristic of a dominant culture is that, because of its dominance, it no longer needs to give an account of itself and or be concerned with its warrantability. It becomes the silently taken-for-granted "way things are," that in relation to which warrant is decided and determined. Research, publication, funding schemes, even the categories of the forms one fills out, are unquestioningly based on the presumptions and requirements of natural scientific research. It is not simply that funding is difficult to secure for interpretive work. It is that the very means of such securing are already, at the outset, cast against its case.

More buried that this, however, and far more pernicious, is another level of dominance: the presumptions and procedures of quantitative research have come to define anything that does not fall in line with those lines of dominance. Under the shadow of quantitative research, qualitative research is said to be about subjectivity, about telling your story, about making things up, about being unaccountably mushy and vague and undisciplined, about being irrelevant and self-involved, overly poetic, emotional, uninformed, "having no proof" (Moules et al., 2017, p. 3), no generalizability, no reliability. It has "little hope of publication."

"Not of practical use."

"Not of interest to readers" (Moules et al., 2017, *en passim*).

It is not especially fundable because it does not cleave to the dominant, recognized and condoned fundamentals.

Interpretive research is, then and, daresay, of course, treated as an object of weird suspicions, like a sort of cultish faith object, something

lurking furtively in some liminal space outside the confines of the surveillances we've come to presume. It is out in the fields (Latin *paganus*),
trod the way of heathens, uncivilized, witches work with familiar cats.

So quantitative research not only "dominates the scene" (Gadamer,
1986, p. 59) but, not coincidentally, has the character of "seiz[ing] upon
and dominat[ing] things [with a] will-to-control" (Gadamer, 1977,
p. 227), thus casting its own shadow over that which slips out of its purview. The dominating character of quantitative research thus *provides
an equally predominant caricature of any alternative to it*. This is parallel to
schools that talk about maybe doing "frills" "later, if there is time."

Sad to say, over many long years, I've seen purportedly "interpretive" work that has fallen hook, line and sinker for this degrading,
bullying, suppressed caricature, and seen good-hearted scholars get
caught in the exhausting, unbecoming and humiliating mugs-game of
attempting to refine and upgrade the contours of this caricature, only to
then get bowled over, over and over again, by stinging questions posed
often out of sheer, I dare say deliberate, ignorance. More than once
over 30 plus years, I have encountered people in positions of power
(for example, external examiners on Ph.D. examinations), literally say,
"Well, I've never heard of hermeneutics!" and who then take that statement as a fully adequate account of why no more needs to be said about
the worth of the work being adjudicated.

Students and scholars alike are often then asked to give, over and
over and over again, a detailed descriptions of a long and publicly available history of interpretive work stretching back, in places, to Aristotle,
even to Heraclitus, and up through the humanist tradition first wrought
at the advent of modern science in seventeenth-century Europe, into
late-nineteenth-century European contestations and detailed quarrels
and concerns over the nature and limits of the human sciences, up
through phenomenology, hermeneutics, into long and complex streams
of refinement and differentiation over the course of the 20th and 21st
century. And all this is the family tree, of course, to contemporary questioning of the value of "the humanities" in a world that is dominated by
market-driven concerns for profitability, and which scoffs as any turbid
and turgid and time-wasting suggestions of the cultivation of insight
into the quarrels and qualms of our living and the potent images, ideas,

and regimes of power that drive our lives "beyond our wanting and doing" (Gadamer, 1989,p. xxviii).

And those demanding this account of this thing they've never heard of often have no qualms in *not remembering any of this*, the next time questions are raised regarding the legitimacy of interpretive work.

Such is the character of dominance.

Only those marginalized need to remember what has happened. Those who are part of the dominant culture can always plead innocence without consequence. Those marginalized must remember their own bloodlines as well as those of the forces of their marginalization. The dominant need remember neither.

Dominance is somnambulant and forgetful by nature, but it sleepwalks and stalks.

How's that for "poetic?" It surely bodes that we are dealing with far more, here, than simply matters of research methods. It is no coincidence that First Nations are speaking up in this fray, that ecological beckonings to heed what lies beyond our will to dominate are becoming increasingly urgent, that those excluded want "in" on what it means to be us.

I could go on. We can't ignore any longer that kin are arising, here, around what only seems like yesterday's war.

Marginalia to the Dominant Text

Those who have become marginalia to the dominant text have always murmured and have been repeatedly turned into a dirty little secret that might go away if we ignore it again. There is a war. It is nothing new. And the quiet urgency of fighting it remains steady and true. Again, make no mistake. This goes well beyond issues of "research methods."

What is at stake in the marginalization of interpretive research is whether scholars have the freedom, and the intellectual responsibility, to explore the lives, often "the pain" (Sanders, 2016), of teachers, of students, of nurses and patients and parents and so on. These varied and varying explorations come via the tough, sometimes vague and nebulous, sometimes contradictory, doorstep stories that are told, voices caught in the confines, for example, of school hallways, stuck, equally, in the confines of the unvoiced and often unvoiceable ways in which schools have been shaped and thus shape teachers and students alike. It is in the voices of those for whom, in advance of their arrival, school has no place or time and can, because of its dominance, abusively blame these exclusions on the very ones it occludes from view. Likewise, parents who, in a moment of profound breathlessness, entrust their only child into the maw of medicalization. Or who know in advance that they will outlive their children. Or who tiptoe their child behind the schoolyard gate and then have an unrecognizable child read back to them by the regnant regimes of schooling that often brook no quarter of response.

The job of Interpretive research is to break these numbing, silencing spells. To go out into the wild "with [a] readiness to be 'all ears'" (Gadamer, 2007d, p. 189) and to gather what we can of the suffering of our living, the language that is used, the images that arise and fall, how and when the joy outbursts, the secrets, the hushed-ness of ordinary life lived. Interpretive work is then charged with trying to give those stories a voice, to "[make] the text[s] ... speak" (Gadamer, 2007b, p. 189) by linking them up to the lifelines of the world that have become hidden from view, "something we thought we'd lost to the work of simply getting by" (Wallace, 1987, p. 12):

> Even those women we dread sitting next to on buses or trains, their bodies swelling with messy secrets, the odour of complaint on their breath, may be prophets. Whether we listen or not won't stop them from telling our story in their own. (Wallace, 1987, p. 48)

This is our work, as scholars, to search and re-search these mixed and convoluted inheritances for tales anciently told, for ancestors that have spoken and written about the matters at hand, so that the doorstep tale becomes a gateway into a larger life, a larger living, a larger commiseration, and I can experience the confines of my own telling opening up beyond the stifle of my own joys and sorrows:

> I don't want to "tell my story." I want to be relieved of it by going to a place (ecos -, topos -/topica -) where I can meet others who can read me back to

myself from beyond my own failings and limits and delusions, beyond the story I've presumed. (Jardine, 2016h, p. xvi).

Interpretive work is charged with not cleaning up these stories, blunting their sting, making them palatable, non-contradictory, smooth and easy. It is charged, instead, with "restoring life to its original difficulty" (Caputo, 1987, p. 2; see Jardine, 1992a, a piece written 26 years ago about what was then "yesterday's war"), a restoration that is necessary because of the oppression and repression of the suffering and hope of, well, all of us, under falsely assuring rubrics and cold steel confidences and marketing gimmicks that want to hear nothing of our living and dying. Interpretive work thus has, I suggest, a deeply political spin:

> *Kenneth Mahea (age 25):* Because of you, I'm actually running for United States representative here in District 34. I want to help the people of this district. What advice do you have for young people like me who are running for Congress and who want to help our nation with wealth and income equality for all instead of just the privileged few?
>
> *Bernie Sanders:* Well, Kenneth, congratulations. It takes guts to do that. Here's my brief message. I've run for office once or twice myself ... many times. First of all, I think you're running for the right reasons. What you have to do is go into your own heart, and you've got to speak to the people in your community, and you've got to have the courage to feel the pain in your community. Go knocking on doors. You've got to become imbued with a passion, you've got to sense the pain, and there is a lot of pain in this country. Talk to people. Learn about that, and then have the guts to stand up to powerful people. Not a lot of people have that courage. That's my message. (Sanders, 2016)

Interpretive work, too, has a deeply ecological spin that links, clearly, to the issues of the exhaustion and apathy of attention:

> It is good to look at what apathy is, to understand it with respect and compassion. *Apatheia* means, literally, non-suffering. Apathy is the inability or refusal to feel pain. What is the pain we feel—and desperately try not to feel—in this planet time? It is pain for the world. It is the pain of the world itself, experienced in each of us. That pain in the price of consciousness in a threatened and suffering world. (Macy, 2003, p. 93)

> Given our culture's fear of pain and the high value it sets on optimism, feel-
> ings of despair are repressed. Hidden like a secret sore, they breed a sense
> of isolation. But when one's pain for the world is redefined as compassion, it
> serves as a trigger or gateway to a more encompassing sense of identity. It is
> seen as part of the connective tissue that binds us to all beings. This self is
> experienced as inseparable from the web to life in which we are as intricately
> interconnected as cells in a larger body. (Macy, 1989, p. 204)

Interpretive work is thus, in this way, a "bridle set with sharp nails" (Tsong-kha-pa, 2000, p. 71), deliberately donned. Through such bringing-to-awareness of the messes we are in, there is the possibility of some relief from, or at least some possibility of commiseration over, the only-seemingly-binding character of our living and our lives by studying the fabric of the world in which we are living and of which my own tale is simply a part:

> This fabric is more abundant, more forgiving and generous and difficult
> than any one of our lives alone can measure, so, in exploring these things,
> in studying thus in the presence and grace of each other, I can be relieved of
> some narrow confine of my "self" by working it out, not simply working on
> it. This is why [interpretive work] feels spacious even when that fabric binds
> and pulls at my attention. (Jardine, 2016h, p. xv)

"The aim of interpretation, it could be said, is not just another interpretation but human freedom" (Smith, 1999d, p. 49), hard won and always in need of re-winning. And this is a freedom *from something* and a freedom, also, *on behalf of something*. It is a freedom from being "bound without a rope" (Loy, 2010, p. 42) to regnant ideas and beliefs, but it does proffer the simple negation of these ideas and beliefs but rather makes visible the causes and conditions of their arising. As goes an old hermeneutic saw, every text, every tale told, can be read as the answer to a question *that could have been answered differently* and therefore, every reading of every text is *possible*, not *necessary*, thus issuing a sort of relief from what appears to be intransigent, dominant confines. The hard-won insights that then arise will, of necessity, mean leaving certain things behind that will no longer support and encourage such precisely such freedom and alertness. It will mean looking foolish and starting all over again. The lifeworld is interpretable. But, too, my own most heartfelt "beliefs" and "feelings" and "opinions" and "experiences" become vulnerable to being read back to me in ways that I could not read them myself. This is true as much of the researcher as it is also true of the one who is the topic of one's study. Self-deception, false consciousness, surround all our confidences like a dark penumbra around a fire. And this surrounding is not some sort of error curable by sheer diligence. It is of the nature of our living that folds of it hide, that parts of it fall behind our backs as we turn our attention here, there, that historical circumstances alter what we thought the past meant and what the future held and what the present asks of us. This is why the language of interpretive work has a weird unsteadiness to it. It is not an effort to "be poetic," but an effort to have one's language do justice to the phenomenon under consideration.

Interpretive work, therefore, is precisely of "practical value" (Moules et al., p. 1). It is why Hans-Georg Gadamer names hermeneutics a "practical philosophy" (2007) with a "practical task" (2007a), because it casts us back into the trouble of living now having seen through and broken the spell of the dominant surface stories that have held us in thrall and held our living aside in favor of mind-numbing words and phrases meant to placate, not reveal. When interpretive work is well done, it is "of interest" (Moules et al., 2017, p. 1) to readers precisely because it is about their lived experience of being-in-the-middle-of-things (Latin, *inter* + *esse*).

There Is Some Relief to Be Had

Instead of taking on the terribly difficult work of venturing, deliberately and with all the poise that scholarship helps us muster, into the roil of living, those of us involved in interpretive research seem stuck, again and still, like recent elections have demonstrated, with having to spend our time going to fund-raising dinners that seem bent on ignoring those doorstep voices, those haunts of lives, in favor of kowtowing, as Moules et al. (2017) show so well, to what wealthy donors want and how they want it served up: "an ordering of things according to the wishes, prejudices, or promptings of the powerful" (Gadamer, 1989, p. 261). We seem stuck, more than ever, with giving an account of what we are doing in such pernicious detail that we have little time to do any of the slow, meticulous work of thinking, of listening, of reading through the life and language we have inherited and the ancestors and elders who whisper, and therefore reading the world more acutely as a consequence.

That is not what those invested in the *status quo* want. They want work that is compliant of this status. They do not want the suffering of life to become legible, especially to those who are suffering and who, in being asked to speak to their lives, just might have the chance to raise their heads out of the tangles when they realize what has been perpetrated, how they have been had by what passes for "the real world," for being "just the way things are."

Thus, the terrible intimacy of this teacher's expression of his lived experience—"this is the real world"—gets *both confirmed and denied in interpretive work.* His exhaustion and feelings of threat are confirmed as genuine (as genuine as the grievances upon which some politicians prey) and, in fact, deeply important, and they seem even closer at hand. And, at the same time, the flat declarations about "the real world," offered as a way to stop conversation in its tracks, stop from "break[ing] forth … a whole [complex, multifarious, power-laden, historical, cultural, etc.] world view that underlies it" (Gadamer, 1989, p. 458).

I must say, here, as plainly as possible, that a very common response to feeling one's deeply felt story shifting and opening, to experiencing forces and ideas that have been lost to memory or deliberately blocked, to find myself acting out a story I had no idea I was in, has often been met with an understandable hostility, a feeling of having been "had." An interpretive desire to untangle the threads of our living can be experienced as blaming those who feel tethered by the "realities" of these threads. Worse yet, daresay, taking on the interpretive work of untangling these threads can *increase* one's sorrow. One finds out that the conditions of one's exhaustion remain dominant *even though the causes and conditions of that dominance are now becoming transparent.*

When one experiences a high school teacher decrying the lack of initiative in his students, it is mere caricature to call it that teacher's "opinion," as much as it is to pin lack of initiative on the wantonness of today's youth. Both of these are outrageous and profoundly illiterate attempts to marginalize these doorstep tales in ways that precisely keep them impotent and compliant and obedient and silent. After all, think of how much is at stake if we begin to ask Derrida's questions: who profits from the exhaustion and distraction of teachers, of students, of scholars? Who benefits from the well-trained compliance of students entering the world, or the naming of that world a "work force"? Who finds it worthwhile that a student learns full well that the only real question is "Tell me exactly what you want, and I'll do it"?

So, could this high school teacher's statement have been interpreted differently than this? Of course, and, I venture, there is some relief to be had. Welcome to the tough work of interpretation that must, as part of its work, always try to make the case for why it makes the case the way it does, thereby sharpening and critiquing its own presumptions in light of the object being investigated and the ever-new circumstances of its appearance. What becomes visible that was once occluded? What is remembered in such an interpretation that has been forgotten? What now seem to be a living issue rather than something over and done with and dead? (see Moules, 2015). Under the heading of interpretive research there is a whole unruly family of ways to take up these questions of waking up and clarifying the conditions under which we are living. And, to repeat, make no mistake, here. Making visible and articulable the roots, for example, of "lack of initiative" in schools framed after the efficiency movement doesn't suddenly make one's life easier. What it does is free us, ever so slightly, from those stories that have held us spellbound to hidden workings (after all, remaining distracted and exhausted is how markets profit from our labor), and freed us for now commiserating and clarifying our individual and collective lot. It is no coincidence that, central to regimes of industrial efficiency is our estranging and disempowering isolation from one another that is, it seems, recapitulated in the often-spoken isolation of separate classrooms of schools, where teachers might want to work together but don't feel that they have the time. And yes, under F.W. Taylor's regime, "time is always running out" (Berry, 1983, p. 76).

A *Mensuratio Ad Rem*

"Is it really 'yesterday's war'? What Gadamer has to say about what gets counted" (Moules et al., 2017) thus raises and goes well beyond issues of "research methods." But it is also about research and its ways and presumptions. As it articulates so well, there are very complex ontological and epistemological issues involve in this reputed war over research paradigms. That it could arise all over again as if we had never been through this before is one more example of that old adage, that when those who fought the war before and won the peace die off or fade from view, the prospects of a new war that remembers nothing of its cost, increase.

I want to add to this conversation about these ontological and epistemological issues by thinking more about the object of investigation in interpretive work. Qualitative and quantitative research are not warring over different ways, different methods, differing criteria of how to properly approach the same object. The object of each is different and each, I suggest, tries to measure up properly to its own.

The object of investigation in qualitative research is not a "thing" with properties to be discovered and named under regimes of "control, prediction and manipulation" (Habermas, 1972, p. 21), but is, rather, a long, contested, and emergent lineage of images, ideas, choices, possibilities, occlusions, inclusions, victories, defeats, silences and voices. The object being considered by interpretive work is this very variousness. "Only in the multifariousness of voices does it exist" (Gadamer, 1989, p. 284). And that variousness varies over time. This is its emergent, living, contested, nature. This is the "real world" of the lifeworld, to be thus. This is why Gadamer (1989) cites the examples of law and art in order to try to get hold of the character of knowledge in interpretive work. In the law, a new case does not just fall under an old law but calls that law to account for its governance. Cases—those doorstep stories— are thus "fecund" (Gadamer, 1989, p. 36). "Interpret[ing]" such cases involves the "the furthering of an event that goes far back" (p. xxiv), summoning precedents or using old images or new nuances, unearthing the work, say, of F.W. Taylor, and making the case for this surrounding of the case of a tale told in a high school hallway. The object under investigation in interpretive work is thus part of a living tradition, as is that interpretive work itself. As with, for example, the history of visual art, the arrival of, say, Picasso was not just the addition of one more case that falls under already-established rules and expectations governing "art history and technique." The arrival of his work induced the disturbing, contentious disestablishing of those very rules and expectations, and then, of course, had a hand in the slow reestablishment of that very history, now revived by a new arrival, now no longer the tradition it seemed to have been. New things become precedents that were heretofore simply ignored or lost to memory. Different things become "old fashioned" or no longer done. Things that were once silent start speaking up. This is "the real world" of a living tradition in the lifeworld, and to expect to have the fixity prerequisites of object of the natural sciences is to violate what it is. Likewise, when I explored with a Grade Two teacher the complex origins of the very idea of "silent reading," and how such a thing seemed preposterous in the early centuries in Europe, and how reading "out loud" once meant carrying the text on one's living breath, well, that seemingly simply, taken-for-granted practice in schools became a wonderful spot of repose for teacher and students alike. Sounding out an unfamiliar word to have it suddenly break out into the open and up onto the voice is not a simple matter of curriculum fulfillment (see Seidel & Jardine, 2014) but of opening up a whole world if relations and kin. And how this very act appears to those in the class whose first language is Chinese—where phonemic strings are not part of the written text—became a place of deep allure, again, for teachers and students alike. This, for me, is how hermeneutics is not simply a means to study pedagogy but is, in its own way, a hint about how pedagogy itself might be practiced.

We can read of a teacher who speaks of the experience of having a dying child in their Grade Two classroom and helping the children learn to live with this reality and to learn to live with it herself (see Molnar, 2014). We can recoil in witness of the case being made that the developmental readers used in schools (so ordinary, so de rigueur in their dominance of classroom practices in the early grades) have an affinity to issues of colonialism and the loss of the tracks of one's people

(Tait, 2016). Someone else writes of the loss of her cousin, Shelby, to cancer (Latremouille, 2014) and the parent of a child of the same fate, writes in response (see Jardine, 2014b, p. 1), and this beckoned me to suggest that "this is why we read. This is why we write" (Jardine, 2014c). The investigation of such things must itself not demand that these things be differently than they are.

This is why I hold this difficult passage from Hans-Georg Gadamer (1989, p. 261) so near and dear:

> Knowledge [in interpretive work] is not a projection in the sense of a plan, the extrapolation of the aims of the will, an ordering of things according to the wishes, prejudices, or promptings of the powerful; rather, it remains something adapted to the object, a *mensuratio ad rem*. [This, please note, is true of and apparent in the natural sciences as well as the human sciences. However, the object of the natural sciences is a different object, and therefore the measure of its adaptation is different; see below] Yet this thing [in the human sciences] is not a factum brutum [a "brute fact" that "is what it is," thus laying out the task, in the natural sciences, of finding and pinning down what it is] but itself ultimately has the same mode of being [being human]. [In the human sciences] neither the knower [the one doing interpretive research] nor the known [the object being interpreted] is "present-at-hand." (Gadamer, 1989, p. 261)

A tough read, literally and otherwise, especially for anyone who thinks that, in interpretive work, you just get to say what you think and make things up and give your opinion.

Here is an elaboration of this passage, including a slightly different and illuminating translation of some of these thoughts. In interpretive work:

> Both the one who understands and the thing that is understood "are" historically, that is, in the process of unfolding themselves over time, and neither the one who understands, nor the thing understood "are" statically present [-at-hand] independently of each other. Both "are" in their interactive development. Hence, understand is still a *mensuratio ad rem*, as Gadamer puts it, or, in another traditional formulation, an *adaequatio intellectus ad rem*, except that the "adequation" of the intellect, its measuring and fitting of itself, is never to a timeless thing that always is what it is, some brute fact, "determinable" and

independent of the one who knows it [or the lived circumstances in which
that knower lives—knowing of Picasso, e.g., is not what it used to be, and it is
no longer adequate to understand the history of art without his fecund influ-
ence]. Hence, I suggest that we might better speak of a reciprocal *adaequatio intellectus et rei*, of the temporary adequation of two entities, intellect [me
attempting to hear of this teacher's experiences with the full weight of what
I have come to learn about our shared and contested circumstances—schools,
distraction, efficiency, initiative, and on and on] and thing [this story, here,
now, pleading both up out of and to that ancestry], to each other, each in
their particular historical development at the given time. (P.C. Smith, 2011,
pp. 24–25)

Part of interpretive work involves studying texts on the nature, history
and practice of interpretive work itself. It involves reading these passages of Gadamer's and Smith's with the very same sort of open-eared
audacity and care and attention that we try to give to our so-called
"participants" in a research study, because each of these clusters of texts
("the literature," the interpreter's background study of the phenomenon
being investigated, and the "data" [interviews, transcripts, anecdotes,
written missives from participants, and so on]) must learn to speak to
one another if the interpretive study is to be successful. Each clarifies
and expands the other and frees it from its limitations while, at the
same time, helps it measure itself against the gatherings of its relations
and kin.

Each thus frees the other. The literature frees the doorstep tale of
its subjectivity ("this is what I experience") by reading it out into a
world of lost relations and occluded ancestries that just might demonstrate that your frustration with lack of initiative is on to something
more that you might have been able to imagine heretofore. And the
doorstep tale frees the literature of its moribund erudition and danger of closing the case, by calling it to account, here, now, the door
just newly ajar. Thus "the fecundity of the individual case" (Gadamer,
1989, p. 38)

Interpretive work therefore tends to sometimes be hesitant and
indirect, not in an attempt to obfuscate an object that is itself clear, but
in order to bring out the obtuse and myriad and unfinished character
of the object itself.

"A Process of Inner Clarification"

After all, who is to say once and for all what might become of grief or schools or politics or children or parenting or ecological anxiety and how we live with such matters and talk about them and open them up, and hide them all over again as the world shifts around us? Who would have thought that this "war" would have reared up again and we'd have to parse our way through it all over again? The hesitancy and indirectness of interpretative work is a way to maintain its *mensuration ad rem*? To maintain its tough rigor.

Years ago, in an informal conversation with Hans-Georg Gadamer in his office at McMaster University, he told me that the care-laden work of interpretation is "internal to Being-in-the-world—a process of inner clarification—rather than its domineering father" (Jardine, 2015b?, p. 16), and it has taken, it still takes, some doing to learn to live with this gentle, encouraging admonition. And to learn how "inner clarification" is inner to the whole living Earth. It is not a subjective inner state. It is the clarification that Ravens can bring back from the edge of the world, my heart, not the one I thought was inside of me.

Interpreting our living is what living does all by itself. It is not the property of research. Research is one of its cousins, one of its specialized forms. What we offer each other is the spell-breaking. What is studied in studying how to do interpretive research is how to remain alert and not be exhausted in the process, and how to invite others into often-hidden and forgotten roils that are already living themselves out in our lives.

You can rest assured that there is no unifying methodology or realm of concern or emphasis or unanimity in interpretive work itself. It is quite akin to a family gathering whose kinships and claims to lineage and importance and urgency are always up for debate, the sort debates that only gatherings of relatives can betray.

You can rest assured, as well, that some in this gathering will find this writing far too heated, while others will find it timid and cowardly.

Welcome to the lifeworld, then, and to the unfortunate circumstance that always faces those marginalized, of being asked to fight a war premised on thin air.

How about this, instead? Welcome, instead, to the doorstep and the troublesome invitation to step out into the wild of things.

CHAPTER THIRTEEN

I Hear Tell It's Happening Again, December 2023 and March 2022

I Hear Tell
There is a war started.
I hear tell that the potatoes are safely
Dug up. Stored.

Four broken limbs.
Lovely crop of tattooed parsnips, too.
For winter beef stews, for rumours.

Rutabagas paraded through the streets.
Each one is crying for good reason. Ruddy
Purple Crowns and broken stems.

The music's festive weeps make the eyes blurry.

I hear tell in great flurries
That God is Great and
Deserving of an Upper Case.

So I've heard for many years.
Come 'round again, reliable as
Potatoes tended.

As reliable as weep and blur from every which a "way."
Remind me, geese.

It's Happening Again

As miraculous as the first time. It's happening again. Just plant. Just wait. Don't even hope. Dreams of sweet future basil must be held at bay, for now. It must do what it can. Just be tender. Use what you've dried and stored from last year. Be still.

But still
And all
It's coming on time to plant in Ukraine.
It's happening again.

CHAPTER FOURTEEN

"A Hubris Hiding from its Nemesis": Why Does the Affirmation of Diversity Tend Toward the Proliferation of Multiple Identities, and to What Consequence?

A Preamble

An easy-to-find cartoon a Corporate CEO at his text on the phone. Outside the window, Occupy Wall Street protesters. The caption?

"Introduce them to identity politics."

Here runs the risk, a tiptoe. I need not reiterate all the ways in which my own "identity" has been handed to me, sight unseen—not marginalized, not silenced, *not even spoken out loud* until quite recently. Yes. And however:

> *For the master's tools will never dismantle the master's house.* They may allow us temporarily to beat him at his own game, but they will never enable us to bring about genuine change. (Audre Lorde, 1979, p. 112)

I worry that "identity" is precisely one of those tools. And however:

> The rule seems to be that the more rigid and exclusive is the … boundary, and the stricter the control within it, the more disorder rages around it. One can make a greenhouse and grow summer vegetables in the wintertime, but in doing so one creates a vulnerability to the weather and a possibility of failure

where none existed before. The control by which a tomato plant lives through January is much more problematic than the natural order by which an oak tree or a titmouse lives through January. The patterns of cooperation are safer than the mechanisms of exclusion, even though they lack the illusory safety of "control." (Berry, 1986, p. 76)

The denial, eradication, displacement and silencing of identities other than that Identity which dominates has led to the suppression of something more than those thus dominated. It has led to the suppressed, perhaps trickster-false belief that the affirmation of a *different identity*, in ape of those dominating, is the way to liberation.

What worn-out metaphor shall we arouse, here? Egg Shells? Land Mines? Guilt and remorse? Buried nameless babies? Popes' *apologias*? Erasing the names of those who erased names as part of their purification rituals?

"Multifariousness of Voices"

Why do the ideas of multiplicity, diversity, and the arising recognition of a "multifariousness of voices" (Gadamer, 1989, p. 285) persistently resolve themselves into talk of multiple *identities*? Identity has the potential to become sealed off, separate, and proffered as self-determining and self-defining independently of any *other*. Can we not be diverse and interdependent without imagining diversity as a splay of separate identities related somehow only *post hoc*? Affirmations of identity have the potential to make all our relations seem "revocable and provisional" (Gray, 2001, p. 36).

It has the potential to be an ecological disaster.

It is war consciousness.

Couldn't our diversity be articulated by complex networks of dependent co-arising causes, conditions, interactions, mutual formations, interdependencies, kinships, and inhabitations, one story inculcated in the other, one voice aroused in the midst of the wide breaths of the Earth, human and more-than-human? I get retold and remade by that Raven's wing-swooping overhead, by my students' suffering, my son's ventures, my language, my foolishness, even by the work of writing this.

In all this unsteady swirl of relations and dependent co-arisings, what is the attraction of *identity* and what does it satisfy?

Identities

Teacher identity. Student identity. Cultural identity. Gender identity. Racial identity. Religious identity. Linguistic identity. Political-affiliation identity. Personal identity. Familial. Geographical. Ancestral. Even this list shifts and flows, adds and omits.

Day to day, we mostly experience these matters fluidly unless and until threat, anger, regret, revenge, suasion, power, violence, and the like arise. Then there is retraction, figurative or literal wall-building, intent on protecting and codifying (and, often, exaggerating, purifying, and clarifying) this hard-won identity from contaminating interlopers.

This movement of retraction occurs no matter the difference between *real* and *perceived* threats. Between real news and fake.

It is ripe and ready for manipulation. I am ripe and ready to easily fall for its roots in distraction and threat, all over again. Animal-body deer-tail white flags, false or otherwise.

Identity Wars

Once started, [wars] ... tend to take on a life of their own. Identities which had previously been multiple, and casual become focused and hardened [and ensuing conflicts] are appropriately termed "identity wars." As violence increases, the initial issues at stake tend to get redefined more exclusively as "us" against "them" and group cohesion and commitment are enhanced. Civilization consciousness strengthens in relations to other identities. A "hate dynamic" emerges in which mutual fears, distrust, and hatred feed on each other. Each side dramatizes and magnifies the distinction between the forces of virtue and the forces of evil and eventually attempts to transform this distinction into the ultimate distinction between the quick and the dead. (Huntington, 2003, p. 266)

The mere existence of an alternative mode of being, the presence of which exemplifies that different identities are possible and thus denaturalizes the claim of a particular identity to be *the* true identity, is sometimes enough to produce the understanding of a threat. [President Bush, in his "with us or with the terrorists" speech (Bush, 2010) has] manifestly linked American identity to danger. (Campbell, 1998, p. 3)

"That's Not What I Meant"

We all know, in varying degrees and in various ways, that language has a life and sway of its own. Despite well-intended attempts to say, "That's not what I meant," the words I've used have sometimes ended up meaning more or different than I meant to mean, and that excess has been a repeated locale of my own humiliation and regret. Sometimes this excess can be a great teacher. I've found myself unwittingly dragged into old, buried implications and arguments, old relations, forgotten inheritances, suppressed lies, new electric charges of insight and uprising, and tangled, unintended duplicities from which "That's not what I meant" provided little rescue or relief. And as with my words, so too my life is often shaped "beyond my wanting and doing" (Gadamer, 1989, p. xxviii), too long lost, just out of sight of awareness, as if every turn of a corner occludes the corner now behind my back.

You're never too old to be humiliated.

I want, here, to meditate on some of the hidden, unintended excess of *identity*, a word full of echoes, a word with its own life and times— variously a declaration, a weapon, a herald, an admission, a hard-won victory, a ruse, a refuge, a moment when a voice is finally heard or how a voice is banished. And on and on and on. Samuel Huntington (2003) and David Campbell (1998) provide hints about how threat, danger, embattlement, can cause the hardening and reification of identity— witness, for example, Donald Trump's recent wall bragging under the guise of fever dreams of rapists and murderers. Or the latest nebulous, slow-moving, creeping, dark Caravan-horde, nestled with possible Middle Easterners, coming to breach and pierce and violate the southern border skin, with small-pox, even leprosy. Funded by Jews. Encouraged by Progressives. Socialists. See how easy this is? We humans have had lots of practice in not learning from experience.

My concern, simply put, is that threat, danger, the pursuit of safety, hardening and reification might be an unintended part of *the very lure of "identity" itself*, its hidden nemesis. It is imagined that if only identity could be pinned down and secured once and for all, uninterrupted by anything outside its purview, definitively bounded and bordered and well walled-off, peace would reign (and this uttered with no real consciousness of how such an urge to secure and pin down *is already an act of war*). Caught inside this circle, cause and effect illicitly interchange fluids, unseen. Those threaten with armed forces and reprisal are the *cause* of their being threatened.

Edward Said (2001) pointedly critiqued Samuel Huntington's conclusions regarding clashes of civilizations, but, I believe, something was overlooked:

> Huntington ... wants to make "identities" into what they are not: shut-down, sealed-off entities that have been purged of the myriad currents and counter currents that animate human history, and that over centuries have made it possible for that history not only to contain wars of religion and imperial conquest, but also to be one of exchange, cross-fertilization and sharing. This far less visible history is ignored in the rush to highlight the ludicrously compressed and constructed warfare that "the clash of civilizations" argues is the reality. (p. 3)

I suggest that Huntington is not saying that identities *are* hard and fast (and therefore that the subsequent clashes are "the [inevitable] reality"). He is pointing out something easy to miss: "left in peace" (Illich, 1992, p. 16), differences and kinships and interdependencies flourish and "flower" (p. 17). *Under threat,* they tend to *harden,* thus occluding a "far less visible history" (Said, 2001, p. 3) of interdependence and interrelatedness, casualness and multiplicity, openness, porousness, cooperation, resilience, resolution, vulnerability, resolvable scuffles and polite avoidance and civility, susceptibility, and even sometimes conviviality and affection. He is pointing to a mechanism (an affliction, Buddhists might call it) that gets hidden once identity becomes hardened and reified. And this even though, perhaps especially when, the resorted-to relief is multiple identities.

Glimpsing this mechanism of threat-based retraction into hardened identity helps me glimpse how *identity* can be both the effect and the cause of a sort of *war consciousness*. Identity is not only *what arises under threat*; it is what, *once arisen*, now needs protection *from* threat, that threat now hallucinated to be monstrous enough to warrant and match the size and urgency with which identity is affirmed. Hubris and nemesis rise up to meet each other.

Such retraction into separate identities is an act, oddly, of self-clarification and simplification and has been offered as a benign means of understanding my "self" and my place in the world out from under various silencing hegemonies. However, no doubt, arises my recent, all-too-familiar grief over how making people *feel* threatened can be manipulated and utilized politically as a form of social control, of marketing technique, of spinning a web to a hidden profit.

That is why the most chilling phrase in Huntington's description is "once started." "Once started," it becomes almost too late to think about identity and how *others* might appear. If we feel threatened, *they* then have to have a hardened identity, too, a clear one, a declarable one, exaggerated monster to befit our own threatened, thus exaggerated and retracted, identity: Environmental Crazies, Muslim Intruders, Gay Activists, Straight People, LGBTQ-ers, Red States, Blue States, Anarchists, Fascists, Right, Left:

> In light of the seemingly secured enclosures of threat-induced identities, any suggestion of boundaries being in any way overridden or "permeable" (Smith, 2006, p. 77) becomes understandable only as *a security threat*. Surveillance, paranoia, border patrols, increased accountability and monitoring, become the order of the day as bi-products of the now-purified "identity" of "us" being increasingly susceptible to "contamination" by "them." Threat produces a situation where the very casualness and multiplicity of day-to-day situations of everyday life becomes identifiable as the *cause* of threat. (Jardine et al., 2012, pp. 30–31)

In light of hardened identity, any suggestion of fluidity, casualness, multiplicity, porosity, diversity, sustainability, and interdependence can become experienced as *the source of threat*, however much they are proffered as its relief.

Perhaps even worse for us in the orbit of education, it becomes almost too late to think about identity because *thinking itself becomes cast as a cause of threat*. Opening identity to thinking and interpretation and to all its casual and multiple interdependencies seems itself like a breach, leading, of course, to increased vigilance and hardening:

> Wanting to know something more than the simplistic, threat-induced clarities about this "us" and "them" become [considered] egregious [or unpatriotic, or at least suspicious]. *Knowledge and its pursuit [which explores those less visible interdependencies that hardening has occluded] become experienced as a threat to security* (see David G. Smith's [2006] brilliant chapter "Enfraudening in the Public Sphere" for more on this point and its telling consequences for pedagogy). (Jardine et al., 2012, pp. 31–32)

This all has the potential to set pedagogy itself on the road to a state of "perpetual war" (Postel & Drury, 2003) constituted by paranoia, accountability and surveillance. Pedagogy, too, retracts under threat and starts to fall under terrible and atrophying auspices for knowledge and its cultivation.

"I love the poorly educated" (Associated Press, 2016a).

This story is an old one—clear and brazenly declared identifiers, simple and easy and unequivocal, get identified with the nature of knowledge itself. Asking after occluded dependencies and relations just blurs what is *in reality* clear and distinct. To know is to identify, codify, and harden into self-containment.

To know a thing is to portion it off from everything else, every contaminating relation. It is to place it under regimes of surveillance and accountability and manageability that know no sway or forgiveness. Zero tolerance. On this basis, to know, then, is to brazenly trumpet without hesitancy or affection:

> An adequate knowledge is thoroughly clear knowledge, where confusion is no longer possible, where the reduction to marks and moments of marks (*requisite*) can be manager to the end. (Heidegger, 1978, p. 62)

"The essence of truth," so this old story goes, "is identity" (Heidegger, 1978, p. 39). Those who don't measure up are marginalized, silenced, taught a lesson they'll never forget. Identity. Colonialism. Proximity or distance from the norm. One story. One teller.

Or, to invert this, we get to say who we are and you don't. Which, on the face of it, sounds like the *inverse* of colonialism? No, that isn't it.

Identity is inherently monotheistic, then? The One True God of my own sovereign person, people, land, faith?

In this light, the urge toward multiple identities can become like a panoply of multiple self-identical gods perpetually warring. (This reminds me too easily of why one could imagine that peace can only come if everyone is armed).

"Sameness, Oneness, State of Being the Same"

Identity: Latin *identitas*, points to "sameness, oneness, state of being the same," (Online Etymological Dictionary). Under (real or perceived) threat, we understandably and often with good warrant tend to retract into barricaded protectiveness, this right down to the animal-body's self-preservation, or the startle of a noise in the night. A terrible irony here is that the outcome of an occasioned and warranted retraction becomes *ontologized*. What is in fact an *outcome* of threat is posited as the way things *really are*: each culture, each person, each gender, each bird species, each bird pair, the tree each bird sit on ... each *is* separate and independently existing. Any relations become understood as subsequent to this ontological reality presumed and formulated under threat.

The affirmation of multiple identities is certainly comprehensible as a consequence of threats of silencing singularity and exclusion and regimes of marginalization and violence. But what if the consequent affirmation of one's own identity in opposition to that singularity takes on precisely the error of that which it is trying to overcome? What if it is precisely *the affirmation of identity* that is the core of exclusion, the root of war? Inside of an affirmation of identity is a sense of self-determining singularity, this, not that. What if our casual and multiple selves could be "left in peace," and thus not compelled with the same urgency toward the seemingly, relatively safe harbors of identity? This, to reiterate (Illich, 1992), is a far less visible history:

War, which makes cultures alike, is all too often used by historians as the framework or skeleton of their narratives. The peaceful enjoyment of [that which is not under threat, embattled] is left in a zone of deep shadow. (p. 19)

As Tsong-kha-pa (2002) says of essence, so too with identity: "It is a concealer" (p. 208). What if *the pursuit of identity itself* is the root affliction, the root error, and carries with it, however multiplied, singularity and silence and ecological disaster?

A Little Buddhist Sidestep

This link between identity and threat, identity and reification, identity and the subsequent suffering of border breaches, links, too, to my interest in Buddhism and its meditations on the self and its ways:

The true mode of being of a thing as it is in itself, is selfless, for its self cannot be a self-identity in the sense of a substance. Indeed, this true mode must include a complete negation of such self-identity. (Nishitani, 1982, p. 117)

In Buddhist thought, this selflessness is not just a selflessness of things, but of my own very self which experiences such things, the very selves of my students, our work, our topics of consideration, our multiplicity and diversity. These words, this breath, the fall air with flecks of snow, September 21, 2016, early morning.

Much of Buddhist thinking and practice is directed toward how, under afflictions such a threat, fear, anger, worry about the future, my sense of self becomes reified and that self then reifies the world into securable objects that it can control, predict, and safely and predictably manipulate. This is why the core of Buddhist thinking speaks about the suffering that arises from a misplaced and reified and false sense of self-existence (Sanskrit: *svabhava*). Buddhism speaks of things and selves being empty (Sanskrit: *shunya*) of self-existence, and, instead, being dependently co-arising (Sanskrit: *pratitya-samutpada*). Buddhism makes an ontological claim counter to the claims of separate identities: things *are* all their relations. It speaks directly against the long inheritance of identity and substance that cascades back through Rene

Descartes' *Meditations on First Philosophy*, to Aquinas, to Aristotle's *Metaphysics*: "a substance is that which requires nothing except itself in order to exist" (Descartes, 1955, p. 255). In this Western lineage of identity, and "on behalf of the truth of things," we must "break things apart until they will break no further" (Jardine, 2012c, p. 86). Please note, in passing, how this logic of breakdown is what underwrites the efficiency movement in industrial assembly and its importation into the ways of schools (see Jardine, 2016c, pp. 179–192).

"The concept of substance [and its consort, identity, and identity's consort, "difference"] is inadequate [and there is] a radical challenge of thought implicit in this inadequacy" (Gadamer, 1989, p. 242). There is a forceful experience that comes from stepping away from this spellbinding lure of identity. Here, then, too, is the urging in Buddhism, one that has a great kinship to current ecological urgings, that every phenomenon requires everything else in order to be what it truly is:

> When we see a phenomenon and clearly understand that the very existence of it is completely dependent on other phenomena, inseparably related to them, then at that time our mind is holding the view of dependent arising. There is no phenomenon [no self, no "thing," no breath, no gesture, no language, no culture, no Raven] which exists independently of others. The only way phenomena do exist is as interdependently arising. To realize the full import of dependent-arising, namely that all phenomena are empty of inherent existence [empty of a self-contained, self-determining, exclusionary "identity"] is an extremely forceful experience that reorients one in the very depths of ones being and bestows peace. (Lobsang, 2006, p. 51)

Again, there is an irony that must be repeatedly noted. Overcoming "the syndrome of grasping at a self-nature" (Tsong-kha-pa, 2005, p. 182) must be accomplished through the application of peaceful means of both studying our arising circumstances in all their dependently co-arising detail and practices that support and encourage this. And what as what then arises *bestows* peace. As with what appears inside the circle of threat-retraction-hardening-increased threat, inside this Buddhist sway (as, I suggest, in the sway of ecological awareness and hermeneutic pursuits), peace is both cause and effect, both "the path and the goal" (Gadamer, 1989, p. 180).

To What Profit

Listen to Alan Greenspan, who, during the height of the euphoria over the economy, was called "Saint Alan," the greatest economist of all time—he testified to Congress, explaining the basis for the success of the economy he was running. He said it was based on growing worker insecurity. Growing worker insecurity. Meaning that if workers are beaten down enough and intimidated enough, so that they can no longer ask for decent wages and decent benefits, then it creates a healthy economy by some measure. All of this has happened. (Chomsky, 2017)

To what profit is maintaining a sense of insecurity and threat and the disturbing of the peace with the promise of walled-off safety? How often is such a sense of danger propagated by precisely those who then offer a solution to what they themselves have caused? It is beyond doubt that this threat-mechanism often inculcates itself into market logic. "Buy this (idea, thing) and things will be fine" is the language of marketing underwritten, of course, with the hidden cultivation and maintenance of a sense that things are precisely *not* "fine" until you do. And then, of course, this sense of all being well must not last too long, else the cycle of insecurity/threat/purchase/ relief will not continue. Read Greenspan's words carefully. The whole mechanism only works if threat is constantly *growing*. Those offering relief must also be in the business of creating what they then offer to relieve.

And, of course, we are witnessing this in the current American election cycle, how incendiary, threatening, clear and provocative images and ideas and promises trump complexity, subtlety and thoughtfulness to the advantage of the one seeking power over us. Make no mistake. All this is explicit, and it is deliberate. Inciting a sense of threat and then offering oneself as its relief and couching that offer in declarations of threats to identity and their solutions is profitable independent of the truth of the claim being made and its warrant. Its warrant is the profitability that flows from its assertion. It *works*. From a YouTube clip of the MSNBC show Morning Joe, August 12, 2016 entitled "How Donald Trump's ISIS Talk Impacts Voter Perceptions":

Joe Scarborough:	He was so cocksure yesterday, and now he's backed off these things.
Gene Robinson:	I doubt it's that planned. I think it's just him. The "Obama the founder of ISIS" thing, it was crazy when he said it; it was absolutely insane when he defended it with Hugh Hewitt, and then today, it's like every day is a new day.
Mika Brzezinski:	And the … it gets "oh, it was sarcasm." But social scientists have found that the corrections never really catch up with the assertion. (MSNBC, 2016a)

Cocksure. Not planned. Just him. Crazy. Insane. Sarcasm:

"So, I said the founder of ISIS," Trump recalled to the crowd, after accusing the president of being "so weak and so bad" that he allowed the Islamic State to grow. "Obviously I'm being sarcastic. Then—but not that sarcastic, to be honest with you." (McCaskill, 2106)

No. Not crazy. A deliberate and strategic linking up of marketing logic with the mechanisms of threat/retraction/hardening and then offering oneself as the solution:

Hugh Hewitt:	Last night you said the president [Obama] was the founder of ISIS. I know what you meant. You meant that he created the vacuum, he lost the peace.
Donald Trump:	No, I mean he's the founder of ISIS. I do.
Hewitt:	but he's not sympathetic to them. He hates them. He's trying to kill them.
Trump:	I don't care. He was the founder.
Hewitt:	But using the term "founder," they're hitting you on this again. Mistake?
Trump:	No, it's no mistake. Everyone's liking it.
Hewitt:	I know what you're arguing.
Trump:	… you're not, and let me ask you, do you not like that?
Hewitt:	I don't … I'd just use different language.
Trump:	But they wouldn't talk about your language, and they do talk about my language, right? (MSNBC, 2016b)

Whew, eh? Such is our shared human psychological vulnerability to this afflictive cycle. Breaking it, alerting to it, seeking out the hidden (and, Trump with Hewitt, not especially hidden) comings and goings, is the purpose of interpretive research in all its forms.

This may seem far from the realm of schools and issues of curriculum or classroom practice. So, well, brace yourself and be glad that what follows was finally said out loud to all those who, under threat, revert to sure-fire, color-coded developmental readers and online reading packages to sure-fire guarantee, against threats of illiteracy, the cultivation of reading skills in the worried and hurried children of worried and hurried parents. Again, make no mistake. Again, it is explicit, and it is deliberate: "I love the terror in a mother's heart when she sees her child fall behind in reading. I made a fortune from that" (O'Leary, 2012).

"Tell Me 'Bout Your Nature" (Lenker, 2020)

Because this [sense of enclosed and embattled identity] causes living beings to be confused in their view of the actual state of things, it is a delusion; ignorance mistakenly superimposes upon things an essence that they do not have. It is constituted so as to block perception of their nature. It is a concealer (Tsong-kha-pa, 2002, p. 208).

In Buddhist thought and practice, things, selves, persons, trees, languages, bloodlines, students, teachers, books, literacy, schools, are considered to be "empty of self-existence (*svabhavasunya*)" (Tsong-kha-pa, 2000, p. 24), "empty of having an inherent self-nature" (Tsong-kha-pa, 2005, p. 183), having an "absence of self-nature" (Tsong-kha-pa, 2000, p. 20), possessing "not even an atom of ... true existence" (Tsong-kha-pa, 2004, p. 215).

These things don't then disappear. They reappear now out from the boundaries of self-containment. Far less visible histories and relations appear in sometimes overwhelming array. Living fields of circumstance, hope, desire, suppression, marginalization, causes, conditions, ancestries, bloodlines and ecosystems of relations. "We are not attempting to get rid of [these things], only of the idea of [them] as self-existent" (Lobsang, 2006, p. 49). "Those objects that appear ... do not stop appearing, but the concepts that take them as having any true existence [e.g. "substance," or "identity" or other reifications] subside" (Patrul, 1998, p. 252). Things, selves, persons, trees, and all, all exist in relations of interdependence and mutual formation. Thus "dependent-arising is the meaning of emptiness" (Tsong-kha-pa, 2002, p. 133).

Only once these multiple mutual inhabitations start to appear (this "far less visible history") is there any hope, I suggest, of their repair and reconciliation. In all this, "identity" has the potential to be a concealer, and simply reverting to "multiple identities" does not relieve this concealment but risks maintaining and simply proliferating and scattering this concealment.

"Always Already Everywhere Inhabited"

If identity has the potential to be a concealer, so, too, then, does *difference* if it arises as the counterpoint of identity. *Difference* carries with it the seeds of the same error. It, too, can be a source of suffering. *We are not just different than each other.* That won't do either. That pine tree over there exudes the oxygen that lets me utter, "I am." And it is not just my ("revocable and provisional") relation but is what my flesh and breath truly are. This is why ecological portends lead to such trauma and grief. *Difference*, as much as *identity*, is not adequate to the fullness of our existence. "We are *always already everywhere inhabited* by the Other in the context of the fully real" (Smith, 2006, p. xxiv). Inhabited, not just "surrounded." Thus:

> One of the great and necessary intellectual challenges is to recover the "lost" dependencies of so much of our coveted traditions, because without such work we become forgetful ... and end up behaving in ways that assume that Others don't matter to who we think we are. That kind of assumption involves a hubris hiding from its nemesis, as 9/11 serves in reminder. (Smith, 2006, p. 40)

> The real challenge is to face the truth that no one tradition [let alone no one person, let alone just humans] can say everything that needs to be said about the full expression of human experience in the world and that what the global community requires more than anything else is mutual recognition of the various poverties of *every* tradition. The search to cure the poverty of one's own tradition works in all directions at once. (Smith, 2006, p. 55)

The search to cure the poverty of my own identity might require letting go, as and if and when I'm able, of the haven of identity itself, instead of simply proliferating it. It might require feeling the full pull of my own breath and blood in the suffering of the world, akin to Thich Nhat Hahn's invocation (David Suzuki Foundation, 2011), hands trembling:

> *Thich Nhat Hahn*:   People who know what is happening but … cannot do anything, there are so many of them, there are so many of them, because they have despair in them. (David Suzuki Foundation, 2011)

No reversion to self-protective self-identity will save me or any of us, here.

A Postscript

> Ambivalence, rather than being overcome … may be developed within its own principle. It is a way in itself. *Ambivalence is an adequate reaction* to these whole truths. The way is slower, action is hindered, and one fumbles foolishly in the half-light. This way finds echo in many familiar phrases from Lao Tzu, but especially: "Soften the light, become one with the dusty world." (Hillman, 2013a, p. 37)

> We seek conversation not only in order to understand the other person better. We need it because *our own concepts threaten to become rigid*; the problem [can be] not that we do not understand the other person, but that *we don't understand ourselves*. We have the hermeneutical experience that we must break down resistance *in ourselves* if we wish to hear the other. (Gadamer, 2007e, p. 371, *emphases added*)

I am white, male, blue-eyed, English speaking, well-off, straight, rather rich and comfortable and, for now, healthy. These are no longer precisely exact identifiers, but rather multivocal nests of complicity and inheritance, a task of understanding to be undertaken, over and over again.

But it is here that the dance of hubris/nemesis can rise up all over again. All this is "easy for me to say" because I do not feel and am not especially embattled.

So, if I may, let this chapter stand as a confession, a lamentation, an admission of my own poverty and the suffering it has caused. And a little reminder of one of the master's tools.

CHAPTER FIFTEEN

"Please Spare Me"

Regarding this passing link between individuality, "my own experiences," identity politics, and property ("owned"), see C.B. MacPherson's brilliant *The Political Theory of Possessive Individualism* (2010). It is about creating threatened and isolated selves that can then be manipulated to profitable ends:

> People whose governing habit is the relinquishment of power, competence and responsibility [the most hidden version of which is "this is just my opinion and I have a right to my subjective opinions], and whose characteristic suffering is the anxiety of futility, make excellent spenders. They are the ideal consumers. By inducing in them little panics of boredom, powerlessness, sexual failure, mortality, paranoia, they can be made to buy virtually anything that is "attractively packaged." (Berry, 1986, p. 24)

If I may be allowed to turn this up one more notch:

> The mere existence of an alternative mode of being, the presence of which exemplifies that different identities are possible and thus denaturalizes the claim of a particular identity to be *the* true identity is sometimes enough to produce the understanding of a threat. [This] manifestly link[s] ... identity to danger. (D. Campbell, 1998, p. 3)

Perhaps it is not a matter of multiple identities that is the solution to this sense of danger. Perhaps, instead, the idea of such danger is inherent in the very idea and cultivation of "identity" itself.

Proliferating identities as some sort of relief to singular, oppressive, silencing identity, might just be more deeply ingraining the original error (what I've often name Democratic Cartesianism). The original error might not be *that* identity and its suppression of others, but "identity" itself:

> The most attractive package to sell to individuals that are thus untethered from the world ["subjectivities" or isolated "we're us and not them" identities] is precisely *the idea of threat itself*. An untethered "I am" [or "we are"] will quite literally "buy into" the idea of "being threatened" since this is precisely the hidden origin of the self-assertive, self-confident "I am" in the first place [Descartes' "methodical doubt" as a systematic threat—shape up, our you'll be banished from the clarity of the "I am." You'll be "them" not "us"]. The abstract "I am" thus produces an equally abstract, threatening enemy: *threat itself*. Allegorical speculation: that the recent War on Terror is a war against threat itself. The fact that this War is currently linked to Islam and the Middle East [or the recent Paris bombings, or Charlie Hebdo about a year ago] is just one more revocable and provisional, historical achievement of a deeper ontological truth both required and produced by individualism itself. As such, the War on Terror combines the perpetuity of threat (which is ontologically linked to the idea of [subjective] individuality) with the need for "a state of permanent war." (Jardine, 2012e, pp. 52–53; Wood, 2006, p. 16)

So spirals the latest talk of walls along the Mexican border. So, too, spirals how one can profit from "the terror in a mother's heart" over fears about literacy and falling behind, leading to clamped-down security measures in the teaching and learning of reading.

So, when an interviewer specifically suggested to Hans-Georg Gadamer that his work in *Truth and Method* (1989), especially the long and tangled explication of "The Subjectivization of Aesthetics Through the Kantian Critique" (1989, pp. 42–81) is a defense against subjectivism through an affirmation, instead, of intersubjectivity, his response is quite visceral and immediate:

> Oh, please spare me that completely misleading concept of intersubjectivity, of a subjectivism doubled! (Gadamer, 2001, p. 59)

CHAPTER SIXTEEN

Really Clear Politics: The Algorithms of Self-Reflection

Our grandson was born on August 4, 2021, and his parents insisted that we not send pictures back and forth over g-mail. Given that their respective fields of scholarly endeavor are criminology and the Dark Web, we simply agreed to other means. He's beautiful, by the way.

Something, here, is not new, hermeneutically speaking. We live in and among causes and conditions, forces and factors that shape what seems to be our own "personal experience," what seems to be "my story" but what is, in fact, an inevitably and mostly occluded, suppressed or hidden or forgotten, manipulated fabric of tides and currents and other mixed metaphors. Self-reflection, in the midst of this weaving and interweaving (note the suppressed Wittgenstein reference) must needs be suspicious (Gadamer). Face value, first blush, deep feeling, my own truth, my story, my lived experiences, are simply fool's gold. Suspicious. Paul Ricouer bumped up against this. Jacques Derrida always asks "Who benefits?" from my somnambulance, my self-assured self-reflections on my own experience? Who benefits from my outrages?

So, the phrase "living in a bubble" is tossed off too easily, because this phrase, itself, allows for too much self-satisfaction regarding its own insight and is itself easily manipulated to ends other than my own well-meaning "author's intent." We must, instead, let ourselves feel our failure and understand how the energetics of electronic spiders which hand us back to ourselves, are no mere child's monster nightmares.

So what follows is a brief story, written a while ago now, about the utter unreliability of my own lived experience and a betraying, most probably, of nothing more than my own naivety. It also hides hints about hermeneutics—the old spell-breaking that the trickster can provide "over and above our wanting and doing" (Gadamer, 1989, p. xviii), some modicum of not simply falling for the trick.

One of the pitiful realities of being a retired academic is that looking oneself up (looking up oneself?) on Google Scholar, Academia.edu and yes, even checking one's books on amazon.ca (I'm Canadian), is (I sincerely hope so. Oh dear.) a commonplace practice. Academic writing, especially specialized things with a small orbit, is the sort of thing that easily disappears into the world with little or no trace. In the old days, one had to wait for the *Social Sciences Citation Index* to be published and then one had to scuttle over to the library and breath in the air of dead tree leafing and crammed study.

Now, of course, things have changed (and, I expect, they haven't changed a bit). After a session of, frankly, checking whether certain of my own books are still in print *at all*, I moved over to real-clearpolitics.com to get a glimpse of the then-current bernie/biden slow-moving train.

Now, I'd only be betraying my age if I were to say that I was surprised by this. I was surprised by this.

"Click *here* for more information."

"Buy now."

Hot links.

Years ago, I remember getting a scrolling ad for "plus-size frilly dresses" and laughing at how the algorithm screwed up. My son let me know that they do that on purpose to help you feel that you're not being manipulated. Even the fake news just might be a fake feigned to cause helpless suspicion and susceptibility to further manipulation.

Be all that as it may, the one thing that hit me hardest is this: this is my first visceral experience of the *solus ipse* what has been called "living in a bubble" or "living in an echo-chamber." My first experience of the algorithmically designed feature of having my own lived experience (the slightly unseemly act of, basically, googling myself) read back to me for the purpose of the profit of those who have designed this very feature *as if* to be helpful.

Even though I'm receiving ads about my own books that I looked up on the Internet, this whole thing is precisely *not a self-confirming echo-chamber.* It is manipulated by principalities and powers bent on *stimulating* that isolation, chambering my experience, stimulating the low-level panic upon which market economics relies, and then selling itself as, not *the cause* but instead *the cure* of that panic. Relief is just a click away.

So now, here's the rub. We are being had "beyond our wanting and doing." That is the nature of the lifeworld, of, well, living. Only now, two things. First, the means of such algorithmic self-reflection are far more pernicious, invasive, and immediate, as was nearly outed about Facebook and Instagram and so on recently. But we've also seen the rise of something else, recently, that is itself not especially new: the outrage over being had is *itself* being manipulated in ways bent, not at untangling what has happened to us, but on maintaining that outrage. Suspicion itself is being stimulated, echoed, and marketed in such a way we are now surrounded by interpretive overload.

What this all means and what, if anything, we might do about it— well, that is the question that hovers relentlessly in interpretive work. *In extremis* this can distort and disable itself out into paranoia or, to the other extreme, being one of the suckers born every minute.

Pay no attention to the man behind the curtain, but once you've got what seems like a glimpse, *then* what?

I know! Want to buy a book?

This is the really clear politics. The "real" topic is that *I am the real topic,* a prospective customer of market advertising that funds realclear-politics.com. All these charts and graphs are just the means to this end of profit and marketing. And, of course, Donald Trump is an ideal avatar, an ideal (but unconscious) embodiment of precisely this reality, is suasions, lies and self-aggrandizements all bent on convincing you, the voter, that you are in full, literally *self*-fulfilling charge (after all, think of the Narcissism of finding your own books advertised to you on a political website, rendering me a minor avatar of exactly the thing that causes me such grief, exhaustion and suspicion).

Ignore the man behind the curtain. Watch out. He looks like you. Ignore the ads streaming alongside the real, clear politics. Unwittingly pay by paying no attention.

"We know what you want. Buy this and you'll feel better."

No wonder that having these slightly-secret amazon.ca ventures outed feels unseemly, like a dirty little secret secreted back to me, they carry a message like this: "I've got front-cover photos of your darkest, most self-serving acts and I can use them for you or against you. Want to buy a book?" The only possible good that getting old might serve is as a reminder of the fact that someone can still be slightly surprised by this, enough, perhaps, so that we don't—that I don't—slip totally into memory loss about what has *already happened to us* beyond our wanting and doing. Don't forget that that is a quote.

Walks over to check out the old social sciences indexes seem like silly old events that are no longer necessary *and* like memory pilgrimages as well that help make our current circumstances seem a wee bit less inevitable. Still not owning a cellphone is just silly bloody-mindedness *and* a quickly fading remembrance of things past—but of what, exactly, I'm not very sure.

But not just this. It is a reminder that there is no *necessity* to our current, apparent (but perhaps not as innocently "real" as we might imagine) echoing-bubbling and, after all, the citation indexes were their own form of encircled self-regard. This is to say, simply, that what is happening to us is interpretable, understandable, de-codable, and that a certain freedom is always ours for the winning (and, of course, losing and having to win all over again).

There is no escaping except for practicing and honing and sharing and expecting a readiness and ability and willingness to be both bubble-burst and bubble-bursting. The art of interpretation, done with affection for our ever-common human foibles, has its portend and opportunity everywhere we breath, even, perhaps even *especially*, in the simplest of events and happenstances. Those ads' appearance is utterly commonplace, so commonplace as to often seem beyond the need, the possibility, of utterance. And such locales of commonplaceness are precisely the places where the repose of interpretation and the leisures (Latin *scola*) of scholarship are often most urgently needed.

What this all means and what, if anything, we might do about it— well, that is the question that hovers relentlessly in interpretive work. *In extremis* this can distort and disable itself out into paranoia or, to the other extreme, being one of the suckers born every minute.

Pay no attention to the man behind the curtain, but once you've got what seems like a glimpse, *then* what?

I know! Want to buy a book?

CHAPTER SEVENTEEN

"Poisoning the Blood of our Country"

Preface

And old musing from 2013. Found just as talk of "Poisoning the Blood of our Country" is rising up, along with a conversation this morning (December 22, 2023, ten years away from what was written below) with Eric about how it works as a double barrel. Arousing the growls of followers and summoning well-buried images and ideas. But also arousing the growls of those who rise up to its baiting on MSNBC and provide entertainment to those very followers. This double logic is why current currents are so powerful and pervasive. Eric and I talked about how news outlets used to be, or at least seem "governed" by a public mandate of broad balance, used to be essentially "loss leaders" on public networks for the public good.

Seems to be from that Gadamer class I taught 25 times. I start with thanks to someone now forgotten. Here be thanks again.

Thanks for your email. It provided a very important opportunity for me, for us, to think through things vital to both of us.

For me, at least, hermeneutics has slowly provided a way to explore and adore what happens when things go right, when we are fully human and treat each other and the broad sways of the earth that way. It involves a type of "letting go" of the troubles of the world that constantly try to drag us back into their fray. This does not mean ignoring these troubles, but finding ways to pay attention that don't simply entangle us all over again, but, rather, free us to think of free spaces beyond their woes, spaces that try to stretch the full breadth open, all the rising and perishing causes and conditions.

When I push up against the troublesome things in our culture, I try, at least, to do so only to the extent that I can then push away from it, release it's grip on me. But I've also found that my worrying over such troublesome things can easily become an end in itself. They can drag me in and will *always* outplay me. I'm very susceptible to their allure. And they are *designed* to exhaust me and to summon me to exaggerate and reify. And when I get dragged in, all I can manage are grand generalizations that never serve to undo these troublesome things. E.g., "our faculty is this or that" or "schools are just assembly lines."

When I generalize like this, they become powerful, hungry monsters. More embarrassing for me, they become monsters, in part, *because of* my generalizing attention to them. They make me forget how much, for example, I love this hermeneutics class, how good our conversations have been, how everyone in the class, myself included, are bringing to it their quirks and qualms on behalf of cultivating a free space.

I wonder if your tendency, like mine, toward over-generalization is linked to your tendency, like mine too often, to precisely axe-grind over the ills of our world and seem, then, to get stuck in the spell of those ills and not be able to look away? [See the chapter entitled "The ... readiness to be all ears," with its meditations on Medusa, an old story]. I have found that those ills feed upon my attention and they become very jealous if I don't pay attention to them. This is as old as the sirens in ancient Greece. They are addictive! My only concern with you in the class is that you sometimes seem to be caught in cultivating a less and less free space for yourself and your thinking. The issue with generalizations is that they tend to "harden" [this is alluding to Huntington] and become more and more intractable. Even a concept like "free spaces" from

Gadamer has to not be taken too "seriously" as an intractable rule or general concept that "everyone should follow." It has to be played with and we have to let it have free play in our imaginations if its effects are to be experienced. Otherwise, it becomes a method that loses track of whether now is the time to enact such an idea. After all, as the Buddha once said, you don't enter a burning building and start describing the principles of combustion. You grab someone's arm, pick up the cat and get the hell out.

Those ills are important and attractive, but they don't lessen with attention—they increase to a size commensurate with the type of attention they are given. They can become nameable generalizations, grand, intractable, immoveable concepts to name our ills (opinionism, isolation, repression, "treating each other like objects" etc.) that then simple entangle us and distract our attention from the fact that we live lives that are often lovely and peaceful and compassionate. Such generalizations can then make a small incident on the bus a terrible and unbearable event that carries the weight of the world on its shoulders and thus then weighs me down with its consequence. The job in hermeneutics is, as David Smith put it, to "free it from the burden of its specificity"—to "lighten" its load and our load. To en-lighten.

I talked, recently, with a grad student who asked me if he should include a very negative example in his work. I suggested that he can do that, but only to the extent that it frees up his ability to articulate the good, difficult work he is doing, only to the extent that it interrupts your readers and grabs their attention. However, we all know life is tough, and we need to face that, but what *for*? Not to become entrapped by it, but in order to free ourselves and others from it. I can lament how schools are entrapped, but a little of that goes a long way. Only when I free myself from it can I free myself for it.

This is why, when I consider ecological matters, I must include myself as a locale that needs to be considered under the term "sustainability." I need to sustain myself—only nourished and fed and air-filled, but also able to think carefully, or set myself right anew if I get too tired or worried or lost or incapacitated.

CHAPTER EIGHTEEN

Meeting an Old Acquaintance

Speaking of old acquaintances, you will have noticed by now how various cita-
tions, passages, ideas, names, come drifting by again and again in this book. I'm
finding, rereading and editing this, that such recurrences can have the charac-
ter of reminding—not simply appearing again, but appearing here, like an old
friend at the door who I haven't seen since my grandchildren moved nearby.
We'll look familiar to each other, but that familiarity is now set to become tested
by my new circumstances, by their new experiences. Even Kongtrul's title
passage—for me, it got mulled over and over—underlinings, writing the page
number in the inside front cover, like a clue to a pathway of some sort that
I wanted to remember. And then what happens is that these things I've studied
in this way "show up" when I write about this or that and they show up under
all the new lights and shadows since the last time we met. More like bedtime
stories with an old, familiar set of characters that shape the mood and cadence
of the places that thinking goes, but that get shifted by an unforeseenness. Such
re-visiting of old acquaintances, old reminders always will have to trip their
way over the new events being discussed, the new contexts of concern or the
like. To have been writing long enough to see so many tides pull in and out, so

many words become antiquated, or newly discernable, and myriad other twists and turns.

This chapter was originally yet another graduate after-class email about that strange moment when one's circumstance suddenly light up, when new practices become enticing to pursue, and when establishing oneself in the midst of these new fields is still to fully come to commiserating realization. "Inquiry in the classroom" had become all the rage, just like so many other rages that can rage through school boards.

> It is somewhat difficult to establish, but once you are used to it, it will be like meeting an old acquaintance. (Kongtrul, 2002, p. 67)

> It's like making a path through the forest. At first it's rough going, with a lot of obstructions, but returning to it again and again, we clear the way. After a while the ground becomes firm and smooth from being walked on repeatedly. Then we have a good path for walking in the forest. (Chah, 2005, p. 83)

There is an arc. Teachers often feel a low-level sense that something has gone wrong, that something is amiss in their exhaustion and panic, but then, without the recourse of study, what can easily occur is mere complaint, negativity, blame and a commiseration based on discontent but not necessarily any freeing insight. Until we are, however briefly, released from the grips of our unease, it cannot teach but only pester. We cannot release this grip by simply calming down.

We must learn to see through it. We must study.

This curves toward thinking about inquiry in the classroom and some of the often--unspoken resistance it encounters. There is a nebulous inheritance that surrounds our work about thinking and questioning: that to think, to question, to explore, is to be negative about, to no longer feel attached, to betray, to "lose one's faith," to be disobedient, to be self-aggrandizing. To think is to lose one's way and start to simply drift. Thinking and exploration can be seen as "uprooting" only.

Perhaps this links to the anti-intellectualism that is sometimes seen as indigenous to education these days (see Callahan, 1964, p. 8)

But we know, in our classroom work, that inquiry is bent on the care, cultivation and *increase* of our sense of rootedness. It is thus radical, once radicalism is itself properly rooted back (Latin *radix*, rootedness.

See Seidel & Jardine, 2016). Inquiry presumes that rootedness is not pre-mised on unknowing (a sort of wordless and silent "being there" and "deep feeling" that has invaded some versions of ecological awareness), and that knowledge is not a sin that expels us, but is, in the world, a deeply human, deeply embodied means of taking hold of our human-ity in all its frail and fleshy countenance. The same thread—a critique of the adequacy of passive, stilling mindfulness for which thinking is seen as the ruin—runs through Tsong-kha-pa's critique of certain lineages of Buddhism. He tells us that "you can't get anywhere with-out [also] reading a yak's load of books" (Tsong-kha-pa, 2004, p. 219). Stillness is certainly necessary here, because inside the panic, one can-not properly and carefully "read," no matter how many books crawl under your nose. It is necessary but not sufficient (an old Aristotelian lesson, that). Inquiry—classroom or otherwise—is:

> not just a matter of achieving stillness in the face of the fray [this, of course, is itself a profound, difficult, and ceaselessly-needing-to-be-re-achieved "per-fection"], but of cultivating a deep and well -studied knowledge of the topic of one's meditations and all the rich lineages and ancestries of thought that have handed this topic over to us and us over to it. (Jardine, 2014d, p. 166)

Consider, then, from Alice Miller's book *For your own good: Hidden cruelty in child-rearing and the roots of violence.* Here, she is citing a peda-gogy manual from 1852:

> One of the vile products of a misguided philanthropy is the idea that, in order to obey gladly, the child has to understand the reasons why an order is given and that blind obedience offends human dignity. I do not know how we can continue to speak of obedience once reasons are given. These [rea-sons] are meant to convince the child, and, once convinced, he is not obeying us but merely the reasons we have given him. Respect is then replaced by a self-satisfied allegiance to his own cleverness. (As cited in Miller, 2002, p. 40)

And another one:

> It goes without saying that pedagogues not infrequently awaken and help to swell a child's conceit by foolishly emphasizing his merits. Only humilia-tion can help here. (From *The Encyclopedia of Pedagogy*, 1851, as cited in Miller, 2002, p. 22)

There is this Romantic atmosphere in our profession's attempts to right itself, that seems, sometimes, to believe that thinking/knowledge will decrease our affection, our love of what we are immersed in, that we will distain what we know and turn our backs on it and become disobedient, cynical, "critical" and the like.

This is where these passages from Miller betray a false equation of obedience and unthinking. Obedience turns on an etymology: *ab audire*, to heed, to listen, and inquiry is bent on increasing our ability to heed what it is we think about, what it is that is happening to us. It can be that our knowledge can make us swell with a foolish conceit - we've all witnessed this happening in those who carry their knowledge like a weapon of dominion over that which they know, where obedience does not mean tending carefully to what we are studying and what it asks of us but, instead obeying the teacher. Period. We've also witnessed people like Wendell Berry who carries his knowledge humanly, as something that grants affection, and also demands a forfeiting of such conceits. We have companions who know this is not a matter of "anything goes." "Anything goes" is simply the nightmare of old, worn-out ways of teaching that cannot imagine schools without their tsk.

When we have watched Joseph Campbell's interviews (Campbell & Moyers, 2013), my affection (and often revulsion) for all those silent threads of ancestry and images and connotation *increases* as I witness his deep affection for knowledge itself and for its sometimes blissful release, there, in the face of his own impending death. I feel drawn *toward* what I study, toward these often—hidden, often miraculous weaves of fabric tugging and pulling "over and above our wanting and doing" (Gadamer, 1989, p. xxviii).

This tug will yield to the loving attention of scholarship if we treat it with the sort of generosity, patience, perseverance, rigorousness, thoughtfulness and wisdom it needs, and remembering that is proper to it: "[the world] compels over and over, and the better one knows it, the *more* compelling it is. This is not a matter of mastering an area of study" (Gadamer, 2007c, p. 115). It is a matter of finding out how to come to live in such an area, such a place, such a tending.

There is thus another arc, here, that points to a sort of freedom, and it is one of the reasons why we might protect and defend rich, difficult, scholarly work in the classroom as worth our while and the whiling spent of our children:

> The aim of interpretation, it could be said, is not just another interpretation but human freedom, which finds its light, identity and dignity in those few brief moments when one's lived burdens can be shown to have their source in too limited a view of things. (Smith, 2020d, p. 49)

Yes, a few brief moments, never won once and for all. This is not a matter of mastering an area of study. So, of course, oh--oh, here comes another yak-load. Remember the nemesis, here, however. We never get "sprung" into some *solus ipse* with a tale to tell and no need to listen.

Get used to it. It can become like meeting an old acquaintance. Declare it: "I am willing to endure the shame of falling short as the price of admission" (Berry & Moyers, 2013). In such falling is our free-dom, our being human, and perhaps a gateway to our itself-momentary, earthly survival.

CHAPTER NINETEEN

Beet Juice

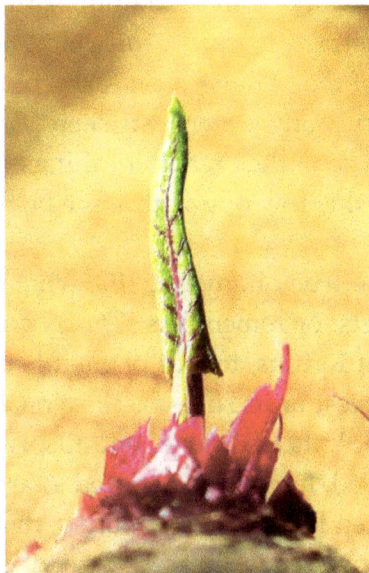

FIGURE 8. BEETLEAF

I'm not trying to *describe* experience—my own or yours. I'm trying to shape my experiences, my immediacies, into more beautiful shapes and contours, richer colors, full of more vivid memories and vivid dreaming, more alert to the relations roiling under the surface of my "lived-experience." My own life—any life—is full of forgetting, is inevitably wrought with inadequacy, is inevitably finite, located, frail and limited. Every tradition, every voice, betrays itself when it feels itself fully adequate:

> The issue today is not simply a matter of making pure choices for one tradition over another, which is psychologically and conceptually impossible anyway, given that there is no such thing as a "pure" tradition. The real challenge is to face the truth that no one tradition can say everything that needs to be said about the full expression of human experience in the world and that what the global community requires more than anything else is mutual recognition of the various poverties of *every* tradition. The search to cure the poverty of one's own tradition works in all directions at once. (Smith, 2020i, p. 334)

And that search only works if those traditions that have been marginalized, silenced, or betrayed come to full voice, not because we might choose this instead of that, but because each voice can only be what it is in the daresay beautifully poverty-stricken admixture of the whole of the breath, the whole of the breadth of things. I can't face the whole of this, though, only this row dug with some better compost, only this up-weeded.

The very same be true of any one life, whatever tradition it beckons, summons, forgets, or remembers. *This* is our collective fate, and it includes the fate of Ravens, too, of planted beets and their harvest, of the fail of that harvest or its success. *These* relations—where my living experience, with all its traditional entrails, is exposed to the open wind—are often buried, forgotten, distorted, marginalized, unheeded, simply fallen for, taken for granted, occluded, distorted, intermingled. And, well, often suppressed, repressed, denied, erased, stolen, subjectivized, objectivized, exaggerated, and so on and so on.

And let me invert this. I'm trying to plumb things *hidden from the immediacies of my own self- reflection*—things lingering in the words we use, I use, ideas we wittingly or unwittingly inherited and this from wherever and whomever. "Neither … is it enough simply to 'let differences be,' as if there could never be any points of address between them" (Smith, 2020, p. 334). The proof? I live on unceded land *and* I breathe the very air *and* my very body is composed of it, has ceded to this land over and over again. These are *both* proofs the attention to which will take more life than I've got left. That attention can *never* be adequate to the full expression of human experience in the world because that fullness keeps coming.

It is the desire for it to finally fully succeed that is the real common enemy in relation to which we must all marshal our poor little gifts (pre-Latin *pau-paros*)—you can spot the word "pauper" here, involving *parare* "to produce, bring forth" and the root *pau-* "few, little" (see the Online Etymological Dictionary entries under "poor" and "poverty").

So, I take a picture and offer it here for good reasons that I am too frail to understand all by myself. I think it is beautiful and that may be part of our locales of commiseration and healing. It is not "enough."

We've all become of mixed blood, Earth blood. Beet juice. It's a joke. Smile. Here we are, all of us. First born. Second born. Indigenous. Exogenous. No one of these locales is fully adequate to the things themselves.

The voles eat up the composted leaves after we've sorted the edible beet greens.

CHAPTER TWENTY

I Am Not a Buddhist

In Buddhism, the central affliction, the central cause of human (and, consequently, much more-than-human) suffering is *identity* and all its requisite reifications. A=A and not B, a topic that's bewildered me since first writing about it 33 years ago (Jardine, 1990c).

Now this is, of course, a common-sense idea—there is the coffee cup, there the light.

And the more desperately we grasp at identity, the more solid it *seems* and the deeper the error becomes. The deeper becomes the *delusion of permanence that lies at the heart of identity and its pursuits*. It is the grasping that is the error, as my creaky aging is slowly teaching me.

I get it. "Easy for me to say." Nice try. It *is* easy to just "say." But struggling to let my footsteps fall outside of my own breath being held is *not* easy.

The solution is not to simply multiply identities. This simply multiplies the original error and makes our loving, compassionate embrace of our strange lot of being alive in the myriad of Earthly relations ever more stained.

Overcoming the tragic, violent, repeated, continuing, historical tendency of one particular [presumed] "identity" to oppress other [presumed] identities is not had by simply giving (and who's doing the giving?) those oppressed a chance to replicate the very error that was key to their oppression in the first place by affirming their own "identity" as different from the oppressor, as legitimate in its own right.

Proliferated delusion is still delusional. You don't beat the self-aggrandized, historically dominant asshole by simply having a chance to be one yourself. The aggressor was *wrong*. And "identity" (according to Buddhism) is at the core of this delusion. And Zen Buddhist practice was key to training kamikaze pilots in the Second World War (see Victoria, 2006). As Christopher Hitchens deftly put it in a YouTube video, "You've got to keep your eye on those guys, too" (I've long since lost the specific reference). Buddhism can become meaningless, narcotizing droning or mindlessly repeated ritualizations as easily as anything else. I don't *believe* it.

We cannot avoid this by simply using the phrase "identifying as ..." as if being asked to perpetrate the error *upon myself* on purpose is some sort of relief. This doesn't open up the threads of dependent co-arising (*pratitya-samutpada*) that weave our breaths together, that elaborate our myriadness. It bypasses the real work of cultivating affection for what is neither the same, nor simply different. In reality, there is no us and them. "Identical" and "different" are inadequate to the matters at hand.

"Identifying as ..." Again, this make perfect sense as an attempt to take back one's own living out from under being identified by others bent on marginalizing my living. However, instead, this is equally in danger of codifying of the root of suffering *as if it is* the route to our individual and collective well-being, as well as the well-being of those Ravens, or the roots of those peas just planted. No.

I do not "self-identify" as a Buddhist. As Christopher Hitchens slyly said, from a source I can no longer trace, "You've got to keep your eye on those guys, too."

I understand, in some just-beginning, wee ways, something of the motives of talking in this very walking-on-eggshells way.

I do not question motives here, not at all. I think, behind our current hyperactive over-stimulation, dwells good heartedness.

However, I am not, nor to I self-identify as a Buddhist. I also do not self-identify as not a Buddhist. I understand full well that this playful seriousness is gained by my own blue-eyed leisure. Please, if self-identifying helps rattle the chains, if this is a step that is timely and needed, I step back in silence and hopefulness.

But please watch out for simply recapitulating the error. In the end, there is one air in which our different breaths linger.

And it isn't a universal. And it is of varying poisonousness and clarity. Differing humidities. Air quality warnings. Disease related.

And these differences are economic and cultural and political and racial and tangled and inequitable. Yes. It is why I am not a Buddhist.

CHAPTER TWENTY-ONE

Cautionary yet Hopeful Thoughts on "Mindfulness Practices" in Schools

Mindfulness in schools. We might have a fanciful reason to expect this—*schola*, Latin, "leisure," "a holding back, a keeping clear" (from the Online Etymological Dictionary). Root of the word "scholar," and readable as a privative term, "not" [Latin prefix *s*] "tilling the land" [*cola*], not caught, then, in these labors and the provisioning they involve. Let's stretch this further while we're here: *schola* perhaps most properly means not being caught spellbound, exhausted and distracted in and by the work we do, tilling land or otherwise.

Of course, "scholars" can get as stuck as anybody in the drudge of the day. And make no mistake. Many universities are falling hook line and sinker for such drudge being precisely what the real work has come to be. But there is a lightness to be had in holding back, in keeping (ourselves and our surroundings and those dear to us) as clear as we are able.

Thus, as per the work of Hans-Georg Gadamer (1989), I've made a bit of a career suggesting that schools/scholarship involves its own type of cultivation (German *Bildung*), of working living fields of knowledge and cultivating them as one cultivates oneself—coming to know our way around this or that patch of the world and consequently *becoming someone* in the process:

> Coming to know a living field of work and its gatherings [is thus linked] to the transformation of the one coming to know into someone who "know[s] one's way around" (Gadamer, 1989, p. 260): "this means that one knows one's way around *in it*" (p. 260), in the gatherings of and in the dependently co-arising gathering presence of mind regarding, a living field of work. (Jardine, 2016d, p. 250)

Scholarship is its own hard work and involves suffering of a very ethereal sort, bent on enlivening the mind to the circumstances of its living and allowing me to think these things through as much as I'm able without panicking or unwarranted exaggeration, despair, or hope. "Breaking open" (1989, p. xxx) the often fragile, often hard and encrusted shells that numb thinking and press in on us from all sides— well, it is no coincidence that Gadamer suggests that "understanding is an adventure and like any adventure, it involves some risks." Leisurely labor, shall we say? Mindfulness—calming the frittery panics that invade such cultivation of knowledge—is not a bad lot for schools to encourage and pursue.

Yet all this is why, frankly, I am so concerned about the rise of mindfulness practices in schools (see, e.g., Campbell, 2013; Saltzman, 2014, and countless recent others). My fear is that such things are unwittingly (and dare I say that I more deeply fear that it is quite wittingly) ways to get kids to "settle down" so they can go back to doing stupid and demeaning things in classrooms, while at the same derailing and marginalizing any "uprising" into a personal problem that needs quelling, rather than see it as an intelligent and intelligible insight into their institutionalized circumstances.

"Increasingly, teachers are using the principles of mindfulness to help make the classroom a calmer place and to improve learning" (Campbell, 2013, n.p.) thus perhaps masking classroom conditions and expectations that might just warrant restlessness and discontent, and leaving in place, too, what "learning" and "improvement" are presumed to be.

I do not want, in any way, to accuse anyone involved in such things of anything. My fear is that, because of the monstrous suasions of schooling, mindfulness is vulnerable to becoming understood instrumentally as a way to simply maintain much of the status quo of school life by calming those being schooled (including teachers) and making their troubles deflect away from interrupting that status. Questioning schooling and feeling restless in its confines thus becomes a personal problem in need (as is always the case in schools) of remediation.

In fact, a leisurely investigation of mindfulness shows it to be well rooted in long legacies and ancestries that belie such exogenous instrumentality. Mindfulness is not simply a "technique" that can be put in the service of some external usage in everyday life. It is, rather, a way of precisely *breaking of the spell(s) of everyday life,* waking up to the delusions and false promises and panics and fears that are encoded into one's circumstances (e.g., as a student in a school, or a teacher on a staff, or a principal in a school system, or a school system under the auspices of Provincial or State surveillance) and learning to act accordingly.

In many Buddhist lineages mindfulness gives rise to and summons and supports relentless insight into the realities of our circumstances. As per Tsong-Kha-Pa (in a work written in 1406 in Tibet), this involves both "leisure and opportunity" (2000, pp. 117–129). In fact, Tsong-kha-pa insists that mindfulness meditation (the stilling and calming and focusing of the mind) and insight or analytic meditation (the thinking through of the hardened reifications in which we falsely believe and the detailed knowledge and study of the causes and conditions of our situation—that situation that calls for calming and stillness and focus) are tethered together. As Gesha Sopa, a commentator on his work put it:

Just as a bird needs two wings to fly in the sky, we also need two wings.

…

What you learn from teachings is exactly what you should put into practice; what you practice is what you should learn about.

…

One wing is the extensive method side of practice, the wing of conventional truth. The other wing is the wisdom side of practice, the wing of ultimate truth. Spreading these two powerful wings in perfect unison, you can fly. (Sopa, 2004, pp. 7, 57, 293)

And then, these, delicious:

Using only joyous perseverance [I think of the enthusiasm of a new teacher, or the quells of mindful, meditative practices], you will end up exhausted. If you practice with the aid of wisdom, you will achieve the great goal. (Tsong-kha-pa, 2002, p. 62)

Do not make study and practice into separate things. Rather, the very thing that you practice must be exactly what you study and reflect upon. (Tsong-kha-pa, 2004, p. 221)

It is like showing a horse the racecourse before you race. Once you have shown it, you then race there. It would be ridiculous to show the horse one racecourse and then race on another. Similarly, why would you determine one thing by means of study and reflection, and then, when you go to practice, practice something else? (Tsong-kha-pa, 2000, p. 52)

Texts are instructions for practice. (p. 52)

Wisdom and the study that it causes are indispensable for proper practice. (Tsong-kha-pa, 2004, p. 220)

You need study. The purpose of knowing them through study is to do them. Therefore, it is vital to put the meaning of what you have heard into practice as much as you are able. (Tsong-kha-pa, 2000, p. 61)

Do not devote yourself just to piling up words in great numbers without engaging in practice. (p. 59)

It is not right to forget what you have studied at the time of practice. Do not make study and practice into separate things. (Tsong-kha-pa, 2004, pp. 220–221)

Note the two directions pulling here—piling up words about "the teachings" without practicing and practicing without pursuing a deeper and deeper understanding of the teachings.

This needs focusing, because this is not just about the teachings of Buddhism, but about teaching and learning itself, about that precarious position of being a University professor fessing up to the ins and outs of classrooms, the prospects of something like a more ecologically sound understanding of curriculum. This sort of thing:

> There are two particular passages in Tsong-kha-pa's work that took me a while to read despite, now, 12 re-readings of those three volumes. They emerge in relation to his response to critics of his work who characterize this emphasis on study in a very interesting way. The context of these brief passages was Tsong-kha-pa arguing against schools of Buddhism that suggest that practice—immediate, non-conceptual, repeated, mastered—has nothing to do with wisdom, with knowledge, with study and reflection. Commonplace in many lineages of Buddhism is the belief that knowledge and its pursuit is, so to speak, mere words, mere concepts and conceptualizations, by which is meant, in the end, mere illusion, mere falsehood and distraction.
>
> One need not study.
>
> One need not read.
>
> In my years working in schools, I had done countless professional development "talks" here and there and was always somewhat taken aback by the heat they sometimes caused.
>
> Then I read this: "Do not explain the teachings without being requested to do so" (Tsong-kha-pa, 2000, p. 65), and this request never works if it arrives pre-emptively from a principal who needs their staff, as one said, "shaken up a bit."
>
> But then I read *this*, where Tsong-kha-pa (2000, p. 110) is voicing a common objection by one of his critics:
>
> What is determined through study and reflection is not intended for [practice] but is merely for promoting superficial knowledge and eliminating others' misconceptions.
>
> Not only is this reiterating this belief: "some think that [practitioners] do not need to study. Only those who explain the teachings do" (Tsong-kha-pa, 2004, p. 220). It is also suggesting that speaking with the voice of study in a Professional Development talk at a school can easily be understood as suggesting you are not only promoting something superficial that practitioners do not need, but that, even more offensively, the reason you are doing it is because those listening need their misconceptions eliminated. Little wonder the heat rose up so often. "Study [is a] mere preliminary to practice to a background support—like mountains at the back of a valley—but not the actual instructions." (Jardine, 2019a, p. 67; Tsong-kha-pa, 2004, p. 22)

This is one of those locales where heat and light dance and dance, and, where I will state outright how comprehensible and sensible was the often-beleaguered relations between university folks and "the field" that I experienced over decades. It is one reason I asked to be given practicum, in-school classes every term that I taught in the Faculty of Education—a chance to get out into the field and experience the exhilarating and frustrating tests to what I might write, what I might think.

So, in the end, mindfulness in schools. Yes. Because, in their deepest root, mindfulness practices are coupled with study and insight and *breaking through*. Like this: "Why study for a future we won't have?"

I always return to a passage that David Smith showed me years ago:

> Meditation is working with our speed, our restlessness, our constant busyness. Meditation provides space or ground in which restlessness might function. Meditation practice is not a matter of trying to produce a hypnotic state of mind or create a sense of restfulness. Trying to achieve a restful state of mind reflects a mentality of poverty. Seeking a restful state of mind, one is on guard against restlessness. There is a constant state of paranoia and limitation. We feel we need to be on guard. This guarding process limits the scope of the mind by not accepting whatever comes. Instead, meditation should reflect a mentality of richness in the sense of using everything that occurs in the state of mind. Thus, if we provide enough room for restlessness so that it might function within the space, then the energy ceases to be restless because it can trust itself fundamentally. Meditation is giving a huge, luscious meadow to a restless cow. The cow might be restless for a while in its huge meadow, but at some stage, because there is so much space, the restlessness becomes irrelevant. (Trungpa, 2003, pp. 218–219)

I must add something here in conclusion. What very often happens in schools when students become restless and encounter difficulties with the work they face is that teachers (and sometimes assessors, testers, curriculum developers, and remediators) *zoom in on that trouble*, narrowing attention, making the "meadow," the "field of relations" available to that restless student *less* huge, luscious, rich and spacious (this defines, of course, precisely what can happen to a restless teacher in a school as well). As Trungpa notes, paranoia and limitation increase in response to restlessness. The restlessness becomes paramount. In a tragic but terribly understandable turn, restlessness begins to be blamed on the fact that the field is *too* big, *too* luscious, alluring and distracting. Abundance, lusciousness, variegation and multifariousness become transformed into threats set on breaching the ever- narrowing security fences.

So much, then, for mindfulness in its fullest sense. Differently put, this is not mindfulness.

Differently put, mindfulness in schools? Yes. And here's to the hope that these new practices are ripe and delicious and luscious, and that the good intent of this little commentary is useful.

One way or another, if it be mindfulness, it will lead to what *schola* portends—the desire for and pursuit of insight into our living circumstances.

CHAPTER TWENTY-TWO

On Bob Dylan's Murder and How Interpretation Takes Time

Part One: November 22, 1963

No matter how quickly that date rings in some ears, this is also the *exact* day of the release of The Beatles' first LP, *Beatlemania*, in Canada. I still have my mono copy and the exact date is printed on the back, as was Capitol Record's habit of the day.

It is perfect that its cover is black and white. So was I, in retrospect. Fall of Grade Eight, with puberty burbles all over the place, all over my face. Something is happening, but I don't know what it is, do I? Not so very sly a reference ahead to the Summer of 1965. Those who know will know.

The following February 9, 1964, The Beatles were on *The Ed Sullivan Show* for the first time, CBS, 8:00 p.m. Sunday.

That black-and-white CBS TV dead-eye-logo creepy-opens, camera-shutter-like, with just a wee dash of Rod Serling, another lover of those days of mine.

I showed my son the video of that Ed Sullivan performance, with all the jugglers and black-and-white comedians, all the near-vaudevillian plate-spinners and dog acts and polite clapping.

And then The Beatles came on and his reaction was utterly revelatory: "Oh, *now* I get it!"

1964. The summer, then off to a new high school, Grade Nine, with a new secret in my back pocket that came to save my life. But then that lull. After the gluts of new songs released, it seems, almost weekly (the English backlog pent up back to October 5, 1962, with Love Me Do) and a movie, silence, silence, weeks, weeks, weeks.

It's over.

And then, like the perfect summation of what had gone on, all the cascades that then came along in their wake, this.

October 18, 1964, starting with a feedback siren wake-up call, I Feel Fine, arpeggiated guitars feeling like a clean scrub, like clean, cold, fresh air.

I Feel Fine. Oh yes, I do.

Part Two: Murder Most Foul

I was going to whip off some comments about Bob Dylan's new song, *Murder Most Foul*, (https://www.youtube.com/watch?v=3NbQkyvb w18&feature=emb_logo), but decided against it (good lyric transcription here: https://genius.com/19399573). That, in itself, is already quite confusing. The Internet is full of reactions across the whole spectrum of opinion, praise and insult. It rattled me to hear it, because our love affair goes back quite a way, to the inglorious origins of being taken by the still-ringing Rickenbacker Angel-Harps of The Byrds' *Mr. Tambourine Man* in 1965, 14-year-old turning 15 that summer, then turning sidelong to Dylan, finding Mike Bloomfield in the meanwhile, and so on.

Angel-headed hipsters. Starry dynamos.

Jingle jangle morning, one hand waving what surely felt like free. And so on. Sh-Boomer reminiscence with a suppressed reference to The Crew Cuts (1954). But don't forget The Chords version, also from

1954, which I found years and years later. The white Canadian boys' version took to the air.

Quick, unread glimpse on the way by of *OK Boomer: How Bob Dylan's New JFK Song Helps Explain 2020* (Hogan, 2020). The immediacies of reaction are so fascinating, so, well, thrilling sometimes, and so unpredictably unreliable, sometimes, too. Actually knowing what I am now experiencing will take some time to sort out. That, by itself, is so strange, when you can get caught right up in the howling immediacies of the day *and* know full well that this, one way or another, will come to something or other, someday.

It is so interesting to note, in passing, that, from long, sometimes funny, sometimes bitter experience, it is difficult to find the proper measure of things in the immediacies of their arrival. This doesn't exactly make me pull back some cynical distance, but, in fact, heightens something. I'm hearing comparisons that put this song in the top measure of Dylan's work and feel myself drawn into that level of affection; and then ones that are more dismissive or at least less rapt, and I don't want them to spoil the party, so I'll go, and take my Internet crawl elsewhere. The thing that is so interesting to catch a glimpse of, here, is that it will take time for this new arrival to prove itself, and the exigencies of that slow-coming, always-uprootable, shiftable and changeable proof cannot be outrun. It can't be nailed down once and for all without rising up again. Dylan once said, somewhere, comparatively recently, that, with his new music, it wasn't just that it was different than "before." It was also that we listeners treated it differently than before as well. That we didn't listen to it the way we used to.

I knew he was perfectly right. I carried around *Blonde on Blonde* everywhere I went for a while in 1966. Not that I understood, 15 years old, June 290, 1966, but I held it in ways that I have held only certain other music. And that hold let it grow—its hold on me and my hold on it. And I'll venture to say that it was good enough to grow. So many other things have faded from view, fallen out of earshot, shown themselves to be not especially worth the while.

OK Boomer, that's enough. Life can be a dream sweetheart. But there's something here about interpretation, coming to an understanding, and the way time passes slowly up here in the mountains.

In other words, I was going to write something about this new Bob Dylan song that I currently utterly *adore* and find *astounding*, but I decided, you see, not to. Well, sort of. One linger of this is that I was going to send the URL and lyrics to my son, Eric (now nearing 38), but realized that this isn't for him, that its cascade of references, musical and otherwise, are of an age of which I am (well, I sent it anyway). I realized that what is happening here is like an ominous moan of some sort whose measure is found, in part, in age, Dylan's and mine. I can recognize many of the musical allusions he drops, and even the harsh precisions of 2:38. They are my very own memory, and they are profoundly old and have long-since fashioned soils out of which I've leafed. They are about being old and fashioned by a life lived and days gone by, not days to come. They are about the right viral-now, about the heartsickness right now.

Maybe it is for Eric, in codes that must sound ancient. After all, November 22, 1963, was 57 years ago. If, on that date, my father were to talk to me about something that old, that'd be November 1905. When he was, what, maybe eight? We were watching *The Simpsons* on what used to be called TV. Lisa was receiving the *Little Miss Springfield Award* at the locale Krusty Burger, and overhead, the Duff's Beer Blimp was filming the event. Kent Brockman, local newsman, was interviewing Lisa when Barney, town drunk and pilot of the blimp, drove it into the antenna on the top of the burger joint, where it burst into flames. Kent Brockman looked over his shoulder and said in a tired, dull, uninterested voice, "Oh, the humanity, the humanity" and then immediately went on with the interview. I turned to Eric and asked if he knew what just happened there and he said, in effect, "It's okay, Dad, I know something happened," and that was the end of it. Referentiality—both that it is there and what it might be and whether is catches your ear and exactly how this all works itself out case to case—is a strange matter indeed.

Meanwhile, someone online mentioned part of Murder Most Foul's litanies of songs is a reverie of Kennedy adrift between life and death. How, just like radio stations that weren't quite able to be fully tuned in, sound drifting in and out, broadcast static, me, southern Ontario, Cleveland and Boston stations drifting …

the beatles are coming wake up little suzie dizzy miss lizzy what'd I say tom dooley st. james infirmary scratch my back I'd rather go blind long black cadillac goin' down slow don't let me be misunderstood twilight time old rugged cross stand getz dickie betts thelonious monk charlie parker down in the boondocks nature boy Lucille key to the highway mystery train

Cry me a River remembering ... play it, ear pressed to the radio, waiting as the white fuzzy sound arc dopplerly like snow-filled sheets of air between here and there, creaking back and forth. Meanwhile, again, I don't know what on earth, if anything, I am going to think of this new song of Bob Dylan's in the however-many years I just might have to come, which is why it sings so electric now, on the buzz-edge of something, something.

There is something to be said for the fact that someone has made a Spotify list of all the music referred to in this new song. That is only a partial list above, with Dylan crying out to Wolfman Jack, DJ, play it.

There is something to be said for how this new arrival rattles its way back through a history I've lived with and a history far beyond me, how older songs become hints *that they never were before,* how being and time fit together in the very being of a simple thing like a new song. How an interpretation, an affection, a musical love affair, can never prove itself once and for all. And how all *that* rattles, over and over again, with the insights and sillinesses of youth and age. The good news is that all this does not ruin the froth of lived-experience one whit. It makes me love it more. Find its giddy innocence more endearing and precious in its precocious certainties. That, in itself, may be one of the draws of this Murder Most Foul.

So, I'll end with that utterly wonderful description by John Hiatt of hearing Dylan's *Like a Rolling Stone* for the first time—that opening rim-shot rivalling the slowly emerging Beatles finely felt siren—and how it expressed something, decades after the fact, that I think I already knew. Or it allowed to form in me something new that, before reading Hiatt's words, wasn't quite there? I don't know which and I can imagine it figuring out, but something of this describes something of the experience of me hearing this new song:

Hearing "Like A Rolling Stone"—that was my first encounter. I heard the song and I felt so transformed by it. My mother, she pulled into a drugstore to pick up something and I felt so changed by the song that I thought, when she came out, she wouldn't recognize me. And I couldn't tell you why. (Hiatt, 2003)

It's like something has happened to the lines on my face and I won't be able to hide it much longer. I just now realized that this ominous sense of waiting, of impending, is exactly what this new Dylan song is about. It is not just a reverie of memory but an uplift halt in how we wait, now, March 2020, wait under a wing of hard-to-decipher impending.

Part Three: "Holding Their Breath and Ours in Anticipation"

Today, tomorrow, and yesterday too,
The flowers are dying, like all things do.

Bob Dylan, from "I Contain Multitudes," released April 17, 2020.

Strange how the past is always turning out to be different than it used to be.

…

Everything now present will become past. But every past will then, *over and over again*, turn out to be something different than it used to be. *This* is the depth of the trauma of linking being and time and part of the pleasure of it as well. (Jardine, 2020a, p. 1)

Yes, part of its pleasures as well. There is pleasure to be had, at times, in the skeins and sinews and muscle aches as things work themselves along. It is part of the secret pleasure of writing and thinking, that the muscle massage, the historical dancing cascades, the way one little flit of insight rattles the whole cage of words all over again, pulls the breath up and in and out. Feels of hidden intimacies that are alive right at the moment they arrive and alive again at the arrival of the next insight that makes the older ones sit up and take stock and be asked to give an account of themselves all over again. You know, "like things do."

The world is always being knit at the front end one way or another, up against arrival, up against the empty chair at the table, await. So then, this morning, waking up to another new Bob Dylan song, "I Contain Multitudes" (https://www.youtube.com/watch?v=pgEP8teNXwY), and the discussion thread about it (http://expectingrain.com/discussions/viewtopic.php?f=6&t=99229&sid=6d1bdae0000624385560fede3538ac23) is already up to five pages (oh, and the "Murder Most Foul" thread is now 55 pages, up one since I started writing this 20 minutes ago). However fast this goes, the chair stays empty, awaiting arrival. Strange thing, this (see Jardine & Batycky, 2016).

Meanwhile great arguments in those 55 pages about how, in Dylan's lyrics, noting that the singer/author of "Dizzy Miss Lizzy" committed suicide by shooting himself in the head, head full of lead in a song somewhat about the JFK assassination, is scraping the bottle of the barrel of referentialities. And how all these posted threads and spins (http://expectingrain.com/discussions/viewtopic.php?f=6&t=99119&sid=6d1bdae0000624385560fede3538ac23) and ghost-images in its lyrics are nothing but distractions should be foregone in favor of just listening. Understood:

> A sort of cascading, post-modern "connectionism" ... In the face of [a] simple event ... one can become simply burdened by unseemly and unending cloys of "relatedness" which can weight down attention and make me simply given up in overwhelmed frustration. (Jardine, 2016f, p. 301)

Chasing ghosts can take me away from this magnificent *arrival*. And the very next thread post says that *summoning those very ghosts* deepen the listening, making it richer and more compelling. So when I next listen to the Larry Williams reference, when I next listen to The Beatles *Help!* Album, track 14, John Lennon singing, it bursts and buzzes, now, like insects around flowers. And then, of course, of course, "Roll on, John" from Dylan's till just now most recent work, *Tempest*, will never sound quite the same again. "What more can I tell ya, I sleep with life and death in the same bed":

> I go right to the edge, I go right to the end
> I go to right where all things lost are made good again.
>   From Bob Dylan, "I Contain Multitudes"

I know full well that someone will find the ghosts in these lines, too and out to the edge I'll have to do all over again. All over again.

And now, we have another song which itself not only contains multitudes, but uncontains anew the multitude of the song that preceded it, uncontains the multitude of the still-living whole of which this new song and that just-now-become-previous one, are both part and apart— this alluding to David G. Smith's still-stunning insight of how "the full meaning of a child, for us, resides in the paradox of being part of us but also apart from us" (Smith, 2020c, p. 405), this from "Children and the gods of war," a piece originally published in 1987.

The utter singularity of the arrival of a new song that sweeps me up in its arms. Yes. Irreplaceably itself. Apart. But then these two songs themselves sing out to and summon their surroundings and those surroundings respond.

The analytic parsing of words and finding of scholarly referentialities can be dead dust. I know this firsthand, as a student and as a teacher, as a writer and as a reader. Yes. But I've found that this is what happens when it all goes wrong, when *senex* loses track of the *puer* spirit and become senile, locked in the closed circle of its own cleverness with no open invitation into those ghost dances:

> [Interpretation, when it works] has as its aim not simply philosophical erudition and the like. The aim of such meditations and work is the cultivation of the intimacy and immediacy of the experience of everyday life, here, as this next child draws breath over a text, here, where reading aloud and learning to pronounce can too often be treated as simply ordinary and commonplace. Not only is "wherever you are … a place of practice" (Tsong-kha-pa, 2004, p. 191). Tsong-kha-pa also insists (and this is a feature that distinguishes the Gelug tradition from other Buddhist lineages and makes ripe its affinity to hermeneutics), the purpose and object of study is *precisely* the deepening of practice itself. After all, "why would you determine one thing by means of study and reflection, and then, when you go to practice, practice something else?" (2000, p. 52). All those complex philosophical and historical twists and turns … are meant, in the end, to make us more susceptible to the beautiful abundance of things as we walk around in the world. (Jardine, 2016f, p. 304)

Yes, even the young child already contains Earthly multitudes, eyes spun up to follow Ravens on air columns overhead, pushing Walt

Whitman into a cocked hat, part and apart, paradoxes and contradictions both contained and uncontained and loosing me out into that very intimate experience of having my life unwoven and wove again, this written over a small gesture of a child sounding out a word full of old and ancient, smelly breath:

> In this smallest of examples, I get to be present as the world ... is being "set right anew" (Arendt, 1969, p. 197). This sort of experience has become, for me, a simply miraculous thing to be around, something almost unbearable in its countenance. What is most deeply experienced here is the lovely, hearty frailness of these strange human ventures of reading of speaking, of voice and utterance, and how the ancients in all human traditions have gather around such ventures, most often unheralded and forgotten. They are right here ... holding their breath and ours in anticipation. (Jardine, 2016f, p. 292)

CHAPTER TWENTY-THREE

"We Arrive, as it Were,
Too Late"

Preamble

> Understanding is not … hold[ing] [my]self back and refus[ing] to take a stand
> with respect to the claim made on [me]. The … self-possession necessary for
> one to withhold oneself in this way is not given here. Someone who under-
> stands is always already drawn into an event. When we understand a text,
> what is meaningful in it captivates us, just as the beautiful captivates us. It
> has asserted itself and captivated us before we can come to ourselves and
> be in a position to test the claim … that it makes. In understanding we are
> drawn into an event … and arrive, as it were, too late, if we want to know
> what we are supposed to [now] believe. (Gadamer, 1989 p. 490)

Much of my work has been centered on hermeneutics as a theory
and practice of human and more-than-human encounter. I have
been involved in not only exploring how hermeneutics can provide
a research "methodology" for exploring classroom practice, but how
classroom practice itself can be understood as a hermeneutic, interpretive act of encounter and mutual formation. Of opening luscious fields,

being drawn into them, captivated, and pursuing "a continuity of attention and devotion" (Berry, 1986, p. 34) to them.

This be the great paradox—a holding back, keeping clear the clatter that might derail, distract or exhaust this attention and devotion, but one that has the aspect of "not … hold[ing] [my]self back."

What follows is an exploration of features of this coincidence and paradox. In particular, I am interested in Gadamer's (1989, p. 366) characterization of understanding and questioning as "more a passion than an action," and how, therefore, understanding ourselves and studying our shared and contested circumstances—including the great topics entrusted to teachers and students in schools—sometimes "presses itself on us" (p. 366), captivates us and compels us into studiousness before we are able to have a hand in gathering what we may from such often-unexpected moments. Before we are able to sort out whether we've been duped or had some sort of insight.

This is as simple and as mysterious as being charmed by an idea, a comment, an image, and event, and being drawn toward it and outside of our zones of real or presumed comfort. Something *happens*. Something *befalls* me.

"We can no longer avoid it and persist in our accustomed opinion" (p. 366)—a telling statement about teaching and learning as well about the conduct of interpretive inquiry *into* teaching and learning.

Identity Theft

"Hermes is cunning … a trickster, a robber. So, it is not surprising that he is also the patron of interpreters" (Kermode, 1979, p. 1). Disturbing the peace, the pacification, the sleepy assurances of familiarity and self-possession. Little god of gateways, borders, boundaries, bent on their opening, their passages, crossing and double-crossing.

Here, now, right at the cusp of where we attempt to hold fast, Hermes pulls a fast one, fleet. Right there comes the trick. There is a hint, here, of how "self-study," at its most effective and telling, does not exactly issue from my "self."

Hermes. Thief. And, in the midst of so much contemporary talk of such matters, most of all, *identity theft*:

> When Hermes is at work ... one feels that one's story has been stolen and turned into something else. The [person] tells his tale, and suddenly its plot has been transformed. He resists, as one would try to stop a thief ... "this is not what I meant at all, not at all." But too late. Hermes has caught the tale, turned its feet around, made black into white, given it wings. (Hillman, 1983, p. 31)

As an author, I know that others have been able to read what I've written better than I am able. Others can sometimes find clues and traces to which I am blind no matter how much I study myself and my own intimate work.

I can even attest that sometimes even what I *intended* is clearer to others than to myself. This, of course, is a commonplace of everyday life, when we find ourselves legible to others and obscure to ourselves. The reason for this is simple, hermeneutically understood. Language and experience, however intimate and close by, are things we find ourselves *in*, not exactly things we find *in us*. They are not exactly internal possessions (although, paradoxically, they are just exactly that). Language and experience are ecopoetic habitats in which we live, contested, multivocal, obscured and obscuring, clarifying, articulate, foolish, poetic, technical, common-sensical, haunted. We live in its implicated folds, often contradictory histories, allusions, precedents, images, prejudices, presumptions, bloodlines, allusions, mixed histories, relations, and agencies. We *find ourselves* in it, such that self-study is not exactly "the self" studying the self. Not exactly. We often can get *found out*.

Just as I sometimes feel frustration with my grandson welling up, I feel the fabrics of my own upbringing welling and pulling and tugging. I feel my breath shortening and my own asthmatic childhood nearby. I get glimmers of James Hillman's (2006b, p. 36) words on breath and *aesthesis* and aesthetics and beauty.

A study line that has helped a bit with the knee-jerk and is useful to have nearby when I fall into this found out and arrive, as it were, too late.

"This Solace"

"Understanding begins when something addresses us" (Gadamer, 1989, p. 299) and if my pretense to self-study doesn't allow me to be addressed by things beyond my self—by the topics I am exploring, the texts I am reading, the voices I hear—self-study risks having the self be caught in and by its own confines.

This is the great risk that this work involves: "Understanding is an adventure, and, like any adventure, it always involves some risk" (Gadamer, 1983, p. 141). Understanding begins when something addresses me, but it only begins there. What also begins there is the sometimes-arduous trek of exploring *what it is that is being asked of me* in this moment of finding my ears pricked. I have to risk venturing toward precisely those moments that interrupt my self-narration, my categories or themes, my expectations, my self-reflections:

> It is truly a tremendous task which faces every human moment. His prejudices—his being saturated with wishes, drives, hopes, and interests—must be held under control to such an extent that the other is not made invisible or does not remain invisible. It is not easy to acknowledge that the other could be right, that oneself and one's own interests could be wrong. This solace … is in truth a basic constant that shapes our whole human experience. We must learn to respect others and otherness. This implies that we must learn that we could be wrong. We must learn how to lose the game—that begins with the age of two or may be even earlier. He, who has not learned this early, will not be able to completely handle the greater tasks of adult life. (Gadamer, 1986, p. 233)

"Yes, It Could Turn out Like This"

"Every experience worthy of the name thwarts an expectation" (Gadamer, 1989, p. 356).

"To begin a story, someone in some way must break a certain silence" (Wiebe & Johnson, 1999, p. 3).

"Something awakens our interest. That is what comes first" (Gadamer, 2001, p. 50). Thus placing the agency of self-study outside the self.

"It would not deserve the interest [I] take in it if it did not have something to teach [me] that [I] could not know by [my]sel[f]" (Gadamer, 1989, p. xxxv). Thus, placing the locale of inquiring into myself outside my own self.

In my former life before retirement, I would often announce to a large class of preservice teachers—a couple of hundred in one of those classrooms where you are, so to speak, "teaching uphill"—that, first and foremost, you stand up in front of your students as an example of how life just might turn out.

I would then gesture toward myself and say, "Yes, it could turn out like this."

The inevitable ensuing laughter betrayed more than I'll ever know, and, I suppose, helped blunt some of the sting that can come with realizing that, despite any and all concerted confidence and effort at identifying myself, my "teacher identity," I'm also, always and already ("too late"!) out in the open, spotted, considered, ignored, presumed upon, sometimes benignly, sometimes otherwise.

Like any fabric of the world (Latin, *textus*) I am readable "beyond [my] wanting and doing" (Gadamer, 1989, p. xxviii).

No matter how much I want to tell my story myself and not be told, I am legible and illegible in ways I cannot imagine all by myself. I must wait, sometimes, for the yellow-eyed side-glances of Ravens. That glance is not *necessarily* a vile imposition. It might be a friend's whisper of advice.

Whatever story I might tell about myself and my experiences, including this one, and whatever comfort I find within the confines of these layers of my self-narration and self-identification, those very same students will read back to me my own most heartfelt gestures in ways that just might be different than I meant, more than I hoped, or far less. More telling is the fact that I may be required to recognize that their readings of what I have said or done are not just sometimes quite *different than my own*. They are, sometimes, *better than my own*. However studious my study of myself might be, their readings may be more insightful, more hale and healing, more honest, more timely, less self-deceptive, more helpful and sound—one whose truth I might have to concede. This is no different than the arcs of smoke this past summer from the British Columbia interior, and the wild-eyed storms setting records to the south, reading back to me my own very intimate self in ways that are sometimes more intimate than I can bear. I am become the object of *their* parsing, *known* as much as knower.

In such encounters, I sometimes get hurt or humiliated and retreat to an afflicted locale of self-possessive self-protection, ashamed of the complicities now outed.

Sometimes, however, I am *relieved of myself* and the burdensome constrictions of my own self-possession:

> I don't want to "tell my story." I want to be relieved of it by going to a place (ecos -, topos -/topica -) where I can meet others who can read me back to myself from beyond my own failings and limits and delusions, beyond the story I've presumed. (Jardine, 2016a, p. xvi)

This is what it is like to "have" an "identity," teacher or otherwise.

We can and must murmur about how easy it is to say this if one has been raised like I have been. However, it is, I still contest, precisely this susceptibility that makes this odd thing, "identity," a living matter. As teachers, we deliberately and repeatedly seek out these interstices of mutual formation, not only with the students we encounter each year, but with the topics entrusted to us in schools (or in research) and with the ancestral voices that lend us their consideration. These topics, too, must lend themselves up to the upcoming encounters, the upcoming queries and questions. All over again, they must show themselves to be worthy of attention and devotion, and students and teachers alike must likewise demonstrate their "readiness ... to be 'all ears' [*ganz Ohr zu sein*]" (Gadamer, 2007d, p. 189).

This gives self-study a truly pedagogical and ecological heart. This strange pleasure spot is exactly the job of teaching: each September, to place our fragile "identity," again and again and again, out in the open fray of arrival, out into "a sort of opening, play, indetermination, signifying hospitality for what is to come [*avenir*]" (Derrida, with Ferraris, 2001, p. 31). And when I consider those right-angled triangles inscribed in circles in a Grade Four mathematics classroom, or commiserate with a colleague over a student's woes, it is as if my "self" is not just studying but *being studied*. I am caught in *its* measure as much as it is in mine—spotted, tested, taught.

These encounters have archaic shapes. The young meet the old. The new meets the established. The familiar meets the strange. The case meets the rule. The story meets the moment of its tell. The elder tells the tale to *this* child just *thus* (the child thus summoning the rightness of the tell). The dead meet the living—not meant occultly, because, see, there? Derrida (1930–2004) and Gadamer (1900–2002) have just now arrived, and Pythagoras as well.

And all this is true far beyond the human orbit of encounter. That Cross Fox that trotted by a few days ago, or that Coyote pair that set the dogs howling, or the Chinook wind that took two trees a month back, can also serve to startle, to interrupt my self-absorption and somnolence.

"The true locus of hermeneutics is this in-between" (Gadamer, 1989, p. 295), this *event* of encounter. My own self-enclosed self-narrations must, shall we say, give way in order for my own narration to become, again, a living one, live, alert, aware, un-self-possessed.

"It Always Involves an Escape"

My story of my living is consistently and persistently read back to me in ways different than I might have been able to read it by myself and from my own point of view. And sticking to my story just might involve layers and layers of pathology—fears, abuses, having my voiced robbed and violated and silenced and sticking to my own story as a defense against such matters, self-delusion, self-denial, self-aggrandizement, defensiveness. My own inner and outer narrative is often the confine of my safety, my self-definition. This is why hermeneutics relies upon a phenomenological source in lived experience, but then enters considerations of such reliance with an eye to the possibility of false consciousness. The face value of experience can sometimes be just a façade, no matter how heartfelt and "immediate."

It is thus the *interruption of narrative continuity*, the *event* of the arrival of insight beyond what my self-narration and self-studying might have heretofore allowed, that is the centerpiece of hermeneutic work:

> Insight is more than the knowledge of this or that situation. It always involves an escape from something [Latin *fugere*] that had deceived us and held us captive. Thus, insight always involves an element of self-knowledge and constitutes a necessary side of what we called experience in the proper sense. Insight is something we come to. It too is ultimately part of the vocation of man—i.e., to be discerning and insightful. (Gadamer, 1989, p. 356)

The droning repetition of the same old story is not remedied by counter-posing it with another story doomed to the very same siloed fate. The silencing of voices is not overcome by simply having a turn at being the one who can now speak without interruption. It is remedied, instead, by seeking out, in each other's presence, insight and escape itself, where the refuge is found in remaining fugitive. That is to say, "You have your story, I have mine" is potentially the site of great ecological disaster, ripe with the odor of the very sort of "possessive individualism" (MacPherson, 2010) that the burgeoning voices of "others" outside the Eurocentric orbit are wont to interrupt. It is not just that "they" have their story "too":

> Our specific human identities constructed through tribe, race or religion can never be ultimately secured, not only because they are always open onto the horizons of others but also, more important, because they are always already everywhere inhabited by the Other in the context of the fully real. (Smith, 2006, p. xxiv)

I am not one to say this without hesitation. I am part of a bloodline that has too long had its story uninterrupted. It may be that other voices need a long time in the light and the sun without interruption.

But still, Hermes scuttles by like a hard-shelled bug. Remaining fugitive in each other's presence: *that* is where self-study can live a wild life, between—porous, always-already-implicated, finite, vulnerable, susceptible, dependently co-arising, ecologically ripe.

"Hermeneutic Experience"

The whole value of hermeneutical experience ... seemed to consist in the fact that here we are not simply filing things in pigeonholes but that what we encounter ... *says something to us.* Understanding ... is a genuine experience (*Erfahrung*). (Gadamer, 1989, p. 489, emphasis mine)

Note, here, that Gadamer uses the German term *Erfahrung* to describe this "hermeneutical experience":

In *Truth and Method,* a great deal of attention is given to the difference between the two German terms for "experience": *Erlebnis* (Gadamer, 1989, pp. 60–80) and *Erfahrung* (pp. 346–361). *Erlebenis* is etymologically linked to the intimacies of one's personal and inner life ([from] *Leben,* to live). *Erfahrung* contains the roots both of a journey (*Fahren*) and of ancestry (*Vorfahren,* those who have journeyed [*Fahren*] before [*Vor-*]). [W]e are drawn out of ourselves, our constructions, our methods, [our established narratives] and invited into something of a worldly sojourn, an *experience* (*Erfahrung*) that does not issue from "myself." (Jardine, 2012d, p. 107)

Hermeneutic experience describes moments of the encounter of my own self-narrative with that which calls it out, calls it to account, calls it to become less finalized and fixated and self-maintaining, more generous and pliable and true to the dependent co-arising nature of being human.

A Proposal on What Self-Study Is For

Like Dogen, the Zen master, said, "We study the self to forget the self. And when you forget the self, you become one with all things" (Snyder, 1980, p. 65). [Self-study] can lead to coming to understand "the self in its original countenance" (Nishitani, 1982, p. 91), as delicately and multiply interwoven in this earthly fabric in which we find woven all things. "One sees one's own self in all things, in living things, in hills and rivers, towns and hamlets, tiles and stones, and loves these things 'as oneself.'" (Jardine, 2016k, pp. 14–15; Nishitani, 1982, pp. 280–281)

Imagine. Eyeing those Ravens eyeing me as self-study, *providing* I let my "self" "come to" in such a moment of recognition—of them, of me, of the arriving spring sun, of our mutually held, conspiratorial breathing. One way or another, we form ourselves, we lose and re-gain ourselves, we forget ourselves or worry over ourselves in concert with the sub-terranean, often-hidden or occluded, roils of the world. These under-roils can be palpably sensed; their workings can be felt and suffered. "The self that we are does not possess itself; one could say that it happens" (Gadamer, 1977, p. 55). Without the endless effort to explore these underpinnings and to maintain alertness, we miss a deep experience of who we *are*—dependently co-arising, earthly beings whose selves are mixed in the mix of air and water and fire and earth, the mix of image and idea, of ancestry and "the fact of natality" (Arendt, 1969, p. 196), of arising and perishing, of living and dying.

Self-study is not mandatory. And study clearly poses its own suffering—facing the sore fleshy mortality of our living *on purpose* and *repeatedly*—that one must become willing, hopefully more *able*, to bear.

I'm reminded, here, first, of a statement by David G. Smith, one of my great teachers:

> The aim of interpretation, it could be said, is not just another interpretation but human freedom, which finds its light, identity and dignity in those few brief moments when one's lived burdens can be shown to have their source in too limited a view of things. (Smith, 2020c, p. 49)

And then, from the Gelug tradition of Tibetan Buddhism, from Tsong-kha-pa's *The Great Treatise on the Stages of the Path to Enlightenment*, citing Buddhapalita's *Commentary on [Nagarjuna's] "Fundamental Treatise"*:

> What is the purpose of teaching dependent-arising? The master Nagarjuna … saw that living beings are beset by various sufferings and assumed the task of teaching the reality of things … *so that they might be free*. [my emphasis] What is the reality of things? It is the absence of essence. Unskilled persons … conceive of an essence in things [something fixed and final and permanent] and then generate attachment and hostility with regard to them. (Tsong-kha-pa, 2002, p. 210)

And finally, from Dōgen Zenji, a lovely, obscure hint at how this bespoken freedom entails studying the self which entails forgetting the self and thereby become one with the myriad of things, those Ravens, this morning, yellow-eyed at the feeder, black-glint and squawking with no trace:

> To carry the self forward and illuminate myriad things is delusion. That myriad things come forth and illuminate the self is awakening. To study the Buddha Way is to study the self. To study the self is to forget the self. To forget the self is to be actualized by myriad things. When actualized by myriad things, your body and mind as well as the bodies and minds of others drop away. No trace of enlightenment remains, and this no-trace continues endlessly. (Dōgen, 2007, pp. 35–36)

CHAPTER TWENTY-FOUR

How to Love Black Snow

New Preamble: A Dangled Participle

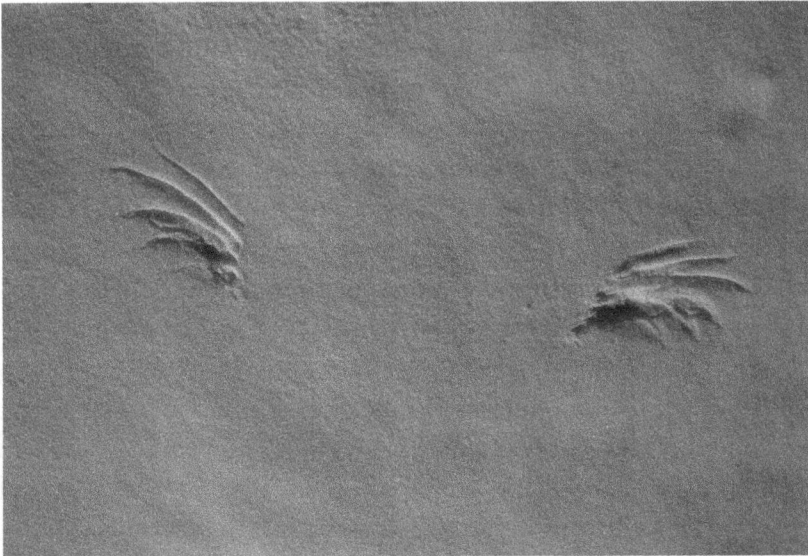

FIGURE 9. SNOWINGS

There is great relief to be had in realizing that the curriculum topics entrusted to teachers and students in schools don't need to be simply covered. They can also be loved and cherished and *experienced*. We know full well that this is terribly hard work, even to imagine this possibility. But schools are already hard work and the course that labour has taken–scarcity, panic, acceleration, impoverishment—is wearing thin and getting worse. Too many wonderful teachers that we know have had to simply quit. There is no use hiding this fact: once curriculum is experienced in abundance, sometimes continuing to live in some schools becomes unbearable. (Jardine, 2006, p. xxvi)

Coming to know, as is the great and terrible task of schooling, can be imagined as *adding to* the abundance of the world, not diminishing it. (p. xxvi)

Schools have been transformed into huge zero-sum games, monolithic delivery systems in which every gain for one turns into a loss or burden for another, while true satisfactions is denied to both. (Illich, 1996, 27)

This chapter was originally the "Introduction" to Michael Derby's book (2015) *Towards a Critical Eco-Hermeneutic Approach to Education: Place, Being, Relation.* I preface it here with this photo caught by chance— always, it seems, by chance—of Raven wings having glanced the snow.

The great black body between these glances is blinked out, absent. It is *not there*, right there before your eyes.

The purpose of this book as a whole is to encourage myself, encourage you, to find the time. To fall in love with the everywhere-present, everywhere-absent luxuriousness of experience and its ecopedagogical undergrowths. We have to become accustomed to expecting this.

Another playground secret, then. Many of the teachers I've taught and who have taught me suffered something shared, something each carried, and some still carry, as a private, intimate burden. It is why we re-gather now and then, for a chance to go oh, yes, I remember.

Wings glance snow. That empty space between, a gathering spot.

When the pulse quickens and some once-commonplace object starts to murmur, and the connections start reeling and roiling, there can be great joy. But they and I (and perhaps you) are also all here, now, in this very world of such frail human distresses and distractions. These are real. They are palpable.

It is no mere swoony eco-meditative hippy-poetic murmur, although I am certainly prone to all that. To remain stalwart in the tough work of coming to unravel the tasks of teaching and learning in a school or, frankly, outside of it—well, welcome. Because such pursuits—let me say it outright—of *wisdom* and *insight* push against the frantics of time. Yes, it is fine for students to simply memorize the rules for the use of commas. And of course, we should help with that. But memorization is an amazing thing to learn the art of (ah, yes, a dangled participle). And there is more to enjoy in the art of commas. And talking of borders and their histories and raising questions of who is in charge of what and what for. There is more world that the world of training up to pass examinations and get it over with so you don't have to think again. I'm guilty, too, of course, of both sides of all these exaggerations.

By the way, a little study done by Sharon Friesen (2010) looked at two large groups of school classrooms. One deliberately maintained their pedagogical practices of getting ready for the upcoming Provincial examinations. The other group took on something of what was then called "inquiry-based" work in their classrooms, of course on the very same topics as the other group. The group that took on inquiry as a pedagogical practice and did not "teach to the test" but rather taught to the *living topographies of what was being tested* performed *statistically significantly better* on the Provincial exams.

Make no mistake, though. This study circulated around the Calgary Board of Education and beyond, but led, as often as not, to what Sharon, Pat Clifford and I named "the yah-buts"—an eerily repeated list of "if I had the time," "if I had those kids," "you just don't understand," and on and on, all deeply and genuinely felt, all signs of how deep are the regimes we've inherited in education, and how sticky the web that binds us all and threatens to:

> This is an important point, and making it greatly accentuates the way that creative teaching must be understood first and foremost as a hermeneutic endeavour. All curriculum requires interpretation. The conservative desire to mandate curriculum as a reified static commodity, to make curricula that are "teacher-proof", to rate teacher performance by student achievement on narrow standardized tests—all of these kinds of measures serve undercut

the one aspect that makes teaching a worthwhile activity, mutually vivi-fying for both students and teachers: teaching as an engagement with the young over questions of life and death, and the way those questions have been addressed by one's own and other traditions in the past, and ways they can be addressed in the present. This suggestion can be read as relevant whether the curriculum subject is mathematics, physics, literature or philos-ophy. What matters is an honouring of the work of inducting the young into the broader human life-stream, without which education can only be an act of human alienation. It requires of both teachers and students that they see their work together as a labour of mutual authentication in which the search for truth in any situation must inevitably trump political expediency. (D.G. Smith, 2020e, pp. 235–236)

And again:

What, then, are the main ways that truth, as truth seeking, truth discovering, and truth sharing, get blocked in teaching? The vivifying quality of teaching-as-truth-dwelling (as it may be called) gets blocked if teaching is understood primarily as an act of implementation, with the curriculum as a settled com-modity emerging from a settled anterior logic heading for a settled posterior conclusion. Teaching itself is reduced in the process to being nothing but a form of procedural manipulation in which the being of the teacher requires no true encounter with the being of the student, or with curriculum as some-thing open and interpretable, something that could show the way to a possi-ble future. (D.G. Smith, 2020k, p. 204)

And, if I may, let this lead you to reading David Smith's work deeply, carefully. This following passage, straight in line with "Why Study for a Future that We Won't Have?":

Teaching, at least in the Western tradition, has always operated inordinately in the future tense, within a temporal frame that privileges the future over the present as well as the past. "When you complete this [course, grade, assign-ment, year, etc.], then you can …" is a turn of phrase that echoes throughout the discourse of all levels of education, from kindergarten through postdoc-toral work. This is an orientation that is honestly come by if teaching defines its role as being the handmaid of market logic, because, as David Loy (2000) has argued, The Market emerged through a template of Christian eschatol-ogy in which future time became now time. Indeed, to extend Loy's sugges-tion, the West lives in a kind of frozen futurism in which what was expected to be revealed *has* been revealed, and what the revelation discloses is that the future will always be more of this, a perpetual unfolding of more and more of this. In this context what education becomes is nothing but more and more of what it always was. The details may vary over time, but the essential grammar remains the same: Education seems like a preparation for something that never happens because, in the deepest sense, it has *already happened*, over and over. So built into the anticipations of teaching is a mask of the future that freezes teaching in a futurist orientation such that, in real terms, there *is* no future because the future *already is*. Hence the ubiquitous icon of the perpetually smiling, young elementary school teacher and its analogues in both consumer marketing and evangelical Christianity. All three celebrate "enthusiasm" as a cardinal virtue, which means, literally, "inside god" (< Gk *en*, inside + *theos* god). They are the bearers of a verdict that, in the name of the future, the future is now closed. Loy's point is not that the future is *in fact* frozen, but only that a particular understanding of it is, an understanding in which the secular and the sacred are conflated within a rationalist schema that provides Western economics with its theoretical justifications. The real work of the contemporary period is to recover a future that truly is a future; that is, a condition that is actually open. (D.G. Smith, 2016k, p. 201)

These long citations reveal a (not so) secret admirations for ventures taken, it seems, on our behalf, on my behalf especially with David's work. This is one aspect of what commiseration and encouragement look like. Go read the whole thing. It blossoms and sings and has healed me more than once.

Go read this, too. *Towards a Critical Eco-Hermeneutic Approach to Education: Place, Being, Relation* (Derby, 2015). This book of Michael's that I introduced is one of so many lovely examples of recent work which wants to provoke affection for the earth-body of the world, for the compost-whiff composures of commas, of noticing Raven wing glances in snow and taking the time to let it teach you something about yourself, about the swirly air-worlds of cold Alberta winters, and feeling of being compelled, to coin a phrase, "to dwell with a boundless heart" (Jardine, 1990b; see Jardine, 2016k).

How to Love Black Snow

Despite the likely alien and awkward feel of the concepts involved, we might, when hearing a sutra, experience a quite innocent sense of wonder—a brief moment of almost childlike, delightful surprise, perhaps colored by a subtle tone of promise and potential. In line with the teachings set out in this book, we might say that just such a brief clearing within simple, unprepared wonder is what constitutes the awakening of faith in the Great Vehicle.

From the "Translators' Introduction" to *Ornament of the Great Vehicle Sutras: Maitreya's Mahayanasutralamakara.* (Doctor, 2014, p. vii)

Now little riverbed stones impress upon my bare feet the aggregate intelligence of form and fit, particular trees stand tall in my memory as pedagogically significant, the cheap yellow paint on my pencil peels and reveals *flesh*—what kind of mushrooms are these? From somewhere deep within the inquiry, beneath the words—*how is it possible!*—a world approaches. (Derby, 2015, p. 2)

[Michael Derby's (2015). *Towards a Critical Eco-Hermeneutic Approach to Education: Place, Being, Relation,* for which this was originally written as an introduction] is worth every moment of while it takes to read it. It must be read as carefully as mushrooms that always just might be poisonous even if delicious, just might be nourishing even if acrid. We are in a fix—pedagogically, ecologically, in body and mind and otherwise—and it's going to take some doing to even start undoing this fix.

The object of concern in this beautiful book is grave and imminent—the tear of flesh that is surely coming in these ecologically sorrowful times. Michael Derby's book is rife with soaring, awakening insight into the often ignored, often trivialized and romanticized, nature of our ecological intimacy, our Earthly Being beyond the confines of the all too human. And it couples these insights with detailed and careful thought to the pedagogy of these matters and to long and tangled histories of human images and thinking in which we have "b[ou]nd ourselves without a rope" (Loy, 2010, p. vii [David Smith's work led me to David Loy's work. This is how this work works]).

Read this book slowly and repeatedly. That is what it needs and deserves. If you read it too fast, the pull of the gravity and imminence of our circumstances will only increase. Read slowly, studied, the panic-pull starts to lessen, and we can then slowly start to see where we are, what has happened to us and our kin, what we have done, what we might now do. The weight will increase with the lightness. Two wings.

Hurry will only lead to panic that is distracting, retracting, and of no use. It will only tighten the knots and the tangle and the confusion.

Here, right off the bat is one great gift of this book. We hurry.

And that last sentence can be read too fast. We hurry, and when our circumstances become dire, we react by accelerating, with little or no understanding of how our hurry is profoundly complicit in increasing our panic, thus increasing our hurry, and so on. And how none of this aids any of us in understanding our lot and our duty.

It is no accident that Buddhists characterize the deepest human afflictions as caught up in a Wheel.

The spell of this ever-accelerating wheeling must be broken. Great and increasingly loud and monstrous hallucinations about how we might Save The Earth (capitalized, and then in all caps, and then bolded, and then in a bigger pitch, and on and on) must stop. This just increases the spellbinding.

In its stead, awakening, brief clearings, little riverbed stones and particular trees, wings uplift.

This book has been of great use and great remind to me in understanding a school I visited last week, listening to and watching French Immersion Grade One children couple together found words and posting them for all to see—and then up goes this accidental couplet, *neige/noir*, "black snow," and how we all gasped a bit at the beckoning incomprehensibility of it: the feel of a world approaching, of aggregate intelligence, of language living instead of dead, and of the warm presence of us huddled together over this classroom happenstance.

So momentary, but just because of this, the true weal of words is felt approaching and whooshing overhead. We duck and giggle. In brief.

Neige noir. I must remember this.

This isn't a big deal, this. It's a small one. One among many pleasures in this book is that, read the right way, it is full of such clear and clearing messages about commonplace and everyday events inside and outside of commonplace and everyday classrooms with commonplace and everyday children and adults and the territories in which they might meet their more-than-human kin. It is about how we might make schools not just *livable* and *sustainable* but *beautiful* and *wise*. It is not just *about* poetry (Chapter Three of his book) or *about* metaphor (Chapter Four) but demands that

> here, where it seems impossible
> that one life even matters. (Wallace, 1987, p. 111)

here, we seek the feel of mycelial pulls:

> right now, in the midst of things, *this*
> and *this*. (p. 111)

This book asks me to stop over things, to stoop, to think. "With *this* bird" (see Chapter Four). I am so relieved to say that this book is *not* about "environmental education" as some sort of subject area (usually a sub-division of Science Education or Outdoor Education or both) among others inside or outside of schools. This literal minded image of environmental education simply abandons the rest of our human inheritance and of the lives of teachers and students to countless ecological disasters, one worksheet after the other.

Instead, this: *All of our thinking and being and imagining is ecological.* All knowledge entrusted to teachers and students in schools comes with place and inhabitation and faces and tales—*fields* of wonder that call for the sort of thinking proper to such fields and their cultivation and care. This is an ancient Aristotelian reminder of *mensuratio ad rem*: thinking which finds its proper measure, not in the methods of human approach, but rather in the thing being thought:

> Thinking is not a means to gain knowledge. Thinking cuts furrows in the soil of Being. About 1875, Nietzsche once wrote (Grossoktav WW XI, 20): "Our thinking should have a vigorous fragrance, like a wheatfield on a summer's night." How many of us today still have the senses for that fragrance? (Heidegger, 1971, p. 70)

From the beginning of Chapter Two:

> Occasionally, we may happen upon the fruiting bodies of this living, subterranean entanglement (if we live, or make time to go, or are taken to the places where fungi still bloom, and if we pay attention) and only then do we become aware of the vibrant webwork beneath us and, perhaps, if our earthly

connection has not been severed or schooled out of us, we are reminded of the interdependent ethos of a "humus filled" existence. (Derby, 2015, p, 18)

We, too, are fruiting bodies, as is Pythagoras and Andromeda and Coyote, and place value, and commas, and this is no more and no less a metaphor than it is of fungi. Coyote always arrives with earthly connections and subterranean entanglements. And when you place something in a place, that place itself is not just an empty, abstract spot, but has a value (Latin *valere*, two meanings of which are "be strong, be well" [Online Etymological Dictionary]) that affects how to think about what happens to what has been placed there. Change the strength and well-being of the place and things in that place change. My work could not have become what it did had I not lived in these Foothills. Place value.

Simple! Mathematics and its Roman and Arabic numeric roots as forms of ecological awareness, of locales and ancestors and relations and imagining. As a Grade Six student once told me, of course Roman numerals have no place value, because Rome was an Empire, and every place it went was Rome—"the vibrant webwork beneath us."

"The way we treat a thing can sometimes change its nature" (Hyde, 1983, p. iii) and we mustn't simply go outside (although we must, we must) and abandon everything left inside the school walls. This is the tough, exhilarating work that this book asks readers to practice right in the midst of the circumstances we face. Here. Grade One. If it can come to be treated the right way, for its fragrances. If we don't treat it that way, our sense for this fragrance becomes uncultivated, unpracticed, dimmed and distant. Its loss of fragrance and our nose for it rise and fall in concert.

Thus, this book lays out a bit of a rescue mission, to learn to read even little Grade One word searches as ecopoetic, ecopedagogical gestures, to become studied and still enough to stop panicking and let ourselves remember how both right-angled triangles and the curves of vines around a tree *both* become *more* radiant in each other presence. Hans-Georg Gadamer (2007a) calls this, in an indirect way, an experience of beauty. Each reads the other out into the open, and releases it from its literal self-absorption and self-containedness. In each other's presence, each becomes exquisite and irreplaceable in the fullness of things and their ways. Treated properly, each is radiant, lighting up the dependently co-arising place of its residing, its strength and well-being, its place value. MOVE "We should apply this to *every* phenomenon" (Tsong-kha-pa, 2005, p. 182), our "selves" included.

My coremediation ([Derby's] Chapter Seven). Inoculation (Chapters Five and Six). Home-making and re-indigenization (Chapter 9)—perhaps overall we are dealing with the ability to read properly, with a honed and practiced sense of place and proper proportion, with enough studied memory and experience so that the "resonant ecology of things" (Chapter Ten) can be sensed ringing in the air. We must allow ourselves the hard labor of this repeated and perennial task of recovery, of waking up, again, in search of brief clearings.

Frankly, there is great joy to be had here, but it has got an ecological sting:

> Everything is teaching you. Isn't this so? Can you just get up and walk away so easily now? (Chah n.d., p. 5)

There are two intertwining paths in this book, one more immediately pleasing than the other. More than any other book in recent memory (I might put Don Domanski's *Bite Down Little Whisper* [2013] alongside here), this book feels and writes and speaks up out of the lift that comes when we step aside from our heavy inheritance and undo its cloak and instead wander, wilder, with stones underfoot and the duty of noticing. It is equally easy to recoil, as it is to rejoice in the deep experience of our conspiracy with trees and other terranean and subterranean entanglements. Coming to still enough to experience for myself such dependency is, as Michael shows in great detail, deliciously, properly and repeatedly humiliating. With practice, you get used to it. "It is somewhat difficult to establish, but once you are used to it, it will be like meeting an old acquaintance" (Kongtrul, 2002, p. 67). In such meetings, our hearts become undone.

This book thus speaks about acts of true teaching and learning in ways that lift and open the heart despite its sorrows, but not in order to turn away to some vaguely stupid Ecological Romance or equally distracting Ecological Panic. No, this lift allows *those very sorrows* to be sung in words and harmonies with Ravens and stones and trees, and not just suffered in silence and isolation.

> *Neige noir* and our huddling over it.
> "Oh sorrow" (Seidel, 2014, p. 112).
> "Hush, child" (Latremouille, 2014, p. 30). Do not panic.

Deep ecological stillness and experience—persistent, repeated, generous, patient, persevering—are vital to beginning to undo our fix, but they are not sufficient. There is another trail in this book that gives heart and courage. It stares dead-on, articulately, and in great detail, into the inheritances of thinking and imagining that have helped get us into this fix. How have schools become so often so deadly and boring and afraid? How has literacy lost its ear for orality? How have the wise ghosts of the land underfoot become lost from memory? How has beauty fled, and why, and what happens if we raise our kids in a world without ears, without ghosts, without beauty? This is the second path, which is at once the same path. *We need to study* in ways that win back our living from its entanglements in unearthly fantasies and fears. Undoing ourselves from the fix we have inherited is going to take some doing. *Our study of our circumstances is going to have to be as complex and as difficult and as entailed as those circumstances themselves.*

There is no way around this and its great ironies. We humans, having disgraced and desecrated the more-than-human world (and, to our shame, the human one as well), have an all-too-human task facing us. We must seek wisdom. We must think clearly and without fear and consequent animal panics. As per hermeneutic insight, seeing the world and our fix only in light of and as an outcome of its imminent and grave impingement on us blocks us from seeing *it* as it is, as it stands there, in its own repose, "over and above our wanting and doing" (Gadamer, 1989, p. xxviii). It takes wisdom to escape our selves and the world that then appears only in light of those worried selves and our projections and fears and repressions. We must break our reflection in the water. We must come to, not in order to turn away from the spell, but toward it, now, finally, a bit awoken and more alert.

"You can't get anywhere without reading a yak's load of books" (Tsong-kha-pa, 2004, p. 219). One must cultivate "an attentive ear for the language in which the thinking experiences of many generations has been sedimented, long before we begin to attempt our own thinking" (Gadamer, 1986, p. 18). Part of the work here in this book, is unraveling how our current ecological concern is, at least in part, a function of how so many of these generations have cocooned themselves (and therefore us, our language, our inheritances, our schools, our teaching and learning) and long since lost an Earthly measure of things. And so many of these generations have demanded of those they met that they, too, must lose such measure and its language, its culture, its places. These circumstances are complicated, historically, culturally, philosophically, linguistically, spiritually. They involve colonialism, gender, dreams of heaven and progress and monstrous hopes for mastery over the world, and on and on and on. They include institutional codifications and market economies and media distractions and the "you're either for us or against us" logic of much political wind. We can step away, momentarily, from this tough work, as I often must, seeking the relief of Ravens and wood to split and tomato seedlings on the sill. But simply stepping away leaves our path still blocked.

This is why this book leans heavily into the phenomenological and hermeneutic traditions of inquiry—Edmund Husserl, Martin Heidegger (see especially Chapter 5), and my old love, Hans-Georg Gadamer (see especially Chapter 6). I've taught a graduate course in the University of Calgary's Faculty of Education on Gadamer's *Truth and Method* over 25 times, and it has proven to be true, over and over again, a hermeneutic adage: "[the world] compels over and over, and the better one knows it, the *more* compelling it is. This is not a matter of mastering an area of study" (Gadamer, 2007c, p. 115). This tradition, at its best and most vital, lends its attention to the lifeworld, the world as lived, the living world. This tradition—part of the very Eurocentric orbit that has cause so much of our fix—seeks the break of the spell, seeks the Trickster who knows the trick, seeks waking up, it seeks beauty and repose, it seeks to understand "what happens to us over and above our wanting and doing" (Gadamer, 1989, p. xxviii)–all out from constructivist cocoons and somnambulant projects and delusions.

Here is where this book becomes slightly magnificent, because the author does not wish to simply swallow whole this tradition of phenomenological and hermeneutic philosophy because it, too and of course, contains sedimented and hardened elements of precisely the unearthliness that has gotten us into the fix we are in in the first place. What the author makes crystal clear is the need for what he brilliantly calls "ecohermeneutic inoculation":

> Ecohermeneutic inoculation in this respect is a deliquescent move—at once critical and remedial—that compels a tradition to reveal what it knows, what it has yet to teach, and where it needs to reconnect in order to remain in resonance with the world and our lives as they are now lived. In this sense, an ecohermeneutic imagination is … concerned with … "salvaging" and revitalizing these philosophic substrates to bring them to bear on ecological pedagogy in a more-than-human world. (Derby, 2015, p. 61)

I do adore the fact that I had to look up the word "deliquescent." This is one of the leisures (Latin *schola*) of study. Unidentified words, like unidentified mushrooms, come to be experienced ecstatically, as a trail with beckonings along it. And, as with mushrooms, getting the etymology wrong can make us lose our way: "from Latin *deliquescere* 'to melt away,' from *de-* … + *liquescere* 'to melt,' from *liquere* 'to be liquid'" (Online Etymological Dictionary). This is why we learn to spell. Because if we don't, the spell gets lost, the threads of ancestral memory gets cut, and we no longer have any aid in finding our way.

We become lost, and, because of our loss, we eat mushrooms that are deadly.

It is an ecological disaster.

Yes. Wait. Here. Got it! Deliquescence. Hermeneutics "makes the object and all its possibilities fluid" (Gadamer, 1989, p. 367) so that we can experience its living arising and living place in our lived experience and that of our dependents:

> All this has as its aim not simply philosophical erudition and the like. The aim of such meditations and work is the cultivation of the intimacy and immediacy of the experience of everyday life, here, as this next child draws breath over a text, here, where reading aloud and learning to pronounce can too often be treated as simply ordinary and commonplace. Not only is "wherever

you are ... a place of practice" (Tsong-kha-pa, 2004, p. 191). Tsong-kha-pa also insists (and this is a feature that distinguishes the Gelug tradition from other Buddhist lineages and makes ripe its affinity to hermeneutics), the purpose and object of study is *precisely* the deepening of practice itself. After all, "why would you determine one thing by means of study and reflection, and then, when you go to practice, practice something else?" (2000, p. 52). And this is why Gadamer insists that hermeneutics, with all is philosophical erudition and study, is "a practical philosophy" (2007f) with both theoretical and practical tasks (2007b). All those complex philosophical and historical twists and turns that typify his work are meant, in the end, to make us more susceptible to the beautiful abundance of things as we walk around in the world. (Jardine, 2016f, p. 304)

A little warning on the way by, of a scholarly temptation, then:

Anything that you want to move has to start where it is, in its stuckness. That involves erudition—probably too much erudition. One wants to get stuck in the history, the material, the knowledge, even relish it. Deliberately spending time in the old place. (Hillman, 1991, p. 154)

Hence, "advice in this liquid midst" (Jardine, 2018): "Texts are instructions for [the] practice" (Tsong-kha-pa, 2000, p. 52) of precisely paying more intimate and proper attention to the resounding. Don't worry. Study, properly practiced, will not ruin the *aesthesis* of ecological reveries, only their limited and limiting naiveties.

Study this book. It can help you become more alert and less afraid. It can provide the courage to face our circumstances full face, and crack the facade that seems so grave and imminent and that beckons us to panic and retreat or to fall prey to useless, however understandable, ecological hysterics.

Come revel, then, and feel the amp of the sun increasing. I end this introduction with a sense of very strange relief. My own work is now being outlived, as Michael ventures into many places that I have not been and many I have trouble going to without too much ache. My work belongs to a different time and place even though I'm in conspiracy with Michael's words, and better for his help.

This book, too, won't last forever. But it is, I believe, what is needed now.

Bragg Creek, Alberta, March 2–12, 2015.

CHAPTER TWENTY-FIVE

"It Will Startle You": Thoughts on a Pedagogical Conspiracy of Birds

Seeing the frailty of your life through seeing the breath is the meditation on the recollection of death. Just realizing this fact—that if the breath goes in but does not go out again, or goes out but does not come in again, your life is over—is enough to change the mind. It will startle you into being aware. (Chah, 2001, p. 44)

Not a Downey Woodpecker

I mentioned during a gathering of teachers seeing a Downey Woodpecker having at the stump in our backyard a few days earlier, how, over and over again, I could not quite resolve the bright yellow patch on the back of its head. I did my best to imagine that it might be an immature boy, and all this work was bent on maintaining myself in its presence and asking, repeatedly, that it yield itself up to my presumptions. Downey Woodpeckers are the only thing anything like this I've seen in these parts for the past 30 years.

Funny black-and-white back design, though.

Then that sudden, oh-so-familiar gulp of air. No, this won't do: "**Northern Three-Toed Woodpecker**: … *yellow* caps … 'ladder' back. The female lacks the yellow cap" (Peterson, 1980, p. 192).

Such experiences are, of course, commonplace, and they involve a strange, experiential reciprocity. As it finally became what it is—freed from my presuming—I became myself all over again, freed from that very same presuming. Humiliation tinged with joy and uplift, just enough to feel fresh air, some buoyancy under the wings. Exuberance ("be abundant, grow luxuriously" [OED]). "Without gut level experience of the other, without sharing his aura, you can't be saved from yourself" (Illich, 1998, p. 6).

These aren't exactly meant to be "metaphors." They are meant, failingly, to describe something bodily palpable about the arrival of this sort of arresting experience. Body-bounded intimacies:

- "the possibility … to see everything with fresh eyes, so that what is long familiar fuses with the new into a many levelled unity" (Gadamer, 1989, p. 16).
- "the readiness of the person who is receiving and assimilating [*des Aufnehmenden*] the text [or the bird sighted] to be 'all ears' [*ganz Ohr zu sein*], [without which] no … text will speak" (Gadamer, 2007d, p. 189).

Eyes. Ears. And both of these framed at the moment in which presumptions "break open" (Gadamer, 1989, p. 360), "break forth" (p. 458) and "reciprocity" (Gadamer, 1984, p. 323) is won by losing myself in order to save myself from myself.

This possibility, this readiness, are things I am still learning about. Here is the ecopedagogical point—this learning is done *in an intimate concert* with these birds and their kin who ask this of me and who, in responding, have shaped my own readiness for that concert:

How could we *be* were it not for this planet that provided our very shape? Two conditions—gravity and a liveable temperature range—have given us fluids and flesh. The trees we climb and the ground we walk on have given us five fingers and toes. The "place" (from the root *plat*, broad, spreading, flat) gave us far-seeing eyes, the streams and breezes gave us versatile tongues and whorly ears. (Snyder, 2003, p. 29)

Thus the lovely paradox of learning that demonstrates that all learning is ecopedagogical: I cannot heed those feeder arrivals if I am not all ears and fresh eyes, ready for what arrives "beyond my wanting and doing" (Gadamer, 1989, p. xxviii). And it is precisely as a result of my repeated, often-failing attention to them that such ears become properly curved and shapely and useful.

"All ears" is somehow both cause and effect. It is a practice that is both my own and the locale of being saved from myself.

This is a phenomenological fact that as those ears shape, the sounds of the world shape in near-perfect parallel.

Conspiracy.

Stellar, Blue

FIGURE 10. STELLAR BLUE

It would not deserve the interest we take in it if it did not have something to teach us that we could not know by ourselves. (Gadamer, 1989, p. xxxv)

First ever noticed arrival of a Steller's Jay over 30 plus years of looking. March 23, 2017, late afternoon. We've long since had Blue Jays, and more recently Grey Jays have ventured into the woods and under the front pitch of our roof for feed. I've seen these Steller's Jays once before up in the foothills to the west.

It is important to note what happens to attention when its object becomes too familiar for words because such familiarity is precisely *not* noteworthy but is still full of pedagogical consequences. There is a numbing comfort in Blue Jays, but familiarity—being a ubiquitous and quickly recognized "part of the family"—can be a type of dulling *an-aesthesis*.

After that Steller's Jay's departure, a good old Blue Jay lit on the same feeder and sent a shiver of strange and thrilling recognition through long familiarity, long-settled memory.

That (with a gasp) is a Blue Jay. I could finally see its smallness, its variegations, the beauty of its Alberta sky-blue, unlike the swarthy dark indigos and glinting metallic-ness of the Steller's Jay. This is a type of knowledge that has an important place:

We do not understand what recognition is in its profoundest nature if we only regard it as knowing something again that we already know. The joy of recognition is rather the joy of knowing *more* than is already familiar. In recognition, what we know emerges, as if illuminated. (Gadamer, 1989, p. 114).

Because of that Steller's Jay's arrival, that Blue Jay is now newly experienced as *among* Steller's Jays nearby. *Everything has changed*, for now, even the once-familiar, ignorable squawk ("a harsh slurring *jeeah* or *jay*; a musical *queedle, queedle*; also many other notes" [Peterson, 1980, p. 208]) is a sound now, fresh ears, among a heretofore-unsuspected surround. For the Steller's Jay: "most common a very harsh, unmusical, descending *shaaaaaar*; also a rapid, popping *shek shek shek*. Also a clear, whistled *whidoo* and quiet, melodious thrasher-like song" (Sibley, 2016, p. 295). Maybe those previously ignorable sounds are *not* all Blue Jays after all. Once-familiar sound-surroundings lift up off the ground in suspense, asking for readiness, freshness.

And when a Blue Jay pitches itself in the lower spruce branches, now, fleetingly, it squawks "as if illuminated."

And a detailed differentiation between two types of Steller's Jays in *Sibley's Birds West* forced me to wait until another one appeared. I didn't notice this differentiation before because I didn't know till now that noticing *that* was notable. So, a sort of anticipation that comes with coming to know. Those moments of waiting for him to return in full knowledge that he may have been passing through in the arc of spring's arrival, never to be seen again. By the way, do they "pass through?" Just checked: They do migrate, but it tends to be up- and downslope, not north–south. Like bears soon to visit the compost heap.

Yes. There, on the feeder. And yes, too, an open-bottom V of white above the beak, and white eyebrows. An Interior West Steller's Jay (Sibley, 2016, p. 295).

Whidoo!

Co-conspirators

"Texts are instructions for [the] practice" (Tsong-kha-pa, 2000, p. 52) of pre-cisely paying more intimate and proper attention to the resounding. Don't worry. Study, properly practiced, will not ruin the *aesthesis* of ecological rev-eries, only their limited and limiting naiveties. (Jardine, 2015, p. xxii)

In our teachers' gathering, it was suggested that the term used for the work of kindergarten classes that are variously called "outdoor schools" or "forest schools" might be "co-conspiracy" with the vivid curiosities of children. And, of course, that co-conspiracy goes beyond them and us and out toward those Steller's Jays as well, then looping back to reappearing Blue Jays and from there over to Peterson and Sibley and other elders and maps and specificities and back again, there, stop, see?

Co-conspirators. Young children are often mytho-poetically figured as heralds of the new, of new life, and the great Romantic hope that they can be reliable sources of fresh eyes and wide ears, saving us elders from ourselves, saving the world from its mortality through the sheer "fact of natality" (Arendt, 1969, p. 196). But then, Sibley and the ancient noticings that he has gathered and detailed, saved me from myself as well. Read properly, study can herald. It, too, can be conspiratorial. Just as was that Jay's reappearance. The conspiracy is broad and rich and unbounded. One breath away.

Co-conspirators. This word sent me back to a nearly impenetrable paper I read years ago by Ivan Illich (1998) titled "The Cultivation of Conspiracy." As a former asthmatic, this image of *"conspiratio,* a commingling of breaths" (p. 8), well, took my breath away when it was mentioned. That first gasp when that once-presumed-Downey Woodpecker yielded to an encroachment of suddenly shared breath whose reciprocity goes far beyond ears and eyes. It is almost unbearably intimate. "Fresh eyes," "all ears." But also, *conspiratio.* My breath halts as it halts on the feeder:

> You draw in your breath and stop still. The quick intake of breath, this little gasp—*hshshs* as the Japanese draw between their teeth when they see something beautiful in a garden—this *ahhhh* reaction is the aesthetic response just as certain, inevitable, objective and ubiquitous, as a wincing in pain and moaning in pleasure. Moreover this quick intake of breath is also the very root of the work aesthetics, *aisthesis* in Greek, meaning sense-perception. *Aisthesis* goes back to the Homeric *aiou* and *aisthou* which means both "I perceive" as well as "I gasp, struggle for breath," as in *aisthomai,* I breathe in. (Hillman, 2016n, p. 183)
>
> *Aesthesis* ... means at root a breathing in ... of the world, the gasp, "aha," the "uh" of the breath in wonder ... and aesthetic response. (Hillman, 2006c, p. 36)

As the Beautiful Captivates Us

> [Some startling event] captivates us just as the beautiful captivates us. It has asserted itself and captivated us before we can come to ourselves and be in a position to test the claim ... that it makes. In understanding we are drawn into an event of truth [Greek: *aletheia,* meaning variously opening what seemed closed, remembering what seemed forgotten, enlivening what seemed dead ordinary and familiar] and arrive, as it were, too late. (Gadamer, 1989, p. 490)

Aesthetic response as a conspiratorial response. Here's a whispery secret. I *adore* these: *jeeah, jay, queedle, queedle, shaaaaaar, shek shek shek, whidoo.* I've often joked about how these make me want to teach phonics to young children. They also make me wonder about what an interesting job it is to be assigned to write these.

Whorly ears.

I'm slowly realizing that, having lived with these Blue Jays my whole life, right back to when, as a child in Southern Ontario, I often mistook their squawks for squeaking clothesline wheels, I'm just now learning all over again about this parade of images and sounds and lives, theirs and mine, too. About a life-long conspiracy that went on despite my attentions or distractions.

The purpose of bird watching is not about getting a longer and longer list of things that I can now ignore. Its purpose is to make almost unbearable the folding layers of sweet and inevitably fatal conspiracy that we live and breathe, such that the next pair of migrating Canada Geese overhead becomes miraculous.

The pedagogical co-conspiracies of teachers, students, old, young, sound, voice, text, memory, will startle you, over and over again, into being aware.

CHAPTER TWENTY-SIX

"Come Fluttering off the Spine"

FIGURE 11. AWAITING. ACCOMPANIED

> To use the hermeneutic adage, [when such an image arrives, when some words or gestures take note of me] the world has become open to interpretation [to *exactly* the extent that I am open to the interpretability of the world]. And here is the great, seemingly paradoxical situation: "keeping ourselves open" and "keeping the world open" (Eliade, 1968, p. 139) are the same thing. As we become experienced, having cleaved with affection and made ourselves "roomier," the world's roominess can be experienced. (Jardine et al., 2008, p. 53; cited in Jardine, 2016a, p. 81)

It's like this, this simple. A picture gets found, long lost to unsortedness. A phrase gets written. Read. And it hits. And the two hits hit together.

A dark geranium, captured from-the-back, front-lit light, encased in grey, a shadow cupped in dark. It is still and it stills me, looking at it. Phototropical. I too, early April, turn to face the sun. It be me sit awaiting. Accompanied. There's a title for it, for now.

And also a lovely opening sentence from an album review whose images ached arc-old when I read them. I never want to forget:

> The steadfast devotion between the women of *Boygenius* is a subject worthy of a dog-eared literary classic, one that's passed from friend to friend until the pages come fluttering off the spine. (Zhang, 2023)

But there is this other aspect to aesthetic arrival that almost inevitably rips past this. As be the nature of words:

> We can never fully know what might come of the work we do, what might fully come of these words, written. "The helplessness of the written word" (Gadamer, 1989, p. 369), which Plato took to be its failing is, in its own way, its generative, interpretive strength. Writing, in its helplessness in the face of new readings beyond the author's desire, is already a portend of the child. Our children always outstrip us. (Jardine, 2000, p. 178)

[An] event's eventfulness is recurrently experienced as "a task that is never entirely finished" (Gadamer, 1989, p. 301). After all, here we are, writer and reader, 44 years on, still struggling with how and whether to learn to live with the entreaties of this event. "By forming the thing [I] form [my]self" (Gadamer, 1989, p. 13). The author—even that CD which they were reviewing—ends up a bit "helpless" to connections stirred (Gadamer, 1989, p. 369, referencing Plato *Phaedrus*). Words can sometimes summon worlds of relations whatever the author might have meant, leaving me, too, a bit helpless. Stillings of words and images and memories, condensing, a-glowing.

Like this.

I'm old enough to see, clear as day, the yellow spine-glue, and smell the yellowed pages, and know full well, half a century ago, more, old friends and those books we passed, hand to hand, and broke open, fluttering off our spines. The books that broke us open just as our reading them broke them open, too. And the commiseration, now, over those days, of friends, of passing in all its forms.

Hermeneutic adages: "breaking open" (Gadamer, 1989, p. 362), "break[ing] forth" (p. 458), both, at their core, aesthetic moments of aliveness, of something summoning up.

Even the images of oxidized sliced-apple browning of those old pages. *Lingin* (Pitctolic, n.d.). Smells of old books.

I looked this up against these old memories—sights, sounds, smells, a whole array of friends, these all gathered up in reading these words. Lingin tends to *add itself* to the myriad. It makes the science of it seem companionable, too.

The palpable physicality—Earth-boundness—of books, passed hand to hand, dog-ear to dog-ear, face-to-face, breath to breath, conspiracies in high school and well before and after, hidden in desks. Sustaining us. Browsing: "feed on buds, eat leaves or twigs from" (Online Etymological Dictionary, under "browse, v.").

The lure of a sort of steadfast devotion passed from friend to friend until the pages come fluttering off the spine that I *somehow, sort of already understood*. This sentence made shiverflutters up my spine, off and away—it does flutter *outwards and off*—now here, trying to compose myself in the face of this image (and all this let alone what might be asked of me if I listen to this album). Made me shiver, energies come fluttering off my spine. Hans-Georg Gadamer talks of how "understanding begins when something addresses us" (1989, p. 299), but then also of how such address happens because of lingering, forgotten, bonds of memory and experience that provide a certain "readiness" to be struck. It is not just that sentence and its properties. And it is not just me and my "perspectives" and "lived experience" and the like. It is an *encounter of off-spine flutterings* and here we go again, yet another cita-tion recited off yellowed pages. After teaching a course on Gadamer's *Truth and Method* (1989), the students in the final go-round gave me the gift of re-binding my aging copy of the book and its cracked glues:

> When we understand a text [or a photograph, or a Raven at the bird feeder], what is meaningful in it captivates us, just as the beautiful captivates us. It has asserted itself and captivated us before we can come to ourselves and be in a position to test the claim … that it makes. In understanding we are drawn into an event … and arrive, as it were, too late, if we want to know what we are supposed to [now] believe. (Gadamer, 1989, p. 490)

Something "hits" and I wanted to write it down, to show you, to pass it along on this yellowing page. It might well end up dead-on arrival. Of course, but as with those old books passed hand to hand— "Check this out!" and hoping to have a cascade of words and whispers come back at me from you, new dog-ears, insights, openings—I want it to see if I could make it "lovely" by letting it work on me, by letting myself write and stay a bit still over it.

Hoping it will flower under a "continuity of attention and devotion" (Berry, 1986, p. 34). Most things simply pass by, unnoticed under tired-ness, distraction, or because many things are deliberately designed to not need care and attention and devotion, flat shiny disposable surfaces not meant to last or root. A Styrofoam cup and not an old, selected, saved, cared for mug.

Differently put, that is a good sentence in that review. It can main-tain itself and grow if taken care of well. And this beyond the confines of what is being reviewed. I know about those things shared hand to hand, poured over, adored, and until this sentence came by, I'd forgot-ten about it altogether.

Good writing. I do agree that "the way we treat a thing can some-times change its nature" (Hyde, 1983, p. iii), and that "sometimes it is necessary to re-teach a thing its loveliness, to put a hand on its brow and say …" (Kinnell, 2002, n.p.), but there is also something about the third thing, the thing itself—not everything can take this teach or treat.

Preciousness.

Both cites say "sometimes." And it is "sometimes" for me, too. Otherwise I'd be inundated. After all, the crest of sunlight this early morning, last day of March 2023, is warm to the forebode of arrivals— of lambs, of sentences, of my grandson's glees, of the upbristle of wanting to write about something I just read, even of my own aging in the face of all that. As Sheila Ross put it, "something like aliveness itself," such that the fluttering off the spine is a description of the wealth and well-being of the thing itself, a wealth it gives me if I treat it right and pass it along:

> Beauty is not radiance shed on a form from without. Rather, the ontological constitution of the form itself is to be radiant, to present itself this way. (Gadamer, 1989, p. 487)

My attention to all this, then, is, of course, phototropical.

CHAPTER TWENTY-SEVEN

"Engage-Abandon"

There is a great interject, right into the heart of "why study for a future we won't have?" that comes from both Buddhism and hermeneutics, and, too from matters ecological. I've long since-cited and recited Wendell Berry's soft encouragement. Again:

The important thing to do is to learn all you can about where you are, to make common cause with that place, and then, resigning yourself, become patient enough to work with it over a long time. And then, what you do is increase the possibility that you'll make a good example. And what we're looking for in this is good examples (Berry, with Moyers, 2013).

And his good reminder that, to be patient enough, here, in the face of our ecologically sorrowful times, is a terrible trial that can cause me to bolt. I'm old. I will leave bolting to others more fit for that worthwhile endeavor. Here, all I can to is again recommend to a class of practicing teachers, once again years ago, that study, even in schools, can be rich, rigorous, ecologically sane and full of living relations. It can be a partner in the world of our commiserating and encouraging sorrows. In real schools with all their shadows and light study can be a strange pleasure.

"Engage-abandon" [Tibtean *blang lor*], i.e., engage in what is to be practiced and give up what is to be abandoned. (Richards, 2006, p. 731)

Exactly because we give up [abandon] a special idea of foundation in principle, we become better phenomenologists, closer to the real givenness, and we are more aware of the reciprocity [engage] between our conceptual efforts and the concrete in life experience. (Gadamer, 1984, p. 323)

Practicing this so-called "classroom inquiry" in ways that are rich, abundant and unafraid is not just a matter of engaging the world and students and our own responsibilities as teachers in a certain way. It is also a matter of abandoning, of giving up, of letting go of something near and dear to which it is easy to be secretly attached.

Abandon "foundations." Foundations: that which is firm and sturdy and unchanged and unchanging no matter what is built upon it, no matter that occurs once it is established, no matter what moves and shifts, no matter who arrives in the classroom or what circumstances rise or fall around us. Hard, final, fixed. That in relation to which everything makes sense but that which does not need anything else in order to sensible. Self-existent, as it is called in Buddhism. Substance as it is called in Western philosophy, or sometimes "essence." Unshakeable beliefs that can no longer learn from the world, that are held in such a way that they fancy themselves as not needing to learn, already knowing in advance what any arrival can essentially be. In light of a knowledge of essence, everything else is accidental.

Engage "reciprocity" instead. Reciprocity: between what we have experienced and learned and come to know, and the arriving circumstances of new questions, new explorations, new arrivals in these living fields.

Increasing experience and knowledge do not result in a firmer and firmer foundation for our lives, but to an increased ability to artfully negotiate our reciprocity with the world and to learn from that cultivation. Increased experience allows me to avoid the false refuge of foundations and the false comforts they offer of finality. This always bears reciting:

The experienced person proves to be ... someone who ... because of the many experiences he has had and the knowledge he has drawn from them, is particularly well equipped to have new experiences and to learn from them. Experience has its proper fulfillment not in definitive [amassed] knowledge but in the openness to experience that is made possible by experience itself. (Gadamer, 1989, p. 355)

We are all accustomed to the quiet comforts of foundations and abandoning their pursuits and our pursuit of them is disorienting, perhaps even terrifying at first.

If I may, the terrifying prospect of abandoning foundations remains terrifying if and only if do not also abandon what we *thought* was the alternative. Under the shadow of foundations, the alternative is thought to be chaos, anything goes, all is meaningless, randomness, spin, fake news with no possibility of repair, violence, and despair. We can experience this roil right now with great intimacy.

This gives a bit of a hint as to why this sort of classroom work based on the intimacies of ecological awareness and the cultivation of reciprocities has trouble, shall we say, "catching on," because it is up against a deep anxiety for which foundations provided the (albeit illusory) panacea. We are, right here, at the root source of our ecological crisis.

To paraphrase Dostoyevsky, if a foundation does not exist (God, in Dostoyevsky's work), everything, it seems, is permitted.

I can attest firsthand to the hostility of some involved in phenomenological pedagogy when such suggestions about not pursuing essences are made [aimed at making these essences foundational, "fix-(ing them) once and for all in a way equally accessible to all" (Husserl, 1970b, pp. 177–178)]—"you think anything goes" was the sad, and repeated, condescending refrain. The speaker, here, shall remain nameless. (Jardine, 2016n, p. 19).

Everything seems to become *hopeless* if we abandon the search for foundations:

Can we console ourselves with that? Can we live in this world, where historical occurrence is nothing but an unending concatenation of illusory progress and bitter disappointment? (Husserl, 1970b, p. 7)

The thing is, what is pointed to in this abandoning of foundations is *not* what the pursuit of foundations has led us to believe. It is not beastly chaos, but rather a summoning of our Earthly relations, dependencies, and kin. Firm and fixed foundations, when abandoned, give way to a net of reciprocal interrelationships (in Buddhist thought, "dependent co-arising") which, with practice, we can learn to experience and negotiate and engage in their interplays. This is, in fact, a very simply, mundane occurrence. It is what you find in Wendell Berry's suggestion, that you should go up to your field and ask "What do you need?" and then become patient enough, knowledgeable enough, to be ready to hear the answer. *That* is reciprocity, pure and simple. Teaching. And learning. And "the consummation of … experience, [what is called] 'being experienced,' does not consist in the fact that someone already knows everything and knows better than anyone else" (Gadamer, 1989, p. 355). It is consummated in a growing readiness and ability to listen, to heed, or, to play with the etymology, to be obedient (Latin, *ab audire*).

"The … readiness … to be 'all ears'" (Gadamer, 2007a). This is not empty-headed gawking but a sever alertness that takes practice to become practiced in. This practice is the practice of *blang lor*. It is commonplace in good, rich, sustainable, affectionate, teaching and learning.

So teachers know what good farmer's know. You learn something every year. But you can never simply bypass the re-winning of that reciprocity with each child that arrives, with each newly gathering field-full of students-full each September. This, of course, is perfectly parallel to how an understanding of this or that topic listed in a curriculum guide is ripe for the re-winning by every student, each in their own way, succeeding or failing or partial or full, over and over and over again, and this intergenerational process of re-winning is not a failure to finally found, but is a sign, instead, of the frail and fleeting success of reciprocity.

What do you need? And what do I need to become in order to be up to the task of understanding what's needed and engaging in it? This is what *Bildung* (German, meaning "cultivation") means in this hermeneutic tradition. It is obvious, then, why Gadamer (1989, p. 356) says that experience is something that no one else can acquire on my behalf, and from it no one can be spared. This points clearly to the type of knowledge and understanding and experience being addressed in ecological thinking, in hermeneutics and in Buddhism: it is not a matter of some anonymous storehouse, but of self-awareness, where I myself, the gracefulness and artfulness of my own interplays with the world, and the interplays I might lay out in front of my students, is at stake. I myself must practice this knowledge in order to become practiced in it. *"All such understanding is ultimately self-understanding (Sichverstehen)*: knowing one's way around" (Gadamer, 1989, p. 260), but this clearly means that to understand myself is to understand my way around in the dependent co-arising of the world, and to become repeatedly ready in making my way in this way. As with experience itself, reciprocity "is always [yet] to be acquired" (p. 356).

So when someone insists that "this is the real world" when pointing to the market-driven, panic-inducing and sustaining realities of schooling, engage-abandon leaves us here:

> "Reality" always stands in a horizon of desired or feared, or, at any rate, still undecided future possibilities. The undecidedness of the future permits such a superfluity of expectations that reality necessarily lags behind them. (Gadamer, 1989, p. 112)

There is nothing foundational or permanent about these panics, this drivenness. It is open to interpretation. It is possible, not necessary. There is no "foundation" here. Reciprocity and its engagement thus have a deeply temporal nature of continuance, of ever-wheeling, of intergenerationality that is ongoingly dependently co-arising, beyond the afflictive desire to finalize and fix and make permanent and over with. Even if we close ourselves off from this "to-and-fro" (Gadamer, 1989, p. 103) and hunker down into feigned certainties, we still suffer it. In fact, I suffer it more if I refuse to become practiced in it. It becomes monstrous and I then repeatedly run into it unprepared.

It becomes, now, almost funny to ask: Why doesn't this sort of teaching and learning catch on more in the local school board? This abandoning of foundations and engaging reciprocity? The vertigo of the venture can easily be too frightening, especially if we are unpracticed in engaging this engagement. Reciprocity is always and necessarily partially out of my hands, because its occurrence *depends* (that good old ecological phrase). And no matter how practiced you becoming in engaging this reciprocity, it can still "outplay" you (Gadamer, 1989,

p. 106) or be refused, rebuked, even ridiculed, bullied. The openness to experience that we win through becoming experienced opens us to be outdone. And then, of course, if, in response to this perhaps inevitable prospect, we retract from that practice, we become simply complacent and silent, we gain no practice in the face of that vertigo, thus increasing the fear we feel when it nears, causing retraction.

This is why the Buddha designated *Sangha*, community, gathering, fellowship, as one of the Three Jewels of Buddhist thought and practice. Gathering together as teachers to become students of this work and its ways is reiterative of an ancient and well-known act. We gather and practice because, in each other's witness, we can become each other's comfort (with its wonderful etymology meaning of "common strength").

We can be a bit of each other's reminder when fear or exhaustion or distraction looms, which it surely will, again and again.

No wonder that Tsong-kha-pa (2000, p. 64) insists, as part of this practice, that we "cultivate love for those who have gathered."

No wonder, too, that he said "you can't get anywhere without [also] reading a yak's load of books" (Tsong-kha-pa, 2004, p. 219). These, too, are our companions, another one of the Three Jewels.

CHAPTER TWENTY-EIGHT

What Should I Tell Them?

Engage-Abandon. High Stakes. This is from the same era as the Red Herring chapter, same school.

What follows happened like this. I was invited to a local high school on a day when the Grade 11 and 12 students were off as a job fair event downtown. I had been working for a while with some of the teachers there. Grade Tens left behind:

"Could you give a talk to our students?"

Tough school comparatively, but not in any grand scheme of things. Got a rep in town, though.

Talk? Sure.

So, as another part of my job, I was teaching a lecture series to all of our University of Calgary, Faculty of Education undergraduate students. Preservice teachers. Over 200 at a time. Sink, taps and gas jets at the front. Teaching uphill.

The lynchpin of the talk I gave at that high school became this: I told them about the class I teach. These people will be teachers. They just may be *your* teachers before you leave school.

What should I tell them?

Handed out index cards. Don't put your name on it. Now's your chance.

Here's what I got back. I have included all of the responses unedited except for removing proper names.

The only caveat I want to add for readers is that this all happened nearly 20 years ago.

And, if I may, read this in relation to the main title of this book you're reading. This list is now 15 years old:

- I would like to see teachers become more aware about what ideology is being taught to students. Severe ID rules, cost and fees, lack of social freedoms, sense of inequality.
- Be more chilled. Make jokes and laugh! Be serious and talk about the things that are happening outside of the class. Talk about music, movies and relate things to life.
- Teachers should encourage discussions about world events more often. I find that following the curriculum tightly makes learning dull and un-useful. Students should have the opportunity to debate and share their opinions about events that matter.
- Be interesting. Stop being so boring. You're not Stalin. Listen to us, I mean if we live in a free country then the students should get to choose stuff, also you should tell everyone about the history behind the thing you're teaching. I know it's more stuff to teach but lots of stick wet gum sticks to tables better than crappy toy gum.
- Be interesting when teaching … involve world news. Don't teach us the old and the past. Don't use the entire class time with pure working. Boring classes will be tuned out. Mix in interesting things. I like it when teachers don't give homework. Teachers who give a lot of homework will make the class stressful.
- Nothing is wrong. Teach what is not taught. There are not bad situations only hard lessons. There are not hard lessons, only forgotten teaching. From the mouths of babes wisdom will flow. Do what is yet to be done. Question what has been done. Explore all teachings past required.
- Lectures and textbook work doesn't do a lot. Students fall asleep during lectures and daydream. It's a waste of your breath and

precious learning time. Make stories. Involve the class. Don't drown us with textbook work.

- Let us work with music on. Don't keep us trapped inside on nice days. Let us work outside. Let us do fun projects. Don't give us assigned seats.
- Do what you think should be done to ensure you have a future. Have fun. We only live once! Do the inevitable and achieve great heights. Peace will overcome violence!
- Class should be interesting. Class should be fun. Teachers should make the students enjoy.
- I would like to have a teacher who is willing to accept a different view on something.
- I want teachers to be more active with their students.
- Teach us the history of stuff. Related it to us. Be happy when we go to class.
- They should all smoke weed.
- They all need to learn the ways of the hippies. Teachers need to be less lazy.
- Take the time to breathe.
- Ok, so, you have got to make sure you not so uptight. Give us some slack, not a lot, but some. Also many people learn better through interacting. So do more things through the arts and find more fun ways for us to learn. That way you won't have as many problems with the kids you teach, especially the teens like grade 7–12.
- More classroom discussions than work sheets. Not repetitive things.
- Break the norm.
- Don't give too much homework because kids have other things in the world to do rather than study all the time. And don't talk about the subject all the time—make the class laugh and fun.
- When in doubt, think like a student. Kids learn best when the matter/info interests or clearly relates to them.
- Be funny and less strict.
- I would like teachers not to give us too much of writing and always give us a reason behind what each thing its, like formulae.

Like one of my teachers was like "Don't ask questions just memorize it" and that puts down the interest of studying. I would like them to talk less, too, or it gets too boring.

- Don't be scared to take a chance—do a project that will cover an entire unit that will involve the students and let them show their strengths in many ways.
- Where should you start? Perhaps from the Arts.
- Be passionate and have fun. Make it interesting for us. If you are bored, we are bored. Add arts and connect through other subjects.
- Don't be uninteresting. Listen to what your students have to say. Ask them what they think of your lesson. They may have valid points.
- Be funny. Don't be boring. Be happy. Don't be sad.
- Kids want to be respected by the teacher. Our principal is loved because he talks to us not down on us. Teach us practical things. In math my teacher shows us clips of numbers and how the things we learn really relate to things and that math does a lot for us. But most of all don't lecture us. Communicate with us. Get to know us. DON'T BORE US.
- Have a laid back attitude for homework and assignments. Explain the material like a teenager, for easy understanding. Don't act like you know what we are going to throw. Go over issues that are impacting us today, not things that happened thousands of years ago.
- Look, please be serious in this situation. Education.
- Don't make us do presentations in front of the class. First of all: it's embarrassing. Secondly, nobody pays attention to what the other student says.
- Make games related to what you are teaching (that will get the students involved and excited).
- Some teachers talk and talk from their notes and it just confuses you and slows you down.
- Try to make the lectures more interesting by presenting the info in an intriguing way. Try to reach out to the students and please, try not to mark hard especially English teachers.

- X is a loser.
- Have lots of fun activities to do with the subject that's being learned so that we don't get bored. And don't rush through things. Y is a loser ☺. [previous two cards were side by side in the pile of cards].
- Teacher should trust the children in school [this phrase was the erased and the card turned over]. School should be [this phrase was then erased]. Waste of trees. Waste of paper.
- To be a good teacher, do not force students to come to class. Just make your class like where students want to come and learn.
- Stop being boring. Have more fun. Loon up and have more fun in class. Make jokes. Get the class involved. Please stop giving so many worksheets and notes. Don't make the class dry, but interesting.
- To be a good teacher, please don't explain the lesson while students are taking notes.
- All people learn in different ways. A mark can mean next to nothing in true intelligence.
- Let kids talk about their issue with current events.
- Don't be confined to the pages in the text. Be special.
- Always incorporate history and philosophy in all classes. If we know the origin of the information, we can connect it better in our mind and give the proper respect to those who shaped our lives today.
- Add interesting tidbits to your lesson. Keep the kids interested. Have something new each day.
- ay.h day.place to go to school.
- Start being funny.
- Give them their dream school.
- Don't be boring. Make class fun, don't be grouchy, go easy on us. Don't assume or judge. Be understandable. Go at a normal pace. Be caring. Be selfless, be serious but funny at times.
- Teachers must be educated. They should be polite.
- Don't bore us.
- Less teaching students like kids, more like adults. More respect/ autonomy regarding schedule, attendance.

- Don't talk too much.
- Respect the students and don't talk for the whole class. Don't be boring.
- Be interesting and let kids understand you. Kids don't tend to do things they don't like
- Smaller classes. Also NO WORKSHEETS. First of all, waste of paper and trees and it should be "hands-on learning" instead. Instead of modern & traditional learning, clear and new ideas.
- Don't be like most of the teachers. Don't make the class boring. Many students want to learn but when teachers make it boring it makes it hard to learn.
- Teachers should be organized and make the room organized too. Teachers should be outgoing and not overly strict. They should make learning fun.
- Explain in detail for all the assignments so that the students get it. Help them and try to give as much time as you can to students.
- Explain clearly, increase your knowledge before teaching to help students.
- Connect with students. Explain lessons straightforwardly. Use examples. Be REASONABLE! Try to be fun and interesting. Have personality. Be open to suggestions. Give us time to do assignments.
- Have at least one fun day a month. A day to just relax and unwind. Play some games, watch a movie, have some snacks, play some music.
- Realize that students are part of a system, family, community, that affects their ability to learn. E.g., if your parents had a fight the night before, you might not care about your math assignment.
- No homework!
- Don't be mean. Don't be boring. Don't make kids your slave. Be cool!
- Put a good story behind history not just keep going on about facts
- Have real life relations to what you teach.
- You teachers need to put some work in the work.
- Try to mix real life with the lessons and speak directly.

- Don't stick to the curriculum. Think outside the box. Don't put your students to sleep. Have them want to come to class.
- Try to be outgoing and not boring.
- The same routine is dull and boring. Mix stuff up and get students to talk about world events even if it doesn't have anything to do with the subject.
- Look, I don't think a good teacher should be boring. Make school fun for kids. Learning and having fun at the same time.
- Teachers shouldn't give students worksheets. Instead, they should say interesting facts with a lot of thought for the students. So that students can start to understand more. Make education more fun.
- While teaching, add a little fun to it so the students actually enjoy it.
- Have the same expectations for all races.
- Don't make your students do worksheet after worksheet
- Make school fun.
- I think teachers should to only teach but also bring students together. Spread your care equally, so you student don't feel lonely.
- Uncover secrets behind the basics instead of uninteresting discussion.
- It seems that whites group with whites, Asians group with Asians, etc. we need to stop that. Every student learns differently. Teachers should get to know how each student learns and learn how to teach them that way.
- Laugh more. Enjoy your job. See the students as works in progress. Curriculum is only curriculum.
- Help kids feel they can trust their own notions.
- Great teachers put students first and truly care about them. Great teachers respect their students.
- There are times for worksheets, but make it less. Watch for the quiet and shy students.
- Stop talking and listen more. Students don't care how much you now until they know how much you care.

- Change the way the rooms are. Should be bigger. Should let student work freely on their own and ask for help when needed.
- All you guys concentrate on books, but not sports or community sources or maybe helping orphans.
- Change the schoolrooms. They are depressing. Change the breaking system of the whole school.
- Changing the school helps change the world.
- Get kids more active with the class. Get them up and interacting with each other.
- Be more expressive. Be outside the box and explore the possibilities which life can teach us, not what the book says. Explore the world of the world!
- I think we don't need exams. We just need knowledge. Everything must be practical, not just reading books.
- Be nice to students. They shouldn't suspect students for no reason because I think that is just stupid.
- Be nice and useful. More test and exam prep.
- Don't get off-topic and tell us useless information. More time on tests and less on unnecessary storytelling.
- No absents
- Don't suck up to your students. And always be the best you can be by not being a bitch or else you'll be hated for life by your students. Be cool, be yourself.
- Don't fall in love with students or date the. You will get busted.
- I think there should be more visual and fun ways of teaching. For example, more games, visual presentations, etc. I also think there should be a different way of teaching everyday. One day a game could be played, the next day something involving art. People learn best when it is entertaining and fun. Guest speakers, movies, dramas, etc. anything worth remembering.
- Always keep your cool with students. Always be willing to help. Socialize with them. Share you thoughts and feelings on a subject. If you treat them like students, you won't be happy with them treating you like a teacher.

CHAPTER TWENTY-NINE

"The … Readiness … To Be 'All Ears'"

This is yet another song of praise for an old colleague, now long gone somewhere or other. Oh, how he would have laughed at that sentence. To be like the space between those snowprint bird wings, that rush of cold air.

Preamble

> Without the readiness of the person who is receiving and assimilating [*des Aufnehmenden*] the text to be "all ears" [*ganz Ohr zu sein*], no … text will speak. (Gadamer, 2007d, p. 189)

What better description could I find for my 30-year love affair with Bill Doll? His unwavering joy in conversation, commiseration, his whiling over a question, a spark, bespeaks a lightness that produces joy while it seeks it. And this, too:

> We welcome just that guest who promises something new to our curiosity. But how do we know that the guest we admit is one who has something *new* to say to us? Is not our expectation and our readiness to hear the new also

necessarily determined by the old that has already taken possession of us? (Gadamer, 1977, p. 9)

There is the coupling, here, of the arrival of the new and the insistence that Bill embodies, that my readiness for that arrival is, in part, determined by what I have already come to know and how I have come to hold myself in that knowing. It is not an amassed blockage to that arrival, but is a condition of it, a condition of recognizing the new when it arrives.

A readiness to be all ears is thus not an innocent, or naive or blank-faced openness, but a studied one, one won and re-won over time. It is an outcome of study properly done. This or that topic "compels over and over, and the better one knows it, the *more* compelling it is" (Gadamer, 2007c, p. 115), not *less*. This sort of knowledge, thus held, is a petition against hardening and closure, a summons on behalf of what can be thus hard won: the lightness of gravity.

Readiness needs to be sought, cultivated. It needs to be taken care of properly and repeatedly and relentlessly. Readiness takes work, it takes energy, *energeia*, "aliveness" (Gadamer, 2007a, p. 211; Ross, 2006, pp. 107–108), and it not only takes it. It *produces* it. And when it works, it hits the still spot between give and take and begins to glow. As anyone who has met Bill or even heard or read him from afar knows full well, his being "all ears" extents such a glow. Such whiling stillness "is not a function of lackadaisical, meandering contemplation, least of all passive in any way, but is a function of the fullness and *intensity* of attention and engrossment" (Ross, 2006, p. 109) and watch out! It's contagious.

In around 1406 CE, Tsong-kha-pa (2000, p. 179) noted that what pleases one's teachers most are not material gifts, but rather "offerings of practice." It is the pleasure taken in the practice of others that allows a teacher to "act as a refuge for everyone" (p. 179). Otherwise they are mere hoarders of their own expertise, weighty but sullen and full of complaint over new arrivals that always and only have nothing new to say. We've all been around enough of that.

In early September 2015, Bill invited me to speak to graduate students and Faculty at the University of British Columbia in Vancouver on a topic of my choice. That talk was given a title cited from Kevin

O'Leary (2012), wherein he described clearly and distinctly how he profits, as an astute businessman, from desperate parental concerns over
"literacy": "I love the terror in a mother's heart"—how one can profit
from those who are petrified and how maintaining one's customers in
a state of terror while providing purchasable relief from that very terror
that one secretly maintains, has become a great contemporary art, in
business, in politics, in education. What follows here is a reconstruction
of some other threads of that talk offered as a wee gift of practice given
to one of my teachers.

Again, we all know this much in having been around the refuge of
Bill's presence. The joy he takes in being "all ears" *creates* joy.

"As in love, our satisfaction [in this joy] sets us at ease because we
know that somehow its use at once assures its plenty" (Hyde, 1983,
p. 22).

Thus, a Fleet

A quick and fleeting scenario from a recent graduate class full of practicing teachers meeting at a local school, where someone on leave from
the local school system visited his old place of work and was surprised
and frustrated by the level of relentless complaint he encountered,
some former colleagues even complaining about how much others
complained. He mentioned how he had never quite noticed it before
when working there and how now, having, shall we say, broken the
fixed stare of living and breathing it day-to-day, he could see what was
once hidden from view.

In our class, we all laughed at first, in recognition and commiseration. But then this: there was an at-first-gradual then ever-increasing
falling forward into this culture of complaint. We all got drawn toward
it, into it, deeper, deeper, so that our conversations became wedded to
its roil, and it became more and more enormously engorged by our
attention which it both fed and fed upon. It loved our attention, especially since that attention was only geared to more attention.

All of us were drawn in because of how very enlivening it *felt* to join
in and how vigorous we each felt in feeling its stirring in us resentment,

condescension, look-at-that-ness, this-bugs-me-too-ness. Everyone had something to say. Anecdotes scattered and shot and ricocheted around the room. Everyone was compelled to listen in that funny way, sitting on the verge of wanting a turn to tell, some urgency, some example, some frustration, some blame, this teacher, that face, those words, tut-tut, and the class of 24 broke up into a dozen ever-louder crisscross sideways conversations.

It *appeared* that everyone was "all ears" but no one was. Each of us already knew the anecdote we had waiting its turn to turn and spin and expend itself in this whirl. The game was already set, already fully determined and there was little readiness to hear something new. You can't be "all ears" if the only audible message offered is "Oh yeah? Listen what happened to me!" Dramatic. Grotesque.

And, admit it, terribly temporarily enjoyable. Arousing.

The Weight, the Inertia, the Opacity

I tried to become one with the ruthless energies that, collectively and individually, was driving propelling the events of our century. I tried to find some harmony between the bustling spectacle of the world, by turns dramatic and grotesque, and the picaresque, adventurous inner rhythm that spurred me to write. Soon realized the gap between the realities of life that were supposed to be my raw materials and the sharp, darting nimbleness that I wanted to animate my writing was becoming hard and harder for me to bridge. Perhaps I was only then becoming aware of the heaviness, the inertia, the opacity of the world—qualities that [can] quickly adhere to writing if one doesn't find a way to give them the slip. Sometimes I felt that the whole world was turning into stone: a slow petrification, more advanced in some people and places than in others, but from which no aspect of life was spared. It was as if no one could escape the Medusa's inexorable gaze. (Calvino, 2016, p. 4)

Here, then a sideways glance at this lovely piece written by Italo Calvino called "Lightness," ever-more-timely for us here, now, perhaps studying for a future we won't have. How the direct stare into these circumstances of complaint tends to harden that stare and therefore, at the same time, turn the object of that stare into its own version of "concrete" reality, thus turning our stare to stone, no longer able to turn away. The snaky roil mesmerizes—it *seems* like "aliveness"—but then it only petrifies. Like terror in a mother's heart, I suppose, stood stock-still and immobilized, susceptible to false promises of relief proffered by precisely that which caused the petrification in the first place.

As the object turns to a stony stare ("Look at that!" "Listen to them!" "You think *that's* bad, wait till you hear this!"—I think, here, of Ivan Illich's [& Cayley, 1992, p. 127] hilariously apt description of this as "apocalyptic randiness"), we become attached to this monster wrought, in part, by our petrified stare, and then we blame it for our woes, turning effect into cause and making thinking impossible. This hostility in its turn once again further hardens and reifies, and this reification invokes hostility ("It's getting worse, don't you think!" "Why doesn't somebody do something!"), and that hostility, in its turn, reifies, adds gravity and weight. What happens, essentially, is that complaint is deeply and sincerely *experienced*, but it is no longer visible as *perpetrated*.

Energy just spent and temporarily exhausted.

Meeting Medusa in a Mirror

Unskilled persons whose eye of intelligence is obscured by the darkness of delusion conceive of an essence in things [things are fixed, reified, concrete, set-in-stone, inert] and then generate attachment and hostility with regard to them. (Tsong-kha-pa, 2000, p. 210)

This is why the "inertia and opacity of the world" is described as a Wheel (Sanskrit: *Samsara*) in Buddhist thinking and imagination. It wheels and, when we become caught in its stare, we are wheeled, around and around, both adoring and complaining of this wheeling. The heavy solidity of "the real world" of schooling is met only with greasy, squirming of snakes. But then, Calvino:

In order to cut off Medusa's head without being turned to stone, Perseus supports himself on the lightest of stuff—winds and clouds—and turns his gaze toward that which can be revealed to him only indirectly, by an image caught in a mirror. (Calvino, 2016, pp. 4–5)

Medusa's roiling can be caught in a mirroring wherein we can remain not simply caught up in her stare and battered in the roil, but somehow "outside" of it: this is Gadamer's (1989, p. 444) "freedom from the environment" that makes us not simply caught in the earth's and our animal-body's immediacies and tethers. We can "rise above what impinges on us from the world" (p. 444):

> This does not mean that [we] leave [] [our] habitat but that [w]e ha[ve] another posture towards it—a free, distanced orientation. (p. 445)

In this free distance, this "free space" (Gadamer, 1986, p. 53), I am not simply caught in the impinging of things, of actual circumstances and heat, but gain a sense of what might be possible, here, over and above the embodied reactions of mutual impingement, what potentialities and powers might be at work in this spell binding immediacy.

But to break the spell of its immediacy and begin to glimpse its perpetration requires a deflected glance. In study, in writing, we support ourselves on the very lightest of things, thinking, but we don't then look away from our lot and up into the clouds:

> As for the severed head, rather than abandoning it, Perseus takes it with him, hidden in a sack. Perseus masters that terrible face by keeping it hidden. His power derives from refusing to look directly while not denying the reality of the world of monsters in which he must live, a reality he carries with him and bears. (Calvino, 2016, pp. 5–6)

Study, writing, carries our burden more lightly.

It may be that in the confines of schools our complaint has little recourse beyond its own continuance. This is why we study. Within the orbits of school and its language and accelerated time, there is not enough recourse available to work *out* what is at work, here. It cannot wing. It has no gush of coolness and musing:

> From Medusa's blood winged horse, Pegasus, is born; the heaviness of stone is transformed into its opposite, and with the stamp of a single hoof on Mount Helicon, a fountain springs forth from which the Muses drink. (Calvino, 2016, p. 5)

As per this class of ours and the uprises of complaint, someone had to simply say, "Stop!" in a voice loud enough to break the spell, loud enough to remind everyone that we are surrounded by ancestors who can help us, quite literally, *out*. So, we read Bill Doll's work. And Maxine Greene. Bill Pinar. Thich Nhat Hanh, Wendell Berry. David G. Smith. Cynthia Chambers, on and on. Without some study of this ancestry, complaint has nothing to draw upon except its immediacy. Once we summoned them, they broke our fixed gaze and cultivated our readiness. We studied our circumstance instead of falling for it. They provided us with a field rich enough to work *out* what was happening, here. They helped us be all ears.

The Bodhisattva Manjushri is associated in Buddhism with wisdom. He carries a sword used to cut through the spell, especially through the petrified and petrifying reifications of "the real world."

Like Perseus' sword, it cuts. It breaks the bound spell.

Studying and the Arts of Writing

Studying and the arts of writing don't precisely make lighter the burden of the world. They can, however, make it translucent, thus, in this small way, lightened:

> When the human realm seems doomed to heaviness, I feel the need to fly like Perseus into some other space. I am not talking about escaping into dreams or into the irrational. I mean that I feel the need to change my approach, to look at the world form a different angle, with a different logic, different methods of knowing and proving. The images of lightness I'm looking for shouldn't let themselves dissolve as dreams do in the reality of the present and future ... (Calvino, 2016, p. 8)

Thus, the wonderful burden of writing and its wonderful reprieve, because, when it works, readers can recognize themselves in it as *already wiser* than they might have first imagined (precisely the act of a good teacher in relation to a student):

> What writers have is a license and also the freedom to sit—to sit, clench their fists, and make themselves be excruciatingly aware of the stuff that we're

mostly aware of only on a certain level. And that if the writer does his job right, what he basically does is remind the reader of how smart the reader is. Is to wake the reader up to stuff that the reader's been aware of all the time. (Wallace, with Lipsky, 2010, p. 41)

And this:

One of the things about being a writer is you're able to give the impression—both in the lines and between the lines—that you know an *enormous* amount. That you know and have lived intimately all this stuff. Because you want it to have that kind of effect on the nerve endings. And it's like—it's something that I'm fairly good at. Is I think I can seem, I think I can *seem* like I know a whole lot about stuff that in fact pretty much everything that I know is right there. It's a very tactical research-type thing. (Wallace, with Lipsky, 2010, pp. 144–145)

In writing, in studying, my own lure toward complaint becomes vivid. I myself am at stake. This sword is for me, for my sake:

I find Ovid's verses (IV. 740–752) extraordinary for the way they show how much delicacy of spirit is required to be a Perseus, a slayer of monsters. "That the rough sand not harm the snake-haired head (*anquiferumque caput dura ne laedat harena*), he makes the ground soft with a bed of leaves, and over that spreads springs that grew in water, and there he sets Medusa's head, face-down." I can think of no better way to represent the lightness of which Perseus is the hero than with his refreshingly tender gesture toward that being who, though monstrous and terrifying is also somehow perishable, fragile yet at the same time somehow fragile and perishable. But the most surprising part is the miracle that follows: when the marine plants come into contact with Medusa, they retransformed into coral, and the nymphs, wanting to adorn themselves with coral, rush to bring more springs and seaweed to the terrible head. Again, this juxtaposition of images, in which the delicate grace of the coral brushes up against the fierce horror of the Gorgon, is so richly suggestive that I hesitate to spoil it with commentary or interpretation. (Calvino, 2016, p. 6)

Don't worry. I'm not citing this because I fully understand it. I'm citing it because I want it nearby because I know it is wonderful even though I *don't* quite understand it. I do love rereading it, though.

Postscript

So, there we have it, this gesture of refreshing courtesy that comes when I think over the past 30 years of friendship and camaraderie with Bill Doll. Study. Light air that bears a sword. Terrifying but not petrifying. Readiness. And, too, somehow fragile and perishable.

CHAPTER THIRTY

It Might Just Be Ravens Writing in Mid-Air

A Small Start

FIGURE 12. SUNBEAK

And the children in the apple-tree
Not known, because not looked for
But heard, half-heard, in the stillness
Between two waves of the sea.

T.S. Eliot, from Quartet No. 4, Section 5 of
"Four Quartets" (lines 36–39)

But then something about the sentence [Bill said] stuck out. *"As a kid, I was just a kid."* It sounds like a line from a Bill Callahan song. Is he saying, "Let's leave that alone," because there is something deeper he doesn't want to discuss, or is it that there is really nothing there? Does it matter?

Mark Richardson (2013, n.p.), from "A Window
That Isn't There: The Elusive Art of Bill Callahan"

It matters, but just *how* it matters and *how much* and *to whom* and *to what end* is not just a tough call but a call that needs to be considered again and again, at every turn of circumstance. This is part of the sweet frustration of the interpretive life, that there is no single declaration. Stories get retold in the bury of the circumstances that call for them. And the pedagogical art of sensing that call is itself a practice part of whose efficacy and worth is linked intimately to the very tale it considers.

Thus, the places, the locales of consideration—with all their convoluted stories and memory and fantasy and desire and inhabitants—have something to say, here, too. An interpretive consideration of my "self," like my consideration of any other considered matter, is not aimed at

a "thing" with properties to be discovered and named under regimes of "control, prediction and manipulation" (Habermas, 1972, p. 21), but is, rather, a long, contested, and emergent lineage of images, ideas, choices, possibilities, occlusions, inclusions, victories, defeats, silences and voices. The object being considered by interpretive work *is* this very various-ness. "Only in the multifariousness of voices does it exist." (Gadamer, 1989, p. 284)

Thus, if there are Ravens nearby, eyeing, can change everything, as can the exhilaration of reading such a lovely line, noting it, citing it, here, now, as a gesture of whiling and remembering, and singing back. Thus, too, the language of interpretive work swirls and dips, not because it is a poetic consideration of something simple, clear and straightforward, but because its object *is* multifarious, voiced and re-voiced from the angles of trees and Ravens and other lives' sounds. Its object calls for a type of expression that tries to cleave well to and to find its measure in that very object.

A Second Start

FIGURE 13. GRADE THREE

A clear, old, August memory of the rail clickities of trains in the distance, dimming light, coming sleep, open hot summer windows, yells of the older kids still up and about, green and young and easy curtains revealing and curtailing what breeze there was. Backyard apple boughs and peach.

Those are the very trains I'd watch roar, sitting squat small boy on the side-track loading docks along the building's south wall, weekends, Burlington, Ontario, when my father would take me to the factory to explore the great and grinding and loud and smelling-of-printing-inks-and-ketone machines as he did his foreman rounds.

Salt pills by the water fountain.

Half-ton rolls of paper you could smell when the machines heated them up.

Polish accents finding wee me a moment of joy relief in their labors of the day, and me, them, too.

And the fact that I'm old enough to have seen in-service *steam trains* go by at all. I didn't imagine this, right? There is a dream-blur to boy-days and 69 years of times and days and daydreaming and stories told and heard and dreamt all mixed with others' lives and their tells and mine.

I am most certainly and reliably a bit of an uncertain and unreliable witness to my very own life.

Click. *As a kid*

And, of course, exactly how uncertain and how unreliable is not for me to answer without duplicity, without, all at once, too much and too little at stake in the game of telling.

Clack. *I was just a kid.*

Single headlight seen at first, train-brightening with cycloptic dream-excitement, and then the great approach of noisy rhythmic chm-chm whooshes and that always-sudden moment of rush-by—with their great hinged armed elbows pushing the wheels and the plume of black, black, black smoke trailing up and over, having just pulled out of the Brant Street Station stop 4 miles west, working hard against inertia for a new head of steam. Part of this a black-and-white Max Fleisher stretched cartoon full of animated and elongated Saturday-morning-jazz-ghosts.

And the Doppler pitch-drop whistle blows in the whiz-by. Factory sat at the Guelph Line level-crossing. Trains audible miles south, Delaware Avenue bedroom window, near enough to Lake Ontario that you could hear the fog horns some nights, and see the sky redden from the slag dumps of the steel plants in Hamilton Harbour, formerly known as Burlington Bay.

"One's Story has been Stolen"

All this invokes, even in me, a least a bit of "So what?" As those involved in interpretive research and the long entrails of curriculum and place and our living relations to the work of teaching and learning as part of a life well-lived, are finding more and more, *everybody* has had a life of some sort or other, *everybody* has a story or two or more, *everybody* hides and lies and distorts and exposes and blends and nurtures and taints, all in a jumble of intent and no intent at all. And this here story's vague closeness and slight preciousness to me is not enough, by itself, for it to be *especially* worth the telling, let alone anyone else's listening or reading, let alone worth even me remembering.

Interpretive work—hermeneutics and the curricula of place and relations and voice and story and life and earth and energy—summons a strange god:

> When Hermes is at work ... one feels that one's story has been stolen and turned into something else. The [person] tells his tale, and suddenly its plot has been transformed. He resists, as one would try to stop a thief ... "This is not what I meant at all, not at all." But too late. Hermes has caught the tale, turned its feet around, made black into white, given it wings. And the tale is gone from the upperworld historical nexus in which it had begun and been subverted into an underground meaning. (Hillman, 1983, p. 31)

Such thievery can break the spell of the "compulsive fascination with my own case history" (Hillman, 2013, p. 30):

> "The aim of interpretation, it could be said, is not just another interpretation but human freedom" (Smith, 2020d, p. 47), hard-won and always in need of re-winning. And this is a freedom *from something* and a freedom, also, *on behalf of something*. It is a freedom from being "bound without a rope" (Loy, 2010, p. 42) to regnant ideas and beliefs, but it doesn't proffer the simple negation of these ideas and beliefs but rather makes visible the causes and conditions of their arising. As goes an old hermeneutic saw, every text, every tale told, can be read as the answer to a question *that could have been answered differently* and therefore, every reading of every text is *possible*, not *necessary*, thus issuing a sort of relief from what appears to be intransigent, dominant confines. The hard-won insights that then arise will, of necessity, mean leaving certain things behind that will no longer support and encourage such precisely such freedom and alertness. It will mean looking foolish and starting all over again. The life-world is interpretable. But, too, my own most heartfelt "beliefs" and "feelings" and "opinions" and "experiences" become vulnerable to being read back to me in ways that I could not read them myself. This is true as much of the researcher as it is also true of the one who is the topic of one's study. (Cited and referenced in full above)

But it is therefore vital to emphasize that, as a writer, *I am not Hermes.* I am not "the 'god' *[even] of [my] own story*" (Melnick, 1997, p. 372, emphasis added) as per far too much of the contemporary self-noise. And this is true even (maybe even *especially*) of these silly stories of trains and summers and finches. Instead, I find myself *in these tales,* being told *by* them, not just telling them, out, somehow, in the wilds "beyond [my] wanting and doing" (Gadamer, 1989, p. xxviii), told by birds and the weight of wood carried.

I find that I'm the tell of a tale. Of remembering this sweet thing that I first spotted, then cited 27 years ago (Jardine, 1992b, p. vii). The lovely two-breath phrase by Rick Fields (1990, p. xiv):

My heart is broken
Open.

It is strange to have a memory stretched back along a stretch of writing itself bent to "make memory last," a phrase that itself just now flitted by from nowhere. I went to look for it, as has become an old habit. To make sure it was still safe and sound. *Truth and Method* (1989, p. 391), Hans-Georg Gadamer citing G.W.F. Hegel. And hah! Look at this:

> [Writing] can detach itself from the mere continuance of the vestiges of past life, remnants from which one human being can by inference piece out another's existence. [Writing] does not present us with only a stock of memorials and signs. [It, like many arts] has acquired its own contemporaneity with every present. To understand it does not mean primarily to reason one's way back into the past, but to have a present involvement in what is said. (p. 391)

"As if Illuminated"

As a kid, I was just a kid. Yes, it does sound like a Bill Callahan lyric. But there is another lyric. Bill Callahan (recording as Smog), "Teenage Spaceship," from the CD *Knock Knock* (1999). When I first heard this song, I sent it to an old friend with only this note: "I know *exactly* what this means. How did he know this?" Flying around the neighborhood at night. Beautiful with all my lights. Spaceship.

Sometimes I need to recite a citation as a chance to breathe the breath of another life and then perhaps come back to myself with better means because of it. Oxygenated like water tumbled over rapid rocks and steeps. What a relief to hear this song. It is both utterly moist and personal *and* an example of intimacy over years, between lives.

Can I have these lyrics as my very own story, please? No, I can't even quote much of them without much hassle and expense (even though I can effortlessly do this: https://www.youtube.com/watch?v=llae AbTSo_k). This song perfectly tells an utterly intimate secret *about my very own life* that I had never before quite imagined having lived. And it does so precisely because of the decades and decades of distance now both collapsed and distended, both. It is profoundly nearby and only heard at a great murk of distance. The weird shock, not only of recognition, but of being suddenly and sharply and unexpectedly *recognized*:

> We do not understand what recognition is in its profoundest nature if we only regard it as knowing something again that we already know. The joy of recognition is rather the joy of knowing *more* than is already familiar. In recognition, what we know emerges, as if illuminated. It is known *as* something. (Gadamer, 1989, p. 114)
>
> Joy, yes, but not just joy:
>
> I need to remember my stories not because I need to find out about myself but because I need to found myself in a story that I can hold to be mine. I also fear these stories because through them I can be found out, ... exposed. Repression is built into each story as the fear of the story itself, the fear of the closeness of the Gods in the myths which found me Thus the art of [interpretation] requires skilful handling of memory, of case history, so that it can truly found. (Hillman, 1983, p. 42)

I listen to this song. It illuminates me just right, just here, years outstretched, and it illuminates some swollen creek through trees, others huddled around, hovering at night, worlds and worlds of images and lives and stories told and hear. Halves of centuries utterly unbelievably in-between.

"Like Archaic Storytellers"

"Telling my story" and speaking of "places" sometimes feels far too literal for my tastes. It is a bit too abrupt, a bit too asthmatic for me, too claustrophobic. Its closeness and closedness doesn't feel like intimacy. "This is my story." Huh. It sometimes feels like confinement rather than release.

My life isn't *inside of me.* There are lakes and trains and spaceships and finches, wild and mint. And Hegel, too, and Bill Callahan. And each one of these is itself not just itself but an ardent world of relations. Radiant beings. Illuminated.

So, to cite these lyrics, these passages, to tell these funny little stories, is to relieve me of some confine of myself, even for just a while. It is to feel myself not just experiencing, but *experienced* from afar and then, bright headlight, suddenly brought near and whooshed by into the Doppler drop of sound memory, "less stuck in the case without a vision of its soul" (Hillman, 1983, p. 28).

Eyed by the Raven at the feeder, not just birdwatching.

It is to exhale and take a breath deep of summerair seaweed and Lake Carp and flushed goldfish now orangeflash lake monsters and Burlington boy-buckets of caught smelts swimming up Rambo Creek and brought home for the rose bushes:

FIGURE 14. DJ

Those trains and memory curtains, deep yellow sunset flickers through branches of Eva and Harry's back yard trees late summer evenings. I was just a kid, picking mustard-colored rose-bugs from the peonies and doing terrible experiments in sealed jars. Life and death arced in my hands and in their squirms for escape.

And then this, written 20 years ago after my first return from Alberta back to Southern Ontario where I was raised:

> How things smell, the racket of leaves turning on their stems, how my breath pulls this humid air, how birds songs combine, the familiar directions of sudden thundery winds, the rising insect drills of cicada tree buzzes that I remember so intimately, so immediately, that when they sound, it feels as if this place itself has remembered what I have forgotten, as if my own memory, my own raising, some of my own life, is stored up in these trees for safe keeping. Cicadas become archaic storytellers telling me, like all good storytellers, of the life I'd forgotten I'd lived, of deep, fleshy, familial relations that worm their ways out of my belly and breath into these soils, these smells, this air. And I'm left shocked that they know so much, that they remember so well, and that they can be so perfectly articulate. (Jardine, 2019a, in press). Like this old thing

> Autobiography porous like
> skin webbed in deep
> Earthwater pushripples. (Jardine, 1992b, p. 40)

Остранение

> It was no thought or word that called culture into being, but a tool or a weapon. After the stone axe we needed song and story to remember innocence, to record effect—and so to describe the limits, to say what can be done without damage. (Berry, 1975/2019, p. 665)

It may be that the familiar only becomes visible and speakable in its truth once it is disrupted and thereby only once our sheer living in its embrace becomes sometimes-suddenly estranged in a rush-by of cold air under the wings of the everyday. The pop-up causes a halt of breath—*aesthesis*—and can set off a nerve shot out of neurasthenic day-dragging. It is the smell of something feral run-off into a life of its own. Energeia. Aliveness. Teenage Spaceship. I get it.

Now to follow this scent without betrayal or usurp or damage is the difficult, practical task of hermeneutics. In fact, part of this task is documenting precisely the lesson that the place teaches about such following. Seeing [*gnosis*] through [*dia*] the place is seeing the place for what it is, and not simply casting it in my own image wrought from living *in* that place. *Being in place* is not enough, and seeing through, diagnosis, is not a habitual recapitulation of the habitual, a droning, familiar repeating of the familiar, a levelling account of levelling. It is not just a meander through the old and the familiar, but a laying down of the nets and a leaving of one's family behind in order, ironically, to experience *these very matters* in proper proportion, beautifully.

In interpretive work, all this has been gathered under a phrase that, ironically, has become flat and all-too easy to toss off offhandedly: "making the familiar strange." It originated as "defamiliarizaton, "*ostranenie* (Russian: *остранение*) in a 1917 essay by Viktor Shklovsky, "Art as Technique":

> Habitualization devours works, clothes, furniture, one's wife, and the fear of war. Art exists that one may recover the sensation of life; it exists ... to make the stone *stony*. (1917/1965, p. 12)

So too with the art of interpretation. To recover the sensation of life over and against the neurasthenia of the day-to-day distraction, absorption, and exhaustion of living itself:

One of the threads of hermeneutic insight is that human consciousness tends toward a certain sleepiness and lethargy and who cares? and what difference does it Make? regarding the ancestral currents that "bear us forward in their fine, accurate arms" (Wallace, 1987, p. 49). Lethargy, *Lethe*, forgetfulness, lethality. A certain "weakness" (Greek, *astheneia*) and heaviness and blandness and flatness and closure, where potentiality, possibility, interpretability, questioning, and venture, seem not only too exhausting to contemplate but, worse yet, simply uncalled-for in light of what moribundly "is." [see Aho, 2018] It was Martin Heidegger (1962) who first gave contemporary hermeneutics hints of the numbing effects of what he called "idle talk," (p. 211 ff.) "levelling down" (p. 127) and the stitched-up-mouths effects of the "it goes without saying" and "everybody knows" and "that's life" familiarities that come from the sways of the "they-self" (p. 163 ff.):

> I take a different approach to the question of what truth, *aletheia*, or uncon-cealment, really means. I invoke the concept of *energeia* here, which has a special value because in dealing with it we are no longer moving in the realm of sentence truth. With this new conceptual word Aristotle was able to think a motion [a movement, motility, animation] ... something like life itself, like being aware, seeing, or thinking. All of these he called "pure *energeia*" (Gadamer, 2007a, p. 213)

The Hermeneutic Two-Step and Then, the Leap

First, "something awakens our interest–that is really what comes first!" (Gadamer, 2001, p. 50). I don't stop. I get *stopped* and this stop is "energizing," "enlivening." A finch in a wild mint vest flies by and I corral it in words and then see what happens next. I quote the line and let it rest a while and see if it nestles, see if it starts to sing.

And there is no method, here, no secret, other than, with practice, cultivating a certain expectancy regarding the abundance of one's living found, often, in its most mundane turns—a CD review, a lyric, an offhand comment or flit of memory, an old story retold with just enough verve to perk and awaken and induce flight:

> The whole leap depends on the slow pace at the beginning, like a long flat run before a broad jump. Anything that you want to move has to start where it is, in its stuckness. That involves erudition—probably too much erudition. One wants to get stuck in the history, the material, the knowledge, even relish it. I gobble everything up, and it gives me appetite to go on. I wouldn't really know what I want to say ... until I've eaten a lot so that my writing is part of a digesting and spitting out what other people say and getting caught by the whole complete of it. Deliberately spending time in the old place. Then suddenly seeing through the old place. (Hillman, 1991, p. 154)

This first origin of hermeneutic work is life-bound, circumstantial, non-replicable happenstance. It is also a secret of the hermeneutic art of teaching "to find that opening in each of us" (Wallace, 1987, p. 13), not by searching our persons, but by finding the open territories of the tale told that might allow each of us to open out into it and perhaps take flight a bit. Curriculum topics as living topographies, places, territories, full of energies and ways. An old idea.

Second, slowly starting to move *toward* this perking happenstance with an eye to taking it seriously and seeing where it might lead, what places it might inhabit and lead me towards. Where, if anywhere. Ground-level animal sense. Grunt work. Waiting, asking around in anticipation. Interpretation fails when it becomes a self-involved, soaring flight up and away from its starts and startles.

Most often, things trail off, scents fail. Red herrings dragged across the path. "It would not deserve the interest we take in it if it did not have something to teach us that we could not know by ourselves" (Gadamer, 1989, p. xxxv), but knowing that it might thus be deserving is a *consequence of taking it seriously* as much as it is a *cause of taking it seriously*. This is the great, intimate, contradictory, and risky first dance of hermeneutic attentiveness. Feeling the grave, detailed, livid resistance to the leap, expressing how fecund is the individual case that provides gravity to the tale being told.

Hence the risk. It might come to nothing. It might take flight. Insight might come, words might come or notes and melodies. It might, too, and just as easily, fly too high and burn up into ashes.

Amazed at the Mazes of Years

So here we go again, recorded 20 years after "Teenage Spaceship": Bill Callahan "Young Icarus," from the CD *Shepherd in a Sheepskin Vest* (2019) (Line 1–4) (https://www.youtube.com/watch?v=owpqArysd-I). Parallel lines and parallel lives.

Hovering at night for years.

I did gasp at this lyric, too, as it bypasses the all-too-familiar sun-soaring of the daytime comeuppance flight for which Icarus is well known. Icarus flew all the time at night. A bit like a Teenage Spaceship, perhaps (Callahan, 1999).

But that Icarus led a nightlife, out of sight of the sun that might tempt him too high, might tempt him to look away from the maze he was born into. This is an old reminder, a warning to those involved in the tough nails of interpretive work. An all-too-familiar life become strange, because now the too-well-known and too-well-worn, old Greek story of not aspiring too high has an unexpected howl and buzz in it: night flights, hovering, a teenage spaceship, peering downward, around and all about. Amazed at the mazes of so many years, stitching graves, feeling dark wings nearby.

It might just be Ravens writing in mid-air.

CHAPTER THIRTY-ONE

I'm Gonna Shine Out in the Wild Kindness

Bluebirds lodged in an evergreen altar.
I'm gonna shine out in the wild kindness.

DAVID BERMAN (1998), FROM "THE WILD KINDNESS"

FIGURE 15. RICTAL BLOOD

That is chin and rictal feather bloodstain. Make no mistake.
Been raw steel-feather shine-out pokes at a carcass somewhere.
No mistake. Nearby. Unmistakable. The lay dead. This Raven I've
cooed over.
Adored.
Far more than once.
Could be entrails of one of white-tails we've come to know. Taken.
No mistake. This wild kindness.
Could be that familiar mother and two daughters come round and round.
Screamed flesh on an evergreen.
Best hope is a clean kill and guts left for Ravens.

The Latin proves it. *Altare*, "for sacrifice" (OED). "The wild silence" (Berman, 1998). My heartbreak is the feel of my own noticing this is no mistake. The Raven will disappear into thin air. I will disappear into thin air.

No err, this, no mistaking this. It is why I write, one reason, anyway. That photograph is beautiful. David Berman's song is beautiful. Him struggling to remain here. He let go in 2019.

And yet there's this: Here: https://genius.com/Silver-jews-the-wild-kindness-lyrics. Here: https://www.youtube.com/watch?v=cIKVJRMv 1T4&ab_channel=usmillie. Here, the cover version that led me after David left, his friends gathered jostling singalong, green-faced funny dancing sorrows: https://www.youtube.com/watch?v=-Xug9Ty0 FD0&ab_channel=DragCity

Maybe rictal blood come from a kill by the cougar that killed our dogs.
Make no mistake. It would be wrong
if that cougar hadn't. "Four dogs in the distance.
Each stands for a kindness." (Berman, 1998)

I wish it hadn't, but then I don't. Old dog. Same trick (ref. me). I love having been caught up in that encircling burying up the hill, branch-and-leaf-covered under low spruce boughs, nose stuck out.

As cougars do.
One white foot visible.
Scavenge with no vengeance at all.
The evergreen altar has blood spills everywhere. Everywhere.

"I'm gonna shine out in the wild kindness.
And hold the world to its word." (Berman, 1998)

CHAPTER THIRTY-TWO

"Asleep in My Sunshine Chair"

Rifling through two-hundred-year-old diaries, unfurling bundles of love-letters like flowers, saying every name in an orphanage registry under my breath, getting lost in a farmer's field, gingerly lifting leaves long folded with perfumey motes, falling asleep in my sunshine chair, drooling spittle puddles onto a crackled map of Nunsmoor. The stories I stumbled across in the archives were often painful, shocking, and occasionally joyous. At first, they seem far away but after a short while they begin to move closer (or maybe it's we who are moving?) and I begin to comprehend, just barely, a great aliveness. (Dawson, 2013/2015a)

"In the Opalescent London Reek"

It was on a bitterly cold and frosty morning during the winter of 1897 that I was awakened by a tugging at my shoulder. It was Holmes. The candle in his hand shone upon his eager, stooping face and told me at a glance that something was amiss.

"Come, Watson, come!" he cried. "The game is afoot. Not a word! Into your clothes and come!"

> Ten minutes later we were both in a cab and rattling through the silent streets on our way to Charing Cross station. The first faint winter's dawn was beginning to appear ... in the opalescent London Reek.
>
> From Arthur Conan-Doyle's "The Abbey Grange"
> (Conan Doyle, 2003, pp. 1009–1010)

Kevin Aho's (2018) "Neurasthenia Revisited: On Medically Unexplained Syndromes and the Value of Hermeneutic Medicine," was a real pleasure to read—that odd scholarly pleasure of not only delicious and meticulous detail, but, with this, sensing folds of intimate, unspoken inheritances peeling back and away, almost from the inside out, almost off my hide. "The joy of recognition is the joy of knowing *more* than is already familiar" (Gadamer, 1989, p. 114) while, in the same breath, experiencing the familiar now almost-embarrassingly brought to life, enlivened, by this "more."

That this particular inheritance of neurasthenia can wake up and I can feel how it has always already "draw[n me] into its path" (Gadamer, 2007a, p. 198) is both startling and humiliating. It "begin[s] to move closer" and then suddenly jumps up, animate and feral and afoot.

I wake with a start from my sunshine chair. That neurasthenia, *of all things,* would come alive on the page—this is the root of hermeneutic pleasure and the source of its insight and curative power.

That I've been long familiar with what is wonderfully called in Old English *grevoushede* makes reading about "the deficiency or exhaustion of ... 'nerve force'" (Aho, 2018, p. 1) a bit like reading an historically detailed, almost-autobiographical reading of how my own life might have already been lived "beyond my wanting and doing" (Gadamer, 1989, p. xxviii). I can nearly imagine living in the late-19th century and understand, barely, how I might carry my own afflictions in language, expectations, ideas and images that have both fallen from contemporary view and, paradoxically, precisely the opposite. Aho's paper lays out a still-existing atmosphere in which George Beard's work (1881) and the history of the dissembling of its insights, arches in and through matters that are still alive and well.

"I begin to comprehend a great aliveness" right there in the "drooling spittle puddles" that Zoloft offers as a relief to and eventual cause of neurasthenia (1881). A good year to finally recognize that the game being afoot doesn't mean only that the alluring puzzle has arrived. It be "a-lives" on hoof or paw.

Darning Needles

I've just been writing another piece and exploring, in part, an old term used by my grandmother to name dragonflies: "darning needles." This, in fact, originates in old, shall we say, "folktales" meant, I expect, to simply frighten or reprimand:

> The devil's darning needles ... sew up the mouths of scolding women, saucy children, and profane men. Even more sinister is the belief that the devil's darning needle will enter a person's ear and penetrate the brain. (Mitchell & Lasswell, p. 20)

The reference to dragonflies and darning has to do with their hovering, crisscross, back-and-forth movement over open fields like the darning of the toes of socks that I'm old enough to recall my grandmother hunched over. Weaving. Latin *textus*, now re-read in reverie. "Dragonflies" was, for me as a child (and lingering since), enough of a name to keep me rather alert. Something about silent, quick, hovering needles, though, was a different matter. The point was received as a boy even though the folktale history was never mentioned and probably not even explicitly known, even though it haunted the tale being told. Reading about it recently wasn't exactly a surprise, and yet it was. The joy of knowing more.

I mention this because of the nebulous ways in which the images and ancestries and mixed and muddled language of the lifeworld, as Kevin Aho demonstrates, find their way down to us, more often than not, apparently (but not actually) untethered from the links that bore them here. Hence the work of hermeneutics. Many of us might have obscure memories of our forbearers talking about delicate or weak nervous conditions, of "the miseries" or the like, or, as my wife's grandmother called one malady "weakness in the body"——full of that now-strange, Victorian distancing and repression. There is even an old, apocryphal joke/non-joke about Victorians covering up bare table legs with linens for fear of offense (*The Guardian*, n.d.). That distancing that is caught in the objectifying/repressing phrase "the body" is itself a mixed and muddled sign of a sort of nervous exhaustion the remembering and naming of which moves it closer and enlivens. I find my own-most life wrapped up in elegant garb somewhat shed over the years.

To move closer and enliven. *Aletheia*. It is most difficult of all to remember that our current formulations of descendants of neurasthenia are not now closer to some pristine objective state of affairs but are themselves wrapped up in the times of their emergence. A deficiency or exhaustion of nerve force can describe the penumbras of auguring ecological disasters, of scattershot news feeds of threat and invasive others, of fake news about fake news, and on and on.

Enough. I give up. Until the next glimpse of "a great aliveness" summons me up.

Reading Aho's piece also reminded me a bit of reading Alice Miller's *For Your Own Good* (1989), and discovering already-all-too-familiar images of the punishing of willful ("saucy") children—breaking their will, darning up their mouths—found in late-19th century "black pedagogy" manuals:

> It goes without saying that pedagogues not infrequently awaken and help to swell a child's conceit by foolishly emphasizing his merits. Only humiliation can help here. (From *The Encyclopedia of Pedagogy*, 1851, as cited in Miller, 1989, p. 22)

> One of the vile products of a misguided philanthropy is the idea that, in order to obey gladly, the child has to understand the reasons why an order is given, and that blind obedience offends human dignity. I do not know how we can continue to speak of obedience once reasons are given. These [reasons] are meant to convince the child, and, once convinced, he is not obeying us but merely the reasons we have given him. Respect ... is then replaced by a self-satisfied allegiance to his own cleverness. (1852, as cited in Miller, 1989, p. 40)

I can't help but read this in light of Fredrick Taylor's insistence on obedience from his workers:

> Have you forgotten? All the children are wild. (LeGuin, 1989, p. 47)

This would have been the imaginal atmosphere in which my grand-mother and my wife's grandmother were raised and taught and thereby my parents and thereby, well, here we are. In the work I have done in with teachers and students in schools, these images are both repressed and rife even though we think of ourselves in education as encouraging precisely aliveness, independence and thoughtfulness.

A link lingers here of regarding a fear of the wild, and the need to domesticate, to tame and tether. Bubbling nearby this, of course, are the root fears of "aliveness" that have led to our current ecological cir-cumstances. It is partly this sense of "great aliveness" that also helps drive the threat-mechanisms of usurpers, invaders, hordes, borders, breaches, walls, death-threats.

The act of seeking out, summoning, and stepping *toward* aliveness, is precisely one of the goals of hermeneutic work in general. We can easily be unwittingly held fast in the binds of these ancestral tethers even though—perhaps especially when and because—they have fallen from memory, fallen from view, become sewn up and hence "unspeak-able." "Insight … always involves an escape from something that had deceived us and held us captive" (Gadamer, 1989, p. 357). It should be noted, however, that Gadamer's point is more complex than it might seem, perhaps more complex than he intended.

The deception is not that what has captured us is simply *false* and that the work of hermeneutics is to disprove something. The decep-tion is that what has captured us in nets of numbing familiarity and goes-without-saying-ness is ontologically reified into what is presumed to be simply "the way things are" (Aho does a nice job of exploring some of this in his explorations of "naturalism" and the nature of "sci-entific/biological reductionism"). It is *this capture itself* that is false—the amnesia-like forgetting, the sleepy taken-for-granted-ness that can lead to believing, for example, that only a biological/medical description is a description of *what is*. The deceit is in thinking that what is in fact a *pos-sible way of giving an account of some phenomenon* is not only *necessary* (i.e., simply "what is," simply "objective") but precisely thereby *exclusionary* of all other ways of making sense of our suffering.

That is the captivity that hermeneutic insight aims to free us from. In that freedom, biological and naturalistic accounts do not disappear in favor of "lived-experience." Rather, these very accounts finally appear as just and precisely that: *accounts of our lives* that arise in relations of dependent co-arising with specific and identifiable domains our language, our hopes, our presumptions, our time, and in light of inherited regimes of methodology, warrant and accountability.

Energeia and Aletheia

Noam Chomsky: Kids are ready for it. They just have to pay attention. Most people just don't pay attention. Because they think everything's hopeless—I mean, it's kind of driven into your head, that everything is hopeless, there's nothing you can do, the power's too great. Some of the most effective kinds of propaganda are the kinds that allow you to see what's going on, but you feel "I can't do anything about it. I'm isolated. I'm alone. I don't talk to anybody [about it]. People like me can't do anything. We just have to suffer, bear it." That's really effective propaganda. That's how slavery lasted for so long. It is how women were oppressed. Let's take my grandmother's generation. If my grandmother had been asked if she's oppressed, she wouldn't even have known what you are talking about. "That's life." For a lot of young people, it's called "apathy," but I suspect that it's more "hopelessness," "powerlessness." (Chomsky, 2017)

Young people want to know if, under the cool and calm of efficient teaching and excellent time-on-task ratios, life itself has a chance, or whether the surface is all there is. (D.G. Smith, 2020, p. 405)

This is always a double-helix—reading these words can both confirm my worst fears and, in the very same breath, relieve me of my feelings of isolation. Someone understands. Some else has seen it, named it. There are companions on those steps with that sign about the future.

The surface. Flat. We just have to suffer it. I can't do anything. It's too much. Hopeless. Powerless. Isolation. Neurasthenia.

So, in reading Aho's work, something popped up that I have found to be perennial in hermeneutic work: that the *topic* of a hermeneutic study (in this case, the long and involved, live-wire history of neurasthenia), and something about the *nature of hermeneutic understanding itself* tend to have an often-secret affinity. I can only sketch some speculative ideas, here, and beg forgiveness in this regard. I am on the verge of being guilty of avoiding precisely the sort of exemplary and careful work found in Kevin Aho's work that led me here in the first place.

One of the threads of hermeneutic insight is that human consciousness tends toward a certain sleepiness and lethargy and who cares? And what difference does it Make? Regarding the ancestral currents that "bear us forward in their fine, accurate arms" (Wallace, 1987, p. 49). Lethargy, *Lethe*, forgetfulness, lethality. A certain "weakness" (Greek, *astheneia*) and heaviness and blandness and flatness and closure, where potentiality, possibility, interpretability, questioning, and venture, seem not only too exhausting to contemplate but, worse yet, simply uncalled-for in light of what moribundly "is." It was Martin Heidegger (1962) who first gave contemporary hermeneutics hints of the numbing effects of what he called "idle talk," (p. 211 ff.) "levelling down" (p. 127) and the stitched-up-mouths effects of the "it goes without saying" and "everybody knows" and "that's life" familiarities that come from the sways of the "they-self" (p. 163 ff.).

This sway can easily catch hold of those involved in interpretive work itself. It sometimes comes coupled with replete irony and condescension, tongue-clucking at those caught in the webs, with little self-recognition of how irony and condescension are themselves anesthetic, numbing, distancing, one more attachment to the very thing one wishes to supplant with insight, love, affection, aliveness.

In light of such interpretive weakness and weakening, the world itself seems precisely equally not in need of my own interpretive energetics. As with depression, this is not merely an internal pathology or state, but is experienced as precisely in sync with a depressed world that has no openings, no hidden bloodlines and memory. Given the time-lines sketched by Kevin Aho, it is no coincidence that the term *Weltschmerz* (German, literally "world pain" or "world weariness") was rife around 1900. As James Hillman (2006a, p. 30; see Jardine, 2016i, pp. 167–172) put it so deftly, "sickness is now 'out there'" and any attempts to then simply turn "inwards" and cure ourselves of our grievousness can end up leaving in place an objectified codification of our suffering in the ways and means of the world itself. This was the great insight of existentialism, the great breakthrough and the great error all at once, that once we concede a sick world, the only recourse is the existential subject set off in its own dire, self-determining isolation. And then, of course, and as a consequence of this withdrawal from the world, the world gets worse. As James Hillman (and Michael Ventura, 1992) put it, *We've had a Hundred Years of Psychotherapy and the World's Getting Worse.*

Just to complicate these matters, Kevin Aho notes that, in *American nervousness, its causes and consequences: A supplement to nervous exhaustion (neurasthenia)* (1881, p. vi), George Beard states this: "neurasthenia is not the result of some new organic pathology but of *'modern civilization* [itself]'" (Aho, 2018, p. 2). (More on this in the Afterword to this Chapter).

So, when we then read "Neurasthenia Revisited: On Medically Unexplained Syndromes and the Value of Hermeneutic Medicine" we can start to sense that those very closures (of our own pathology *and* the closure that the world itself invites and promotes and sustains) are themselves open to interpretation, and to the slow unwinding of ancestral threads, of live bloodlines, of movement instead of "sedimented" intransigency and inertness:

> To use the hermeneutic adage, the world has become open to interpretation [to *exactly* the extent that I am open to the interpretability of the world]. And here is the great, seemingly paradoxical situation: "keeping ourselves open" and "keeping the world open" (Eliade, 1968, p. 139) are the same thing. As we become experienced, having cleaved with affection and made ourselves "roomier," the world's roominess can be experienced. (Jardine et al., 2008, p. 53; cited in Jardine, 2016a, p. 81)

Even the insistent reductionism of naturalism is itself an old wive's tale oft told and retold, often precisely as a condescending rebuke to the sauciness, the scolding, the profanity, that can seem to come with hermeneutic insight.

And hence the great irony, that the opening of such burgeoning alertness regarding neurasthenia is *precisely* what tends to fail under the shadowed suffering of neurasthenia itself. That is why, in reading Kevin Aho's piece, I found myself searching out this:

> I take a different approach to the question of what truth, *aletheia*, or uncon-
> cealment, really means. I invoke the concept of *energeia* here, which has a
> special value because in dealing with it we are no longer moving in the
> realm of sentence truth [to which reductionist and naturalistic means and
> measures might apply]. With this new conceptual word Aristotle was able to
> think a motion [a movement, motility, animation] ... something like life itself,
> like being aware, seeing, or thinking. All of these he called "pure *energeia*."
> (Gadamer, 2007a, p. 213)

In an alternate translation, Sheila Ross (2006, p. 108) renders part of
this passage as "something like aliveness itself" and she links it directly
to the sort of whiling or "tarrying time" (p. 108; see Jardine, 2008; Ross
& Jardine, 2009) requisite of interpretive work. As Aho's piece shows,
lingering intently over this long and long-buried history with the sort
of loving suspicion of interpretive insight wakes it up and simultaneously wakes up in us our deeply suppressed complicity in its wakes. "It
is only through these shared self-interpretations that we can experience
and make sense of our suffering" (Aho, 2018, p. 12) and, I suggest, this
very commiserate sense-making is itself something of an alleviation of
precisely that which it studies. And this is true of any topic of hermeneutic interest, even though it is especially apt in this particular case.
With the interpretive study of *any* topic, the topic draws near, and we
and it are enlivened in a single, affectionate gesture. This gives a hint of
why and how hermeneutic insight has an especial affinity to pedagogy,
because its work is precisely centered on the enlivening arrival of the
new in the midst of the world grown old and numbed.

It is not just that we can counterweight the reductionist and naturalistic accounts of our ennui with those of living accounts of those living
with such matters. In interpretive work, as Aho's piece demonstrates
so vividly, *those very reductionist and naturalistic accounts themselves*
come alive. They are not just the inert, dominant accounts of "what is."
Instead, we see that *they themselves* have dependently co-arisen out of
(and into) our living, in response to circumstances and streams and
forces and hopes and desires. (Again, see the Afterword below).

"They begin to move closer," just as we, now, are moving. Reifying
reductionism into feigns and sought-for objective permanence is thus
foregone in favor of arising and perishing, since even our confidence in

and need for such reification comes and goes. "Gadamer explains [that] Aristotle apparently coined [*energiea*] in his exploration of the question of the being of becoming" (Ross, 2006, p. 107).

Suffering Itself Is Impermanent

As you continually experience whatever suffering is appropriate to you, you absolutely must know how to bring it into the path. If you accept the suffering, you let the basic suffering be and do not stop it, but you never have the suffering of worry that creates discontentment when you focus on the basic suffer. Since you are using a method to bring even basic sufferings into the path, you greatly lessen your suffering, so you can bear it. (Tsong-kha-pa, 2004, pp. 172–173)

The *energeia* that comes from the interpretive venture is not just a way to study one's *grevoushede* through studying the dependent co-arising of its ins and outs and the intimate body auras of its licks and shifts and crisscrossing darts and darnings. Interpreting it can also help ameliorate it to some small degree. Even my own decision to not use the phrase "seasonal affective disorder" and to come to deliberately call it, instead, "seasonal affectedness" allowed me, in some small way, to sidestep or at least deliberately and consciously interrupt the pathologies of disorder and to more deeply experience how *profoundly* well-ordered is this seasonal affectedness. "Disorder" was simply an added layer of, following Tsong-kha-pa, a sort of "secondary suffering" that, in fact, masked and occluded the "basic suffering" and did not allow it to be brought onto the path of interpretation, the path, that is, of un-reifying its grip on me and my grip on it.

Key to hermeneutic work, then, is that "the concept of substance [permanence, the A=A of objectivism and reductionism] is ... inadequate. [There is a] radical challenge to thought implicit in this inadequacy" Gadamer (1989, p. 242). Part of the challenge to thought is that grief and suffering themselves, like depression or nervous exhaustion, have no substance, only emergent and re-emergent causes and conditions of dependent co-arising.

From Robert Bly (n.d., p. 11): "Grief is not a permanent state; it is a room with a door on the other wall."

Our relation to grief is an "infinite task" (George, 2017) taken on by a finite being. But this is not because grief is permanent but precisely because *it isn't*. It is, rather, perennial, seasonal in its affectedness. Go through the door on the other wall and, sure enough, another waiting room in which things will once again accrete, forgetting will again accrue, and then, also sure enough, Coyote will rustle in the bushes outside (see Beamer, 2017) and the whole thing, all over again, will jump up unexpectedly when something just happens to happen, slobbering spittle on your face and then biting down hard and fast into the quick of memory.

Welcome. Again. This is the tough work of hermeneutic insight:

The First Noble Truth is all about accepting or welcoming unsatisfactoriness or suffering (*dukkha*) rather than trying to resist it. You will notice then that its nature is to change and drop away. (Sumedho, 2010, p. 37)

It drops away, arises, drops away, *providing* we remain, as steadfastly as we can, ready to escape its capture all over again.

Escaping its capture does not mean that it will simply disappear and I'll be "cured" or "saved" or "redeemed." It means, well, don't sit too long in that sunshine chair, but if you do, enjoy the sunny sleep and spittle drooling over a "crackled map of Nunsmoor," only to be startled all over again by aliveness, nearing.

Afterword

[George] Beard [in *American nervousness, its causes and consequences: A supplement to nervous exhaustion (neurasthenia)*, 1881] attributed the rise of neurasthenia both to a hereditary predisposition as well as the wrenching social upheavals of modernization in the United States at the end of the nineteenth century, as large swaths of the post-Civil War population migrated from slow-paced rural communities to chaotic and bustling cities in the Northeast. Beard also cited new technologies of industrialization such as the periodical press, the telegraph, telephone, and steam engine, as well as the ubiquity of mechanical clocks and watches that "compel us to be on time and excite the habit of looking to see the exact moment" (p. 103). These factors, taken together, contributed the excessive strain on mental and physical life, and help explain Beard's claim that the "chief and primary cause" of neurasthenia is not the result of some new organic pathology, but of "modern civilization [itself]" (p. vi). (Aho, p. 2)

In the early twentieth century, schooling was ripe for the arrival of the efficiency movement as proposed by Fredrick Winslow Taylor (1903, 1911), whose images of industrial assembly took educational reform by storm (see Raymond Callahan's now-classic [1964] detailing of this [still ongoing] storm in *America, education and the cult of efficiency*; see Ayres, 1915; Boyle, 2006; Braverman, 1998; Cubberley, 1922; Dufour & Eaker, 1998; Gatto, 2006; Friesen & Jardine, 2009; Kanigel, 2005; Wrege & Greenwood, 1991). As with the worker on Taylor's assembly line (here cited from one of his lectures from June 4, 1906), ideally one is aiming for a situation in which "we do not ask for the initiative of our men. We do not want any initiative. All we want of them is to obey the orders we give them, do what we say, and do it quickly" (cited in Kanigel, 2005, p. 169). The worldly correlate to such obedience and, so to speak, "disinitiative," is to require of the worker the doing of an increasingly narrow and meagre task, one that *does not require* initiative but obedience, not only to what is to be done but to precisely how, when and for how long it is to be done. "What [Taylor] really wanted working men to be [is] focused [to use the language of education, "task oriented"], uncomplicated and compliant" (Boyle, 2006); parallel to this, the world inhabited by the worker at the same time becomes degraded, retarded, ugly and demeaning. (Jardine, 2016i, pp. 171–172)

Thus, in a great and predictable cascade occurs, where school tasks, as per the conditions of the "exact moment[ness]" of "modern civilization" render the work at hand as something that needs no initiative (and therefore *requires* and *rewards* a sort of neurasthenia), so, too, does "initiative" itself become pathologized:

When this shadow falls over schools, even if initiative and interest might accidentally rear up in the midst of the endless lines of disconnected, meaningless, rote work, there is, so to speak, nowhere (no "where," no "field") in the world of such a classroom that might warrant or reward or embrace such rearing up. In fact, the opposite becomes true. A world of bits and pieces under managerial surveillance *rejects* and *rebukes* rearing up. Initiative becomes a *detriment* to efficiency. The rearing up of initiative and interest becomes subjectivized into a *property of the restless student* and not at all something called for by the work at hand. Such rearing only meets reprimand for its interrupting of the uniform movement of "the line" (Jardine, 2016i, p. 172).

Thus, initiative itself ("kids these days"), not only its lack (again, "kids these days"), is ripe, under the conditions of "modern civilization," for medicalization. Haunts of Alice Miller's (1989) ghosts of wild and willful children all over again. We can only speculate how a deficit in one's attention is produced by the alienating fragmentation of the world, each fragment of which brooks no sustained attention and only compels one to get on to the next screen flickering. This becomes an odd after-image of industrialization. "For the machine, time is always running out" (Berry, 1983, p. 76):

> One [phrase] every foreman had to learn in English, German, Polish, and Italian [and now Hindi, Urdu, Arabic, Mandarin, and others] was "hurry up." (Cited in Watts, 2006, p. 154)

In the resultant atmosphere of machine-consciousness that constituted "modern civilization," even our efforts to "connect" and "stay in touch" suffer the surface flicker flicking by, inducing a sense of acceleration, of always missing out on something no matter how often you check, thus thinning the surface of attention again, leading to the atrophying of the skill and art of attention itself, leading to thinning, to skittering. "It is not an accident that Buddhists call the world and it's suffering a 'wheel'" (Jardine, 2016g, p. 225).

Just as lack of initiative was medicalized into, among other things, brain chemistry, so, to was aliveness itself summoned to a similar fate. Initiative, questioning, studying, seeking to break the moribund surface story are seen as equally problematic:

> In an essay written about 1908 and entitled "Why Manufacturers Dislike College Students," Taylor would observe that college-educated engineers were so spoiled by interesting studies, by the sheer pleasure of learning ...

that shop life almost always disappointed them. Better to stick them in a shop for a year right from the start. "They then begin to learn the greatest lesson of life, that almost nine tenths of the work that every man has to do is monotonous, tiresome and uninteresting. They then start to develop the character which enables them to do unpleasant, disagreeable things." (Kanigel, 2005, pp. 138–139)

I have to say, on the way by, that I have heard similar arguments made regarding enthusiastic student-teachers who are entering the profession. I recall more than one "experienced" teacher insisting that they, too, were enthusiastic when they started out in the profession.

So, here is the non-hermeneutic question: is neurasthenia "really" a medical condition, now even a brain-chemical, serotonin-related matter, or is its cause "really" "modern civilization?" Hermeneutics, frustrating to many, has no answer to this question. It asks a far more terrifying cluster of questions: what might be at stake, who might profit, what might be lost and gained in these alternatives?

More pointedly is the current ecological nightmare that surrounds our "aliveness"—the conditions under which it might cease to be sustainable. Let me put it this way. Let's us practice a hermeneutic commonplace in its attempts to understand our circumstances. *Think, for a moment, just how very much would loom up if we let ourselves believe that "modern civilization" is the cause of our current woes.* What would this ask of us? What would we forfeit and gain? Can I bear it?

It is little wonder George Beard's original speculation about "modern civilization" being the cause of neurasthenia was not able to stand as a summons to thinking and action. Think of the unbearable weight of current ecological insight into the effects of "modern civilization" and the near-neurasthenic that can repeatedly loom up when we hear of it. It had better not be that little wonder is all we are left with.

I end with thanks to Kevin Aho once again for opening up this ambiguous, inherited pathway nearly lost to memory but felt more intimately than labored breath itself.

CHAPTER THIRTY-THREE

Quickening, Patience, Suffering

A New Preface, 2019

"The Cruelty Is the Point" Adam Serwer. *The Atlantic* October 3, 2018. Online: https://www.theatlantic.com/ideas/archive/2018/10/the-crue lty-is-the-point/572104/

"The Cruelty Is the Point." David French. *National Review*. June 7, 2019. Online: https://www.nationalreview.com/corner/the-cruelty-is-the-point/

It is essential to understand that the suffering caused by a form of schooling premised on breakdown is not a *personal matter* even though the suffering experienced is often profoundly personal and intimate. This is one of the greatest and most pernicious lies that issues from breakdown: that issuance of a sense of isolated, individual malaise geared to simply deepening one's mire in the throes of breakdown and tightening its grip. Breakdown leaves us with silence and a suffering [and a form of resigned obedience] that cannot possibly lead to commiseration, since precisely any sense of a community of work and obligation is precisely what has been effaced [made irretriev-ably suspicious in advance—it is the irretrievability that is killing us]. Even though the consequences of breakdown are deeply and intimately felt, and the pathologies of suffering and violence and paranoia that breakdown engenders are right in the melancholic faces of many teachers and students … what is needed is a seeking out of the origins of such matters. The origins of such suffering (and therefore a clue to the uprooting of such origins) are historical, philosophical, ancestral, culturally rooted, economically and industrially underwritten *inheritances* that have been handed to teachers and students in schools. (Jardine, 2008c, pp. xiii–xiv)

Schools have been transformed into huge zero-sum games, monolithic delivery systems in which every gain for one turns into a loss or burden for another, while true satisfactions is denied to both. (Illich, 1996, p. 27)

The contemporary conservative attack on public education, desiring to make education accountable to a transcendentalized market logic rather than to liberal/modernist ideas, is indirectly a way of securing the kind of psychology necessary for the preservation of the militarist state itself. If market logic is constructed on principles of competition, comparative advantage, victimization of the weak, and the commodification of everyday life, then the *management* of this particular universal ideal, pedagogically speaking, can only be brutal. It turns schools and classrooms into places where winner and losers are determined, not on the basis of ability *per se*, but on the basis of particular abilities necessary for success within the market, such as physical attractiveness (especially for women), personal aggression, contempt for the weak and so on. (D.G. Smith, 2020e, p. 233)

Quickening, Patience, Suffering: A Fortuitous Email Exchange

Jodi [Latremouille]: Hi, David, I was reading *The Spell of the Sensuous* (Abram, 1996) and was reminded of that paper you sent us a couple of weeks ago. There is a passage about the Australian Aboriginal tradition of "songlines" or "ways through" the continent, meandering trails, auditory route maps that are composed of a melody with various verses to be sung in different locations. It speaks of the Dreamtime Ancestors, while chanting their ways across the land, depositing a trail of "spirit children" along the trail. They are described as "life cells," children not yet born; they lie in a potential state within the ground. When a woman is pregnant, the actual conception is thought to occur with the quickening, when she steps on a song couplet in the earth. So the spirit child "works its way into her womb, and impregnates the fetus with song."

> Wherever the woman find herself when she feels the quickening- the first kick within her womb- she knows that a spirit child has just leapt into her body from the earth. And so she notes the precis place in the land where the quickening occurred, and reports this to the tribal elders. The elders then examine the land at that spot, discerning which Ancestor's songline was involved, and precisely which stanzas of that Ancestor's song will belong to the child … In this manner every Aboriginal person, at birth, inherits a particular stretch of song as his private property, a stretch of song that is, as it were, his title to a stretch of land, to his conception site. (Abram, 1996, pp. 166–167)

I woke up this morning way too early and couldn't go back to sleep! Maybe if I send you this, I can sleep again :-)

David: Well, I woke up this morning thinking of that paper and how I might either finish it or abandon it again for now. This almost reminds me of what Abram is describing—this fortuitous email just leapt! And that that leap is an ancestral one in its own way—what quickens is not just this life but also the lead lines of song that bear it here. And, as with much of my writing, it reminds me too of Hillman's passage, and Tsong-kha-pa's which are the headers of that paper, about patience.

To Begin, Singing

There's another word for objectivity, which I feel is much better, and that is "patience." Suffering with it.

> James Hillman, from *Lament of the Dead*. (Hillman & Shamdasani, 2013, p. 156)

It is very crucial that you generate the patience that accepts suffering.
> Tsong-kha-pa, from Volume Two of *The Great Treatise on the Stages of the Path to Enlightenment*. (2004, pp. 172–173)

This title term "quickening" is an apt image for something that is phenomenologically recognizable in hermeneutic work—that moment of suddenness, when an idea comes alive and starts to become full of a *life of its own*. It is an apt term because it designates the deep ontology of hermeneutic work: that we live in a living world whose life is, in turns, generated and degenerated, renewed, transformed, handed over, ailing, near death, newly born, occluded, woken up and fast asleep. And this points to something evident in the work of an alert classroom—that beautiful and difficult and often sudden arrival, when students and teachers alike lean inwards toward a topic, a topography, a place, and feel life rising up in and through its song lines.

Its lives.

Our lives.

It lives and so do we, now, again, caught in its new radiance.

Hermeneutic work is both the "furthering of an event that goes far back" (Gadamer, 1989, p. xxiv) and the embracing of the new such that that furthering and those events henceforth appear differently that we could have heretofore imagined. Both of these insights must be held together—like David G. Smith's (2020, p. 406) image of "living in the belly of a paradox" wherein the child, the new, the arrival, arrives as "both part of us and apart from us." This is why quickening quickens us, because we recognize ourselves in its stirring even though it is not me stirring but rather me being stirred. The purpose of hermeneutic work is not to solve this as if it were an error, but to find ways to abide this ever-just-arriving irresolvable and make it, once again, livable.

Upstartings gone beyond startles to become "possible ways of shaping our lives" (Gadamer, 1986 p. 59). Tough work, this going beyond.

This tough work bespeaks the especial affinity between hermeneutic work and pedagogy.

It summons, too, Jacque Derrida's image of the Seder table's empty chair, awaiting, biding, leaned forward into a future's portend with "hospitality for what is to come [*avenir*]" (Derrida & Ferraris, 2001, p. 31).

A Grade Three teacher and I wrote a piece on the work she did with her class on the paintings of Van Gogh, and his frequent use of the image of an "empty chair." We found deep water there, as did the children themselves. One student wrote:

The sad and lonely chair sits alone in a cold and empty room. The only warmth is a little smokeless pipe. So as the chair sits alone with still only a little warmth, the chair waits for something. But what is it? It still waits for the moment, that moment that the chair thinks will never come. The brick floor gives a chill in the air. The chair still sits by the door, waiting for the moment. But the door doesn't budge. Days pass, but everything is still. Still as a rock. So everything goes like this day after day after day. This goes on and nobody sits on the chair. Nobody even notices the chair and that's how it will stay. (Cited in Jardine & Batycky, 2016, p. 108)

The responses Jennifer received when she showed some other teachers were well-meant and predictable:

"Nathan is so thoughtful. He always says the most amazing things." "What grade did you say you teach?" "You are so lucky. I could never do that with the children in my class. They just aren't capable." "Nathan is really gifted. He really ought to be tested." "Well, how are you going to extend this child's learning now? Perhaps he should have an opportunity to take his own writing and create his own picture." (p. 109)

When David [Jardine] came into the class later that week, I asked Nathan to read his work to him. They went out into a quiet spot in the hall, and after reading his work to David, Nathan said "He's buried next to his brother, you know." (pp. 109–110)

Jennifer and I became lost in the wilds of Dutch Calvinism and its ban of certain iconographies. We spoke in detail about how she cover the walls of her classroom with reproduction of artists, surrounded the children with what seemed like a surround of stained glass windows. A lovely parallel to explorations with Michelle Bastock, a teacher in a Catholic schools, on how children's books are rife with illustrations, but education leans toward thinking of them merely as "supports" for learning the text itself, this being, of course, a deep delve of Protestantism (Jardine & Bastock, 2005).

Part of us and apart from us. This "apart from us" is a locale of great trauma and joy in hermeneutic work as well as the work of pedagogy—an experience of an "other," asking us to be other-wise. We could not experience it as apart from us if it were not part of us and us part of it. Paradox. Belly laugh in recognition.

Such giddy composure is both "the path and the goal" (Gadamer, 1989, p. 180):

> It's like making a path through the forest. At first it's rough going, with a lot of obstructions, but returning to it again and again, we clear the way. After a while the ground becomes firm and smooth from being walked on repeatedly. Then we have a good path for walking in the forest. (Chah, 2005, p. 83)

Quickening: "*it* draws *you* into *its* path" (Gadamer, 2007a, p, 198, emphases added).

Quickening thus bespeaks the quick of it, that, even though all this work of mine on some particular topography of the world has set out the conditions of possible insight—all the reading, thinking, writing, exploration, repeated mulls and conversations, transcriptions, finding citations and etymologies and dates and names and places, copying things out by hand, falling in love with an image or recoiling into thick nickel-spittle fear and inaction in the face of it, receiving emails and waking up singing unexpectedly, looking and looking through literature, writing things and reading them aloud and scratching them out, revising, rejecting, trying again, reading things to others, trying to memorize phrases and finding these phrases in the voices and faces of those I meet day to day, hoping they will say just the right thing that I need to break the spell, clear the way, or whatever that hesitant block might be called—the breakthroughs and disappointments, and, often, leaving the work behind, for now, in sad abandonment, filed away like a corpse in a cold drawer, darkened and chilled for possible later exhumation, sickened by this thing I'm trying to write, wanting to get away from it, failure, the dark valleys of shadows and death ... *all of this* suffered roiling only makes insight *possible* not *necessary*. There is no *necessary* pedagogy to such suffering.

Teachers know this, that the plan does not assuredly *cause* the quick of arrival and engagement. Teachers know this weird gap—like a silence in a songline, suspended—and, if they become experience, they learn the painful less of how to not panic over it. A great trial with its own sufferings.

Patience, here, is necessary but it never ensures.

"I am willing to endure the shame of falling short as the price of admission" (Berry & Moyers, 2013)—over and over to stand failed in the face of the work I undertake, "outplayed" (Gadamer, 1989, p. 106) all over again.

A hermeneutic secret, then, that my failure to measure up to the work I do is a sign of why *its* success is not *mine*, a sign of how the child must outrun its forbearers if it is to have a quickened life of its own and how, paradoxically again, my success in such matters is found in precisely this failure. This is part of the careful suffering at the heart of teaching, that students get up and walk away, just like my own child has done, and how this necessarily leaves me haunted by his death even though he is alive and kicking.

Even in walking away, these young things then walk amid song-lines. Thus, caring, in hermeneutics, for the well-being of these lines is my only comfort. It is how the suffering of such matters might just be Noble.

Might be—that "might" is why compassion is always necessary and why sorrow (German, *Sorge*, translated in the work of Martin Heidegger [1962] as "care") always necessarily ensues upon the joy of quickening. This is why the hermeneutic affection for quickening must learn to be about love and not attachment, about compassion, not rescue.

Again, all of this roiling work only makes insight *possible* not *necessary*. This gap between the possible and the necessary cannot be bridged by an act of will, by methodologism, or by increases in funding or earnestness or drive. This bridging, if it happens, "happens to us over and above our wanting and doing" (Gadamer, 1989, p. xxvii):

> The whole leap depends on the slow pace at the beginning, like a long flat run before a broad jump. Anything that you want to move has to start where it is, in its stuckness. That involves erudition—probably too much erudition. One wants to get stuck in the history, the material, the knowledge, even relish it. Deliberately spending time in the old place. Then suddenly seeing through the old place. (Hillman, 1991, p. 154)

And oh, the tales that can be told of being simply stuck seemingly endlessly in that old place (that, too, is quite a topic). Just like this chapter that has taken *so* long—it's taking its own sweet time tastes bitter sometimes. Just like me repeated the citation of that quote *yet again*. Like re-playing an old 45 used to be.

But here is the hermeneutic hope. There can be a moment when the effect outruns such efforts and causes, such erudition and history and material, such relish. It is a moment when *the outcome becomes uncaused by the efforts to cause it*, when it becomes, in the old Latin coinage, *causa sui*, something generated within itself, something with a "life of its own," literally, from the Latin, something that is the cause of itself. Until this happens, I do not have a topic for the work I am doing, only frail and patient suffering and scuttling around in stuckness.

Quickening, with all the startled witlessness that comes with it in the act of composing a text, when it rises up of its own accord and I am asked to act accordingly. I become a follower, a guardian, a cautioner, full of affection for something now both part of me but apart, it stood turned facing me now, full of "the … intrusive power of a being reposing in itself" (Gadamer, 1977, p. 227). I become an object of *its* quick regard ("it would not deserve the interest we take in it if it did not have something to teach us that we could not know by ourselves" [Gadamer, 1989, p. xxxv]).

I become the outcome and *it* becomes the cause. It seeks to outcome me, to make me and my words and actions into what it needs. Now I must marshal what I know, what skill I've gained, what experiences I've gleaned, what practices I've practiced, what patience I've tested, and bring them as offerings to this meeting of the afoot quick:

> If one pursues a hermeneutic study, it is not enough to write about different things. I must also write differently, in a way that acknowledges, attends and waits upon the agency of the world. Hermeneutics is therefore akin to the opening up of "animating possibilities presented by each event" (Hillman, 1983, p. 77). Hermeneutic writing is premised on the eventful ("understanding proves to be an event" [Gadamer, 1989, p. 309]) arrival of animating spirit. This is why its name is the name of a god of arrival, of youth, of fecundity and fertility and agency. It is premised on the belief in a resonant, animate world, full of voices and spooks and spirits which require a form of attention that extends beyond one' s self, out into the living ways of things. It is premised on the arrival of the young boy Hermes, flitting and flirting. Hermeneutics represents a conversation with the old borne on the breath and in the face

of "the new, the different, the true" (Gadamer, 1977, p. 9). This is not precisely a leap that I do, even though I must prepare myself through immersing
myself in the voices of the ancestors, spend time in the old place. And then,
"the leap"—some insight arrives, it seems, from elsewhere, a "provocation"
(Gadamer, 1989, p. 299) carrying its own agencies and consequences and
desires. "To understand … hermeneutically is to trace back what is said to
what wishes to be said" (Grondin, 1994, p. 32)—just imagine, things *wishing*
to be said. (Jardine, 2008a, p. 110)

What do you want from me? And what will become of me if I concede
to this urging? And, perhaps most telling, what is the right thing to
do, now, here, in this turn of a sentence? It is thus that such quickening
is linked to the fact that I, as one trying to compose myself in the face
of such quickening, must now suffer its arising. Trying then to settle
myself and compose in the face of these arising and quickening topics
is, in part, trying to figure out what attention I now owe this arrival.
I owe these topics something of my life because they are already intimate parts of that very life (part and apart), some of its organs and
blood, some of its memory and regret and sudden joy.

This is a deeply ecological occurrence, this recognition that my
life is in debt to the surroundings and territories and topographies of
its emergence, and that my research is, in this sense, always already
underwritten, already "funded" (Latin *fundus* meaning, among other
things, "piece of land").

An Elongated Political and Ecological Chorus

The concoctions that are beneficial to the rich and powerful, they'll tend to
propagate. The ones that are harmful to the rich and powerful tend to be
marginalized and suppressed. But that has nothing to do with the reality of
the world. That has to do with how power systems function. (Chomsky, 2017).

What becomes of the function of education within the state? Insofar as market logic determines the value of *all* social practices, only forms of education that serve the market have value. Hence the recommendation of Hon.
Mike Harris, Premier of Ontario, at the beginning of Hayekian reforms in
that province in 1989: "The humanities should be removed from the university, since they serve no economic benefit." More recently, the *Social Sciences*

and Humanities Research Council of Canada (2009) has passed policies that give priority funding to proposals that directly serve the interests of the business community. (D.G. Smith, 2020f, p. 379)

This matter of a quickening that arrives over and above those things that cause it causes institutions to "waver and tremble" (Caputo, 1987, p. 1) and often respond with disdain and condescension because such institutions are premised, perhaps inevitably, on the market-accountabilities of causation. Unfunded research has become a suspicious waste of time in the Faculty I am now leaving. Rarely a minute goes by without the marshaling workshops to increase the chances of getting grants, getting published, and on and on. Equally rarely does anyone feel that there is any time at all to talk about the territories we are researching—*what is being thought about* rather than the *fact* that it is funded. Flippantly put, if it is funded, *it doesn't matter what it is about*. It is already deemed worthwhile because, in advance, the only object worth whiling over is funding. All of this is premised, of course, on the neo-liberal movements of withdrawing public funds for public work, a fetish for the individualistic privatization of scholarship which equates with linking it to market-economic productivities and outcomes. Faculties are now underfunded, so they need external funding. But such externality then feeds the atrophying of the *fundus* of the work itself in favor of its productivity of its outcomes.

Without external funding, scholarship is simply time wasted. Mal-lingering.

Just now, in writing this, overhearing (March 22, 2014, 2 p.m. EST) the Premier of Ontario, Kathleen Wynne said at a Liberal Caucus Annual meeting, "in government, impatience is a virtue." "Time is always running out for machines. They shorten our work … by simplifying it and speeding it up, but our work perishes quickly" (Berry, 1983, p. 76). We are instructed to erase any references in our reference lists that are older than 5 years, because such matters are considered "out of date." Under such auspices, songlines and our blood relation to them are *deliberately being cut*. Their memory traces and language are deliberately being suppressed, marginalized, and ridiculed—too wild and out of view of productivity surveillances and accountabilities—as we rush, instead, into work that is premised on outdated-ness as its deliberate goal. Our work is deliberately designed to not last, to not mature and age well but simply become disposed of in favor of what's next—the fetish for the new, so odd, as we both recoil from the wild and summon new arrivals at accelerating rates. That is why there is a great analog, here, to First Nations lamentations and hopes, to ecological nightmares. Thus, too, the great bullying of market consciousness—when Xi Jinping was announced as the new President of the Peoples' Republic of China, the Canadian Broadcasting Corporation introduced him in its radio broadcast as the new leader of the world's largest *economy*. And, too distraction becomes the requisite mood whereby a low-level panic is maintained just enough to propel insatiable consumption and production. Satiation, of course, would spell the end of the spell. There must be no "development of the concept of *enough*" (Berry, 1983, p. 79).

A Side-note on an Iatrogenic Loop

There is a reason that Buddhists call this world and the delusions that sustain it a Wheel. We find, here, a terrible, heartbreaking loop, where the attempts to ameliorate our troubled situation are suddenly seen to be its causes. Fear of arising leads to panic setting in, and once panic sets in, procedures, rubrics, mandates and methodologies rush in, in good-hearted attempts to save the day, further foreclosing on future quickenings and further confirming the fear of arising that set this sequence in motion in the first place. Hence "outcomes based education" and ever-louder calls for "teacher accountability" that are *causing the panics for which they are touted as the cure*, with little or no consciousness of there being ancestral songlines that lie buried under these scurrying surface loops. We then seek relief inside the very loops that cause us to seek relief, unable to decode our circumstances because we've lost track of what might bring relief outside of this loop.

The loop is experienced to be all there is and the promises to "fix" education with this or that or this skitter and skip across consciousness like stones on water. Many teachers I know correctly sense that there is "something else going on" here, but memory has been lost. Meditating on these matters and singing over them is deemed impractical because, of course, we don't have the time, not here, "in the real world." As one teacher noted in a recent class, if you just nebulously sense this iatrogenic loop but have no way of unraveling its spell, if all you have is an ever-new sense of "trouble" with no songline recourses, all you can do is complain. This is why our relationship to the culture of complaint that ravages many schools must be one of love and affection for those suffering from the forestalling of quickening, from the disparaging of patience and the cultivation of "the old place," from the loss of any memory of what has been done to us. The complaint is correct ("something is going on") but incorrect (it feeds on uneasy without recourse to study, composure, practice, and patience).

Little wonder that attempts at enlivening such memory and suggesting patience in the face of the quickening of the world are often met by anger. We've place a lot of stake in our attempts to avoid the suffering that comes from learning to embrace the suffering of the world and its arising. It is little wonder that we unwittingly dreams of a pedagogy premised on "'a state of perpetual war' (Postel & Drury, 2003), given the perpetuity of the world's [natality and] mortality. After all, a war against our response ('terror') to the very existence of uprising is, of necessity, perpetual" (Jardine, 2012a, p. 5).

Little wonder that the scholarship feels so embattled, that many of my colleagues feel under siege and exhausted, that no effort is ever enough. However un- or semi-conscious it may be (I'm willing to allow that some of those "in charge" are simply living out this wheeling and think it is simply "the real world," or "the way things are these days"), *perpetuating this state of siege and exhaustion is deliberate*—it is, quite literally, de-liberating. In fact, to enter into such a state of perpetual war is now seen as a cause of great pride in the academy. There is no other way to explain how a university can have "being in the top 5"—i.e., "beating" all but four other universities in some battle, some race to be "first"—as its stated goal.

Thus, quickening becomes terror, a perpetual insurgency that must be perpetually fought with ever-new sources of funding. And, as market logic dictates, *it can never be enough.*

This is not a logic of speed. It is a logic of acceleration. The faster we speed over the Earth, the less likely our foot might fall somewhere long enough to experience the leap, the quickening.

Hence unable to be "interpreted," quickening becomes broken in two. It makes more likely, on the one hand, our increasingly stunned fascination with the skittering surface stimulations of our own latest and shiniest devices (where quickening becomes sheer speediness of access, and promise, and novelty, and flight between one site and another) and, on the other hand, our equally stunned fascination with a world that feels full, as so many recent movies and television series show, of the walking dead, evacuated of the quick but seeming to summon us and our attention nevertheless.

"Just Start Doing It"

> Berry: The country and, I think Vandana [Shiva] can tell you, the world, is full of people who are seeing something that needs to be done and starting to do it, without the government's permission, or official advice, or expert advice, or applying for grants or anything else. They just start doing it. (Berry & Moyers, 2013)

There is no way out of this iatrogenic loop-logic except to simply step out of it. I am on the verge of retiring from my job and realize full well how easy that is for me to say. That ease comes with great sorrow, but rest assured that such ease is hard won and won't come unless it is practiced. Hermeneutics is a practice that must be patiently practiced if you are to become practiced in it. Just start doing it.

Hermeneutic work (as with worthwhile work in the classroom), in its love of the patient work of attending to quickening ("to know the world, we have to love it" [Berry & Moyers, 2013]), provides a modest way, however embattled it remains in the eyes of the academy.

Along this way, I must suffer the disjuncture between the lingering time called for by such arrivals and what time they need from us, and the terrible market-logic panics that have caught us spellbound and halt with a sense of low-level emergency and a deathly silence.

A terrible trial.

This is the trial to which hermeneutics is dedicated. This is why Hans-Georg Gadamer (1989, p. 356) invokes the words of Aeschylus in his invocation of *pathei mathos* as key to understanding the sort of experience and knowledge sought by hermeneutic work: *learning through suffering.*

Sure, we must remain clever in and about the machinations of the world. Go ahead. Just don't fall for it and start believing that the getting of grants is the real work. The getting is the cover story, the lie needing to be told to those who brook no quarter for the truth. So here's the impudence (shush and keep this to yourself). The real *fundus* of this funding must itself be hermeneutic: its "ground" must be the patient and suffered ground of the Earth, the topic, the stretch of song, and the path and goal of composure that such a ground requires of me:

> What we call the modern world is not necessarily, and not often, the real world, and there is no virtue in being up-to-date in it. It is a false world, based upon economies and values and desires that are fantastical, a world in which millions of people have lost any idea of the materials, the disciplines, the restraints, and the work necessary to support human life, and have thus become dangerous to their own lives and to the possibility of life. The job now is to get back to that perennial and substantial world in which we really do live, in which the foundations of our life will become visible to us, and in which we can accept our responsibilities again within the conditions of necessity and mystery. (Berry, 1983, p. 13)

> People whose governing habit is the relinquishment of power, competence and responsibility, and whose characteristic suffering is the anxiety of futility, make excellent spenders. They are the ideal consumers. By inducing in them little panics of boredom, powerlessness, mortality, paranoia, they can be made to buy virtually anything that is "attractively packaged." (Berry, 1986, p. 24)

Any grant will do as long as it is attractively packaged. But hell, advice to young scholars: get the grant if you can. I did it. Repeatedly. Shut up. Stay alert. Do what you can. Study. Try not to get in too much trouble with the authorities. Remember that they, too, are suffering under precisely the delusions that they present to you as real. They are not the authors of this delusion, just bit players in its weaving.

Their suffering is worse. They have to *believe* it. The purpose of scholarship, its "end" no matter what its topic, is to break this spell. Just give up expecting much thanks in return from those living "in [delusional spell of] the real world." You will be understood to be causing suffering ("rocking the boat"), not offering a way to ameliorate it.

Second-Last Mull

Berry:	A lot of my writing has been, when it hasn't been in defense of precious things, has been a giving of thanks for precious things.
Moyers:	What are the precious things that you think are in danger right now?
Berry:	It is might hard right now to think of anything that is precious that *isn't* in danger. But maybe that's an advantage. The poet William Butler Yeats said somewhere "Things reveal themselves passing away." And it may be that the danger that we have inflicted on every precious thing reveals the preciousness of it and shows us our duty. (Berry & Moyers, 2013)

One of my classes this year takes place at a school I've been working with for decades. This fall, for the first time, my hand hit the door and it was locked, and there was a new security camera pointing at me, and a buzzer. That such a circumstance was good-heartedly considered, I do not doubt. That such new arrangements both aim at *increasing a sense of security* while at the same time *increasing the atmosphere of insecurity* in which we now live, I also do not doubt. I just no longer know who to tell about such experiences except you, now, reader.

Sing, if you're able.

Such securing takes me back to thoughts of F.W. Taylor, about whom I've written often, but who is now making a new appearance that sounds too familiar:

A little more than a century ago, Frederick Winslow Taylor introduced "scientific management" to American factories. By meticulously tracking and measuring the physical movements of manufacturing workers as they went through their tasks, Taylor counseled, companies could determine the "one best way" to do any job and then enforce that protocol on all other workers. Through the systematic collection of data, industry could be optimized, operated as a perfectly calibrated machine. "In the past the man has been first," declared Taylor; "in the future the system must be first." (Carr, 2013)

The links between my faculty's funding fetish and the desire to put scholarship under surveillance cannot be avoided, even though this may be no one's intent. And then this:

> There is, for example, the Hitachi Business Microscope, which office workers wear on a lanyard around their neck. "The device is packed with sensors that monitor things like how workers move and speak, as well as environmental factors like light and temperature. So, it can track where workers travel in an office, and recognize whom they're talking to by communicating with other people's badges. It can also measure how *well* they're talking to them—by recording things like how often they make hand gestures and nod, and the energy level in their voice." Other companies are developing Google Glass-style "smart glasses" to accomplish similar things. (Carr, 2013)

The fear of quickening (like the reactionary ecological fear of "the wild" ["the child," as Alice Miller (1989) noted]) is ripe and rampant.

Kids these days!

"Understanding is an adventure and, like any adventure, it always involves some risk" (Gadamer, 1983, p. 141). And then "adventure is 'undergone', like a test or a trial from which one emerges enriched and more mature" (Gadamer, 1989, p. 69)—one hopes this is the emergence. It is a bit comforting to know we are fully surrounded by ancestors that know something of our suffering and what we might do to live well in the face of it. Elders who don't just work our woes to their own advantage.

Ah. Do you feel that songline? Fear of the quickening wild child (fear of Hermes) is at once a fear of aging, of "maturing." And a fear of aging, of maturing, is being overly enamored with the child, the new, with "what's next" coupled with a steadfast desire to not learn from such arrivals: Hans-Georg Gadamer (1989, p. xxii) brilliantly names this temptation "the naive self-esteem of the present moment." This is another hermeneutic insight, that we can become simply ravaged by the "onslaught of the new" (Arendt, 1969, p. 185) if we become spellbound by arrival itself and have no time for the patience required to let such adventures ripen us. We fear quickening because we fear mortality.

So the whole of this chapter's venture into quickening now inverts: we are perhaps *too much in love with the new* as a way of forestalling insight into our own mortality, of forestalling our own aging. With patience comes experience, and the impatience of modern scholarship that eradicates old references eradicates my becoming an experienced teacher, an experienced scholar. Just because I've published a lot and got many grants and taught many courses does not necessarily mean that I am "experienced" in such matters.

So, we have, here, in the efforts to avoid the great suffering that comes with insight into patience and quickening, a delusional complex that cannot bear the belly of this paradox, actions in praise of the child ("the new," "the latest," "next") while also hating and fearing the child and its quickening arrival, wanting to outrun it. Wanting to no longer suffer.

As a consequence, our well-intended responses, our questions, become Utopian (literally, "nowhere"), Titanic, Gigantic, distorted under ideal eyes raised too high, that no longer know the ground they walk, no longer having the patience to ready themselves for the leap.

What can we do to make schools better?

"We don't have a right to ask that question. We have to ask, 'What's the right thing to do?' and go ahead and do it and take no thought for the morrow" (Berry & Moyers, 2013).

CHAPTER THIRTY-FOUR

"Tears Run Down Heaven's Gaunt Face"

We are always educating for a world that is or is becoming out of joint, for this is the basic human situation, in which the world is created by mortal hands to serve mortals for a limited time as home. Because the world is made by mortals it wears out; and because it continuously changes its inhabitants it runs the risk of becoming as mortal as they. To preserve the world against the mortality of its creators and inhabitants it must be constantly set right anew. The problem is simply to educate in such a way that a setting-right remains actually possible, even though it can, of course, never be assured. (Arendt, 1969, p. 192)

Preamble

First, a very brief confession. I read over the following lovely, cascading, funny, painfully familiar passage quickly on first reading, laughing, commiserating from certainly having stood on both sides of that lectern. It is from David Foster Wallace's *Infinite Jest* (2006, p. 911) and seems to be tossed off as a vivid, well-read joke and then left behind:

These academics' arguments seem sound as far as they go, but they do not explain the incredible pathos of Paul Anthony Heaven reading his lecture to a crowd of dead-eyed kids picking at themselves and drawing vacant air-plane- and genitalia-doodles on their college-rule note-pads, reading stupe-fyingly turgid-sounding shit—"For while *clinamen* and *tessera* strive to revive or revise the dead ancestor, and while *kenosis* and *demonization* act to repress consciousness and memory of the dead ancestor, it is, finally, artistic *askesis* which represents the contest proper, the battle-to-the-death with the loved dead"—in a monotone as narcotizing as a voice from the grave—and yet all the time weeping, Paul Anthony Heaven, as an upward hall full of kids all scan their mail … silently weeping, very steadily, so that tears run down Heaven's gaunt face.

There are countless examples like this in *Infinite Jest* of great elaborations, meticulous, detailed, sometimes even nauseating scenarios.

This one hit close to home with its scene of professors smothered in their own words and overcome by their own sentiments, and students numbed by what might as well be a "voice from the grave."

But it is also about pedagogy, its conduct and its failures, not only in what Paul Anthony Heaven is trying to speak about, but in the very scenario of his self-involved failure, at that very moment, of exactly the same thing.

The Original Plan: To See if Heaven Has a Point

What might happen if I didn't pick at myself while reading this passage, didn't just laugh and moan and feel very slightly humiliated but, instead delved a bit to see if Heaven has a point? After all, "the possibility that the other person may be right is the soul of hermeneutics" (H.G. Gadamer, July 9, 1989, cited in Grondin, 1994, p. 124).

Clinamen, tesserae, demonization, kenosis, askesis. That list alone is enough to set an old scholar's mouth to watering. Just imagine the circuses of images: patterned mosaic pieces (*tessera*) like shells picked up on a beach that remind me of them fitting in somewhere, or broken-heart necklaces that memorialize their belonging together; the *clinamen*-like "swerve of events" (Rai, 2008, n.p.), "an ancient 'shiver' sent up the new spine, a clinamen or turbulence" (Kunze, 2018, p. 38), of happenstances that can have a "generative capacity" (p. 48).

Then, too, the cold and morbid imposition of what is settled beyond question. The interruptions of what seemed settled. Imps, tricksters, Coyotes, Hermes, the young child's innocent question, animal spirits, the death of someone that rattles the roof. *Daimons* (Hillman, 1983, pp. 54–55) everywhere you look—Raven's head crooked at the feeder, watching, animal energy, signs, messages, familiars on the backs of brooms. Ecological myriads of lives and living and voices and myriad stories and energies, versus heavenly dreams of the One self-emptied (*kenosis*) of all Earthly relations. Innocent lamb's bloods shed to recapitulate warding off death, to ward of the ghosts of dead ancestors or various real or imagined evils. Interpretation and "opening the mouths of the dead" (Hillman & Shamdasani, 2013, p. 1), so they don't just haunt us in the dark but can still speak, teach:

> It is the ancestors. It is the dead. This is no mere metaphor. This is no cipher for the unconscious or something like that. When [Jung] talks about the dead he means the dead. And they're present in images. They still live on. (p. 2)

So that newly arriving cases no longer just fall helplessly under an old established rule or category or pigeon-hole but instead be "fecund" (Gadamer, 1989, p. 38). The newly arrive life, the newly arriving case (literally, something that "happens," that "befalls" [Online Etymological Dictionary (OED)]) can sometimes correct the exaggerated self-confidence of the proffered and presumed fixity, humiliate its feigned clarities, "productively supplement" (Gadamer, 1989, p. 38) even "correct" it (Gadamer, 1989, p. 39). These uprisings, through "responding and summoning" (p. 458) can demand that these fixities account for themselves here, now, in the face of current circumstances. Why are we learning this? Why do you drone on?

First Nations elders' tales. Greek gods. "Chance and necessity, conservation and dissipation" (Johnson, 1993, p. 198) Revise. Renew. Remember. Revive. Forget. Repress. Genitalia doodles and airplanes. Of course, these—both youthful uprisings and flights and fancy and bodies and genitalia and brains.

Dead-eyes and weeping.

But then, Italo Calvino speaks of "quickness" (2016 pp. 31–54) in this light compared to the "narcotizing" lectern voice. "Lightness" (2016, p. 33). "Lightning flashes" (p. 16). Martin Heidegger, too, uses this image to denote the moment of sudden, unanticipated insight (1977, p. 44) that illuminates its surroundings, like a good question asked or a new arrival unforeseen that stops the drone and demands that it wake up. As teachers and students, we all already know something of this odd, physically palpable terrain.

Perhaps I should take each term and elaborate it? Pages and pages of references and citations. Maybe even footnotes if they are still allowed. Maybe I could rescue that list and make those students perk up. *Askesis*. Disciplined carefulness. But artistic. Aesthetics. Beauty and its craftiness.

After all, in the matter of pedagogy, these all hint at compelling, often ambiguous relationships between the teacher and the student, the old and the young, between the established and the new, between tradition—"the loved dead"—and what Hannah Arendt (1969, p. 177) simply called "the fact of natality" (p. 177) that are being sorted and re-sorted, generation after generation.

And, in schools, even here in Paul Anthony Heaven's classroom, we have an example of these very matters which are the topic of his droning, he and his students unwitting participants in a great irony. Heaven's conduct is legible as precisely this "battle-to-the-death" contest, one, at that very moment, he is losing, *as are his students.*

Equally tragic, *the topic itself*—despite all its rich, scholarly aromas and temptations—is losing its life. I always feel, perhaps over-optimistically, that if that list of his was held open with some joy and deftness, some of that hall of kids would recognize their own living suddenly clarified right before their eyes—"to recognize ourselves in the mess of the world as having been engaged and always being engaged" (Hillman, 1983, p. 49) can come, in pedagogical waves, as a great shock, sometimes a great relief.

So, I decided that this was not a good plan, to follow that itch to elaborate each and every one these terms and all their relations and all its revivals, revisions and repressions, off shoots, consequences. First, that plan would take a lifetime. And second, furthering this elaboration would miss another particular point in this scene of Paul Anthony Heaven's tears and gaunt face and his doodling students.

Given hermeneutics' interest in tradition, history, ancestry, consciousness, the fecund nature of the individual case, generativity, the relations between the new and the established, the young and the old, history and the event, and in aesthetics, memory, discipline, etymology, experience-as-venturing (*Erfahrung*) and ancestors (*Vorfahrung*) (hiding in plain sight the root German term *Fahren*, "to drive," "to travel," and hiding the English ter–to fare")—my own interest in this scene needs a sharper point.

Moreover, given my having stepped away from my old, regular job of supervising student-teachers in local elementary and high schools, and teaching on-campus classes on how we might, despite the contemporary shape of many schools, find abundance and pleasure in our work, this scene brings something else into view, even in some old anecdotes I've told before about mathematics and schools and kids.

Senex and Puer

Young people want to know if, under the cool and calm of efficient teaching and excellent time-on-task ratios, life itself has a chance, or whether the surface is all there is. (D.G. Smith, 2020c, p. 405)

A story to be retold, here. When "teaching uphill" to a group of around 225 prospective teachers in a third-year lecture series: What is the deep lesson we teach? This: *Every time we stand up in front of a group of students, we stand as an example of how life—their lives, perhaps—could turn out.*

"Yes," I would say, gesturing to my own long hair and odd disposition and affection for thinking, "it can turn out like this."

After the lovely, hard-to-fully-decipher, myriad and multifarous laughter subsides, we would then get down to business. Some students would drift away, others not, when we came to talk about the pleasures of exploring rich living fields of work with student of our own in classrooms, and how schools are too often set up as places of exhaustion and acceleration, and that they might need to cultivate themselves in order to tactfully and articulately resist this prospect. And this for the benefit of themselves and their students and the life of what they are teaching And that they needed to learn about how things got this way so they can decode what is happening to them, understand some things about what is remaining silently at work and learn about what alternatives there might be, and so on.

This is why I decided early on in my career to take on practicum students every single year, so that I could wend my way with these students about their school placement experiences and not just speculatively weep over theories of "schools" but, instead, when I was able, proffer practical advice here and there about this and that that they encountered. Learning from classrooms we would visit where rich and abundant work was being done had to come to learn to live with the darkened hallways of other locales. Such is the deep ambivalence of this profession, and such is the decision that each new student-teacher faces: "What will you now do?"

What happens when the relationship between the new and the established, the young arrival and the tradition, the student and the teacher, *fails*? Perhaps the characterization of these relations as a battle-to-the-death already betrays that something is *already broken*. Perhaps only once broken apart can we then imagine one side needing some sort of "victory" over the other. Perhaps Paul Anthony Heaven's own classroom betrays his having arrived, one might say, too late.

James Hillman provides a wonderfully graphic and playful way to think about this matter of the failure of the pedagogical relationship. In line with his own Jungian background, he describes puer and senex as a "complex" whose most healthy, whole and sane manifestation is how they *belong together*. Each, shall we say, "shadows" the other and helps keep it in place and in proper proportion and, in doing this, keeps itself in such proportion as well. They are thus vital sides of each other. They strengthen each other and bring out the most livable, viable versions of young (puer) and old (senex).

This only becomes a "battle to the death" when they lose sight of one another. When healthy and whole, it is a sort of tense "balance" that needs to be won and re-won over and over again, as any teacher can attest in thinking of each September's arrivals of new faces in the classroom. Each side comes to proper life *in relation* to the other.

Senex in its positive aspect bespeaks the senatorial, the wise, the elder, the whisperer, the old man, the old woman who knows something about the old ways and their comforts and dangers, full of stories that make you fall in love with coming to know your way around the worlds of heroes and villains, right angles and histories and periodic tables. Rich, alluring, tough stories that ring true and clear. The field guide. The good counsel. The eye-twinkle and assurances that you might be on to something, that you should watch your step here and there, senex always wary of the difference between being properly protective (of the young, of the territories explored) and over-protective, always read to find out that they may have misjudged and start all over again.

James Hillman's meditations on these matters focus, in part, on what happens when this relation gets broken. It is not just that we now have two parts now apart instead of together:

> Not only is fragmentation a disease, but the dis-eases [hyphen added] of the disconnected parts are similar or analogous to one another. Thus, they memorialize their lost unity, their relation persisting in their disconnection. Any severance produces two wounds that are, among other things, the record of how the severed parts once fitted together. (Berry, 1986, pp. 110–111)

This very description of Wendell Berry's rings of the *tessera hospitalis* but points to something more troublesome. Fragmentation *wounds*. It *changes the nature of each of the separated parts* because each part has lost that which gave it a healthy measure of itself.

There is an endless stream of these matters in the varieties of human experience. One could even consider David G. Smith's (2006) explication of the workings of Enrique Dussel's (1988, 1995) "myth of sacrifice" and "myth of salvation"—you will submit and become "us" or you will be sacrificed, to use Alice Miller's (1989) chillingly familiar term, "for your own good." This fragmentation is also an omen of ecological disasters as well. Breaking down mathematics, for example, into fragmented and separate bits and pieces is an ecological disaster happening upon what is, in reality, a living field of relations.

Fragmented, each becomes transformed into something that loses track of the way in which its lost part helped keep it in check, help ameliorate its excesses, helped beckon and confirm its strengths. Out of relation, *each side becomes monstrous,* and it is too often these monstrosities that meet in schools.

Just consider how familiar is this extended description of what James Hillman calls "negative senex":

> The negative senex is the senex split from its own puer aspect. He has lost his "child." The archetypal core of the complex, now split, loses its inherent tension, its ambivalence. Without the enthusiasm and eros of the son, authority loses its idealism. It aspires to nothing but its own perpetuation, leading but to tyranny and cynicism; *for meaning cannot be sustained by structure and order alone.* Such spirit is one-sided, and one-sidedness is crippling. Being is static, a pleroma that cannot become. Time—euphemistically called "experience" but more often just the crusted accretions of profane history—becomes a moral virtue and even witness of truth, *"veritas filia temporis".* The old is always preferred to the new. Sexuality without young eros becomes goaty; weakness becomes complaint; creative isolation becomes only paranoid loneliness. Because the complex is unable to catch on and sow seed, it feeds on the growth of other complexes or other people, as for instance the growth of one's own children [telling words for pedagogy]. Cut off from its own child and fool the complex no longer has anything to tell us. Folly and immaturity are projected on to others [see Immanuel Kant's "overcoming of immaturity" (1774/1983, p. 33) and Rene Descartes' "repudiation of childhood" (see Bordo, 1988, pp. 97–98)]. Without folly it has no wisdom, only knowledge—serious, depressing, hoarded in an academic vault or used as power. The integration of personality becomes the subjugation of personality, a unification through dominance, and integrity only a selfsame repetition of firm principle. (Hillman, 2013a, p. 41)

Likewise the risk of senex becoming senile when it loses its "child," the puer-aspect, cut off from the wisdoms of things become merely puerile. Familiar is this positive aspect of puer:

> The puer aspect of meaning is in the search, as the *dynamus* of the child's eternal "why?", the quest, or the questioning, seeking, adventuring, which grips personality from behind and pushes it forward. (Hillman, 2013b, p. 50)

Enthusiasm, renewal, energy, life, liveliness, a new beginning, a fresh start, a new group of students pumping through the hallways into the organs of the classrooms "to see with fresh eyes" (Gadamer, 1989,

p. 16). And even vis a vis the arrival of student-teachers into classrooms, new life in the living profession of teaching itself:

> We keep hearing from principals that some of the best people are the new, young, fresh blood in the system. Jon Ed, Human Resources Superintendent, Calgary Board of Education. (*Calgary Herald*, March 23, 1993, page B1)

But then, here, too, there is a danger of this puer-aspect becoming untethered. Again, a familiar description for those who teach:

> Negative puer may become hyperactive and we find all the traits accentuated and materialized but without inherent meaning. When the falcon cannot hear the falconer, wingedness becomes mere haste and fanaticism, an unguided missile. Everything new is worshipped because it gives promise of the original, while the historical is discarded because it is of the senex who is now enemy. Personal revelation is preferred to objective knowledge so that minor epiphanies weigh more than the classics of culture. Eventually meaning declines into a philosophy of the absurd, action into the *acte gratuite* or violence, or intoxication, or flight into the future; and the chaos returns, which the puer as archetype is itself called to oppose. By refusing history, by pushing it all down into the unconscious in order to fly above it, one is forced to repeat history unconsciously. In the unconscious the senex position builds up with a compulsive vengeance until with all the force of historical necessity it takes over in its turn, reducing new truths to old cliches again, switching the only-puer into an only-senex, split from the next generation. (Hillman, 2013a, p. 51)

Again, exhilaratingly, terrifyingly familiar. More than once I overheard a teacher saying to one of my student-teachers in their staffroom that they, too, were once really enthusiastic when they started out.

These two descriptions of negative puer and negative senex always remind me of the sort of repressed footing of talk of "teacher-centeredness" and "child-centeredness" in university classes about curriculum and pedagogy. David G. Smith provided me with good guidance in an old essay of his, originally from 1988:

> The old unilateral options of *gericentrism* (appealing to the authority of age, convention, tradition, nostalgia) and *pedocentrism* (child-centered pedagogy) only produce monstrous states of siege which are irresponsible to the matters

at hand, that is, to the question of how life is mediated through relations between old and young. (Smith, 2020c, p. 406)

Such talk of centerdness is understandable. It seems to be an effort to try *to put to rest* something whose very restlessness is at the heart of a healthy pedagogy. Both teacher-centeredness and child-centerdness seem to bypass the terribly difficult work of maintaining a healthy relation *in-between*, a relation that must always be re-cultivated, occasionally moment to moment in a classroom.

It was actually David Smith's writing that helped me find James Hillman's work legible in my own efforts to work in schools, coupled with a glimpse from Hans-Georg Gadamer's *Truth and Method* (1989, p. 295): *"The true locus of hermeneutics is this in-between."*

But what, then, of Paul Anthony Heaven's students, doodling, scratching themselves?

We can easily picture a more contemporary audience of the young rife with phone messages and clicking and flighty, headlong, surface-stimmed screen flipping and accelerated, frantic stay-in-in-touchedness. I even find myself flinching at a now-27-year-old, rather prescient description:

The subject of postmodernity is best understood as the ideal-type channel-hopping MTV viewer who flips through different images at such speed that she/he is unable to chain the signifiers together into a meaningful narrative, he/she merely enjoys the multiphrenic intensities and sensations of the surface of the images. (Usher & Edwards, 1994, p. 11)

But this isn't Paul Anthony Heaven's audience. If we dare say that the tears running down Heaven's gaunt face betrays negative senex:

If persuaded into the temporal world by the negative senex, the puer loses connection with its own aspect of meaning and becomes the negative puer. Then it goes dead, and there is passivity, withdrawal. (Hillman, 2013a, p. 51)

Puer energetics and liveliness withdraws because *that is the lesson being taught* by the negative, narcotizing voice standing, weeping at the lectern. And again, one way or another, we teachers stand before our students as examples of how life might be for them and for their students, and their responses to my own standing feed back to me my own regard of them regarding me.

Three Anecdotes

In education [we] assume responsibility for both, for the life and development of the child and for the continuance of the world. These two responsibilities do not by any means coincide; they may indeed come into conflict with each other. The responsibility for the development of the child turns in a certain sense against the world: the child requires special protection and care so that nothing destructive may happen to him from the world. But the world, too, needs protection to keep it from being overrun and destroyed by the onslaught of the new that burst upon it with each new generation. (Arendt, 1969, pp. 185–186)

To be true to one's puer nature means to admit one's puer past—all its gambols and gestures and sun-struck aspirations. From this history we draw consequences. By standing for these consequences, we let history catch up with us and thus is our haste slowed. History is the senex shadow of the puer, giving him substance. Through our individual histories, puer merges with senex, the eternal comes back into time, the falcon returns to the falconer's arm. (Hillman, 2013a, p. 59)

Missing in these two lovely citations is that strange third factor skipped over so often in battles between teacher-centeredness and child-centeredness, between fixity and openness, energy and wisdom: the topic, the terrain, the topography, the place and its relations and ways. The locales *in which* we come upon our students and they us. I have argued elsewhere, as have so many others, that the loss of this third factor is a pedagogical and ecological disaster. Mathematics, for example, which has a role to play, alongside all the other living inheritances handed to teachers and students in schools, in the amelioration of fragmentation and the quelling of battling.

What follows are three quick scenarios—some you'll see again below or above—from my days supervising student-teachers and working with practicing teachers in their classrooms in the field of mathematics. I'm reiterating them here because something about my previous attention to these has been newly perked by this long and winding road through Paul Anthony Heaven's gaunt, tear-stained classroom.

...

First: Grade Two? Three? Visiting a practicum student. Kids doing the fourth worksheet before morning recess. Like this: put an overhead up. Show the kids. Do the first question. Hand out the xeroxes. Give a time limit. Wait. Collect. Next.

Little girl calls me over as I walk in, I expect simply for something to do as much as anything.

"I don't get this question." Jodi goes to the post office. She has five packages and three letters. "How many more packages than letters does she have?"

Blank space to put your answer.

+ and - signs. Circle what operation you used. Flummoxed.

I squatted down and held up one hand, five fingers: "He has five packages." The other hand, three fingers up.

She stopped, reached out and bent down two of my five fingers; then bent up two fingers on my "three" hand. Paused. Shouted "2!"

I said, "Yes, yes, put that on the line."

Then this from her: "But I don't know whether I added or subtracted." Breathtaking question. We had a lovely little back and forth with me putting fingers up on one hand, down on the other, back and forth. All I could manage was, "This is really good. You're right. This isn't a mistake. All is well."

When we told the teacher what happened, she said that the question was confusing, and she would delete it next time.

Then duck, watch out! Incoming puerile child-centeredness from the (I think, I hope) good-hearted teacher: "Why don't you just circle the answer that you think is best?"

Admission: I knew right away that this young child's query was *good* even though I still don't quite know the fullness of what it opened up. Her teacher's response an example in our on-campus class of how having a question doesn't mean something has gone wrong. My own on-campus students—most of them, when told about this event, didn't quite get it and got confused themselves about what was going on. Of course. They learned mathematics in school. That classroom teacher was precisely a victim of the leadenness of her own lifeless schooling. She is the victim of something as much as its perpetrator.

Second: Outdoors. Playground. Winter. Us at 52 degrees North Latitude. Been inside visiting right-angled triangles and their ways. Now, boy, Grade 6. Facing straight south. Toes on the tip of a tree shadow south of him with sun low and winter-creamy behind that. "When I was out here in the summer, this shadow was way over there" (pointing south to where a much shorter shadow would tip with a higher sun arc).

"But Pythagoras says something is the same." Me: "Yes," with a voice amazed as much at this kid as at Pythagoras, imagine, showing up here in the deathly cold and bright Alberta blue sky.

Third: Student-teacher, Grade Five class at the chalkboard (yes, that long ago). Multiplying by fractions was the topic.

"They [the students, now out for recess] just don't get it no matter how I try to explain it." So me, practicum supervision, here, in an age-old territory. Let's start again. You have the example here of $\frac{1}{2} \times 6$. Let's do 5×6. Student-teacher blurted "30," more like a belch than an answer. Yes. Right. But tell me what you *did*. Then that wonderful writhing.

"I multiplied."

"I just know." And more, each as hard and unforgiving as concrete. Then, slowly, six five times. I wrote down 5 6s on the board.

"Yes. You have six five times. Okay, let's go back to the example you were doing."

$\frac{1}{2} \times 6$.

The student-teacher at the chalkboard, sort of whispering and shouting at the same time over $\frac{1}{2} \times 6$: "You don't even have it once!"

A little gasp of part surprise, part bewilderment, part exhilaration Smile. Me. "Yes. You don't even have it once."

Gasp of breath. His breath. My breath. Breathtaking. Yes. Look. There it is! A weird, humiliating pleasure, something beautiful, something demanding something of us standing there at the chalkboard.

Askesis. Carefulness in the face of bursts of energy. Stopped still, both of us at this opening event. Happy.

James Hillman calls this eventful arrival *"aesthesis,"* and I read this passage while thinking of Paul Anthony Heaven's "artistic askesis":

> The familiar idea [is] that beauty arrests motion. You draw in your breath and stop still. This little gasp—*hshshs* as the Japanese draw between their teeth when the see something beautiful in a garden—this *ahhhh* reaction is the aesthetic response just as certain, inevitable, objective and ubiquitous as a wincing in pain and moaning in pleasure. Moreover, this quick intake of breath is also the very root of the work aesthetics, *aisthesis* in Greek, meaning sense-perception. *Aisthesis* goes back to the Homeric *aiou* and *aisthou* which means both "I perceive" as well as "I gasp, struggle for breath," as in *aisthomai*, I breath in. Does this not suggest that if beauty is to appear, we must be stopped still? (Hillman, 2006a, p. 183)

And this:

> Things speak; they show the shape they are in. They announce themselves, bear witness to their presence: "Look, here we are." They regard us beyond how we may regard them, our perspectives, what we intend with them, and how we dispose of them. (Hillman, 2006b, p. 33)

"You don't even have it once!" is this student's insight *into* something *other than himself,* finally being caught in the regard of that which he is trying to understand, me, standing there, smiling, saying, somehow, yes, there it is. It is *there.*

Yes. It is *beautiful.*

Meanwhile, the Grade Five students had come back in from recess and had all quietly sat down, most simply listening and watching us.

"I don't know what to do now."

"Just tell them about the conversation we just had, that's all. And then listen and see what happens. I'll stay here."

. . .

These, of course, are just moments, full of the exaggerations and distortions and revelations of recall, memory and the shapings of forgetting. However, "it is the moments that are momentous, the pearls, not their string" (Hillman, 2013b, p. 104) and in these, there is something that I haven't admitted out loud in so many words: *the strange, satisfying pleasure to be had* in happening to be there when these things happened. An exhilaration. Just imagine chancing upon Pythagoras being rescued from memory at the tiptoe shadow of a winter playground tree.

And once a pearl rises up, writers tend to string.

Or getting to not only feel the back and forth of adding and subtracting and their intimate relations right there, literally in my fingertips, but suddenly recognizing it to be true all over again. Yes. I forgot. Yes.

And having the opportunity to stand by the troubles of a student-teacher and being there when the outburst happens—not even once! Adding or subtracting. Something is the same. Two things here.

First: "understanding [in these moments] proves to be an event" (Gadamer, 1989, p. 309), something that "happens to use over and above our wanting and doing" (1989, p. xxxvii). And that event is precisely such: and opening up of something, a coming-forward, an arrival that flutters full of relations scattering all around it. "An event that 'appropriates us' into itself. It jolts us, it knocks us over, and sets up a world of its own, into which we are drawn, as it were" (Gadamer, 2001, p. 71). Adding and subtracting are relations in a world of relations of their own, even if the worksheet deems otherwise. Shadows and right angles and old Greek cults belong together and show up in playground sun-shadow events.

It is the following of these events, the recognizing of these *as* events in the field of mathematics that is the lynchpin, and the pleasure and exhilaration can often be the very clue that is needed. Thus the second point of eventful recognition:

> We do not understand what recognition is in its profoundest nature if we only regard it as knowing something again that we know already—i.e., what is familiar is recognized again. The joy of recognition is rather the joy of knowing *more* than is already familiar. In recognition what we know emerges, as if illuminated. (Gadamer, 1989, p. 114)

So it is not just a matter of training up student in my University classes to know things, but to know them in such a way that they cultivate in themselves and start to carry with them the ability to recognize what is happening in front of their eyes and step into the living fields these events open up. And to learn ways to recognize the footfalls of their own students as they come to know and take pleasure in it. Pleasure.

In all these cases, it wasn't just a matter of a "student" finally "getting it." It was also somehow me "getting" something about *my own presence* to these events. *And something of the life of mathematical relations jumping up suddenly before both our eyes*, both of us startled a wee bit and happy. Plunging, cool water.

And the agencies and rough beast beauties of the field itself rising up and surrounding us. Aesthetic, but then, to *askesis*, asking for care, discipline, catch-your-breath-settle-down and look carefully Great ecological advice, just as a Cross Fox skipped by this morning.

Maybe, in the end, Paul Anthony Heaven had a point.

End

May I insist here that we cannot over-estimate the importance of this rapprochement. It is worth every attempt, not for the success or cure that it might bring, but because each attempt makes us aware of the split and thereby begins healing. (Hillman, 2013a, p. 36)

As an early sign of this re-union, we may expect new experience of ambivalence. (p. 36)

Ambivalence is the adequate reaction to ... the whole truth. To cure away ambivalence removes the eye with which we can perceive the paradox, whereas bearing ambivalence places us within [the] reality where we perceive both faces at once, even exist as two realities at once. This way works at wholeness not in halves but through wholeness from the start. The way is slower, action is hindered, and one fumbles foolishly in the half-light. The way finds echo in many familiar phrases from Lao Tzu, but especially: "Soften the light, become one with the dusty world." (p. 37)

To make meaningful and beautiful—th[is] primary paradox that human beings *have* to live with. (Snyder, 1980, p. 30)

The paradox. Feeling as much a student as a teacher when teaching student-teachers in university classrooms or school classrooms full of students who have their own teacher and a student-teacher and a

university supervisor sometimes all at once. Being present to classroom events and being slightly suspect as a bearer of all the old news,
good and bad, about "The University" and "The Field." Adoring how
Pythagoras outruns me every single time, cool water:

> We ought to be like elephants in the noontime sun in summer, when they are
> tormented by heat and thirst and catch sight of a cool lake. They throw them-
> selves into the water with the greatest pleasure and without a moment's hes-
> itation. In just the same way, for the sake of ourselves and others, we should
> give ourselves joyfully to the practice. (Pelden, 2007, p. 255)

CHAPTER THIRTY-FIVE

Baby's Blue … See Through

FIGURE 16. SHADOWCAST
"Shadowcast" photo by the Author

A Poem for a Space of Forty Days
I'm not sure if I don't expect
That this just might be how things appear as life
Ebbs. As consciousness starts giving up
Its sometimes terrible sway.
And things have a chance to become themselves again.
Back to normal. Ungripped.
Like timid birds finally able to peek out safe and sound.
To peek out safe, and sound the air around.

A sort of over exposed burn out in
Psychedelic Expectation.
An olden boy a sucker for
Translucent Beauty. Just like always.
Just like for years.
Ravens just out that window.
I'll just bet I missed their wing shadows by
Lost Seconds.
Just like 70 Years Gone, just like that
Just Like That.
Upper Cases
Proper Names
Yes.
Windowsuns.
Baby Pinks.
Baby Blues.

Baby's blue and it's sweet as can be.
A Yellow Ring.
I feel like Yarrow.
See through.

Things speak; they show the shape they are in. They announce themselves, bear witness to their presence: "Look, here we are." They regard us beyond how we may regard them, our perspectives, what we intend with them, and how we dispose of them. (Hillman, 2006c, p. 33)

[It] would not deserve the interest we take in it if it did not have something to teach us that we could not know by ourselves. (Gadamer, 1989, p. xxxv)

Quaranta giorni. Literally "a space of forty days" (OED). An old Italian term naming the 40 days that ships from plagued countries had to lay in harbor.

Quarantine. Forty days and 40 nights. Forty days in the desert. A strange linguistic hangover from Biblical imaginings.

Strange thing to find when you've got a bit too much time on your hands. *Schola.* Leisure. "A holding back. A keeping clear" (OED). But don't forget, when doing interpretive work: "Even when etymologies are right, they are not proofs but achievements preparatory to conceptual analysis, and only in such analysis to they obtain a firm foundation" (Gadamer, 1989, p. 103). And this noted right after Hans-Georg has analytically detailed and lamented the "subjectivization of aesthetic experience" (pp. 42–81) and proposed *Truth and Method* as set squarely on "retrieving the question of artistic truth" (pp. 81–100).

Time to pick up new habits, or, perhaps, to think through old habits anew. That last phrase is as good a definition of interpretive work as I can currently manage.

A relatively new habit, this picture taking stuff. "Don't wait" is the only thing I know that I know. It has become, lately, a way to demonstrate to myself something of the immediacies of attention and what they can yield in the lingers of dying ever so slowly so far. Some sort of fecundity of the individual case. Something of the irreplaceability of the case. Something of remembering not to skitter away, but rather, stay, sit and see what happens.

Momentariness. Temporality. Sunarcshifts across a worn old oak table.

Such goes ephemera. But, as per cases well attended to, their very particularity betrays, to equivocate, a sort of universality of irreplaceability, irreducability.

But this universality does not *govern* them. Nor is it ever complete. It always stands in abeyance of the arrival of the next case, or the arrival of the fresh experience of the very same case returned to and differently the same because of that. Looking again at that photo. Falling in love as its gravitational pull "increases in being" (Gadamer, 1989, p. 40) and purrs from the attention.

And must be experienced as such to be experience for what it is, freed-moving, but never free from the archangel eye of subjectivity that beholds it. Abeyance. Suspension. Something of Edmund Husserl's (1970 a, b) phenomenological aspirations. And also, expectant waitfulness or hopefulness (OED). Like whiling. Agape. Daresay both pronunciations of this last work: open-mouthed, amazed, and also some deep, sensuous attraction to what seems to be the truth of what is experienced. Drawing closer, waiting. Writing.

There is breath here, too, both gasped and held:

> The word for perception or sensation in Greek was *aesthesis*, which means at root a breathing in or taking in of the world, the gasp, "aha," the "uh" of the breath in wonder, shock, amazement, and aesthetic response. (Hillman, 2006c, p. 36)

An *aesthesis* unsubjectivized, that bears witness to an experience that "something [just might be] is going on, (*im Spiele ist*), something [seems to be] is happening (*sich abspielt*)" (Gadamer, 1989, p. 104). I add these square brackets, because aesthetic response, like etymologies, is not proof, but is, rather, an ambiguous clue that needs love and attention. And it just might turn out to be little more than a fleeting affair that goes nowhere, that does not deepen or last or return. We all know this sort of experience full well, I expect.

Just look at that picture (I say to myself as well). I write this secretly because I want to know: it's not just me, right? *It's* quite stunning and strange and provocative. Provoking voicing, showing, sharing, and writing. *Its* voicing, *its* showing. It

> is an *Ereignis*—an event that "appropriates us" into itself. It jolts us, it knocks us over, and sets up a world of its own, into which we are drawn, as it were. (Gadamer, 2001, p. 71)

A little recessed space whose recess—withdrawnness, hidden enclave-ness, increases with the right attention. It becomes beautifully less capturable and beautifully more drawing in the same working gesture of interpretation.

There is a great old word for photographs: snaps. I deleted far more photos that the ones I'm offering here. And that decision has a suddenness and immediacy that I cannot unfold further, except to say that it is like what happens when a story is told and you know immediately that *that* is worth noting, remembering, saving, caring for, not forgetting. This happens, too, when I read, too, and a strike will occur and the text will beckon a pen underlining, making it a locale to which I just might return, and the work, then, is to properly attend to it so it doesn't end up simply being reduced to the fact that I got struck.

Okay, then, time for a wee deluge. I take each of these in the very same way I take that photo—dwell-spots.

What if this were true? And, not to forget old J.D., who benefits if it were? And let's not forget to recite something cited so many times before:

> The familiar idea [is] that beauty arrests motion. You draw in your breath and stop still. This little gasp—*hshshs* as the Japanese draw between their teeth when the when they see something beautiful in a garden—this *ahhhh* reaction is the aesthetic response just as certain, inevitable, objective and ubiquitous as a wincing in pain and moaning in pleasure. Moreover, this quick intake of breath is also the very root of the work aesthetics, *aisthesis* in Greek, meaning sense-perception. *Aisthesis* goes back to the Homeric *aiou* and *aisthou* which means both "I perceive" as well as "I gasp, struggle for breath," as in *aisthomai*, I breath in. Does this not suggest that if beauty is to appear, we must be stopped still? (Hillman, 2006b, p. 183)

Some words for a former asthmatic to hear, I'll tell you. What good would it do to know about this, to remember this? *What if this were true?*

> Below the ecological crisis lies a deeper crisis of love. For love to return to the world, beauty must ... return, else we love the world only as a moral duty. (Hillman, 2006b, p. 175)

What if *this* were true?

> Only beauty can save the planet. Even the strongest combination of guilty feelings, economic reasoning and scientific evidence are not enough to turn the tide so that our planet's life may continue. Nevertheless, if you love something, you want it to stay around and stay close, and keep radiantly well. And

> it is precisely beauty that makes you fall in love. [It] gives you the feeling that what is here is to be treasured and not misused or harmed, and certainly not to be regarded in terms of functional usefulness or economic return, for such is to look at the world as a slave or a whore. (Hillman, 2006a, p. 192)

This?

> It captivates us just as the beautiful captivates us. It [that photo, this citation, that bird call, that child's query] has asserted itself and captivated us before we can come to ourselves and be in a position to test the claim ... that it makes. In understanding we are drawn into an event of truth [Greek: *aletheia*, meaning variously opening what seemed closed, remembering what seemed forgotten, enlivening what seemed dead ordinary and familiar] and arrive, as it were, too late. (Gadamer, 1989, p. 490)

And these repetition, too, are left in this book on purpose, because each recitation bumps up against the circumstances that are surrounding it—the topic of the chapter, the example being used, the point being sharpened. It is also an age-old memory tool:

> Told and retold in almost ritual repetitions, worrying over bones or the great and ancient monastic murmuring of texts out loud and under the breath, seeking the truth of what it repeats, seeks its redemption in words. Monkish practices of scholarship. Telling and re-telling are attempts to let it find its freedom from my own obsessive remembering of it within the confines of a life whose imposture is both too great and too small by itself to think this through. (Jardine, 2016l, p. 275)

> Consider: When a young child tips forward into a word and finds herself struggling to sound it out, humming and murmuring over its sonority and the ancient, specific, detailed links lurking there with the look of its letters, its words, its spaces, tossing it around her tongue and breath, tripping unknowingly over all those old mongrel roots of English, all inbred and tangled together and pushing and pulling of attention this way and that, perhaps not yet sensing the haunting presence of such forgotten ancestors and ancestries that are ripe and ready to be known even though we can get along quite famously in sheer ignorance of their life and lives. This simple act of pronunciation is at once the most ordinary of classroom events and a great, roiling thing, a great nexus full of the "silence of a world turning"
> (Domanski, 2002, p. 245). And then suddenly, yes! Pronounced.
> (Jardine, 2016f, p. 291)

Here's the tough thing. Not every story, not every case, not every event, lasts. Not everything "makes memory last" (Gadamer, 1989, p. 111). And nothing comes with a money back guarantee, with a tag that ensures that yes, this one will last, this one's good, I need to remember *this but* not *that*. Becoming proficient in interpretive work is, in part, getting good at the practice of recognition, the practice of seeking the last of things and the weird risk of making something public. No matter how diligent, being practiced is no sort of guarantee. Things fall apart. No centers hold even when they sometimes once did for a while. Things change and surround and erode. The past is constantly turning out to be different than it was. This year's events will become re-readable no matter what we do. Statues will go up and be torn down no matter how careful we are.

So here's the trick. I'm erasing things. I'm sorting. I'm emptying the trash. Me. And my own limitedness will be an intimate part of how this operates, where and when these parses occurs. And I am and remain profoundly susceptible to tragic, awful errors in this regard—of ignoring, of following old habits, of losing precious light and shadow through distraction, exhaustion or mere happenstance, of numbly repeating deeply buried presumptions, prejudices, unnoticed bile and guile, picking away mindlessly at the same scab.

And *no matter what I do*, no matter how good-hearted the effort, I cannot outrun this prospect. That is why I write and publish these things, because my own light and shadowcast inevitably proves itself to be inadequate to the case itself. I cannot live up to that photo's sweet demand, or that one, or that.

There is no outrunning this. A reminder to myself: Stop running.

CHAPTER THIRTY-SIX

An Obituary at the Very Last Minute

Their last dying words are, "This can't be happening. It's not real." And when they should be spending time facetiming their families, they're filled with anger and hatred. I just can't believe that those are going to be their last thoughts and words. When you try to reason with people, "Can I call your family, your kids your wife, your friend, your brother?" and they say, "No because I'm going to be fine" and you're watching their oxygen levels max out …

> Jodi Doering, South Dakota ER nurse. https://twitter.
> com/NewDay/status/1328319845012824065

I write this confused. Simply put, I feel culpable for helping, in a very minor and small way, to set loose a beast that seems to have become dangerous. Perhaps it was always dangerous. Interpretation run amok into utter self-enclosed self-referential self-isolationism, this-is-my-story-ism or, more simply "I think this. Done."

This worry doesn't take sides in advance. This worry is always easy to try and pin on "them" and not "us." That, too, floods with guilt.

It is too easy to see this as an attempt to revert to exactly what the interpretive impulse had freed us from. Hegemonies of grand

narratives. The unsuspicious (Gadamer, herm of sus) naiveites of surface stories that satisfy without illumination or interruption. It appears
as a re-summoning to silence this voice or that. To even suggest that
things might be otherwise that "my experience" suggests seems to belie
the freedoms finally hard won.

"No, I'm going to be fine." No, you're not. "That's what *you* think."
Yes, it is. Done.

The slippages between signifier and signified felt like such a liberation at first and long since and still. To emerge out from under
sedimented presumptions, dominating voices, long-writ stories told
numbingly frequently, to find the fresh airs of interpretive possibilities
and the utter thrills of how language and bloodlines and ancestries
and new voices can crackle and spark along unforeseen lines and pathways, quickening us, challenging, refreshing, humiliating who this
"us" might be.

Oh the joy of language let loose and soaring, sparking the wires
finally hearing my own voice rattling and humming in the rafters. An
old, lovely urge captured here so clearly: Yes, but "the uninitiated," the
unpracticed, "have no proper vessel. They carry water in a sieve and
pour it into a perforated jar" (Hillman, 2013c, p. 220). Hermeneutics
is, in part, the preparation of a proper vessel (with the full knowledge
that each new life, new idea, new arising, new perishing, will involve),
in part, preparing the vessel all over again in ways that *it* needs that
I couldn't quite foresee without it. It is a practice that takes practice, but
it doesn't result in being practiced, but in being perhaps a bit more *ready
to practice all over again*. (Jardine, 2020a, p. 8)

"Proper vessel." Stated by a white guy citing a white guy. See? There
it is again:

> What can occur, what seems to have occurred, is that, in the face of the trem-
> bling insight about the groundlessness of foundations, it has become all too
> easy to *almost* accept this insight except at the very last minute. At the very
> last minute, I too-easily can take my own experiences, my own story, my
> own beliefs, my own emotions, my own presumptions, my own opinions, my
> own attitudes, as all I've got to go on. "I just believe in me," as John Lennon
> exhorted after excoriating this and that grand narrative. And the excoria-
> tion had its own warrant, but the result has ended up with simply multiply

the grandness of "my own warrant," now equally impenetrable and unaddressable. What can occur, what has occurred, is a sort of unravelling into competing claims of fakeness or naivety, mixed and muddled positionalities, indeterminacy manipulated into strategic lying, suspicions pumped up into wall-building, haunts of scheming and blames of counternarratives, us and them-nesses run rife and deliberately manipulated to hidden ends, and on and on and on. Once signifiers lost their point, once the silencings of grand narratives became more and more evident, the future was sketched. What was intended as an opening up and making more generous and forgiving, what was intended as a gesture toward genuine conversation, listening, and good will, too easily becomes narrative overload in which every word is both exquisitely precious and utterly suspicious at the same time. It too easily becomes the too-clever cynicism of "anything goes" and "who is to say?" I'm reading over the chapters that are to follow [in a book I've published on- line, itself a sign of my exhaustion over public speech] and I'm realizing that they are, one way or another, the measure of the person who reads them, not just the measure of me as a writer. But then, even though I've urged practice and caution and stillness as often as I dared do, I do feel responsible, just a wee bit, for our collective current malaises. Don't read this if you're not up to it. And don't think for a moment that I know exactly what that means. Just don't let it get to you. It is meant to be good news, exhilarating, liberating news, even though the *mens auctoris* is one among many of the usual post-modern suspects. (Jardine, 2020a, pp. 2–3)

This phenomenon doesn't manifest as isolation but as *precisely the opposite*. It *appears* as finally *belonging* to a realm whose interiority is quite literally *self*-confirming. "My voice," "my people," "my opinion," "my experience," "my story" as a presumed inoculant, not *against* self-isolation but on its behalf.

Death-bed refusals to summon one's relations now see as freedom. Fear that it is *your* relations you are summoning, not mine, and doing this in advance so that what can happen next is not a conversation between us in which we both risk thinking more or differently or more richly. Rather, we both risk nothing but violation, violence. Such that, as we've seen too often lately, only violence is feasible to "connect."

Add to this the treasure of electronic devices geared, as the word suggests, to make divisiveness simple and easy and to hide the question of who or what might conquer/profit from such divide, and we've got a weird dead end. "Device": "the method by which things are divided"

(Online Etymological Dictionary). In a recent *New York Times* cross-word, in fact, the answer to the clue that asked for one who doesn't own such a device was "loner."

A dear old friend of mine circulated a video link a while back of a German doctor that claimed that the COVID-19 *lockdown* was the worse crime against humanity in human history. And I can proclaim without hesitation that the infectiousness of this is real, and it is catching, and no mask is adequate to it, no social distancing is effective except simply blanking out and becoming as shouty-adamant as those whose shouty-adamancy annoys my own slumbers. Trying to carefully make the case seems like dancing solo, here, right now, typing. I'm left not wanting to say anything about Jodi Doering or about this sent-out video or about that dear old friend. I don't know what to do.

I watch as the inverse-that-is-no-inverse happens to Robert Kennedy Jr., where any concern about government actions, any warrant for any suspicion about what is happening to us, any interpretation that interrupts the narrative, is mocked, exaggerated, lied about and dismissed.

But there it is. I've been as perfectly coerced into the very silence that can no longer tell who is coerced and who coercing as has my old friend now down a rabbit hole, calling me the rabbit holed-up in fakery. As the smoke gathers in the air.

"No, you are!"

"No. You!"

An uttechere only Blake fans and Frye weasels might get the joke. *Someone's* dreams are fulfilled in all this, but I can't tell who. Doesn't feel like mine. Perfect. A mumbly murmuring under the shriekings. Fake news seems fake. Or maybe not. I've had it.

I'm not going to be fine. I've learned that, right at this juncture, I should "up" my medications *and* that they are a deliberate, surreptitious plot to quell the uprising of the masses.

It becomes like a mantra murmured under my breath, inside the CPAP machine, nights when I roll over and play near-dead:

"What you're seeing and what you're reading is not what's happening" (Trump, 2018). "This can't be happening. It's not real."

"What you're seeing and what you're reading is not what's happening" (Trump, 2018). "This can't be happening. It's not real."

"What you're seeing and what you're reading is not what's happening" (Trump, 2018). "This can't be happening. It's not real."

My oxygen levels feel maxed out. I don't know who I might call even if I could. After all, who might you trust? *Something* feels like a death-threat. The Ravens no longer seem quite so benign.

Okay, well, I'm going to try something, then, if only for my own good. Perhaps the interpretive gesture becomes dangerous *precisely when it does not go far enough* in its dissembling of foundations. Perhaps the interpretive turn results in a feeling of being out in the open in such a way that it is easy to retract, to retrench into something like what appears like subjectivity.

Okay, ready? *I myself alone* is not a proper vessel, not a proper practice. Why? *Because there is no such a thing.* This existentialist, hallucinatory, alluring nightmare is the last grand narrative that tries to rescue this human-flesh-me from the fray of living by giving me what seems like a safe and impervious locale of self-isolation. *There is no such locale.* It is no place, utopian, pathetic. This language, that people, our history, theirs—these are all feigns and fakes. Make no mistake. There have been good reasons for such retreats because of the profound abusiveness that grand, white-boy narratives wield by their very nature, by their very grandiosity. And make no mistake. I'm white, I'm rich, I'm English speaking, I'm male, well-educated, from European blood lines. *Now* what are you going to do? And what am I to do?

But the point must be made that all those retreats, *all of them,* even my own private interior selfhood, are produced in response to the very abusers one is attempting to self-isolate against. The greater the abuse, the higher the walls of the isolation chamber. As per a thread of Buddhism, the Grandest of the Grand Narratives is the Self that has become the hidden escape hatch for cover against the rise of interpretation and its terrible countenance:

I know well of the Gadamer-Derrida conversations (see Michelfelder & Palmer, 1989) in which Jacques pointed out that Hans-Georg was presuming the "good will" of the partners when he spoke of conversation. But presuming good will doesn't mean that you simply goofily continue in such a presumption come what may. It only means that one seeks out reliable companions and can test that reliability only by risking assuming it, and then seeing what happens, whether trust builds, whether expectations are treated with open-mindedness and dignity. And getting better at taking those risks and considering open-mindedness and dignity. And getting better at taking those risks and considering those matters I know. Sloppy words—friendship, trust, dignity, open-mindedness. Antiquated all, but that, of course, is part of the whole point of this, that antiquatedness. All I know going in is this. There was a cluster of honeybees in the greenhouse a couple of days ago, in the tail end of autumn. five of them out for one last buzz. I stopped when I saw them and slipped into a recent under-breath muttering—"Stop. I may never see this again in the remains of my life. Stop, just a breath or two. There." My own exercise of one last buzz. They were very beautiful and utterly ordinary. I wouldn't recommend this if you're not up to it. Given the tempo of many people's lives, coming to a dead stop at the sight of some bees could be injurious if you're not careful, if you've had no time to practice such things. And, of course, the reason that there is no time to practice such things is because of lack of practice. How's that for a conspiracy theory about bees and distraction and breaths shared? This be the perplex. (Jardine, 2020b, p. 3)

I wrote a while back (Jardine, 2020b) about the Arizona couple who ingested chloroquine phosphate, an aquarium cleaner used to clean fish tanks, in sway of misunderstood presidential advice (Beasley, 2020). I mentioned the assertion "I loved the poorly educated" (Quartz Staff, 2016).

And I know, now, that *being poorly educated has nothing to do with it*. It is far more mystical than that, far more deeply rooted in our animal bodies. Far more psychopathological, socio-pathological, worming down into dying body meat and gut-fears and beliefs that there must be *something* behind the curtain, there must be *some* foundation. *There must be!*

The slippage of signifiers signaled by the rise of interpretation, once it seeps into the groundwater, makes one ripe for the picking of the next trickster:

"What you're seeing and what you're reading is not what's happening" (Trump, 2018). "This can't be happening. It's not real."

"What you're seeing and what you're reading is not what's happening" (Trump, 2018). "This can't be happening. It's not real."

"What you're seeing and what you're reading is not what's happening" (Trump, 2018). "This can't be happening. It's not real."

Siren's wails, and you're damn right I'm being equivocal. The seeming liberatory effect of interpretive work makes all of us *even more susceptible to abuse*, to fakery, to the Neo-con- man, to the click-bait, to the marketing ploy. Hermes being a trickster does not mean he was cute and benign. *That* is the trick. Coyotes will rip apart your flesh if you let them, or prey on your spent carcass. My oxygen seemed used up, and I'm not sure I want to win it back:

> You know what else they say about my people? The polls, they say I have the most loyal people. Did you ever see that? Where I could stand in the middle of Fifth Avenue and shoot somebody and I wouldn't lose any voters, okay? It's like incredible. (Trump, 2016; RealClear Politics, January 23, 2016) In a source I can no longer trace, one commentator suggested "This wasn't meant as a compliment." Believers think it was, of course, of course and the commentator's comment is only heard as infidelity. (Jardine, 2019b)

I'll end by expressing as simply as I can my love for that nurse and those dying patients and whatever it is that has been perpetrated on all their failing breaths. I am so sorry for any hand I may have had, through action or inaction, in all of this.

CHAPTER THIRTY-SEVEN

Two Arced Fishes and a Raven's Eye: Thoughts on Selfies, Pandemics, and a Door, Ajar

Preamble: Two Arced Fishes

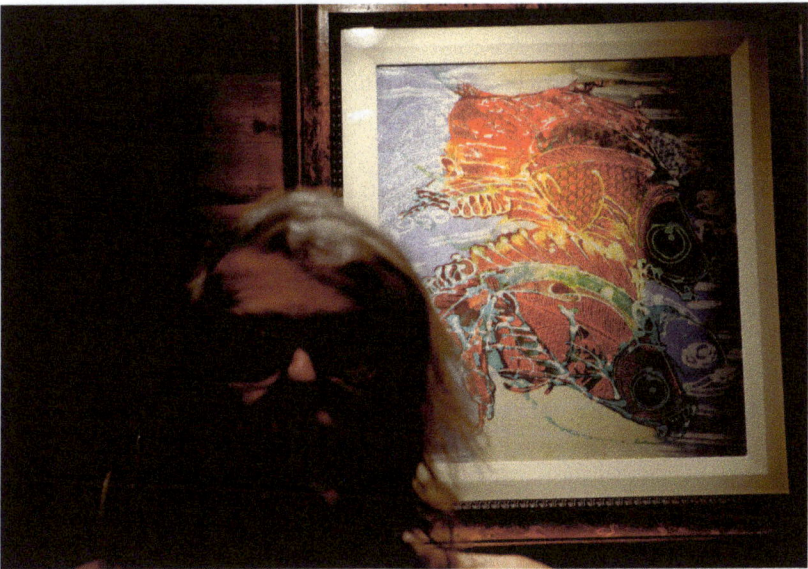

FIGURE 17. TWO ARCED FISHES

Sometimes
Selfies betray arced fishes.
Imaginaries
Far more bright and brilliant than the imaging self's self-regard.

Unbeknownst. Face-darkening.
Swum behind one's back.
It's how to write, I've heard
Tell. Eyecast
Back and around
To what got meant
Even if I didn't sense I meant it. Even if I didn't mean it.

Arced fishes
Betraying a giveaway
Right when,
Could be especially when
I thought it was just me.

Collective Stress Disorder

Animals under various forms of threat—the continuous presence of predators, lack of adequate food, drought, and the like—tend to play less and less.
They tend, quite naturally, to revert to those kinds of activities that will aid
them in gaining comparative control over their environment, activities that
involve little or no risk. They revert, so to speak, to what is tried and true,
what is most familiar. (Jardine, 1992a, p. 119)

Finding out what we have imagined to be most tried and true and most
familiar, isn't necessarily happy news. It just might be requiring mandatory, state-sponsored study for a future that will not be.

Okay, stop. Breath a moment. Where is that citation? Here:

Unwholesome mental formations are like a tangled ball of string. When we
try to untangle it, we only wind it around ourselves until we cannot move.
These mental formations are sometimes called afflictions *kleshas*. Sometimes
they are called obscurations because they confuse us and make us lose our
way. (Hanh, 1999, pp. 73–74)

Thank you. I don't say that often enough to these teachers whose words
dwell near me and help me out. One small reason for scholarship is

finding comfort—common strength—to help lift up my own frailties into something more air-borne, a suffering that is lighter, more livable, more companionable. Again, a pedagogical image of the meeting of the old and the new, the established and the arising, the ancestral and the new baby born. An aside, that my wife and I, all things being well, just might be grandparents in a few days of this writing, August 2, 2021, due date August 6. One more reason to keep reading, keep writing.

So, there is a phenomenon, here, that I would always caution my student-teachers about. In their practicum placements, there will always be a little worry of this, a larger one over that, there's another, another that, and that, and that—these tend to coalesce into what I half-jokingly named "collective stress disorder" where the sense of threat, distur-bance, anxiety, frustration or exhaustion of *all of these collectively* can come down upon the head of *any one of them* and make my actions and reactions any one of them exaggerated, inappropriate and monstrous.

> Ivan Illich (& Cayley, 1992, p. 127) almost playfully names the inflaming and exaggerating urge in these matters a sort of "apocalyptic randiness"—basi-cally framed, "I have an even more horrible example to tell you! Let's imagine an even worse situation!" (p. 127), spoken or written with a sort of energizing, arousing, inciting, conspiratorial glee coupled with a strange tinge of superi-ority, distain, and moral indignation. This, of course, is reminiscent of school staffroom conversations: "You think *that* kid is trouble? A couple of years ago, I had a kid in my class who …"
> …
> When speaking of apocalyptic randiness, Illich (& Cayley, 1992, p. 127) also warns of falling prey to its opposite, Romanticism, where, with equal exag-geration, simplification and thoughtlessness, one sees good news every-where. (Jardine et al., 2010, pp. 27–28, 35–36)

Our panic-reaction gripping onto things creates reifications towards which one then becomes hostile. And, again, the more we grip, the greater the grip we are in:

> Like trying to grab cornstarch dissolved in water, the faster and harder and more desperately we try to seize these matters and cling to some-thing hard and permanent the more substantial they *feel* and the more is aggravated our desire to grip even tighter. (Jardine, 2012b, p. 219)

The result of this gripping work is a "Titanic mind-set," (Bowers, 2008, p. 11), caught up in what Edward Said calls the "vocabulary of giantism and apoca- lypse each use of which is plainly designed not to edify but to inflame" (2001, p. 4). (Jardine, 2016m, pp. 208–209)

Utterly embarrassing for me to read and be reciting so many, many times. Things written *years ago* and still I fall prey. Stop. Still yourself. Untangle first. Always a good idea. Otherwise, we lose our way.

I lose my way

"A Consciousness that must Leave the Door Ajar"

A consciousness that must leave the door ajar. (Hillman, 2013b, p. 98)

Restoration and renewal. The arrival of these moments of stilling can be great gifts, hard to handle. The good news is that the bad news, here, can be good news—it forces my hand, shows me my patience, com- posure, trust, paranoia, exhaustion, suspicions. Our circumstances, as teachers, as students beckons our careful attention. Covid-19 has been a terribly passive and patient *teacher* along with all its collective surround- ings of stress and strain. It shows me how easily I can be preyed upon by click-baits. How easily I can discover how I've been entrenched, how I've forgotten what my work is after all these years under the relatively minor. Discover, as David Loy (2010, p. vii) put it, that I have, we have "bound ourselves without a rope." This trick is age-old. It shows me that it would be so easy to simply revert to the old saw of what's "tried and true."

The door is ajar, the opportunity at hand, of rethinking schooling, of releasing ourselves from its pent-up fears and worn-out inheritances and prejudices and presumptions. But equally on hand is the threat- based, knee-jerk, unthought "idea" of simply "getting back to normal."

"If It Actually Exists, it Must be Possible"

It's coming back to us one way or another. This is what can happen if the anxious, mindless rushing of schooling gets interrupted. There is a lot of talk about the vital need for kids to get back to school because of how important it is. I agree. *But it need not be the same old efficiency-model, panic-based acceleration, and exhaustion* (see Jardine, 2017). What we've witnessed is that there is no necessity to the things we have being doing.

One of the most pernicious and intransigent and most deeply buried falsehoods squirming around with those fishes is that schools as they are contemporarily often constituted—the ones we want to "get back to"—are simply "the real world." Schools, "normal" schools, can cleave toward "a demonstration hidden within … deeper harmonies and deeper simplicities" ones more in line the etymologies of that word "school" itself. Consider this: School, Latin *schola*, "leisure for learning." Greek *skhole*, "originally 'a holding back, a keeping clear' " (Online Etymological Dictionary [OED] under "school"). This is what can happen if the frantic forward push of our living gets paused. This is the terrible, tough, pedagogical gift that Covid-19 has offered us.

Schooling will always be difficult and hard work *no matter how you do it*. Finding a way into the re-emergent harmonies and simplicities of the abundant relations of living disciplines and living fields of relations, human and more-than-human is at least a difficulty that bears with it the potential of repeated uprisings of great relief and joy:

> I am not sure I have much more to say that hasn't been already said over and over again by so many. The complex and difficult insights of ecological alertness are known and have been for aeons. The complex and difficult insights of how education might shape itself in light of this alertness has been well documented in recent decades. Witness the papers in this collection [referring here to Lyle, Latremouille, & Jardine, 2021] and their references lists, full and abundant [see also the previous issue of this journal, and so many other classroom examples and scholarly back up to their rigors and delights and difficulties]. Witness how those [reference lists] referred to have their own family trees listed. Follow them, too. Find your way. It's a lush, tough field. I've witnessed dozens of schools where these matters of teaching and learning and curriculum ecologically imagined are accepted and practiced.
>
> …
>
> After all, it is not as if curriculum guides don't describe living fields of knowledge, locales, places, terrains wont of attention and affection. The invitation is lying nearby, right on-hand. The theory has become well-wrought and is burgeoning with new stings and insight as we speak. The practices have been

well-documented. But, as per Bill Callahan (2019b), "God's face on the water, though plain to see, it's still hard to read" (n.p.). (Jardine, 2021c, p. 38)

There we are. Learning to read, all over again. I recall, for example, the utterly strange example of the following list that was common at the beginning of the pandemic, about what to think of this, about what to do, to understand, to study, to remember, to lament. I can no longer be assured that all the URLs are still "hot," but it does give pause to the rush to get back to and unthought, knee-jerk normal when placed alongside Gary Snyder's insistences about the grain of things:

Spreads of lions laying on warm paved roads in South Africa. (https://www.cnn.com/travel/article/lions-kruger-lockdown-scli-intl/index.html).

Sea turtles thriving on empty Florida beaches (https://www.cnn.com/2020/04/18/us/thriving-sea-turtles-lockdown-florida-beaches-trnd/index.html).

Wild goats taking over Welsh towns (https://www.theguardian.com/uk-news/video/2020/mar/31/goats-take-over-empty-welsh-streets-llandudno-coronavirus-lockdown-video).

Squirrels taking over Santa Monica parks (https://patch.com/california/santamonica/watch squirrels-take-over-santa-monica-park-amid-coronavirus).

Sheep wandering golf courses in England (https://www.reporter.am/sheep-take-over-golf-course-in-england-act-as-greenskeepers/).

Wild boars on the streets of Barcelona. (https://twitter.com/CarolineLawrenc?ref_src=twsrc%5Etfw%7Ctwcamp%5Etweetembed&ref_url=https%3A%2F%2Ftheconversation.com%2Fcoronavirus-what-the-lockdown-could-mean-for-urban-wildlife-134918).

Shoals of fish back in bluer and clearer canals of Venice (https://www.theguardian.com/environment/2020/mar/20/nature-is-taking-back-venice-wildlife-returns-to-tourist-free-city).

Europe breathing fresher air

(https://www.euronews.com/2020/03/30/europe-breathes-fresher-air-under-lockdown-as-coronoavirus-measures-ease-pollution).

Nitrogen Dioxide levels plunging in northern China
(https://earthobservatory.nasa.gov/images/146362/airborne-nitrogen-diox
ide-plummets-over-china).

This pandemic, and all the sundry surrounding panic-based, media-overkill-click-bait-based hysterics hopefully have allowed moments of pause, because the rich and abundant fields of relations that house us and that are entrusted to teachers and students in schools are simply awaiting us.

Make no mistake. This is no Romantic joy-ride. This work often *hurts*. One's new students, in many cases, are already well-schooled in being schooled, and have been taught to not be taught this way. And, let's face it, surrounding circumstances and panics and presumptions and parental worries and arced fishes are not necessary working in our favor toward favoring exploring abundant, living fields of relations as a way to proceed. Working this way is not easy. It is not quick. And, in our current circumstances, it might seem like an emergency. It is. Therefore, it is bone-wearyingly laborious, but it is good labor, honorable labor for teachers and students alike. To rigorously seek out the threads, the connections, the details, to push back against the tendencies to fragment, to trivialize, to accelerate, is tough work in which we need to find comfort—common strength, as goes the etymology—in each other.

But again, don't get light-headed, here. There was a study done involving 26 elementary and secondary schools, 12,800 students in Alberta, Canada, that demonstrated that following the ways that a disciplinary, living field of knowledge is practiced instead of the old industrial model of schooling lead to markedly higher performances on Provincial Standardized Tests (Friesen, 2010). I gave this study to a principal who dismissed it out-of-hand, saying "we just don't have time for that sort of stuff." My dear colleagues and co-authors, Patricia Clifford and Sharon Friesen, and I used to call this "the old list of "yeah-buts ...":

Up against the too often pronounced exhaustion and desperation and despair of "this sort of thing is not possible in my school/with my sort of students/in this part of town/at this grade level/with this school administration/in this school board/in this subject area/with these parents/under these economic conditions," and so, on and on, we offer an old and pointed response of our late colleague, teacher and friend, Patricia Clifford: "if it actually exists, it must be possible." (Seidel & Jardine, 2014, p. 2)

An Old, Familiar Face

Perception of opportunities requires a sensitivity given through one's own wounds. Here, weakness provides the kind of hermetic, secret perception critical for adaptation to situations. The weak place serves to open us to what is in the air. We feel through our pores which way the wind blows. We turn with the wind; trimmers. An opportunity requires … a sense … which reveals the *daimon* of a situation. The *daimon* of a place in antiquity supposedly revealed what the place was good for, its special quality and dangers. The *daimon* was thought to be a *familiaris* of the place. To know a situation, one needs to sense what lurks in it. (Hillman, 2013b, pp. 101–102)

This is the lesson I carried into all those University classes I taught and into those school classrooms where I ventured with student-teachers and on my own in friendships with teachers in schools, in graduate classes, and so on. The open door is *everywhere*. Every topic is a potential clue, a possible hint. Every topic listed in every curriculum guide is the center of an elaborate and elaborate-able and venture-albe field of living relations. Opening up those fields for our students—for ourselves as well—is at the heart and in the grain of things pedagogical.

As a general pronouncement, this can seem simply overwhelming and chaos-inducing and Romantic and unrealistic and frightening and woozy and all that. It can also seem subjective and "letting kids do what they want" chaos and so on. It is none of these. These, too, are knee-jerks that are understandable if you have not experienced and witnessed this sort of pedagogy. What is always needed to make it a viable, practiceable matter, is an good example of "a demonstration hidden" always nested here and here and here.

So here we go, an old, familiar *familiaris* squat on the back railing, a frequent visitor, utterly easy to ignore or let glide by. Normal.

FIGURE 18. LILAC IRIS

"Right here, where it, where it seems impossible that one life even matters" (Wallace, p. 111) comes the moment that teachers understand on their good days, and students, too, when something heretofore simply fly-by stops and stills us into stopping and stilling and whiling. Just imagine, for a moment, the multiple stories to be told, the new stories to be ventured, photos to be taken, feathers to be microscoped and drawn by hand, Latin etymologies of *Corvus corax*, myriad cultural depictions—more stories than could be read in a lifetime, the sciences of flight, the details of habitats, of territoriality, the analogies of this to tribes and political allegiances. Life-spans (10–15 years). Wingspans (100–150 cm). Typologies. Kinds. Relations. Linnaeus's branching work. Relations: Jays, Crows, Magpies.

Monogamous, this picture being one of a pair that has been around for quite a while.

My wife and heard they were nesting nearby, and the neighbors saw four little heads popping up. We thought of how cute it might be if the parents brought the kids over to our feeder. Well, they did, full grown, loud, boisterous, each vying for position, chasing others away, pecking and yakking. We knew they were territorial, so we knew, sooner or later, the "kids" would disperse. We took the feeder down temporarily and mom and dad have, for now, returned.

Whiling over this and all its adjacent fields of relations is itself an extraordinary "normality" that as commonplace as can be. We can all recognize it from those times where something of "interest" (Latin root, *inter-* and *-esse,* essentially, "being in the middle of something" [OED]) has grabbed our attention and our attention deepens as we continue to explore. This is not some sort of subjective, touchy-feely flight of fancy made up on the spot, this idea of whiling and the time it takes. It is a deeply scholarly matter:

> It is not merely one's "taking time" to linger over something, as in the slackening or slowing down to contemplate. [This whiling] temporality ... is not a function of lackadaisical, meandering contemplation, least of all passive in any way, but is a function of the fullness and *intensity* of attention and engrossment. (Ross, 2006, p., 109)

> We become enthralled and "enveloped in a time that does not pass" (Ross, 2006 p. 106), a time described by Hans-Georg Gadamer with the German term *Verweilen*—translatable as "tarrying" or "whiling" or "gathering." (Jardine, 2016d, p. 250)

> In this tarrying the contrast with the merely pragmatic realms of understand becomes clear. The *Weile* [the "while" in *Verweilen,* tarrying] has this very special temporal structure—a structure of being moved, which one nevertheless cannot describe merely as duration. In it we tarry. (Gadamer, 2001, pp. 76–77)

> This possibility of, shall we say, "absorption" and being moved and addressed and, shall we say, summoned or beckoned by the work itself, is phenomenologically familiar. When the work undertaken is worthwhile, the inquiry, the topic, the images, the ideas, the story:

>> truly takes hold of us. [I]t is not an object that stands opposite us which we look at in hope of seeing through it to an intended conceptual meaning. Just the reverse. The work is an *Ereignis*—an event that "appropriates us" into itself. It jolts us, it knocks us over, and sets up a world of its own, into which we are drawn, as it were. (Gadamer, 2001, p. 71; Jardine, 2016d, p. 250)

Difficult to grasp, but the irony is that it is worth taking the time to think about and study this temporality that teachers already understand when a group of students get taken hold of by a topic, and idea, an image, a story, a mathematical diagram. We know this from our own lives as well, this weird uplift. We can all find it in ourselves when we linger over something that opens our hearts, sparks our ideas, in which we find companions who also love this place, this thing, this idea, this field, old ancestors found lingering there with advice and warnings and details. The work of art or words of a student that brought me to a halt on day. Beautiful things:

> And the Raven, never flitting, still is sitting, *still* is sitting
>
> Edgar Allan Poe, from "The Raven," final stanza
> (https://www.poetryfoundation.org/poems/48860/the-raven)

Or this from the *Prose Edda* chapter entitled "Gylfaginning: Here Begins the Beguiling of Gylfi":

> The ravens sit on [Odin's] shoulders and say into his ear all the tidings which they see or hear; they are called thus: Huginn[1] and Muninn.[2] He sends them at day-break to fly about all the world, and they come back at undern-meal; thus he is acquainted with many tidings. Therefore men call him Raven-God, as is said:
>
> > Huginn and Muninn hover each day
> >   The wide earth over;
> > I fear for Huginn lest he fare not back,—
> >   Yet watch I more for Muninn."
> (https://www.sacred-texts.com/neu/pre/pre04.htm, p. 51)

The footnotes in square brackets indicate that Huggin means "thought" and Muninn means "memory."

I fear for thought lest it not come to me. It is difficult to remain alert in the clustering gatherings that classrooms can be. There are worthy companions who've written about their work in schools (see Seidel & Jardine, 2016, which contains writings of classroom teachers pondering and practicing this sort of work).

I watch out for memory traces in that Raven's arrival. I know there will be doors, ajar, if I can sit, still.

A Lilac Iris

At the center of a stone or at the axis of a tree there's the silence of a world turning. (Domanski, 2002, p. 245)

   The center is everywhere. (Nishitani, 1982, p. 146)

Of all things, COVID-19 has most disastrously aggravated our feeling of time running out, of all this having taken too long, of stretched and snapped patience. Many have suffered in this lingering, no doubt about it.

But again, there is a hint. Many teachers have expressed to me in this meanwhile their desire to rethink the old familiars of school. Rethink what might be found in the eyes in mirrors, or the ones of Ravens:

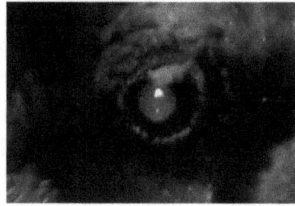

FIGURE 19. CLOSE EYE

I've never noticed this before, a lilac iris, probably colored out of reflects of the surroundings. A quick look on Google Images shows that this reflect is not frequent. Now what?

There is no "everyday," no "normal" day. We all pretend there is. We all add to the myth. It's an act of pretense which helps us survive, to feel there's ground under our feet, when we know full well that beneath that ground there is an eternity of stars and galaxies, a great unknown which, on one of these normal days will swallow us whole. (Domanski, 2002, p. 249)

We don't need to be afraid, even though this might feel like a sort of misty dissolving or the like. It isn't. It is "too much to take" but it need not be swallowed whole. Just take that as your starting point and *let it be the center* of your ventures. That will help you settle down from this sometimes too-large invocation of living relations.

A lilac iris probably reflecting its surroundings.

The fires in the West are teachers. The smoke that stings teaches as it stings. The First Nations children buried in unmarked graves would like a word with you. The drought across the prairies has a lesson all planned, as do the European floods, as does COVID-19, as does January 6, 2021.

Teachers every single one. I've often advised student-teachers that when they move from the hard work of having elaborated a living field with their students, on to the next topic, they will, of necessity or at least frequency, run smack into a solid wall *all over again*.

Starting all over again. You can become practiced at this over time, but our everyday lives mitigate against such openness and necessitate setting off, deep breath, all over again, into the work of remembering and thinking, Odin's lovely, horrible pair of familiars.

Even the well-being of my inhaling is rained down from the trees overhead. And this said as the smoke from fires to the West choke a bit. "I can't breathe" come round all over again as a consequence, all over again, of what we have trouble facing, behind our backs and right before our eyes, all over again.

And to sit here, writing, and you, reading, all over again, *textus*, weaving. "Threads interweaving, criss-crossing" (Wittgentstein, 1968, p. 33):

> Certainly one can call this process a "while" [*Weilen*], but this is something that nobody measures and that one does not find to be either boring or merely entertaining. The name I have for the way in which this event happens is "reading." With reading one does not imagine ... that one can already do it. In reality, one must learn how ... Now the word *Lesen* ["read," a German kin to the English word "lesson"—I think, for example, of an old commonplace in Anglican church services, of saying "today's lesson is taken from Matthew,"

meaning both literally "a reading from Matthew" but also *reading* that reading for its "lesson"] carries within it a helpful multiplicity of harmonic words, such as gathering together [*Zusammenlesen*], picking up [*Auflesen*], picking out [*Auslesen*], or to sort out [*verlesen*]. All of these are associated with "harvest" (*Lese*), that is to say, the harvest of grapes, which persist in the harvest. The word *Lesen* also refers to something that begins with spelling out words, if one learns to write and read, and again we find numerous echo words. One can start to read a book [*anlesen*] or finish up reading it [*auslesen*], one can read further in it [*weiterlesen*], or just check into it [*nachlesen*], or one can read it aloud [*vorlesen*]. All of these point toward the harvest that is gathered in and from which one takes nourishment. (Gadamer, 2007a, pp. 217–218)

Lesson plans: harvesting, sorting out, and gathering together. Wonderful things to re-consider in the face of the grain of things.

An Old, Familiar Face Takes Nourishment

So, then, whence the lilac in this Raven's pupil? It is unclear. But as per one of my lingering habits, I zoomed in on that lilac eye photo, just to see what I can see, like the bear who came over the mountain. And, well, whaddya know?!

FIGURE 20. PEEK A BOO

See? White shirt with sky-blue stripes. Pale skin halo pinkish, sparse-long white-grey hair, elbows akimbo with camera held up, blue/white striped shirt below, pixilated. That's me in the spotlight, losing my religion (as the saying goes), right in the midst of a lilac arcing eye eying that very spotting.

Be still. Click.

CHAPTER THIRTY-EIGHT

Being at the Trembling

FIGURE 21. BEE BETWEEN

> `... endless afternoons lost
> in their own alchemical sense of surfaces and shadows
> bees hyperkinetic across meadows each takes at least
> sixteen days to make sixteen afternoons of heaven's push
> and heed transubstantations afternoons into flesh
> flesh into honey.
>
> From Don Domanski (2013, p. 9), "Madonna
> of the Diaphanous Life"

> I wrote a letter to a wildflower
> on a classic nitrogen afternoon.
>> From David Berman, (1998), "The Wild Kindness"

Being at the trembling, shimmering cusp of things.

Can't include photos of my grandson here for quite unspeakable reasons of caution. But still, you know this. Here he is, here they are, brand-new fabrics, brand-new familiarities being knit, brand-new excitement and pleasure and accomplishment and pleasure and care and affection and all that, all that:

> A new flower on the pea vine.
>
> From Bill Callahan (2022a), "Coyotes"

A brand-new spring sun rising up. Right here, right now, like never before.

And, of course, something age-old, the ancient, tough work of uprising onto your own two feet, and the giggly surroundings that uprise with you, the vertigos, the repetition, the imitations, the love. An old, old story. Hands reached out. Hearts reached out.

Me stretching and cooing as grandfathers have done long before his arrival made me one for the first time.

These two collide, ancient and brand-new. Where's my bee picture, floating between the garden flowers? Ah, okay, there it is. Header. "The true locus of hermeneutics is this 'in between'" (Gadamer, 1989, p. 295). The knit and the re-knit.

And then bloody-well undone:

> Dreams are thoughts in lotus and chains
> Chains are broken in the morning by the first bird's first song
>
> Singing sha-sha-shadow
> Sha-sha-shadow's of dawn
>
> Shadow of my boy coming down the hall
>> From Bill Callahan (2022a), "Coyotes"

I have to beg forgiveness for enjoying the newly arrived photos of him oh so much, given recent events in Uvalde.

And I have to let myself enjoy this more than I might have ever imagined, given those very same recent events in Uvalde. This and writing is all I've got, a meagre, little, quiet witness, useless, inadequate in a surround where there is no adequacy.

Bill's voice raises up in almost-fear with every tall repetition:

> And as the sun moves away
> A boy's shadow grows tall, tall, tall.

From Bill Callahan (2022a), "Coyotes"

This enjoyment, this untangling and entangling and re-tangling always has the penumbra of its disappearance, of my own disappearance, otherwise it wouldn't be what it is. One more breath in-between. Those bee flowers long-dead. That bee perhaps surviving one more year. My old hands reaching out in await.

The bees I saw last year, late in the season, in the greenhouse, shimmering over wee basil flowers at the last minute. Knowing full well it might be the very last time I see this. And that this has always been so.

Did I tell this story already?

Jackie, teetering, take an elbow, help me. "Oh sorrow" (Seidel, 2014, p. 112). Sorrow. *Sorge*, who's root also means "care."

I remind myself all over again of my own two feet:

> This lift [this loft in between] allows *those very sorrows* to be sung in words and harmonies with Ravens and stones and trees, and not just suffered in silence and isolation. (Jardine, 2016c, p. 184)

Bee be between. Jodi, help. "Hush, child" (Latremouille, 2014, p. 30). It's good to be surrounded in these constant in-betweens.

CHAPTER THIRTY-NINE

Sunflowers, Coyote, and Five Red Hens

Preamble

Not everyone is beguiled by the hunt for double meanings, the decoding of references, the connection between sub-rhythmic dots of syllabic emphases, or the tracing of narrative arcs. [But] I do believe that those buried layers of syntactic, semantic and symbolic meaning give life to the songs, regardless of whether the listener gives a hoot about decoding them. They deepen the saturation of the colours, the concentration of feeling and the verisimilitude of the small world the songs describe. (Newsom, with Paytress, 2015, p. 86)

Sight-Lines

I feel uneasy stepping into the great territories opened up by Nancy Moules (2017) and Kate Beamer (2017) at the tail end of last year's *Journal of Applied Hermeneutics*. It is not (yet) a territory I have endured as deeply. That bracketed "yet" is little more than a feeble attempt at trying to remember not to forget what surrounds us all, whatever its proximity.

There is no real refuge out of the sight-lines of impermanence, death, and grief. A shuddering thought, that this makes persistent and practiced mindfulness of these sight-lines the only reliable refuge. It is no accident that contemporary hermeneutics, in its ventures to speak about our living circumstances, is inevitably surrounded by penumbras of finitude and its ins and outs, and how, or whether, or to what extent, I have come to live with this inevitably.

This is wound into the flesh of *any and all topics* of *any* interpretive delve: "the concept of substance is … inadequate. [There is a] radical challenge to thought implicit in this inadequacy" (Gadamer, 1989, p. 242). The challenge is simple. What shall we say, what shall we do, in the face of the reality of impermanence? We want to speak clearly and openly but without foreclosure or finality. We want to invite others into this open wound and help them calm themselves and become composed and undistracted if they do. That is what these two authors have done for us.

When their teacher, Edmund Husserl (1970b, p. 7), desperately asked "Can we console ourselves with that? Can we live in this world?" his students' answer was a resounding yes, yes, *this* is the locale of our solidarity and hope. The good news, the hermeneutic consolation, is that "everything around us teaches impermanence" (Tsong-kha-pa, 2000, p. 151). Everything around us teaches us precisely this consolation. Everything is an opportunity for practice and commiseration, for comfort in its lovely etymological origin—common strength.

Thus, the secret of interpretive work is that this impermanent dependent co-arising is full of relations, full of often-hidden or occluded voices and ancestries, mixed bloodlines, secrets. It is full precisely of the voices and images and ideas and lingerings of the quick and the dead.

Opening the Mouths of the Dead

In *Lament of the Dead* (Hillman & Shamdasani, 2013), James Hillman repeatedly introduces a stunning image to help formulate his experience of first opening Carl Jung's then-recently published *Red Book*

(1999): "I was reading about this practice that the ancient Egyptians had of opening the mouth of the dead. I think we don't do that with our hands" (p. 1). Sonu Shamdasani soon elaborates:

> It is the ancestors. It is the dead. This is no mere metaphor. This is no cipher for the unconscious or something like that. When [Jung] talks about the dead he means the dead. And they're present in images. They still live on. (p. 2)

This is an ecological as well as a mytho-poetic presumption, and it has some affinity to threads of Buddhist thought as well. It is a presumption that "transforms the world and its beings into a most extraordinary vision" (Tsong-kha-pa, 2005, p. 125):

> The land of the dead is the country of ancestors, and the images who walk in on us are our ancestors. If not literally the blood and genes from whom we descend, then they are the historical progenitors. (Hillman, 1996, p. 60)

Likewise, the linguistic progenitors hidden in words (like "comfort"). And the earthly progenitors hidden in the plain sight of the animal-body's tracing of places and footfalls. The dogs sniffing old piss trails as the snow melts.

> Transforming according to circumstances, meet all beings as your ancestors. (Hongzhi Zhengjue [1091–1157 CE], 1991, p. 43)

We "are always already everywhere inhabited" (Smith, 2006, p. xxiv). The ancestors, our *relations*, human and other-wise, are always already among us and we among them, in the most ordinary of objects or words or images, in the texts, in the trees, in the dreamstates, in the gestures, even in the flesh-ache of muscle-born dry wood for winter and the panicky bugs that scurry over it. Or in the distant, unwarranted and perhaps inevitable fear for one's child, care sometimes gone amock, monkey-mind in the midst of impermanence.

And this is just as true of ravens nearby and long since disappeared, of trees long gone to soils, of the outbreath of this forest, here, now, around me, inhaled under the sun's slow returning.

Sunflowers and Five Red Hens

Every road leads to an end
Your apparition passes through me in the willows.
Five red hens—you'll never see us again.

> Sufjan Stevens (2015), from "Death with Dignity"

A delicate Helado Negro remix of "Death with Dignity," these shreds and patches have the poignant, half-there quality of going through the possessions of someone dear who has died. Its incompleteness, then, is as apt a reflection of grieving as you could hope for. (Harris, 2018, p. 107)

Pennants. #239, 2nd floor West, Trueman House, 1947. The still,
Colourless memory of a colourful past Still
Embedded with pins. (Adapted from Moules, 2017, p. 3)

Five red hens whose deep saturation of color is palpable in those lines that took my breath away, even though I don't quite know what it means:

We are drawn into an event … and arrive, as it were, too late, if we want to know what we are supposed to [now] believe. (Gadamer, 1989, p. 490)

But I do know *how* it means. Its specificity holds and intensifies and "breaks forth as if from a center" (Gadamer, 1989, p. 458). Images are sites of power and prickle, pins that beckon attention and ask something of us—to take good care of them. They *are* incomplete, and an elegant interpretation of them leaves them as they *are*, deepening the saturation of the colors.

I didn't know John Moules well. Only a wee bit. Only once upon a time sat in his backyard, with seven-foot—were they eight-foot? 10? 20?—sunflowers laced to the garage and singing in the full-bore summer light, all heads, ours too, turned in phototropic obedience, and all this burned into memory traces whose graces come and go. We are all sat still. Still there. Motionless.

And he came to see my garden and it now seems like a near-mythic event, his frail gait and determination under ravens overhead soaring on summer thermals, black oily wings glinting and curving in thin air.

All things teach as they alight and gurk-gurk and click and burble and yellow-eye the compost.

We check the greenhouse and check the smell of the tomato leaves. That smell like nothing else. Furry vines thick with the perfume of red pulses. Grieving can be just this acrid sweet:

> Silhouette of the cedar
> What is that song you sing for the dead? (Stevens, 2015, n.p.)

I grew up around cedar trees and there aren't any hereabouts. They haunt me still from little boy days near Lake Ontario and the Niagara Escarpment, where they clung to limestone edges and aged in place for centuries. As did I, feeling my age as this image flits by and flirts and teases. Like cicadas, even this passing reminder is full of teachings (Jardine, 1998a)

Red hens, cedars, ravens, sunflowers, all new and fresh. There is some relief to be had in feeling already somewhat outlived. Of dropping the heavy weight of me feeling necessary to the well-being of the world.

"A radical challenge to thought." It is an escape from something.

Held Captive and Coming To

> Insight is more than the knowledge of this or that situation. It always involves an escape from something [Latin *fugere*] that had deceived us and held us captive. Thus, insight always involves an element of self-knowledge and constitutes a necessary side of what we called experience in the proper sense. Insight is something we come to. It … is ultimately part of [our human vocation]—i.e., to be discerning and insightful. (Gadamer, 1989, p. 356)

> [Insight is] is not [simply about] this or that particular thing [but] insight into the limitations of humanity. Thus, experience is the experience of human finitude. The truly experienced person is one who has taken this to heart. The idea that everything can be reversed, that there is always time for everything and that everything somehow returns, proves to be an illusion. (Gadamer, 1989, p. 357)

We are reifying beings and such reification belies impermanence and such belying of impermanence leaves us haunted but not necessarily insightful. Images can spellbind as much as they can release us into the tumult of things. Remaining fugitive is the art of interpretation.

Martin Heidegger's *unheimlichkeit*, "un-home-like-ness" (1962, p. 233) sensing the uncanny haunt of things under the icy surface calm, just looked up in an old hardcover bought in 1971, held together with tape, aging in place on the shelf, still with the notes from a conversation with Gadamer from 1976 scrawled inside the cover, with his note back to his own teacher:

> Care [German *Sorge*, root of "sorrow"] is internal to Being-in-the-world rather than its dominating father. (see Jardine, 2015a)

It is sometimes true that the dead are more among us when they are no longer alive, that they are "with" us in more lively and haunting ways in their death than in their living.

> Back and forth, between memory Love, anger,
> Disappointment, reality
> Romance, gratitude, admiration, regret. (Adapted from Moules, 2017, p. 2)

Every death bursts forth as if from a center. Their living, in death, gets tossed up into thin air and scattered outwards, an energy out beyond the thicknesses of a body, lying, stilled. It is getting these grave gravities back in motion again, back "in play" (Gadamer, 1989, pp. 101–109), that is the work of undergoing grief—Aristotle's *energia*, that very thing that grief can drain faster than it fills up, "aliveness."

"The Claim"

> After this recognition—the image as ancestor—there is the experience of the *claim* that images make upon me.
>
> …
>
> We do not make them up, so we do not make up our response to them but are "taught" this response by them.
>
> …
>
> Our way … does not interpret the image but talks with it. It does not ask what the images means but what it wants.
>
> …

How do we know whether they mean well with us or would possess us? (Hillman, 1996, pp. 60, 61, 93, 75)

"Shifted Toward a Rustling"

Something outside of the funeral hall window caught my attention and my gaze shifted toward a rustling in the bushes. Coyote. It was one of those bone chilling winters, a harsh climate, that provided comfort to me in its barren, hollow form. Yet still, there was movement. (Beamer, 2017, p. 1)

Still. There was movement, animation in a barren, hollow form. Back and forth. Between. *"The true locus of hermeneutics is this in-between"* (Gadamer, 1989, p. 295). It is the fugitive spot where we can sense, in the smallest or largest of events, sing this out all over again: "something is going on, (*im Spiele ist*), something is happening (*sich abspielt*)" (Gadamer, 1989, p. 104), or as the German etymology betrays, *something is at play* (German *Spiel*).

But watch out. Hiding here, too, is a Yiddish-English usage of a tricky tale meant to deceive or persuade or to allow the teller to escape unharmed or elude capture. Thus summoning pitchman Hermes all over again and Coyote's trickiness.

In taking up the trick, walking through the open gate, then, we must remain alert and not just fall for it.

The wound of grief is thus a locale of the unexpected, rustling arrival of "something outside." Coyote is just such a familiar figure, and it is how Hermes might be cast as well, both like the sweep of a black cat on a witch's broom. Familiars. The bush-rustling portend of *energia*, aliveness. Coyote's trick, Hermes' opening of the gate, can bring hope and a sense of futurity, opportunity out beyond grief and its thickness and gravity and haltedness. Opportunity, portals, pores, openings, wounds. A hint, then, of *aletheia* (see Moules, 2015). Sensing what lurks. Pins and hens and sunflowers turn to face me. What do you want? What shall I do that is proper to this turning?

Imagine. Death's swerving halt sets things in motion. Its arrival is not adequately understood as simply the causal outcome of previous events or circumstances. Instead, it *happens* and its happenstance cascades out into the future and back into previous events deemed finished and over with. In this sense, it makes sense, but does not make enough sense to speak of the "cause of death." Death enlivens—memory, presumption, desire, hope, imagination, expectation, regret, anger, and grief, yes grief. Precisely its eventful finality makes it an unfinished swerve, back and forth, and sidelong into surroundings, multiple.

Summoned "to see with fresh eyes" (Gadamer, 1989, p. 16) It is full of "lightning flashes" (Calvino, 2016 p. 48)

The suddenly found object, the suddenly arisen smell or word or little totem having been left behind here on a table, sometimes unbearably and unexplicably full of significance, reminder, or portend. The ghost of a forgotten habit run into over coffee spilled in the morning. "I see dead people" in the quickening light glanced in the window. Even those words about fresh eyes are precisely such, remembered here, memorably risen up seemingly of their own volition.

Repeat after me. Italo Calvino (2016) speaks of "quickness" in this light. Things *happen* and no amount of well-wrought themes or rules or the like can outrun the fact that "the rule does not comprehend it" (Gadamer, 1989, p. 39)—the event outruns and such outrunning keeps the rule alive and alert and in play. It becomes a live wire that must prove itself again and again in the face of events.

Oddly, so oddly, death in the experience of the living as an experience of "lightness" (Calvino, 2016) and "quickening." And this just as the very opposite also occurs, where the live body, in death, becomes a thick thing in an instant and how the dead body seems to weigh so much more than one that is alive.

"Afflicted by Openness"

Repeat. We can become "afflicted by openness" (Hillman, 2013a, p. 55) as those grieving know full well. What might have portended quickness and enlivening can shift: "wingedness [can] become mere haste" (p. 51) or the repeated, even relentless rush of moments, swerves, waves of memory and gut that simply push and stab. Those doing hermeneutic work understand this full well, too. Suddenly, unexpectedly, "every-thing points to some other thing. Nothing comes forward just in the one meaning that is offered to us" (Gadamer, 2007b, p. 131).

Repeat. We can be "outplayed" (Gadamer, 1989, p. 106). Or, perhaps worse "through his[/her] own wounds, ["wound" as locale of vulner-ability, pain, sensitivity; "wound" as hole or portal, Latin *porta*, root of opportunity] may feed others, but may himself [/herself] be drained thereby" (Hillman, 2013, pp. 19–20). In grief, we can end up spent, drained while all the while there is the buzzing of event. There are those times when the memory of the dead starts to flit and cascade and buzz and tremble and skitter and scatter and it won't stop. It won't stop.

That deaths summon repeats. This is so much like those first becom-ing involved in interpretive work. "How do I get it to stop?"

Repeat: "The uninitiated," the unpracticed, "have no proper vessel. They carry water in a sieve and pour it into a perforated jar" (Hillman, 2013c, p. 220).

"The Green Signals"

> How their deaths quicken the air around them, stipple their bodies with a light like the green signals trees send out before their leaves appear. (Wallace, 1987, p. 40)

This is such a lovely hint at the nature of interpretive work when it works. It reads like something I knew all along but had forgotten, some-thing that allows us "to recognize ourselves in the mess of the world as having been engaged and always being engaged" (Hillman, 1996, p. 49). Even if we leave such engagement undecoded, it increases the richness of the colors of red hens.

There is a passage from the first volume of Tsong-kha-pa's *The Great Treatise on the Stages of the Path to Enlightenment* (2000, p. 111) that I find myself returning to: "I compose this in order to condition my own mind."

If I may be so bold, I compose this, I write, in order to compose myself, in order to gain some fleet and failing composure in the face of the onrush of things. Writing, when it works, does not despoil the richness and saturation of the colors. Paying proper attention to experience breaks through the illusion of permanence. It can deepen the colors and can expand me beyond my own means of consolation: "By making the object of meditation extensive [you] expand your [own] mind" (Tsong-kha-pa, 2002, p. 63).

"So that they might be free"

From the Gelug tradition of Tibetan Buddhism, from Tsong-kha-pa's *The Great Treatise on the Stages of the Path to Enlightenment*:

Buddhapalita's *Commentary on [Nagarjuna's] "Fundamental Treatise"* says:

> What is the purpose of teaching dependent-arising? The master Nagarjuna ... saw that living beings are beset by various sufferings and assumed the task of teaching the reality of things ... *so that they might be free.* [my emphasis] What is the reality of things? It is the absence of essence. Unskilled persons ... conceive of an essence in things [something fixed and final and permanent] and then generate attachment and hostility with regard to them. (Tsong-kha-pa, 2002, p. 210)

And from Longchenpa's *Finding Rest in the Nature of the Mind* (2017, p. 47): "Through wisdom, freedom is achieved." But it is not just my freedom that is frailly and momentarily won. Interpretation *frees its object of investigation to be what it is*—dependently co-arising, rather than caught in the binds of grief and other afflictions that might reify.

It lets John Moules catch the thermals and fly up above the sunflowers even as my chest heaves at the thought.

Away you go, then, so we can console ourselves. So that you can remain with us beyond these dead and silent remains.

CHAPTER FORTY

"Things Reveal Themselves Passing Away"

Preamble: An Ode to a Long Love Affair

Bronwen Wallace (1945–1989) was a writer I discovered only upon hearing of her death and reading Dennis Lee's obituary in the Toronto *Globe and Mail* in 1989. I then sought out her last published book of poems, *The Stubborn Particulars of Grace* (1987) and images from it have appeared and reappeared in my own work ever since.

Such can be the fate of long-standing love affairs, this one now nearing 30 years. They can become like haunts that frequent one's life, and that bring the remains of the dead alive again and again. Such is the weird way of words, of images, of bird calls or insect screes, of forgetting and recalling and forgetting all over again.

It has become, for me, wrapped up in the weird ways of writing, of becoming someone who feels wonderfully, even if sometimes painfully, answerable to the world in words.

This is how I've learned to steady myself. It is my most practiced way of bearing. With all its failings and foibles, it has become a practiced refuge of a sort: Shantideva, in his *Engaging in the Bodhisattva Deeds* and *Compendium of Trainings* states "I compose this in order to condition my own mind" (Tsong-Kha-Pa, 2000, p. 111)

I compose this in order to compose myself—to both settle myself and to make up my mind out in concert with the wild composition of the world. Remembering myself, but this said with a great caution: "Like Dogen, the Zen master, said, 'We study the self to forget the self. And when you forget the self, you become one with all things'" (Snyder, 1980, p. 65). "One sees one's own self in all things, in living things, in hills and rivers, towns and hamlets, tiles and stones, and loves these things 'as oneself'" (Nishitani, 1982, pp. 280–281).

The Insistence in Bronwen Wallace's work was on behalf of "the stubborn argument of the particular, right now, in the midst of things, *this* and *this*" (1987, p. 110). This iterates an old hermeneutic adage, that any particular case worth whiling over—of lives, of images, of moments, of arrivals, of a written phrase that halts and beckons attention like a Raven-borne wing whoosh overhead—never simply falls helpless and silent under a rule or type or generality or theme that aims to already know it in essence in advance of its arrival. Instead, in interpretive work, *this* stubborn particular summons those always-too-broad insights, calls them to wake up and learn something (both about themselves and about this arriving case). The case (literally, something that "happens," that "befalls" [OED]) corrects the exaggerated self-confidence of the proffered essence, humiliates their feigned clarities, "productively supplements" (Gadamer, 1989, p. 113), "correct[s]" (p. 114), "set[s] them right anew" (Arendt, 1969 P. 197). Setting them right, then, does not make them now more fixed and final, but makes them, instead, readier for the arrival of the next case that just might make all the difference in the world all over again. It makes the rule freshly *just*. It makes generalities *generous*. Fore-giving.

This is how contemporary hermeneutics differs from its Husserlian origins and the desire to "fix [the life-world] once and for all in a way equally accessible to all" (Husserl, 1970b, p. 178). Hermeneutics is deeply phenomenological, but it is not and does not aim to be "eidetic" (Gadamer, 1989, p. 254) or foundational: "Exactly because we give up a special idea of foundation in principle, we become better phenomenologists, closer to the real givenness, and we are more aware of the reciprocity between our conceptual efforts and the concrete in life experience" (Gadamer, 1984, p. 323).

It should be noted in passing that this is from an essay entitled "Hermeneutics and Suspicion." Hermes watches over gates and door- ways like a bit of an animal *familiaris* and is not above letting the swing- ing door hit you in the backside just at the right moment. Hermes is a trickster bent on tickling the sombreness of eidetic sureties. He is the slip on the ice, the goof, the happenstance, the alerting animal-body sniff and snort, alert to the reciprocities of arising and perishing (Sanskrit, *pratitya-samutpada*, "dependent co-arising" in contrast to fan- tasies of permanence and fixity), in-breath and out ("a swinging door" [Suzuki, 1986, p. 29]):

Hermeneutics is thus based on those fumbly grace notes that can come from "a consciousness that ... leave[s] the door ajar" (Hillman, 2013b, p. 99), the grace, shall we say, of "experience" properly named:

> "Being experienced" does not consist in the fact that someone already knows everything and knows better than anyone else. Rather, the experienced person proves to be, on the contrary, someone who ... because of the many experiences he has had and the knowledge he has drawn from them, is par- ticularly well equipped to have new experiences and to learn from them. Experience has its proper fulfillment not in definitive knowledge [essences, generalities bent on finality and, shall we say, "once-and-for-all-ness"] but in the openness to experience that is made possible by experience itself. (Gadamer, 1989, 355)

Openness to experience—to the ongoing porousness and interpret- ability of the world—is not simply a given in human comportment. The animal-body can feel threatened and can easily hunker down and "harden" (Huntington, 2003, p. 221) and close and lock the gate. Sometimes, in fear, in threat, it is warranted to temporarily hold our breath, but this, too, must pass. It cannot be held as a permanent state. This is why the openness of/to experience needs concerted, repeated practices that will allow it to be nurtured, cared for, emulated, deliber- ately protected from distraction, threat, and fret. It must be "won [and re-won] by a certain labor" (Ross & Jardine, 2009, n.p.), but labor of a certain ilk, free from the exigencies that might harden attention and lock it up and build a wall. This is why I have often mulled over the Latin roots of the word school: *schola*, which means not only "leisure" (this is ironic—or tragic—enough when one thinks of the state of many schools). It also means "a holding back, a keeping clear" (OED) so that the gate can swing, so that the deep reciprocities between our conceptual efforts and the concrete in life experience can reveal themselves.

But right here is the weird paradox of our situation: something of the agency of our openness is "beyond our wanting and doing" (Gadamer, 1989, p. xxviii), "We are possessed by something and precisely by means of it we are opened up for the new, the different, the true" (Gadamer, 2007, p. 82). *And* responding with practiced propriety and grace to what thus possesses us and takes our breath away increases our ability to be possessed and to take good care of it when it arrives. The readiness for new experience is itself made possible and made more hearty and whole by enduring and learning from the very readiness it is wont to win.

Thus, the paradox: openness to "the stubborn particulars of grace" is both cause and effect of openness to "the stubborn particulars of grace."

In our current circumstances, we each face the task of finding ways to maintain ourselves, over and over again, out in the open, and to not let real or perceived threats and distractions exhaust us and betray us and distort our insight and companionships. This is especially urgent "these days," but it is also "truly a tremendous task which faces every human moment" (Gadamer, 1994, p. 233):

> This is the true vocation of life-long work; namely, to live freely yet without certainty, except the certainty that clinging to concepts beyond their functional ability to serve the human prospect well will result in ever-deepening forms of estrangement as the concepts fail to address the new realities that confront them. An ability to face the necessary disillusionment points paradoxically to the source of our hope. (Smith, 2020g, p. 291)

Dennis Lee's paean to Bronwen Wallace's work lovingly frames the potent effect of what Gadamer called "the fecundity of the individual case" (Gadamer, 1989, p. 34) which portends precisely such frail freedom: Bronwen Wallace left a total of some 130 poems. The best join[s] the stock from which the living will draw nourishment for generatios. They help to trigger:

That spark in a synapse somewhere ...
saying look, you have time, even yet
To come to love this too. (Lee, 1998, p. 109)

Each site, a threshold
Into this slow discovery,
the random testimony gathered
As best we can, each of us down
To essentials, as the failed are
and the dead, who bear us forward
in their fine accurate arms.
From Bronwen Wallace (1987, p. 47), "Testimonies"

Just consider the relieving grace of this. I have the time to love this, too.

Such wee attention to these moments and that rough look of that Raven at the feeder this morning makes the open-ended possibility of spring arriving arrive right in the midst of—more pointedly, *because of*—limiting my attention to this very moment:

Her final book took its epigraph from Flannery O'Connor: "Possibility and limitation mean about the same thing." By hunkering into the lives and stories that define *this* particular place, she achieved a universal gesture of being human. Her poems were acts of dwelling, acts of love. (Lee, 1998, p. 261)

Again, this, for me, is a pedagogical insight and an ecological one as well. We must remain cleaved to the particularity of things and to the fields of relations that cluster around such things, *and* to the tough knowledge that these things are not only surrounded but *are* their surroundings. Otherwise, insight, if and when it comes, can too easily become as abstract and otherworldly-- utopian, "nowhere"-- as the afflictive regimes of distraction and distortion which ecopedagogical insight wishes to critique and elude. Unlike the "ordering of things according to the wishes, prejudices, or promptings of the powerful" (Gadamer, 1989, p. 261), insight into our living and its locales of energy and dwelling and love, "slips out the back door and thus slips back in and under: The hope is rather than it being a battering ram to the door you can be a fog that drifts underneath the door and gets up in the cuffs of your shirt rather than tears your shirt off" (Dawson, 2017a, n.p.)

"Things Reveal Themselves"

Berry: A lot of my writing has been, when it hasn't been in defense of precious things, has been a giving of thanks for precious things.

Moyers: What are the precious things that you think are in danger right now?

Berry: It is might hard right now to think of anything that is precious that *isn't* in danger. But maybe that's an advantage. The poet William Butler Yeats [2010] said somewhere "Things reveal themselves passing away." And it may be that the danger that we have inflicted on every precious thing reveals the preciousness of it and shows us our duty. (Berry & Moyers, 2013)

This insight is almost unbearable, that the direness of our current ecological circumstances just might be the lynchpin for insight into the preciousness that surrounds us. That such preciousness shows itself right at the moment of its falter subtly places grief at the center of insight, but only to the extent that we don't simply lose ourselves to and in grief itself.

It can show us our duty by showing us our debts. Make me feel a bit "like a prisoner whose cell gate has never been locked" (Loy, 2010, p. 41).

There is an analog to interpretive work, here, that the manifest character of the topic we are investigating only arrives once our grip on it (one might better say, once *its* grip on *us*) has failed and faltered, only once we stop simply living captive in our presumptions and start, instead, catching glimpses of what has been often-secretly at play all along, glimpses of its makeup, its dependent co-arising. As its grip passes away, its grip on us reveals itself. "Insight … always involves an escape from something that had deceived us and held us captive" (Gadamer, 1989, p. 357) and, at the very same time, our capture, our reliance, our affection, reveals itself. Instead of being attached to it in grips of fear of losing our grip on it, we can now "come to love this too."

Only when this capture starts to shift do things start to reveal themselves. We start seeing worlds arising and perishing, tucked in the folds, lifted on the air and lodged in the most wee of things:

> The [spring] water's now down the driveway in the full mix of things, still, shining in the mixes of road gravel and horse shit. It's why the dogs scurry back and forth when we walk the road. So much, so much, in every whiff. Great saints following the paths. There go the Ravens, my dears, again caught and uncaught on the warm air foothill uplifts. To be dying under their wings is a weird miracle. To realize that this dharma-order has been in play all along, noticed or not, is a weird embarrassment. "Where have I been?" Right here. Writing. Trying to right myself. (Jardine, 2018, p. xiii)

When I dare to quote myself from over *20 years ago* asking, "Where have I been?", I must ask myself, well, "Where *have* I been in these nearly twenty years since?"

Distracted. Fraught. Exhausted. Heads-up only to bend low again. Often simply wasting away.

At the very beginning of the 2,584-page, five-volume commentary on Tsong-Kha-Pa's *The Great Treatise on the Stages of the Path to Enlightenment* (originally completed in Tibet in 1406), Geshe Lhundub Sopa (2004, p. 1) starts thus: "So, here we are. Right now, you have a life that is precious and valuable."

So here I am, placed right back in the ripple of this year's snowmelt that I've perennially loved for as long as I can remember.

This silly, precious thing betrays me as much as does my old *grevoushede*. My own life reveals itself passing away, streaming in the sun and down the drive.

Just this is the time I have to love this.

"What About Foxgloves?"

You have had many and great sadnesses, which passed. And you say that even this passing was hard for you and put you out of sorts. But please, consider whether the great sadnesses have not rather gone right through the center of yourself. Whether much in you has not altered, whether you have not somewhere, at some point of your being, undergone a change while you were sad? Only those sadnesses are dangerous and bad which one carries about among people in order to drown them out. Almost all our sadnesses are moments of tension that we find paralyzing because we no longer hear our surprised feelings living. (Rilke, 1904/1962, pp. 63–64)

This nebulous shift to finding the world interpretable—to "hear our surprised feelings living"—holds true whether we are parsing the babbles of presidential stutterings, or studying some line of taken-for-granted practice in a school classroom, or whether we are reading song lyrics about enduring the loss of a young wife:

> What about foxgloves?
> Is that a flower you liked?
> I can't remember.
> You did most of my remembering for me.
> And now I stand untethered.
> In a field full of wild foxgloves. (Mount Eerie, 2017)

Remembering, here, isn't necessarily something I *do*. It can often *befall* me, happen to me, overcome me.

"It is necessary that a man should dwell with solicitude on, and cleave with affection to, the things which he wishes to remember," this being one of Thomas Aquinas' four precepts for the cultivation of memory (Yates, 1974, p. 75). That line, "you did most of my remembering for me," is so full of how memory shapes itself and forms itself in the harbors of particularities, their locales. "Whence the Philosopher [Aristotle] says in the book *De memoria*: 'some men can be seen to remember from places'" (Yates, 1974, p. 356).

This is a profoundly ecological point, that places harbor memory (and therefore the composition of myself) and cleave around the stubborn particulars of such places of which my self is but one player in this round. Foxgloves are nearby. And, it happens, cicadas, too:

When [cicadas] sound, it feels as if this place itself has remembered what I have forgotten, as if my own memory, my own raising, some of my own life, is stored up in these trees for safekeeping. Cicadas become archaic storytellers telling me, like all good storytellers, of the life I'd forgotten I'd lived. I'm left shocked that they know so much, that they remember so well. (Jardine, 2016b, pp. 83–84)

Experiencing such moments involve both "the joy of recognition" (Gadamer, 1989, p. 114) and their link to a certain hermeneutic truth. Hans-Georg Gadamer invokes the words of Aeschylus in his invocation of *pathei mathos* as key to understanding the sort of experience and knowledge sought by hermeneutic work: *learning through suffering* (1989, p. 356). This does not entail a type of morbidity, but is a more fine-grained reminder of the character of experience and learning itself, a certain lovely ache that it is best to become accustomed to while time and attention allows.

Experience can thus move from the immediacies of what is suffered or endured toward a sort of insight that no longer remains simply victim to, paralyzed by and captive of what is suffered.

It is not just cicadas or foxgloves or my own life-course intimacy with such things. "The whole … to which [they] belong [] resonate[s] … responding and summoning" (Gadamer, 1989, p. 458). Experience, in its very particularity, shall we say, *worlds* out into fields broader than my own bearing, broader than my own memory and woe:

Lavenders an echo of the beeswing …
Dazzling foxgloves ashake in the salty wind. (Dawson, 2017b)

Foxgloves. "Every word … carries with it the unsaid" (Gadamer, 1989, p. 458)

"That Declaration of Readiness"

I awake to the screech of a fox in the street
Carrying your soul in its teeth. (Dawson, 2017b)

That declaration of readiness, no matter what the outcome, that's a part of everyone's soul. We are all motivated by deep impulses and deep appetites to serve, even though we may not be able to locate that which we are willing to serve. So, this is just a part of my nature and I think everybody else's nature to offer oneself at the moment, at the critical moment when the emergency becomes articulate. It is only when the emergency becomes articulate that we can locate that willingness to serve. (Cohen, 2016)

In response to Leonard Cohen's words regarding "readiness, no matter what the outcome" and his invocation of an old Abrahamic invocation of a "Hebrew word, *hineni*, which translates as 'Here I am' or 'I am ready.'" Rufo Quintavalle (2018) raises a specter regarding the old tale of Abraham's readiness, at God's behest, to sacrifice his son. This tale mirrors, of course, the *New Testament* willingness of God to sacrifice his own child as a scapegoat for human foibles. Just as lamb's blood smeared over doorways allowed the angel of Death to pass over in ancient Egypt, now the Lamb of God's blood, spilled on a wooden cross, effects a parallel salvation, now with the promise of everlasting life. The sacrifice of precisely that which provides me with some nebulous sense of life perhaps lasting beyond my own fading breath calls out a fox-screech. We are saved, it seems, by the death of the child, no, by the deliberate *sacrifice* of the child, but it is assuredly odd to think of who this might be, this "we" who are saved:

> Victims of a desperate event. Evidence for the largest single incident of mass child sacrifice in the Americas— and likely in world history—has been discovered on Peru's northern coast, archaeologists tell *National Geographic*. More than 140 children and 200 young llamas appear to have been ritually sacrificed in an event that took place some 550 years ago on a wind-swept bluff overlooking the Pacific Ocean, in the shadow of what was then the sprawling capital of the Chimú Empire. The 140 sacrificed children ranged in age from about five to 14, with the majority between the ages of eight and 12; most were buried facing west, out to the sea. The llamas were less than 18 months old and generally interred facing east, toward the high peaks of the Andes. (Romey, 2018)

Quintavalle links his meditations on Leonard Cohen's final interview and his invocations of *hineni* to our ecological condition, that we seem, however unwittingly, ready, in our blind and panicky ecological ravages, to sacrifice our children to perilous, perhaps irreversible fate of no longer being able to "set [things] right anew." Obeying the call to such a sacrifice might bring with it the prospect of continuing grace and favor in the eyes of God but heeding such a call to sacrifice "the child" sacrifices *precisely* the prospect of continuance itself. And this is especially telling when we consider what "gods" are being served by our ecological ridiculousness and the ruins of our distractions and afflictions.

Or, perhaps, this places the prospect of continuance out of our hands? Perhaps *this* is a sign of how captive we have become by the ecologically disastrous gods we've decided to serve? How drastic the alert to wake up to this emergency needs to be? That things reveal themselves just as we raise our hand against continuance itself?

Forgive me. This goes further than I have the ability to follow, even though I stubbornly remain faced this way. I become untethered and pause. And just happen to catch sight of the sun stream:

> ... in that endless pause, there came
> once again the sound of bees.
> (J. Jóhannsson, 2009)

CHAPTER FORTY-ONE

Early Morning Blues

FIGURE 22. BABY'S BLUE AGAIN

A hitherto concealed experience that transcends thinking from the position of subjectivity. (Gadamer, 1989, p. 100)

Baby blues again.

2021, The specific locus of interpretive work is working out the conundrum of who is looking at who, of how to work this out, how to remain still enough to see *myself* behind bars, how to remain open enough to understand what being thus seen might mean. Working out why this matters, why study this, why let myself be drawn into this weird dance. Because the shape of the Aspen tree bark shapes my grandson's hand and he is handled by it. My younger grandson, now nearly two weeks old, fixes on light and shapes and you can almost hear the electrical brain traces being laid down regarding such a thing as these plant leaves in sunlight.

What to do? Fall silent. Take a picture. Open a document. Spill some ink. All of these. Searching out for something more intimate than seeing: "… to be felt seen" (Jardine, 2022) and how the consequences will never be outrun. How I want to show my boy. His boy. To other blue-eyed wonders. The wee one not yet named.

Relations. Aliveness. Love (Latremouille et al., 2021, 2024). I'm writing as slowly and as carefully as I can about this aching world of ours, that deer's lovely garden munch and stare, my own heart breaking for its trot-bys. I'm trying to avoid making self-references from the position of subjectivity.

I don't know much else to do. Except read about places, beings, relations (Derby, 2015) written in a place by a being, a relation for whom I have great affection. And then write about elementary schools and *neige noir* in honor of his work and his stalwartness, (Jardine, 2015) in response, loving mulls of the mullings of languages and French word searches and the sparkling images that spark up:

> Reflection [as with this sort of writing] does not withdraw from the world. It steps back to watch the forms of transcendence fly up like sparks from a fire; it slackens the intentional threads which attach us to the world and thus brings them to our notice. (Merleau-Ponty, 1972, p. xiii)

And how "ecologically sorrowful times," that glaring phrase (Jardine, 2015, p. xv) is a glaring phrase repeated and repeated in the other (Latremouille et al., 2024). And how the buck stills and looks as we murmur that phrase in cloistered hums, meditative repetitions, low voices, lowing voices, mooing sleepy drifts. How citing Merleau-Ponty cites one of our kinfolks, one among bucks and blue-eyed camera flashes and early mornings.

And what to say to the 1-year-old, years from now, days from now, or sooner (now 2 years old) if the buck stops coming around because of my own ecological neglect. Damn it, it is why I do these silly things, because there are songlines, teachings, and lessons lying all around us all the time, even in the words we use:

> past participle of *neglegere* "to make light of, disregard, be indifferent to, not heed, not trouble oneself about," literally "not to pick up," variant of *neclegere*, from Old Latin *nec* "not" (from PIE root *ne-* "not") + *legere* "pick up, select," (Online Etymological Dictionary, under "neglect.")

And, too, teachers at hand even when my sorrow gets to overwhelm. The monstrosity of "The Environment" is, in the end, a distraction, a point of exhaustion and frustration:

> *Tim DeChristopher*: Because we don't know what to do. That's what I'm trying to say. It's really complicated to live in love, at this time.
>
> *Wendell Berry*: We do know what to do. We need to take care of the responsibilities that we've got. The effective boundaries of responsibility are your own limits. There's so much you can do, and you ought to do it. That's all. (DeChristopher & Berry, 2020)

All I've got for now, for us, for you, reading this, are these warm and living trace lines, and another little forthcoming story (Latremouille et al., 2024):

> I was picking up the daily [compost] load last Friday and in the back of the local grocery store there was a Grade Four class, about twenty kids, talking w. the owner who just then, by coincidence, was telling the group about what I did daily. [An aside: to be back in the middle of such a gathering nearly brought me to tears. Old memories of invigoration and clarity and teaching and learning].
>
> So, I packed the car, got the mail, and meanwhile the store owner had given the kids Macintosh apples as a treat.

As I left the parking lot where the kids and teachers were now gathered, I swung by to give the teacher my phone number, and mention that the compost heaps I keep are just around the corner if they want another short field trip—greenhouse, gardens, etc. Kids started coming up to me with their apple cores. I opened the car hatch and they started tossing them in the boxes I'd just picked up. I got to say something bland and true like "Yes, it is a simple as that" as some hurried up to finish and toss.

Got back in the car with the window rolled down, ready to go, and one utterly beautiful young girl came near, stood still and looked at me, softly, and nearly smiled, no words.

Transfixing. In retrospect, feels like another vivid dream that lasted hours, even though it was only a few seconds. Caught in her regard and she in mine.

As is my weakness, I just checked the etymology regarding "regard": not just looking at and seeing each other, but that other sense of "kindly feeling which springs from a consideration of estimable qualities."

CHAPTER FORTY-TWO

The Unfinished Work
of "Getting Back to Normal"

FIGURE 23. OVERHEATED COYOTE

Every generation occupies itself with interpreting Trickster anew. No generation understands him full, but no generation can do without him. And so, he
became and remained everything to every [one]—god, animal, human being,
hero, buffoon, he who was before good and evil, denier, affirmer, destroyer,
and creator. If we laugh at him, he grins at us. Whatever happens to him
happens to us. (Radin, 1956, pp. 158–159; cited in Clifford et al., 2008, p. 78; see
also Ignace [Stsmél'ecqen], 2008, p. 95)

A Prelude and Some Overdue Praises

We, here, in this class, belonged together under the mark of these words [we were reading together] and could take some comfort here, some common fortitude and strength. We all had to not only live individually with having read and understood these words. We had to live with the fact that these others, too, were here with us [reading]. All the relations, our teachers, our childhood's, our schooling, our children, our elders, all called to account, a Great Council of Beings gathered, huddled around fires lit over ages, listening to the tales that hold us here. We, here, had a brief glimpse of what it might mean to say that pedagogy has to do with wisdom, communities of relations and small, meticulous obligations often hidden under the cool and calm. A deeper cool and deeper calm. Of course, we are all living under the newly fashionable education jargon of "community" that has already ruined these words before they even had a chance. The lamentation continues: jargon is rooted in an old Welsh term *iargoun*, which means "the warbling of birds." At least the warbling of birds is done with some tilting pleasure at the sun add the air-blue arch … this broad Chinook sky and the prairie abyss and the wind, and oh, the cold that cracks your bones, Alberta. (Jardine, 2016j, p. 94)

The arc of time passing is always an odd thing since it often feels like no time at all. The above passage was written as part of the *Foreword* to David G. Smith's book *Pedagon: Interdisciplinary Essays in the Human Sciences, Pedagogy and Culture* (Jardine, 1999a, pp. xviii–xix). The words being mused over by the class I mention were part of an essay of his, "Children and the Gods of War," originally published in 1988, 32 years ago, as of this writing. That this very sentence will not age well is part of the point in mentioning this.

Here is the passage that caught us up, recited here from David's wonderful new collection *Confluences: Intercultural Journeying in Research and Teaching*:

It is as if you people ask for, above all else, not only a genuine responsiveness form their elders but also a certain direct authenticity, a sense of that deep human resonance so easily suppressed under the smooth human-relations jargon teachers typically learn in college. Young people want to know if, under the cool and calm of efficient teaching and excellent time-on-task ratios, life itself has a chance, or whether the surface is all there is. And the best way to find out may be to provoke the teaching into showing himself or herself. (D.G. Smith, 2020c, p. 405)

I can't count how many times I've recited this passage as a reminder to myself. And a strange reminder at that. Because these words have a strange unfinishedness to them, a strange provocation that performs the very act of provoking me a reader that he is speaking about. He is asking *me* "Is the surface all there is?"

Can you hear the Ravens going to the edges of the earth and returning with a heart we forgot we had, that we thought was inside of us but was instead rife across the world, between us?

A burned-out image of a Coyote to start. A little reminder from years ago, a young student's picture made during weeks and weeks of Coyote stories in Sharon Friesen and Patricia Clifford's classroom became a cover illustration and whose name she gave it became a book subtitle for *Back to The Basics of Teaching and Learning: "Thinking the World Together"* (Jardine et al., 2008):

FIGURE 24. THINKING THE WORLD TOGETHER

Coyote as Trickster. Coyote as messenger. Denier. Affirmer. As a royal screw-up whose foibles teach us. One of the chapters in that back-to-basics book was called " 'Whatever happens to him happens to us': Reading coyote reading the world" (Clifford et al., 2008, pp. 67–78):

> While laughing at Coyote with their friends and family, native children learn how to behave and how not to behave. This is why Coyote is a sacred fool. This clown gives us a way to know and accept ourselves. His foolish

mistakes and his heroic imagination teach about balance and respect. This
is the balance in ourselves and in our interrelationships with all life-forms.

Anges Vanderburg, Flathead Indian Elder.

(Cited in Clifford et al., 2008, p. 74)

This is a clue to how carefully done must be the task of having students read things, of choosing well, whatever that might turn out to mean. Because, when it works, it can become like a great love affair with all the exhilaration, tragedy and release that might involve. This is why there is something about writing that is, to put it blandly, "open to interpretation," because it not only allows but requires me, as a reader, to step forward into its unfinishedness in a risky game of give and take:

> *Bill Callahan*: I think pretty much every song is either unfinished or proves to be inadequate or lacking in some way. And that's the whole reason for me continuing to make music—because there's always room for improvement. And then having a listener and/or critic really helps finish the song but they point out the holes that songs have on purpose. I think songs are probably supposed to be unfinished so that each listener can finish them in their own personal way and that's why people are so passionate about the music that they like, 'cause something in their psyche has finished the song, so they feel like it's a part of them. (Madden, 2020).

This is why it was so on-edge when, in a just-released song of his, 35 (Callahan, 2020), the first line reads "I can't see myself in the books I read these days." But then, then, as the song ends and "the road was pulling out so soft, fast and black" (an image so full of childhood memory for me of nighttime road trips and staring out the car's back window), he evinces having found a deep love: "I've got your book on my lap."

Yes, you just might fall in love and start carrying words around with you, almost like familiars on the backs of brooms or parrots on your shoulder. Just like I did when I first read David Smith's work, or when I first went into Sharon Friesen and Pat Clifford's classroom. Feels like it is part of me. Little alerts that help you start, sometimes, over a single word that has become too easy to hear but near-impossible, as goes the etymology, to heed:

Genuine literacy is most creatively a discursive activity that does not rest with a pedagogic literalness that puts language at the service of the will. Reading the world, inscribing and being profoundly inscribed by it, has to do more with deep attunement or hearing and involves a kind of obedience to life's deepest resonances (< Fr. *obeir*, "to obey"; > L. *ob audire*, "to hear from"). (Smith, 2020b, p. 158)

David Smith taught me, and still teaches me, a great deal about such things:

The best qualitative research might be more like outstanding literature: on reading it you feel joined to the broader world in new and refreshing ways. Hermeneutic/interpretive research [requires] elucidat[ing] the political, philosophical and cultural ground out of which the subjectivity of experience is formed. Without this ... gesture, subjective experience remains both self-enclosed and then left dangling helplessly in the winds of broader world events. (D.G. Smith, 2000d, p. 48)

How to take offhand comments or words or gestures or newspaper articles or advertisements or school-board declarations, or a musician's interview, or a sign or photo posted online, as *teachers* that just might beckon exactly the right sort of attention needed to wake me up out of the slumbers of ordinary, to see the stars and galaxies crackling right beneath the seemingly-solid-and-placid surface. If my students can't see themselves in the books they read and find themselves read back to themselves out into territories wilder and more abundant than they might have first suspected, then reading is just a cut-and-paste.

But when you hit that spot and feel spoken to, this, just for you, come on, dance. Forget yourself and find yourself "roomier" all at once, this image from St. Augustine as a way to describe the ventures of learning (cited in Carruther, 2005, p. 199).

Again, a weird dance when something rises up and compels me to leap out into the unfinished thought I'm reading.

Just like the Ravens at the feeder can sometimes startle me back to some level of awake. This bee's 'tween a nice bad pun.

Thinking the world together.

But we know, each of us in different ways and in different tongues and to different extents, how easy it is for attention to dull and how a low-level disease comes with it, of boredom, of complacency. We each know, variously, how that dulling can sometimes be deliberately perpetrated, so that even Coyote's appearance can be pre-numbed. This seemingly-solid-and-placidness is nothing new. Our attention, our language, tends to get flattened, stuck. The story gets retold often enough that it loses its tell. It turns into "the way things are," "the real world" and thereby, of necessity if not intent, belies the arrival of the new, belies, therefore, the arrival, literally and figuratively, of "the child."

Therefore this, from an essay originally presented at the *World Council for Curriculum and Instruction* in Hiroshima, Japan, in August 1986.

It is called "Brighter than a thousand suns: Facing pedagogy in the nuclear shadow" and is again cited here from *Confluences*:

"Education is suffering from narration-sickness," says Paulo Freire. It speaks out of a story which was once full of enthusiasm, but now shows itself incapable of a surprise ending. The nausea of narration-sickness comes from having heard enough, of hearing many variations on a theme but no new theme. A narrative which is sick may claim to speak for all, yet has no *aporia*, no possibility of meeting a stranger because the text is complete already. Such narratives may be passed as excellent by those who certify clarity and for whom ambiguity is a disease to be excoriated. But the literalism of such narratives (speeches, lectures, stories) inevitably produces a pedagogy which, while passes as being "for the good of children," does not recognise the violence against children inherent in its own claim. Because without an acknowledgement and positive appreciation of the full polysemic possibility which can explode forth from within any occasion when adult and child genuinely meet together: a possibility which resides precisely in the difference of every child, every person, a difference about which one can presume nothing despite the massive research literature (e.g., about children) available to us, and despite the fact that our children come from us, are our flesh and blood. Without an appreciation of the radical mystery which confronts us in the face of every other person, our theorizing must inexorably become stuck, for then we are no longer available for that which comes to meet us from beyond ourselves, having determined in advance the conditions under which any new thing will be acceptable, and thereby foreclosing on the possibility of our own transformation. This radical difference of every child, every other person, renders our pedagogical narratives ambiguous but at the same time hopeful, because the immanent ambiguity held within them opens a space for genuine speaking, holding out the promise that something new can be said from out of the mists of the oracle of our own flesh. (Smith, 2020i, p. 116)

"Ambiguous but at the same time hopeful." Like unfinished songs longing to be fallen in love with. I've got your book on my lap.

Oracular Ears Budding. I feel like a sacred fool, tricked out and better for it.

But here it is again, 1999 echoes of that Smith forward I wrote, full of consumptive panic, and of Don Domanski's (2010, p. 121) ravens "go[ing] to the edges of the earth and returning with our hearts in their beaks":

The critical edge here is the crisis of a spirit dancing on the edge of the world coupled with a certain deadly playfulness, deadly because that is precisely what is at stake here: whether life itself has a chance. Many of us understand this crisis and the ways in which our children's live, my child's life, my own life and the demons in the trees and Coyote howls in the wind are becoming co-opted by consumptive panic endemic to our so-called postmodern era. As the fragments crack, the genuineness and spirit and address of David Smith's work are only understandable as hopelessly naiveté. Let us all be naive, then. Let us all give up hope. There, in that place of hopelessness, when the eschatological hallucinations of a "better world" are given up, genuine love and compassion are possible. There, life itself has a chance out from under the vicious, well-meant glare of "improving our schools." (Jardine, 2016j, pp. 94–95)

Hah! Panic-endemic indeed. We're right back to our burned-out Coyote near an empty bench.

So, Then, Where Were We? Oh, Yes, Getting Back to Normal

And here's the sentence to pull forward after that long and goofy Prelude: "Whatever happens to him happens to us." What better ecopedagogical poem to this four-legged, not just a matter of Trickster fables but of flesh and blood and suffering and breath stories, here, today, Sunday September 13, 11:39 MT, 51 Degrees North. Eastern slopes of the Rockies, under a canopy of smoke from Oregon and California wilds fires:

> Whatever happens to him
> happens to us
>
> Whatever happens to him
> happens to us
>
> Whatever happens to him
> happens to us
>
> Whatever happens
> Happens

It is fascinating that the google search item that was found was the Golden Gate Bridge in San Francisco. The photo, over treated above, shows a lounging coyote in the sun near an empty bench taken sometime early in the 2020 viral lockdowns.

Lockdowns. Even though this word was probably chosen with great ease and intended to be simple and straightforward, one of the things that plagues teachers is that your ears can get easily pricked by unintended nuance. What might count ordinarily as an ordinary word can start to bristle and twitch. Lockdowns. It can cause trouble, and it can be deliberately used to deliberately cause trouble. Of course. No words are innocent.

Getting back to normal. That, of course, is a phrase in itself, a trigger, a longing, an often-unexamined—what is the scholarly word these days? Trope?

Imagine this spoken in a chorus by those googled Coyotes in that search picture above. Oh, they'd be howling it, singing off key, forgetting the words, coming in late. Or just snoozing through it all.

So, okay, getting back to normal. Whatever happens to him happens to us. There are countless ecologically minded writers talking of the Earth sending us messages about "normality," about how, right now, right in this crack in what has long since counted as normal, some light is being let in. With even further apologies to Leonard Cohen, we asked for a sign and a sign was sent.

Coyote. Sun. Bridge. Beauty.

I'm thinking of Bill Callahan's (2019b) lyric about how "God's face, plain to see over the waters, is still hard to read." What shall I think of this, given that I have on hand the full array of human good heartedness and foibles, words and images and gods and monsters right on hand, ripe and ready to pounce?

Welcome back to a normal that never left. The normal that seems to be killing us. Why Study?

The trick—ah, Coyote!—this is where the pedagogical act is such hard work. Standing toe to toe with a student, trying to understand, trying to open up and find my own wherewithal in this roil of images and words. Then this: "The possibility that the other person may be right is the soul of hermeneutics" (H.G. Gadamer, July 9, 1989, cited in Grondin, 1994, p. 124).

Just like Coyote stories, though. Exaggerations meant to teach? Distortions meant to reveal? *Teach* what exactly, then? Take another breath. They may be right, as may that laze of Coyote by the bench. They may both have something to tell us that we might not have known.

How my own "look at that!" screeds about men and white and guns and threat-making exaggerated shapes of "us and them" rears up, my own "us and them" in response. Its sea turtles on the cleaner beach all the way down (how's that for an egg-headed allusion?).

I'm in just the right shape to consider what all the ecological falderol has been about in these recent years right at the very moment when I'm also full of the all-too-human tendency to blind clarity that the affliction of threat can produce. Not only have I been made raw and alert enough. The signs are there ready for the treacherous work of reading them.

It is hard work to look at that basking Coyote, not as an interloper into human "normal," but as a teacher *about* that very real and presumed normality, its costs, and this not just its cost to Coyotes and sea turtles. It is hard work to look at that scant and partial list of fish arrivals, bright air full of boars and sheep. Hard work to see that that space that is opening up because of the retractions of human actions is an open space *other than* one to simply mindlessly filled right back up as quickly as we can once when we get the chance.

It's hard work to look at that cluster of wild humans armed on the steps of the Michigan legislature as teachers. Plain to see, but hard to read. Hard to take that they might be teaching me as much about myself as about them. To stay with these matters long enough that they might become moments when insight inverts, and our human "back to normal" is finding itself under the measure of the *actual Earthly surroundings of its sustenance.* It's hard, I must say, to see any Earth on those government-building steps. Mostly wills-to-power:

> Let's take this further down Nietzsche's treacherous trail: "The will to power can manifest itself only against resistances; therefore it *seeks that which resists it*" (Nietzsche, 1975, p. 346). Once that resistance is found, I can then revel in the power felt in overcoming an uprising—"a desire to overwhelm, a forming, shaping and reshaping, until at length that which has been overwhelmed has entirely gone over into the power domain of the aggressor and has increased the same" (p. 346). This then increases the possibility that this sort of seeking out of resistance [to my will] will itself increase. Not just "we are seduced by them" (Chodron, 2007, p. 76) [these things that resist our will]. *"We welcome them"* (p. 91, emphasis added) because they confirm the feeling of ego power and the reality of my [now-feeling-empowered] self. (Jardine, 2016g, p. 225)

History teaches that there is a direct line, here, between the "will to power "and the "triumph of the will." "Heil," reads one sign in one crowd shot. We frail humans are certainly feeling embattled. We are embattled. Jobs lost. Friends dying. Movements restricted. We want to burst.

Whatever happens to them happens to us, whomever be this us and them.

Meanwhile, lions come out and gather in the warm sun. A pride of humans on the steps. Meanwhile, too, such touts of trying to think through what is happening to us all are scorned by a sort of inverse elitism, where "thinking" becomes the *cause* of woe, not its amelioration.

Oh, we humans, eh? We're plain to see dancing all around Coyote and his sun-hot furry curl, even when we're out of sight on the empty bench and the empty bridge and the waterways empty of pleasure craft and working ships, but full of bright fishes, glint and flint in the sun. We're play to see on the steps in gun glints. In the disciplined police responses to white men.

Here sits the pedagogical agony (to once again lift up an insight of David G. Smith). The multiple readings that are aroused around all these matters are themselves unfinished, and it is only when one reading collapses into itself and declares itself no longer in need of heed outside its own orbit that things become full of danger. Closure is the danger. No longer capable of a surprise ending because the story is done—that is the danger field. No longer open to interpretation, to furtherance, to elaboration, to the *relief* that can come from such opening up.

But there it is, eh? Opening up is the answer! Hah! Damn Coyote playing with my words! How about a really bad Covid-19 joke, then?

The same guys who refuse to wear a mask in a bar refuse to order Corona beer. "I love the poorly educated" (Trump, 2016). I apologize.

"If we can catch the seduction [of distended, disproportionate arousal and anger and threat and fear] at this subtle stage, it's much easier to nip in the bud" (Chodron, 2007, p. 223; then again, her book is entitled *No Time to Lose*). The thing is, though, that, once the spell is broken, do I have on hand the wells from which to draw that might allow me to start elaborating what is going on in ways that are adequate to the circumstances that have arisen? Can I think well enough? Write well enough? Settle myself well enough? Am I able to be generous, patient, persevering, discipline, still enough to seek some wisdom, some insight that will be useful? Am I able to be wrong open-heartedly but not just cowardly and weak, and able to know the difference? And know that knowing the difference needs precisely the multifariousness that self-enclosure precludes?

An Unfinished Postscript

Everything that is experienced is experienced by oneself, and thus contains an unmistakable and irreplaceable relations to the whole of this one life. Its meaning remains fused with the whole movement of life and constantly accompanies it. One is never finished with it. (Gadamer, 1989, p. 67)

And yes. These are the things to ask, also, in my own cultural appropriation, with Pat Clifford and Sharon Friesen years ago, and now here, again, of Coyote stories as a way to elaborate our shared and contested circumstances, a way to open them up to the fresh air:

> Calling to us from the boundaries of our own world, Coyote howls holes in the taken-for-granted, the assumed, the unuttered, and the unutterable. But he doesn't simply howl such holes: he incites us "in" through such openings, such opportunities for understanding, with his silly grin and his all-too-human foibles and the energy and foolish wisdom he exudes. That is, he teaches. And he teaches by teaching us the limits of the world. And he teaches such limits through their violation, through "keeping the world open" (Eliade, 1968, p. 139) so that the lessons of balance and respect can be learned once again, here, by this child and that. (Clifford et al., 2008, p. 71)

And our work on the Blood Reserve (Friesen et al., 2010), and those lovely young children armed with cameras and taken out on the land by Elders and their names of plants paired with Linnaeus' Latin binomials, and the stories collected, some left untranslated on the website we all developed together, and the Elders we consulted about all of this at the time, despite the care we took, over and over again.

Stop it. It is too easy to become too fast and easy. It is always too fast and easy from a position of historical and contemporary dominance. It's too easy to plead innocent.

CHAPTER FORTY-THREE

To Be Dying under Their Wings Is a Weird Miracle

FIGURE 25. THERE. WINGS

Thelma's Other Side

I only met Thelma Moules once, on exactly the same day that the sunflowers appeared and housed themselves in my memory, a vivid day, strangely more so now than then, as per the exacting and often exaggerating, vagaries of memory. This image cluster buff and come to shine with attention. It seems, once again as before, that it must have coalesced of its own accord into something that could be tucked away in a recess and called up, now, reading "Watching my Mother Die—Subjectivity and the Other Side of Dementia" (Moules & Estefan, 2018).

To be honest, I only barely recall Thelma's face. I'd even forgotten her name but recognized it right away while reading. Thelma. A great old-as-the-hills name, that, as is the phrase "old as the hills." Of that meeting day I mostly remember her even-then thinning hair and the brightness of the shine of her skull's skin amid the sparse stalks of sun and sparkle of light.

Reading Nancy's words, the very first thing that jumped up was that grief is always *someone's*. General concepts, expressions, ideas, theories, descriptions, themes, necessarily leave out one of its primal features—its *closeness*, its *rattling immediacy* up and down the spine, in and out the in- and out-breaths, its being *mine* and no one else's in a way that is not diminished no matter how much I share, how much I write or tell the tale or hug or weep.

It does not exhaust even when it seems it has.

But it does round back in memory apses, naves and niches, tucks and folds, images, glimpses and nods. It composes itself and thereby composes me and thereby decomposes, slowly, only to be shred open again at the whiff of something that reminds. Dying and its reaches are long-lived, even in forgetting.

I Am Not a Subject

"Subjectivity is a distorting mirror" (Gadamer, 1989, p. 276). Funny advice, then: "Don't take your life personally" (Jardine, 2016a, p. 82; Sumedho, 2010).

But all this doesn't make my experiences subjective, because I am not a subject. Me being cast as a subject is an existential cast-off of the very objectivism that hermeneutics is *also* not especially interested in kowtowing to, contesting, or vying for or against—or allowing to define and limit it. Me as a subject is the axial point of ecological disaster, of ancestral disaster.

I am not a subject. I am one of us, one of your kin Nancy, Andrew, John, Thelma. I grieve right out in the full, dark sun of the world and even my experience of isolation and loneliness in grief is long since understood as one of our lots in life, one we share variously, in weird and familiar ways, proximally, and at a distance. My having and interior life not fully out in the sun is already out in the sun. Just like you'd recognize how a deer will stand stalk still, thinking it can't be seen. We love them for this. Even in the intimate moment that I feel that it is mine to suffer alone, this feeling is confirmed by paging through Picasso's blue period, or through speeding past that very deer's carcass at the side of the highway and see the Ravens cackily, joyously gathering, feasting.

These Ravens betray me, give me away. All praise for that happening.

These multifarious voices, stories, glimpses, and images, don't replace one another but cumulate, with each added tale rattling spinning like fiber on fiber, making it new and old at the same time. Thelma Irene Moules. Reta Lenore Jardine becomes weirdly legible again having been long since forgotten. "Only in the multifariousness of voices does ['my experience'] exist" (Gadamer, 1989, p. 284). It is not an inner state once you exhale. It is not exactly "outer" either. These words are inadequate—of course. Try to get out more. Speak. Write. These are ways to not only "make memory last" (Gadamer, 1989, p. 391) but to let my own experiences be borne up where they belong, in the *Familienähnlichkeiten* of the earth's fabrics and tugs and pulls.

Like air under wings.

And even if I pull back "inwards," this interior is familiar territory. I am not alone in my lone. This is an ecological truth. Containing multitudes is itself a story as old as the hills. Even the hills contain multitudes. Subjectivity, borne as a buttress against the vagaries and irrationalities of the early twentieth century, hides the fact that, in its retreats, it affirms precisely that which sent us, full of anxiety and dread, scurrying into ourselves, forgetting that these very selves that seemed a refuge against those vagaries were, to a hidden degree, the invention of that *from which* we retreated.

This is why stories must be allowed to speak *out*, why they must be placed in broad and abundant fields of living relations and not be caught back in the captures of retreat.

Grieve *out loud*. Like this: why study for a future we won't have? Otherwise, it is an *ecological*, not just personal, disaster.

The Past Is Turning Out to Be Different Than It Was

I get it. All this seems contradictory. One can't rescue the lifeworld from its multifarious contradictoriness by trying to portion off the varieties of its ways into the "moist gastric intimac[ies]" (Sartre, 1970, p. 4) of various subjects. The contra, in the lifeworld's contradictoriness, is not just in and between the dictions underneath or behind which there is a non-contradictory world. *The lifeworld itself is full of contradictions, occlusions, variegations, mixed blood, unclear turns, upheavals, impenetrable mysteries and revelations that come and go, rise and fall, emerge and perish.*

We all know this. It does not—or certainly doesn't always or necessarily—follow the logic of identity and difference, of "it is" or "it isn't." It is woven, instead, in an ecologic of interrelatedness, of *textus*, weave and catch-a-thread unraveling and weave again. The one new thread suddenly makes the ones that have become old and familiar different that they used to be. The past, as Nancy's writing hints, is turning out to be different than it was. Even finished events are unfinished. Her father died. Now her mother.

It is no more or less mysterious that how Picasso's work did not simply add itself to an already closed-case history of art but changed how we might understand that very history, that art, this case of Picasso and the ones that followed. Precedents, exemplars, turn out to be some different than they used to be. Nancy Moules was not born as just one more in a line of blood but renders that very line re-spun. John and Thelma turn out to be something different that they were, and they will again, even in this wee way of having their names mentioned in writing, their names read in reading. I've turned out differently because of them and her. We are not subjects simply subjected to this *post hoc*. We are earth beings who *are* in this weird way and even the differences between them and what I've become because of them and Nancy, too, is full of relations. There is no self-identical substance hiding here. That is why this work we do is so freeing and so annoying all at the same time.

The summer after I wrote about John Moules death and recalled those monstrous sunflowers at his house, my own back garden got inundated by sunflower-volunteers grown from the happenstance scattershots of bird seed over the winter. And Nancy and I are caught to wonder what it means. And it doesn't *mean* anything. And yet it does. We are both weavers and woven, and which is which is which is always "yet-to-be-decided" (Gadamer, 1989, p. 119), again, again.

The Job of Hermeneutics and an Old Biblical Matter

> We welcome just that guest who promises something new to our curiosity. But how do we know that the guest we admit is one who has something *new* to say to us? Is not our expectation and our readiness to hear the new also necessarily determined by the old that has already taken possession of us? (Gadamer, 1977, p. 9)

The job of we face—the job hermeneutics puts center-stage—is not to step in and stop or clean up or fix this process. It is not a problem to be fixed, as David Smith (in press) has warned so well. Hermeneutics is not bent on straightening this out or solve this puzzle, but to puzzle over it and gather us together around our bespoken kin, Nancy, here, and Thelma, and John at a greater distance, but nearer because of it. And Ravens, too, and sunflowers each lean in to listen to the gathering.

This is why hermeneutic work needs to use language that fails in the task to name its topic once and for all, not because of a desire to be vague or "poetic," but because such halty, stumbly, gooey, etchy, sly and hinty words bespeak the tremble of how lived experience is lived, what lived experience *is*. It's the old *mensuratio ad rem* thing again. Objectivity is too dumb-ass a thing to ask of living, and subjectivity, its modern consort, also fails the test of *adaequatio*. Objectivity and subjectivity are equally/oppositely *inadequate* to lived experience. This the great value of Andrew Estefan's part of "Watching my Mother Die—Subjectivity and the Other Side of Dementia." It takes great detail and careful study to see through these inheritances we too easily presume. To take what seems to be a given, what seems to be something obvious, and to "make the object"—in this case, "subjectivity"—"and all its possibilities fluid" (Gadamer, 1989, p. 367) is part of the "skilled art of questioning" (p. 367) that is vital to hermeneutic insight.

The tough task of hermeneutic work is that, in order to be understood and communicated and commiserated-over, lived experiences are not to be tossed, shall we say, "upward" into a regnant idea or generality or theme or pattern and then fetched down by others to apply to their situation too, or in order to adjust the soaring idea so as to better ensure its flight. Grief shall not be lifted up. It graves. So even when "what is fixed in writing has detached itself from the contingency of its origin and its author and made itself free for new relationships" (Gadamer, 1989, p. 395), these new relations are now drawn into the orbit of this contingency through a recognition of the contingency of their own living and the slap-back echo urged in the arches of air and sun.

Understanding, here and therefore, is always, shall we say, a lateral pass, a toss of likeness, of verisimilitude (Gadamer, 1989, pp. 20–21), analogy, allegory, metaphor, interruption, startle, familiarity and the strange be-wariness that familiarity makes possible. This is like that but—tricked you!—no it's not. This brushes up against an old biblical matter that I wished I had discussed with John Moules. It is the non-monotheistic, hermeneutic logic of a non-believer, of one who, instead, finds everywhere the experience of "breaking open" (Gadamer, 1989, p. 362) into relations of dependent co-arising. There is not one True Incarnation of the Eidos, no one True Word that is sovereign over all that it governs, that is the Perfection, the Essence (or, more softly put as per "interpretive research," the Theme) of that which it names. Instead, there are multiple incarnations, each of which are suggestive, not of the One True Logos *of which* they are the variegated incarnations but instead, *of each other.* We live our lives akin. Each suggests all the others, laterally and each "stubborn particular" (Wallace, 1987) is thus "whole" without each needing to be being redeemed by some univocal singularity which arches overall and in which, to use the Platonic image, each "participates" in relations of proximity and distance. *Neither* the singularity of "this is the object" *nor* the singularity of "this is my subjective experience."

"A Special Effort of Memory"

Now the trouble with this is at least double. First, the receiver of such a lateral pass—the reader of a hermeneutic piece—must engage in a precarious, deeply risky calling up and:

> … running up and down the known *range* of cases to which [the topic being discussed] applies, by actually calling up the spectrum of *different* exemplifications and then *catching the point.* (Norris-Clarke, 1976, p. 67)

That work of "the spontaneous and inventive seeking out of similarities" (Gadamer, 1989, p. 432) is what hermeneutics names as the "basis of the life of language" (p. 432). *Here* is where the counterpoint of "objectivity" resides:

> It requires a special effort of memory to recall that, alongside the scientific ideal of unambiguous designation, th[is spontaneous and inventive seeking out of family resemblances constitutes the] life of language itself [and] continues unchanged. (Gadamer, 1989, pp. 433–434)

The topic must be allowed to "to expand to its full analogous breadth of illuminative meaning" (Norris-Clarke, 1976, p. 72).

That, by itself, is tough work enough and it points to how, in order adequately be myself, I must read, I must study the vagaries in all the forms I can muster. And here is the rub. Read well if it is well-written, *my own living will find itself at stake,* summoned up to bear witness, to sing, to lament. To understand.

Having to be Not Remembered

Understanding is the expression of the affinity of the one who understands to the one whom he understands and to that which he understands. (Gadamer, 1983, p. 48)

From Old French *afinite*, "relationship, kinship; neighbourhood, vicinity." (On-Line Etymological Dictionary)

I can't stop thinking about the intertwining of two things. Two special efforts of memory.

First, losing the memory of one's loves—that weird and seemingly inevitable time-fade, where the voice cadence can't quite be recalled, where the old photo startles with something lost to the wear of living, where a small, forgotten object hides unbeknownst and unexpectedly triggers memory.

Second, remembering how one's loved one lost their memory. Lost their memory *of me*. My own mother drifted off into a playful spot, with a clutched Teddy Bear, and when my son visited her in her final days, she thought he was perhaps me? Perhaps just back from World War II, from overseas? And her husband (actually long-dead) was off getting the bags out of the car for vacation and the lovely restaurant they have here, where you can eat for free! Lucky me and her and us to have it happen that way.

But Nancy writes, and I read. It's not just losing a parent but having to live with the fact that they lost you in their waning days and *then* died. They take something of you with them in any case. But to take the memory of you ahead of time is a tough matter—to be unremembered, to somehow disappear, right before the eyes of your parent.

In Alzheimer's, it is as if I have died, *as if I had never lived*, right in front of their eyes, even though, well, *here I am*. To be alive to witness my own death in the eyes of a loved one is a strange, strange thing. To be able to write about, to be able to have that writing read, is an old cluster of our deeply human arts of living and dying.

When her mother died, Nancy was no longer having to live with being not remembered. What an utterly weird relief, eh? Same as with my own mother, whose traverse into final reverie was far sweeter than most. For Reta, it became a family resemblance mix-up and mash-up and she was not frightened or angry. Just lucky happenstance, that. It wasn't like I wasn't remembered. It was like I was part of the mix-up. Freeing, in its own ambiguous way.

An Ecological Aside Regarding Memory and Place Value

More thoughts on the special effort of memory. Another happenstance drifted by in the orbit of "Watching my Mother Die—Subjectivity and the Other Side of Dementia" (Moules & Estefan, 2018). I haven't worked it out adequately, yet, but it is the closest I've come to glimpsing this land. Just a broken-up journal-scrawl sketch, then:

> … This very same sort of memory/forgetting … driving into south Calgary on Saturday along hwy. 22 … all the construction, with many of the old, familiar signposts and figures and trees and fields torn up … had the feeling, not simply that I didn't quite know where I was, but that I knew *exactly* where I was, but that *this place doesn't remember me being there at all*. Like I'd been forgotten, erased from tree-memory, earth-memory, or something … after all those drive-bys, all that attention and devotion … right there in the midst of me lamenting its shifts and trying to remember its shapes, it forgets … me, trying to be so in touch with the place and feeling its perishings, and having it spurn like that … it's not just that I've lost something, but that something has lost me. This happened to me a lot when I was young. The town I grew up in had these repeated ravagings of the living grass and field and bird and flat dirt path surroundings to make way for spiking population growth … and it wasn't just that places I remembered were gone, but that *the places that remembered me were gone* … could no longer remember. That I had become forgotten by the land itself … a small version of a First Nations lament that I can hardly stand to have so near …

> Great moon, eagle moon, goose moon, frog moon
> Tethered
> Here.

> Lesley Tait

From Latremouille et al. (2024, p. 219)

Like five red hens, I don't know precisely what this summoning of moons means, but I do know *how* it means.

And then this, first written, my oh my, 20 years ago after my first return from Alberta back to Southern Ontario where I was raised:

> How things smell, the racket of leaves turning on their stems, how my breath pulls this humid air, how birds songs combine, the familiar directions of sudden thundery winds, the rising insect drills of cicada tree buzzes that I remember so intimately, so immediately, that when they sound, it feels as if this place itself has remembered what I have forgotten, as if my own memory, my own raising, some of my own life, is stored up in these trees for safe keeping. Cicadas become archaic storytellers telling me, like all good storytellers, of the life I'd forgotten I'd lived, of deep, fleshy, familial relations that worm their ways out of my belly and breath into these soils, these smells, this air. And I'm left shocked that they know so much, that they remember so well, and that they can be so perfectly articulate. (Jardine, 2016b, pp. 83–84)

A Terribly Shareable Incommensurateness

And, of course, to be not remembered by a mother, the very one whose remembering of me shaped me for good or ill as much as anyone and for a long stretch of my life, back when none of this was able to be articulated enough to be anywhere near free of, well, *that* has a terribly shareable incommensurateness.

The very one whose remembering of me greatly shaped my way in this family resemblance (and this, of course, for good or ill, well-meant or otherwise), in losing their memory, loses me, but loosens as well:

> So, here's to my own pate glowing red in the hairbrush sparsenings of grey and white. To mothers. To fathers. To sunflowers and the loft of Ravens.

So, there go the Ravens, my dears, again caught and uncaught on the warm Spring-air foothill uplifts. To be dying under their wings is a weird miracle.

And brightness and darkness, remembering and forgetting, here in this great commiseration.

I hope it is arced just a bit by yellow looms of sunflowers.

Afterword

Nancy Moules, 9:03AM, November 15, 2018: I noted that you wrote that you only met Thelma once. You actually met her a few times and she had a bit of a crush on you because you gave her a kiss. The first time was at a graduation party that Lori Limacher had for me. Then there was the time with the sunflowers, but I know there was one more time. She liked that you acted interested in her and listened to her.

Memory. Turns out I'm sweeter than I recall. Or so someone else remembered me in ways I'd forgotten.

CHAPTER FORTY-FOUR

You are Walking Near Your True Home

My eye is caught by an article in *Business Insider* (Moss, 2014): "Now You Can Buy a Bulletproof Blanket Specifically Made for Kids to Use During School Shootings." The company's advertising is cited above one photo: "When seconds count, Bodyguard blanket can provide a quick, simple solution for maximum protection against a school intruder." Fortunes will be made. (Seidel, 2016, p. 146)

Clay County Development Corp. director Pamela Ramsey Taylor made the post following Donald Trump's election as president. Her post said: "It will be refreshing to have a classy, beautiful, dignified First Lady in the White House. I'm tired of seeing a Ape in heels." Clay Mayor Beverly Whaling responded: "Just made my day Pam" (November 14, 2016 / 12:22 p.m. EST) (*Associated Press* (2016b)).

Pamela Ramsey Taylor runs a local non-profit group in Clay County, West Virginia.

"She acknowledged her Facebook post *could be* 'interpreted as racist, but in no way was intended to be'." So much for author's intent, or "I didn't mean it." You're right, it *could be* interpreted that way, and no amount of feigned intent can save these words:

Local mayor Beverly Whaling responded with "just made my day Pam." "I was referring to my day being made for change in the White House! I am truly sorry for any hard feeling this may have caused! Those who know me know that I'm not of any way racist!" (http://www.bbc.com/news/elect ion-us-2016–37985967)

Oh, okay, so, fever dreams. Waking dreams. Getting back to normal? Where might relief lie?

Relief might lie.

This is part of the profound twist we are living in, that the lie of relief is bend on maintaining that from which we want relief.

Here's to the *mens auctoris*—literally, the mind of the author, more figuratively, what they author *meant* as the great and terrible escape hatch.

In long retrospect, there was good reason to name that since-disappeared self-publishing press I started in 1992 Makyō Press (Japanese: 魔境; see Jardine, 1992b, e.g.), and good reason to have cited Robert Aitken (1982, p. 46) in this regard:

> Makyō, "mysterious vision" [is] a deep dream experience. Certain religious traditions place great importance on makyō. Visions and heavenly voices are seriously considered to be signs of enlightenment and salvation. These phenomena may be of general interest, for they reveal the rich potential of human experience, but they reveal little of the true nature of the one who experiences them. If you do experience it you can recognize that you are walking near your true home [but] no matter how interesting and encouraging makyō may be, they are self-limited.

Near your true home, but be careful in reading these postings about Apes in Heels, these ads for bulletproof blankets. The crack is trying to let in a certain light even though Lenny's gone, too. Don't just fall for what they might uprise.

Stand up, and, if you're able, slip your hand under the arm of those deliberately weakened by this sped-up slow violence. Sing! It's stupid. It's useless. Yes! Sing *anyway*! Full-throated. Open-hearted!

> *Air-gulping again. Washing my hands more often will certainly help with something, but instead of singing Happy Birthday over the sink, maybe, in order to not forget again, I can sing like a bird dreaming of flying in clearer air. Nightmares. Corona. Mexicans. Invaders. Foreign Bodies. Walls. Infections.*

Violations. Rapist. Murderers. Coming to get us! It all fits together terribly well. So, I'm sitting here, clickty-clackty, typing. In-breaths and out-breaths whilst all the while breath being held in suspense for the latest news. Meanwhile, in what was called a "kind of triumph of spirit," locked-down Italians in the north of Italy are seen and hear "singing from balconies" (Higgins, 2020). And then there are those before-and-after maps showing full well how the air for singing has been freed up a bit by the very inducing panic shortness of breath. Ready?

I feel it. Sleep disturbed. Old asthmatic lock-down memories. Lots to consider, even though the conditions of careful consideration are themselves well-infected.

To speak and to write even though we fully understand that we are only near our true home and we are working in a realm of ghosts and tricksters and temptations, these words:

> To be the dream of which we are the sleep. A listening, an awakening that passes through us, the rhythm that knows us and that we do not know. It is the organization in language of what has always been said to escape language: life, the movement no word is supposed to be able to say. And in effect words do not say it. (Meschonnic, 1988, p. 90)

Many of us have long since felt this uplift, seen this creep of light through the cracks, and sensed how it might be tough, good news to feel the fabrics we are caught in, to fondle the thread-spins, to untie knots when we're able, and smooth brows over rich field furrows. We're being proven somehow right to plant apocalypse tomatoes, to have bees in the yard that we now notice, that we now *adore*, to let ourselves feel our animal bodies noticing the warming sun:

> This work asks for love and takes care of that very same love, all at the same time, along with the blushing of it and with the coupling of hard-nosed and hard-won composure, the tears and the embarrassment all. Let the tears come and then sit up. Stop. Think. Write. Carefully. With all the care that this work musters and measures and needs. Get the citations in line. Don't quote the wrong page. Get the years right. You need accuracy. Don't let yourself get poisoned in the rush of things. Don't let yourself forget to listen for the old voices in the air. (Latremouille et al., 2024, pp. 138–139)

Don't lie. Don't look away unless you need a break and if so, take one deliberately, alively, in full breath and hard bone. Take care of yourself and your surroundings, the Ravens and the kids, the students and the teachers, old and new. Smile at the distant customers that are so nearby. Don't let your fears become little Klesha-imps that haunt and entice. Easy to say. Hard to do. Practice.

Meanwhile, I write. Again:

> [Writing is] a tool, a net or trap to catch and present; a sharp edge; a medicine or a little awl that unties knots. (Snyder, 1979, p. 29)

When it works, "clear water flows from my pen" (Callahan, 2019a).

Oh, we humans. Oh, wee humans. And I'll include myself and Donald Trump and his sons in this lament as well. Oh, the sorrow, the sorrow:

> An Arizona man has died and his wife is in critical condition after they ingested chloroquine phosphate—an aquarium cleaning product similar to drugs that have been named by President Trump as potential treatments for coronavirus infection. The couple, in their 60s, experienced immediate distress after swallowing the drug, an additive used at aquariums to clean fish tanks, according to Banner Health Hospital in Phoenix. Chloroquine phosphate shares the same active ingredient as malaria drugs that President Trump has touted as possibly effective against COVID-19, the potentially life-threatening disease caused by the coronavirus. On Saturday, Trump tweeted about the combination of hydroxychloroquine and azithromycin, saying it had "a real chance to be one of the biggest game changers in the history of medicine." (Beasley, 2020)

It is amazing what can happen when blind allegiance couples with fears that are not ameliorated by the very one to whom you have allegiance, one that lies and exaggerates and stokes those very fears to increase your allegiance and then offers precisely himself as the cure for your fears.

Without me, you'll burn in hell forever, but I love you and if you love me, I'll save you. Very old news, all of this.

Poor wee humans. We humans. Me.

I'll say it, though. I *almost* laughed when I read this thing about the Arizona couple. Almost. Almost fell for the they-get-what-they-deserve-it-is-their-own-fault thing. And it has nothing to do at all with being poorly educated (although I did presume this: "How can you be so stupid?").

I remember a commentator a year back or so commenting on Trump's "I could shoot a person on Fifth Avenue and they'd still vote for me." The comment was: "This wasn't mean as a *compliment!*"

So, to that Arizona couple, I confess any witting or unwitting part I may have had in this collective circumstance that led you to this. I hope you can forgive me. I nearly laughed at your suffering. I am so sorry that this happened.

I love you both. How hard it is to say all this and not smirk at the thought of it.

CHAPTER FORTY-FIVE

"A Dark Saying": On Temporarily Regaining a Measure of Well-Being

My grandson and I barefoot over them swept up on the deck. We be swept up in the crunch and toss and giggle. Ah, these leaves' sounds once again live up to their deep familiar smell. I can smell them more in this first fall of good ears in years. With the great aid, too, of [his] focussed abandon. Autumn. In-breath. I can hear its scents.

I know only too well how illness can make us insistently aware of our bodily nature by creating a disturbance in something which normally, in its very freedom from disturbance, almost completely escapes our attention. Here it is a matter of the methodological primacy of illness over health. But of course, it is the state of being healthy which possesses ontological primacy, that natural condition of life which we term well-being, in so far as we register it at all. But what is well-being if it is not precisely this condition of not noticing, of being unhindered, of being ready for and open to everything? (Gadamer, 1996, p. 73)

This second passage is from Hans-Georg Gadamer's *The Enigma of Health* and, as per his example, I looked up the etymology of this word "enigma," a word easily used but full, as with all words, of secrets. "From Latin *aenigma*, 'riddle,' from Greek *ainigma*, 'a dark saying,' from *ainissesthai*, 'speak obscurely …', from *ainos*, 'tale, story, proverb' " (*Online Etymological Dictionary*, under **enigma [n.]**). Gadamer warned that such etymologies "are not proofs" (1989, p. 103), but they can help loosen up things that have become, as Edmund Husserl (one among many of Gadamer's teachers) described it "implications of meaning which are closed off through sedimentation or traditionalization" (1970b, p. 52) and "the sediments of passively accumulated experiential residues, analogies, etc." (p. 303).

Thus the core of interpretation to puzzle over such obviousnessses, things taken for granted, things that go without saying—hidden, forgotten, unspeakable, commonplace, and so on, such that, when you try to write about it, words struggle and trip, because it is precisely a locale measured by no need for words. Health. Well-being.

"Freedom from disturbance." I started wearing hearing aids for the first time on Friday, January 7, 2022. I re-gained a measure of "well-being," a well-being whose gradual *loss* I had hardly registered till recently. I was thrust into a condition of noticing a well-being whose loss I hadn't been noticing and whose characteristic seems to be precisely being in not being noticed. I suddenly experienced not only becoming (relatively) unhindered, but also experienced how I had become hindered *and* had not noticed. Trying to get these sentences to be properly fitting is a bit of an hilarious exercise which, in a way, proves Gadamer's point, that well-being tends to escape notice, and registering its return is an odd thing, since something of it, he claims, not only lives in a condition of the unregistered, but has this as its defining characteristic. Health doesn't exactly "register." So arises old echoes of the task of interpretation itself: "the great problem here is to *understand* what is so obvious" (Husserl, 1970b, p. 187), breaking the spell of the "tranquillizing self-assurance [of] 'Being-at-home' with all its obviousness" (Heidegger, 1962, p. 237).

The amount of available literature on this subject of hearing loss and gain is utterly mind-boggling. I could make a list, here, but will leave that to others better qualified in judging this literature. For now, I will follow some experiential trails in hope of elaborating what has been a fascinating, frustrating, and occasionally joyous venture.

What follows are all caught up in the new glimmers of sound. What also follows are brief thoughts on the analogs between this temporary re-gain and noticing, and the nature of hermeneutics itself, along with parallels to the fleeting noticing of our current ecological circumstances and the often-accompanying tranquillizing self-assurance that comes from not noticing its increasing prevail.

> *One news item talked about how the returning fish and animals felt wrong and also felt right. This sounds like new hearing aids sound. Bringing to notice their previous absence. There is much talk of ecological troubles, but we did have glimpses of the momentary return of a strange, distorted measure of forgotten well-being. Here:*

> *"Nature is taking back Venice": wildlife returns to tourist-free city. (https://www. theguardian.com/environment/2020/mar/20/nature-is-taking-back-venice-wildl ife-returns-to-tourist-free-city).*

All this new onslaught of sounds at the same time as nebulous, widespread pandemic talk of wanting to "get back to normal"—these emerging fishes, read as signs of "not normal?" Or a notice of well-being that we can't handle?

A Notice of Well-Being that We Can't Handle? An Anecdote to Start

First, an anecdote of how I just happened upon taking the step of getting my hearing tested. The anecdote itself is simple but was utterly disturbing. My partner and I were watching a DVD and I was, as per recent occasions, having trouble hearing the dialogue clearly. The voices seemed too wrapped up in the ambient noises of the scenes being played out. Sound had become two-dimensional, so to speak, without foregrounds and backgrounds, without a "field" in which things were sounding here and there. Flat. Singular.

As I expect might be commonplace, I've simply become less and less interested in even bothering with DVDs or CDs. So, I cupped my hands behind my ears and could hear a little bit better and make some better sense of what was going on. It worked a bit.

So far, so ordinary. I'm old enough to clearly find familiar the images that come up when you search for "ear horns" or "ear trumpets" in a simple online search. *Of course*, cupping your hands behind your ears will change the sound you hear, help you quite literally *gather* more of what is auditorily happening.

But here is the crux that made the difference in this case. Utter happenstance. I went out into the kitchen and for no reason I can remember, I cupped my ears and started talking out loud, basically to myself and about what I can't recall. Of course, what I heard sounded different because of the cupping,

However, my voice sounded, not strange but *shockingly familiar. It sounded like a voice I knew intimately but hadn't heard in years and years.* I *recognized* the voice I heard and *recognized* something hard to express accurately—I sounded like I used to sound. I blurted out [several expletives deleted]: "I sound like I'm 18 years old!" Frightening, comforting, not exactly either of those.

It was a sudden and utterly bright and disturbing looming up of something long-lost, long-forgotten and *utterly, intimately, almost secretly familiar*: recognizing, right now, *my very own voice* from years ago suddenly appearing as if out of nowhere. Not new. But also, brand-new. Enigmatic, this. I didn't know I hadn't been hearing it—a slightly spooky, slightly dreamlike experience.

And so, as happens with this sort of writing that I do, I went to find counsel and see if it might help me elaborate these dark sayings, this enigmatic uprising. Conversations with loved ones nearby, emails to friends and colleagues, reading and rereading old sources of consolation and clarification. The usual as happens when the urge to write arises as well, my own long-since refuge of trying to compose myself over experience and its wafflings. The very thing sought by hermeneutic work is the very thing often eluding notice:

> We do not understand what recognition is in its profoundest nature if we only regard it as knowing something again that we already know. The joy of recognition is rather the joy of knowing *more* than is already familiar. In recognition, what we know emerges, as if illuminated. (Gadamer, 1989, p. 114)

I might say here, as if sounding and resounding.

Sounds and Opening

We went down the driveway with the dogs, down the road a bit where the fields open up. *I can hear them opening.*

This finally sounds like it looks.

I expect that anyone might be able to notice this, that fields *sound* wide? I don't know this for sure about others. To actually *explicitly* experience what it is that is so obviously experienced is not a trivial matter.

There is also a renewed *kinaesthesis*—hah, the aesthetics of movement—to this shift because we carry hearing with us as we move, and it is one of the ways that our moving is measured—this over and above issues of balance and so on. *Hearing* turning the corner of the room, hearing the distance of things, hearing them nearing, me nearing them, and now, looking out the back door at the bitter cold spell finally broken for a bit, not just "seeing" out the door, but hearing its openness and anticipatorily hearing what is to come as I step out into the open, bare feet on the snow, open sky above, light just coming up.

Those small blinks of snow crystals melting underfoot. The cascades of small energies upwards, seems a different pleasure, but the same, now. *Aletheia.*

> *The word "splash" is onomatopoeic. Of course, it was before when I heard the soft roundness of water filling a tall glass and said the rounded word. And now, the word hisses and sparkles and glistens as does the sound of filling water. The empty neck smalls, slowly up-pitches, just like it looks.*

So, a bit of *synaesthesia* as well, that the light has a sounding bristle to it—as if the increasing visibility is trying to stimulate my hearing as well, showing my eyes what I'm hearing full well already. Or the new ability to hear is expecting sound from brilliant sights? Hearing the wind in the distance—hearing that there is a distance which is plainly visible. Hearing, not just wind but its *approaching*.

Almost like these new-old sounds are themselves doing the sketching and I'm just trying to keep up, name, gather, embrace ... even the audible slitting sound of a sharp knife through a red pepper. The slit sounds sharp. Can humans "hear" knives being sharp? Of course.

So wonderfully mundane, that cascade upwards of sound when filling a glass with water, poured from a height just for fun, just for the sound of it.

It really is a complex thing—the rising pitch of sound, the rising water. So very ordinary, like the face of an old acquaintance or some such thing? That none of this is exactly a brand-new thing being experienced (I've walked roads, filled glasses, and cut vegetables, after all, for years), but is a brand-new noticing of the unnoticed. So, the hermeneutic point: the joy of recognition is coming to know more than what is familiar. This sentence is getting more and more enigmatic *and* more illuminated.

Ah, of course: *Aletheia*

"The Lean Toward Noticing": Warns of the Overwhelm and Further Signs of Dis-Ease

The effect does leak "sideways" into other senses. Coming down the darkened stairs to the basement office, the light was left on in the bathroom and the light it cast ahead of the bottom of the stairs—not that it was literally brighter than before, but its notice-ableness [?] was brighter? Huh? A result, I think, of the hearing aids increasing the lean toward noticing more generally than just noticing hearing. "Health does not actually present itself to us" (Gadamer, 1996, p. 107).

It may be, too, that if health suddenly *does* present itself to us, we may, in a way, withdraw.

Suddenly having hearing aids can involve, to coin a phrase, the fright of hearing but *not* recognizing. On the first day of having hearing aids, I could *hear* that the hallways was narrow. Hearing that and not knowing what it was, at first, was troubling.

Right here is a grand hermeneutic analog of the summoning of the desire to interpret which can get scared off if the "address" is too much to take, too unfamiliar, too loud, too hardened to budge under consideration.

I'm remembering graduate classes from years ago when the idea of the interpretability of things started to settle in on us all, that one person said: "I took the C-train home and I looked at the sign above the person's head across from me and it *meant something* stranger than I'd noticed before. Everything started to mean something." We laughed in recognition and commiseration, and also over pleas, in another class, of "How do you get it to stop?" once the interpretive uprising starts to gain notice. IN analog, I've talked with many folks over the past months about how they've simply shelved their hearing aids. Lots of reason for this, of course. This be its own myriad of inquiry.

One thread, then another. This overwhelm of hearing aids is somewhat like the experience of hearing a noise or maybe thinking that you may or may not have heard a noise outside in the dark of night and not knowing what is happening or what to do or whether anything needs to be done.

To "decode" this strange plenitude ... and I can easily imagine what might happen if one couldn't exactly do this ... I can see why some people might profit from a guide of some sort who can take them for hearing walks, rolls, and enjoy the joys of recognition, help stop over and name what they are hearing, sometimes for the first time in decades ... how all this incoming, with an incommensurate amount of stilling oneself over it, could easily be mistaken for madness or demons everywhere.

This is why I'm writing this, in part. To turn upside down ("English *whelmen*" [OED]) is, to a certain degree, the clever and too-easily tossed about desire of hermeneutic work—the trickster opening closed doors, tripping you when you least expect it and so on, all on behalf of checking out the red ant colonies under the rocks near my mother's roses as a child, the bursty, lemony smells hidden underneath.

It can be fun. It can be joyous. And it can be terrifying, to be summoned to interpret an unexpected onslaught. It is important to avoid the sometimes off-handed, post-modern glibness of upsetting other peoples' applecarts, so to speak. I'm having enough to do with my own. My happenstance and practiced ability to hear *as well as* my practiced ability to write and ponder, has been helpful and have made the overwhelm more noticeable than it might have been, more bearable.

So, a second thread of other dis-eases muffled in hearing loss:

Today [3 days post -aids], the water-delivery-guy-dog-barking was just unpleasant. No startle at all, no panics and breathlessnesses. I got to say out loud to him that I'd got these hearing aids and he mentioned that he remembered, last time, how I had to leave when he arrived. Meanwhile, Gail woke up and came out for coffee and I mentioned all of this to her, and she said "Yes, I could hear it all out the window, your reactions were completely different. Calm. Well, calmer."

Coming into view in this yawning new gap are a myriad of dis-eases that accompanied my hearing lost: anxiety, impatience, and [low-level] paranoia, anger, suspiciousness, the startle reflex that kept getting cued off by loud sounds, And, of course, how the whole matter got blurred and deferred by masks and plexiglass and muffled voices already muffled at the grocery store. Depression. Enclosure/enclosedness. Withdrawal. Distance. Retread. Isolation. Masks. Plexiglass.

Gail has mentioned more than once that it had become slightly frightening to be around me. That is making more and more sense. She wasn't alone in this. I had become frightened to be around myself, feeling out of control of these monstrous, sudden, violent, terrifying uprisings. Gail's beautiful patience (whose beauty is now radiantly clear).

How the illness was spread around, as illness will do. Not like others catching the same ailment, but others having to live in the wider orbit of someone with that ailment. This is not just "I have/had and ailment and they didn't. They just had to cope with me having/having had an ailment."

No. They were ailing in the orbit of my ailment. Family nursing. It is not just a matter of me becoming accustomed to hearing again, but how that accustom goes, must go, far beyond that. All of us overwhelmed. And me properly single out as someone bearing part of this and, well, just not listening when encouraged to get tested. This is neither ironic nor a joke, but it is both.

Might be good to think of this as all one ailment and our locales in it being different? This line of thought needs its own meditations.

Feeling out of it. Being out of it.

Even a spoon or pot lid dropped on the stone counter—I'd get set off, short of breath, having to retreat somewhere and settle back down. These were really like brain-stem bolts of energy, piercing, frightening. When I went to my doctor and we talked about the startling, he mentioned that part of it can be simply not being around loud sounds and losing a sense of proportion when one arrives out of the blue. All this, of course, is now wrapped up in how my hearing had become, for the most part, a huge, muffling cushion.

Too much and not enough reading online of the links of hearing loss to Alzheimer's. Me aging enough to have memory glitches becoming more common.

"As Before—and Yet Not Quite as Before"

For the life-world—the "world for us all"—is identical with the world that can be commonly talked about. Every new apperception leads ... to a new typification of the surrounding world and in social intercourse to a naming which immediately flows into the common language. (Husserl, 1970b, pp. 209–210)

Is it not an extraordinary thing that the lack of something, although we do not know precisely what it is that is lacking, can reveal the miraculous existence of health? It is only now, in its absence, that I notice not *what* was previously there but *that* it was there. (Gadamer, 1996, p. 74)

Gadamer speaks of the sometimes "violent estrangement from ourselves" (1996, p. 70) that can come from the sudden disappearance of well-being. It can also come from its reappearance. This blanket "world for us all" proves increasingly enigmatic, especially once disturbed, and this both through loss and/or gain.

This summons up what happens when one starts stepping into the odd locale of an hermeneutic/phenomenological alertness to lived experience. Everything is *exactly like it used to be* and yet also, somehow "as if illuminated":

With the break with naïveté [perhaps better to say "goes without saying-ness," "unnoticedness"] brought by the transcendental-phenomenological reorientation, there occurs a significant transformation .... As a phenomenologist I can, of course, at any time go back into the natural attitude.

...

As before—and yet not quite as before. For I can never again achieve the old naïveté; I can only understand it. (Husserl, 1970b, p. 210)

There is an amazing parallel, I'm now seeing, between the effects of hearing loss and how it makes uprisings startling, and the effects of interpretive work and how, initially, uprisings can be startling, like too-loud sounds. With practice, the startling sort of still happens with hearing aids, but they allow it to be located in a rich field that helps them seem less monstrous and dizzying. With interpretive work, becoming practiced in it has the same sort of effect, that there are still startling uprisings—like these emails we're doing and me getting almost bowled over by this parallel itself—and then … well, I'm used to then cutting and pasting it and seeing if I can compose it into the paper on hearing that I'm trying to write … this situating turns away from my own "overwhelmedness" and toward the topic of hearing, of interpreting sounds, and my writing about it.

There is a layer in here that is vital: whatever my topic might be, my efforts are, in part, to find the verities of hermeneutics in it, to find its relations, threads, ancestors, familiarities, unspokennesses, what is at play, what is going on in it—to find **its** "hermeneutic." This is why, w. students starting out, the first question always is "what is your topic?" because *that* will help the rampant connectionism … slow down and sit somewhere—in a topic, in a field, over this, regarding that. This is where composure comes back in … it is not a general or empty category or practice. As per some forms of meditation, it is a meditation *upon something* from which one gains composure from *its* composition/composure—e.g., loss of hearing and getting hearing aids. what *its* composition is, is where I get a source for *my* composing of myself over this new arrival.

The enclosedness of hearing-loss. Think of all the recent media tailspins about folks all living in their own echo-chambers.

One Last Speculative Exaggeration, for Now: "Sloping to Severe Loss"

Hearing-loss becomes downright Avatarial. Narrows. Suffocates. Barricades. Exhausts. Enrages. Harsh, echoey ping-pings with not enough space to calm and ameliorate themselves outwards into hearing the regard of trees off in the distance, and incoming winds, nearing. And Ravens overhead.

It may be that well-being is better located in the notice of it, that the non-notice *squanders* its being what it is. Squanders our relation to what is, weakens us into the numbing of everydayness. Noticing well-being, noticing the unspoken, is, in and of itself, a form of well-being that is deserving of some sort of attention. It is a noticing indigenous to hermeneutics and to never quite being able to go back. I can't go back to the "Don't worry. You'll get used to them" well-meant consolations about hearing aids, my ear-things, my earthings.

Hans-Georg is a bit correct, though, and I use his first name because of the intimacy of this last cluster of notice. He talks of the feeling of "weightlessness" that comes the equilibrium of well-being (1996, p. 113). Something *is* disappearing from notice. It is fading a bit. It feels like childhood having come back around and now having it slowly dissipate, dreamlike, as I re-gain my equilibrium, the not-notice of aided hearing.

And this feels anything but weightless.

The good news is that Hermes helps a bit. Having my grandson nearby also helps, him and I loving Barred Owl hoots in the grocery store. There is well-being to be had in being disturbed out of not noticing. Him and I all ears as the leaves crunch underfoot, as the snow crunches underfoot and the drainpipe water-melting rings inside the metal pipe and down and off down the driveway. You can *hear* that it is metal, there, waiting to be heard.

Water down the drive, out into the field that still sounds like it looks.

CHAPTER FORTY-SIX

An Ode to 215 Babies Tossed Away Unmarked

> All things being well
> We have a baby coming.
> All things being well.
> A baby.
> Where we become, so they say, grand.
> All things being well.
> Such are my words, here, now.

The changing of names. The suppressing or erasing of memory and language. Parents and grandparents who we taught that Cree, for example, was ugly and against God himself. Forgetting, figuratively and literally, where the bodies are buried. As Gail Jardine (2012) noted so clearly, with reference to Duncan Campbell Scott (1862–1947): "Our object is to continue [with 'enfranchisement'", which means giving up ones First Nations status], "is to continue until there is not a single Indian in Canada that has not be absorbed into the body politic and there is no Indian question" (cited in Miller, 2004, p. 34; see G. Jardine, 2012, p. 36 valuable detailing of this and other relevant Canadian legislation). One deals with difference, diversity, interrelationships by the *eradication of difference* and diversity such that no further dealing is required. "I want to get rid of the Indian problem" (D.C. Scott, in Miller, p. 34) by getting rid of the Indians. Colonialism as precisely and exactly the epitome of *cancel culture*.

This is precisely the sort of thing *against which* applied hermeneutic work works. It is about *not* forgetting (*aletheia*), opening up wounds and occlusions wrought by regimes of power, silences foisted and fostered and often then denied. It is about suffering all the pain released in finding out about relations lost and found. It is about calling out attempts to replicate these silencings, bringing forth marginalized voices and letting one's own voice fade back and come forward in hoped-for good measure, uncancelled. As happens in such work, my own voice and expectation and memory and prejudices get called out in this work. Hermeneutics does not provide methodological immunity or a means to "enfranchise" its topics into the anticipations and presumptions of the day.

And there is always, always the open-wound prospect that all my efforts leave me and you unprepared for the arrivals that arrive. Unprepared for what they tell us about the world and, perhaps even more so, unprepared about what they tell us about ourselves. What they tell me about *myself*. This is the locale where hermeneutics is not "subjective" but far, far more intimate and immediate than that. I find that I have been precisely *not* subjective but instead complicit in a world of relations and ancestries "over and above my wanting and doing" (Gadamer, 1989, p. xxvii)

We've all heard that a local school in Calgary, Alberta, just had its name changed from Langevin School to Riverside School. It had previously been named Riverside but was changed to Langevin in 1936. Hector-Louis Langevin (1826–1906) was one of the "Fathers of [Canadian] Confederation" and was considered the architect of the residential school system in Canada for First Nations children.

This name-change followed up on the discovery in late May 2021 of the remains of 215 previously undocumented bodies of dead young children found buried and unmarked near a former residential school in Kamloops, British Columbia:

> The children were students at the Kamloops Indian Residential School in British Columbia that closed in 1978, according to the Tk'emlúps te Secwépemc Nation. (Paperny, May 29, 2021)

One of the main blocks of the Canadian parliament in Ottawa, Ontario, is called "The Langevin Block" (Hayday, 2017). This story is still unfolding. The Calgary Catholic Board of Education has been asked to consider renaming Bishop Grandin School, Grandin also having had a hand in the "work" of residential schooling in Canada. And now, more recently, a statue of Edgerton Ryerson was torn down outside the university named after him, and calls have arisen to rename that, too. I know this without knowing one single thing about Ryerson. I can easily simply get caught in the outpouring and end up as unknowing as I did before, but perhaps weirdly slaked by the chance to get roused up.

Tough to say, and even tougher, this. I had never heard of Langevin in all my 70 years except as the name of that nearby school. I had to look up even these mere facts. There comes a great deep breath of air with these new [to me] revelations and, frankly, a gasping for air as well— this, too, having provided us all with recent images and halts. Say his name: George Floyd. How about the 1921 Tulsa Oklahoma massacre that just had its anniversary? How about this revelation: Duncan Campbell Scott's "no more Indian problem" document was a Parliamentary Memo, written, not in the 19th century, but in 1920? (see G. Jardine, p. 36):

> The *Gradual Civilization Act* (1857), the *British North America Act* (1867), the *Gradual Enfranchisement Act* (1869), the *Indian Act* (1876) and Duncan Campbell Scott's parliamentary memo (1920) appear to intend to assimilate Aboriginal peoples through treating them as "minors," as "wards of the state" with no ability to make their own decisions. (G. Jardine, 2012, p. 30)

Shock but not surprise. A great, deep breath of humiliation once again about what is known, what is said, what is suppressed, what is revealed, how easy it is for me to live a life not knowing. Privilege means not only not knowing about "them" and "this" and what has been perpetrated upon First Nations people.

But it also means something more severe: not knowing *about my own relations*. Great networks of relations now rising up out of the earthbowels *full of unnamed, re-named children's flesh*. Looking, now, for names and family lines. Petitioning the Catholic Church to open its records. Stay tuned. Stay tuned. But now that the school's name has simply disappeared, so has even the possibility of the tricky confrontation. Like it never happened. Like everything is now set right by erasing the name and replacing it with an English name ... oops, no, sorry, that's what residential schools did. It's a joke, this cancelling, a terrible one. And those who swoon over land acknowledgments and exploring First Nations language and knowledge—I'll say it. Don't think for a moment that they have explored their own language, their own ancestries.

I would never impugn motives, here. There is most often a real affection and real, valuable learning happening in the interweavings and acknowledgments. Again, a note toward hermeneutic work and an acknowledgment of the careful work needed to go beyond a simple attraction to leaving one's own tongue, one's own people's doings, behind. There is nothing to be gained by leaving one's own living forgotten but still vividly, secretly at work. Would that just once some well-meaning person would start a meeting with reading from the Treaty promises that their people wrote. Acknowledging my own impugnments.

And now, amid all the scurrying talk of "cancel culture" (Gerstmann, 2021) at the change of that school's name, I settle in to thinking, yes, change the name, but don't simply replicate the erasure of names and languages and memory perpetrated by residential schools in the first place. Put a placard with the old name's stone out front of Riverside School. Name what happened, who, and when and their reasons, with all the detail you can muster. This is one of *my ancestors* whether the name is changed or not. This *happened*, name change or not. Don't let me forget what happened *again*.

Give Hector-Louis Langevin his full due in full view. Otherwise, we simply name-change as a sort of high-handed moral duty and then risk forgetting *all over again*. This field must be dug up, relation after relation, named, shown and *I will not change that terrible image of a field dug up*. I will say it loudly in the face of images of 215 babies tossed away unmarked. The purpose of hermeneutics is to read the marks, make the marks, not erase them. It means to remember, to open, to enliven. This is true of *every topic that hermeneutics confronts*. And this sort of forgetting, suppressing is itself tragically endemic. Pandemic, perhaps.

I must learn, once again once again once again, to not turn away, to love the terrible griefs as good, harsh, demanding teachers. There are terrible courses still to come and I hope we can bear it. I hope I can bear it. We're told by Elders that this 215 is a mere drop of rain in a storm more terrible than we can imagine. More terrible than *I* can imagine, because many of our fellow beings have long since heard of it and many still suffer it. Many suffer it without knowing about its whence and whither. And ah, yes, literally as I began to write this, Pope Benedict, June 6, 2021:

> "I follow with sorrow the news that arrives from Canada about the upsetting discovery of the remains of 215 children," Francis said in his customary Sunday noon remarks to the public. "I join with the Catholic church in Canada in expressing closeness to the Canadian people traumatized by the shocking news," Francis said. "This sad discovery increases the awareness of the sorrows and sufferings of the past." "May the political and religious authorities continue to collaborate with determination to shed light on this sad affair and to commit to a path of healing," Francis added. (D'emilio, 2021)

"The sorrows and sufferings of the past." No. The open wound is *now* and simply changing the name of that school, or that university, does not serve to cleanse that wound. Tearing down statues might be required as a locale of action and pain and anger and its outworking. But don't erase. None of us will be healed by cancelling and forgetting.

And yet, I step back, right here, because I cannot adequately imagine what actions might be right, proper, needed, helpful. It may be that rage and outrage are hermeneutically acute explications—there's a sentence for you and for this journal and for my own work and its limits and usefulness.

My work is feeble, here. Like this: it is ironic, perhaps even tragic, that "Benedict" means "well-spoken." It is ironic, perhaps even tragic, how much sway the Catholic Church still holds over First Nations people. But what do I know other than bending my cupped ear again and falling, right here, right now, into silly words?

We need the repressed and marginalized stories of schools, of deaths and births, of illness, of joy, of Earthly Raven arrivals, of entangled ancestral howls in the night. All of us need this. And we need this whatever our topics may be. We don't fulfill our summons by all simply rushing off toward the latest news. But this latest news-that-is-not-new can provide a moment of renewal whatever work might then ensue, now, again, hopefully more alert, more full of the energies that hermeneutics provides and demands (see Aho, 2018; see D. Jardine, 2018)

But who am I to say much more than that, knowing so very little of any of this till just now? I can only hope that something of the blackened pages to follow struggle to be true to that howling familiar's whisperings. We all have work to do. I have work to do.

CHAPTER FORTY-SEVEN

An Early Childhood Education

Introduction

I am a long since retired Professor of Education, where my main job used to be the teaching and supervision of preservice teachers, mainly in the very early grades of school. Alongside this, I taught graduate-level courses on interpretive research and its especially pedagogical nature and interest. This combination became the ever-abundant source of my own writing and research over the full stretch of my career (from, e.g., Jardine, 1988b, 1990a, b, 1992a, b, 1993, 1994, 1996, 1998a, b, 2000, 2006, 2008c, d, 2016 b, c, d, f, 2017, 2022 and what follows).

An old adage from Hans-Georg Gadamer helps clarify the twist in the title of this paper: "The possibility that the other person may be right is the soul of hermeneutics" (H.G. Gadamer, July 9, 1989, cited in Grondin, 1994, p. 124). This is an eminently pedagogical statement. It capsulizes how teachers will lean toward what children are saying, what children are doing, and look to find what might be the lesson *for them* in these often simple moments, and then lend this interpretation back into the back and forth with them—over the drawings, over the walks in the leaves, over the oo-oo-whowho that my grandson and I are learning from the Barred Owls video clips and the lovely painting upstairs (see the cover of Latremouille et al., 2024).

He was the one whose ear caught this sound off in the distance of a clip of wee lambs gamboling.

Together, we saw that a horse colt did this gamboling as well, as did a calf. His giggles over it let me note it and name it and see it anew with him. Our walk down our snowy road after made him kick up his heels and laugh, made me laugh, too.

There is something very simple about hermeneutic/interpretive work and simple about precisely *who* gets educated in an early childhood education. I tend to be the one, over this keyboard, who finds it utterly adorable that an etymological search of "gambol" (see Online Etymological Dictionary, under "gambol (n.)": "from Greek *kampē* a bending" (on the notion of "a joint") is then directed toward the word "campus (n.)").

This chapter, once again and in its own way, is an old professor's gambol. However, as such things often go, the plays and interplays of lived experience often hide wounds and troubles and grief. I want to add a bit of context that has already been cited in this book, to an issue that comes up in what follows, and state outright that this bit is not itself enough and sits still unresolved, but now solvent, "loosed, released."

The red fox that heads the next pages is a soft cuddle of childhood and also, a summons, too, to myriad histories, personal stories, dreams and deeds.

An Early Childhood Education

Make no mistake. We each bear "those private, irreducible histories that no one else would get a piece of, ever" (Wallace, 1987, p. 110). Still and all, here, writing, editing, I lie, I exaggerate, as per the trickiness required in the tricks of images and words, in the hopes of forming something useful, healing, even just a bit.

We're not stuck. I'm not stuck with myself. Stuffed foxes can help.

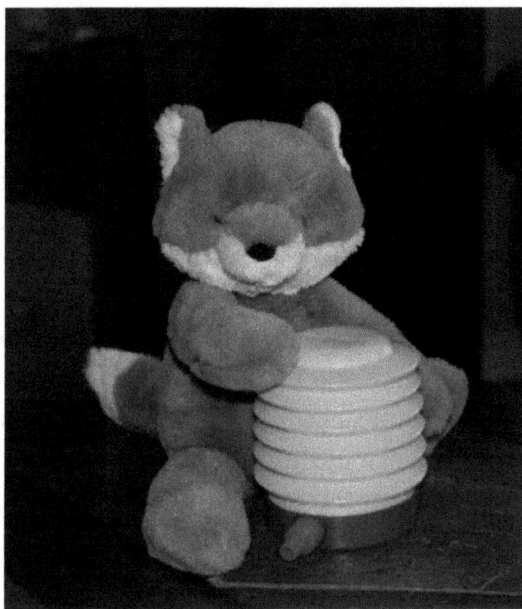

FIGURE 26. FOX IN REPOSE

No matter what we write, readings of it "happen to us beyond our wanting and doing" (Gadamer, 1989, p. xxviii). Even my own readings of my own writings seem that way most times.

Foxes can still see us moving, can still us.

Simply a lovely, silly picture of a stuffed toy set to rest that unexpectedly became part a transfer locale of personal overwhelm, familial joys and treats, and a great nearby reminder to remember, to imagine, to sorrow as fully as can be, and not let the image's allure simply swamp me inward.

My grandson was 14 months old at the time. This was a brief early childhood education won over the weeks and months that followed.

First Blush, 1953

We let it in We let it in. (Brian Eno, 2022)

That this song has a low, repeated growl to it is just right. It has a bodily effect of comfort and fear mixed, cues the animal-body, the animal alert, the purr, the snore, the possible dangerousness of something beautiful ….

… the only image I can recall was a red light flashing regularly on the top of a building outside the hospital window, me in for allergy tests, 1953, pre-scratch-test flat racks of needles, tethered to a chair. Three-year-old, thereabouts.

Someone mentioned, years later, that I had a stuffed animal with me, apparently one I liked, one I still do not exactly remember. But, on hearing that I had one, a near-sickening downward glissando of a too-close-too- moist-experience pulling back away from my face so I could slowly picture myself from the foot of the hospital bed and see myself sitting up, holding on, hugging bear-tight, red light flashing out the window. Dreamworlds of very real things.

Imaginal synesthesia gently held in those images, still slightly nauseating.

Still beautiful, drawing me nearby. Hugging close.

Be wary.

Second Blush, September 28, 2022

I've long since known of the joy and comfort of these sorts of stuffed foxes, little side witnesses to the young'un on my lap as we leaf through books or trundle wooden cars with vocal "brummmmms" and laughs. He'll bring the three foxes over to join us. Then toss them overboard and giggle. Stack them up in the new wooden truck and drive about.

Lovely, taken-for-granted, old knowledge, soft stuffed patient red fox witnesses, hugged, tossed, forgotten, remembered, and grabbed again. A great field of quiet safety. Okay, so far, so ordinary. Orderly. Culturally shaped and inherited. Little loves, blueberry stains on fox and boy, both. And the floor. And me. A curricular matter, this: a matter of a course whose sweet familiarity hides bitters. Not so ordinary, making me love it all the more in the soreness of that flittering by. Lucky us?

Privileged us? Families. Histories. Memories. Theirs. Ours. And who is who and what's what as bloods blush?

Given all that, what to do? There is no grand instruction at such a turning, and no grand task that is adequate. Just because there seems to be an opening, does not mean *at all* that it is a "plain, clean gift." It is stuffed, often over-full. "Dark attachments ... luring us further ... we find ourselves drawn *out* ..." beyond the comforts of home (Hillman, 2013b, p. 94, *en passim*). The blands of dull and taken-for-granted familiarity become, instead, animate animal familiars, with lurks and bites and messages, ever so slightly fearsome. Educations, one hopes. I hope.

Away we go, then.

Off the boy goes for a nap, and the old guy gets his own chance to do the same. To dream in the sunlit air. Couch. Red Fox on the table a hand's-reach away, him waiting there, as they do, the anthropomorphism mixed with a wee drift of *vulpemorphism*—full, of course, of our deeply human, deeply mixed and multifarious accords over foxes and them over us, and long, shared and contested ancestries and stories of fox presences and children's toys and their proper, lovely work, their proper and lovely comforts.

We meet our very own shared and contested ancestors and ancestries in that soft, familiar stuffing.

And there are voluptuous red foxes sometimes out the back window, curling up in safe sunpatches to snooze after circling and pawing the snow. The simple, hard work of trying our best to adore these pass throughs, shushing each other and smiling in the snow-glitter staring and waiting and watching. What a thing, this threesome, us holding each other, her holding our gazes, our affections, rapt.

Third Blush, a Meanwhile Worth a Little While

Before sleep came, we were out on the deck waist bents gather-tossing fall leaves fallen crackles.

Two threads might help this blush make more sense. My son and his lovely family moved from Virginia to 10 minutes away this past summer. Our grandson is now 17 months old. The joy and strangeness in this alone is spectacular to bear, home, safe, sound, nearby, fallen leaves. Armfuls.

Meanwhile, I was able to purchase hearing aids this past January, and that, too, has made an as-yet-beyond-me difference, now being able to recover a measure of well-being that had been unnoticeably lost over a long stretch of time.

So therefore, this sprung up:

First, An Autumnal Ode to Synaesthesis, Enthusiasm and Energy
Just now the leaf
Crackle. Autumn's old and wayward slouch toward rest.
Me and my grandson barefoot over them swept up on the deck. We be swept up in
the crunch and toss and giggle, them over us. Downshowering.
Ah, these leaves' sounds once again live up to their Deep familiar smell.
I can smell them more in this first fall of good ears in years. Earthings. Just break the
word apart.
With the great aid, too, of the focused abandon, 14-month-old entheos and energeia.
Yes, I know. Great Greek Boy God pretentions,
With his golden curled air in the sunlight.
(Best unintended typo ever). His glee saves me for just a fleet. This most common-
place of stories told.
Full to the leaf brimming I can hear its scents.
Hush now,
We all have bare toes, blood blushed.

I must credit, here, Sheila Ross's translation of *energiea* as "something like aliveness itself " (2006, pp. 107–108)—out from under the numbing neurasthenia (Aho, 2018; Jardine, 2018) of the rushes and dumbing-downs of everyday life, coupled with the hysterias of relentless, distracting, exhausting electro-stimulations. We be out, alive, in the leaves and the smells, lucky us.

Lucky me, murmuring back over James Hillman's recall, I've heard how things like this can too easily be understood simply as nothing more than poetic and emotional upwellings:

Within a senex cosmos [premised on old age, order, fixity or the quest for it] … [it] will be either reduced to meaninglessness by calling it [a] "random events[] or fit into order as [a] "statistical probabilit[y]." (Hillman, 2013b, p. 91)

In such light, it reads only like mush, sheer "opportunism" bent on manipulating and deceiving and rattling the cages of order. Hillman outsmarts this. Watch:

> Let us begin with the world "opportunity: the word derives ... most probably from *porta, portus (angiportus)*, "entrance," "passage through," ... associ[ated] ... with ... the Roman *porta fenestella*, a special opening through with Fortune passed. (p. 91)

Such is the privilege of autumns close and hand, of open "windows [*fenestra*]" metaphorical and literal (p. 91) and in the blurs between which is which, patiently waiting to be tossed off the deck and loved as they cascade to the ground. Why drag up and out into such etymologies? Because my grandson and I know full well this: "Pores are [also] openings in our skins" (p. 91). And these felts mix with the blushes of how our openness is wound up in wounds felt in the body. This is my own age's lovely soreness felt in holding this little boy and feeling the aches in my shoulders as part of all that loveliness. With thanks to James Hillman for teaching me how to let me own woes become, if and whenever possible:

> *Perception of opportunities requires a sensitivity given through one's own wounds.* Here, weakness provides the kind of hermetic, secret perception critical for adaptation to situations. The weak place serves to open us to what is in the air. We feel through our pores which way the wind blows. We turn with the wind; trimmers. An opportunity requires ... a sense ... which reveals the *daimon* of a situation. The *daimon* of a place in antiquity supposedly revealed what the place was good for, its special quality and dangers. The *daimon* was thought to be a *familiaris* of the place. To know a situation, one needs to sense what lurks in it. (Hillman, 2013b, pp. 101–102)

Ah, yes. Familiars. A tough practice, this. A loving, reliable teacher, this practice. I cradle my grandson near, but safe. More like a fire in the woodstove. I protect him from it and demonstrate (monster that I am) its wonderfulness and dangers, mixed. I will not, as per Hannah Arendt's important meditation:

> ... expel [him] from our world and leave them to their own devices, nor ... strike from [his] hand [his] chance of undertaking something new, something

unforeseen by us, but [instead] to prepare [him, and, vitally, re-prepare myself all over against under his witness and trust] ... for the task of renewing a common world. (Arendt, 1969, p. 196)

Simple as that. Early childhood education is not just the education of young children. Of course not.

Fourth Blush on a Shoveled Deck

So, six weeks later, we went back out on the deck for the first time since the snow got shoveled off it, and he bent over and scooped up leaves that were no longer there and tossed them up, with a little glance and grin up toward me nearby. An early childhood education lesson so astounding in its layers and forth-comings and complex dependent co-arisings. There's a Ph.D.'s worth, right there, about familiarity, memory, how locales and places cue it, how having had an affectionate time made its barefoot imprint print and cue recall and side-glance and all. This is extraordinary. This is why I've committed to memory lines from Bronwen Wallace, and why I have her book, like a stuffed fox, easily to hand: "surprised [all over again] ... to find it here, where it seems

FIGURE 27. HUGGIN AND MUNINN

impossible that one life even matters, though … [like her] … I'll argue the stubborn argument of the particular, right now, in the midst of things, *this* and *this*" (Wallace, 1987, p. 111).

We let it in. One set of my own great grandparents—this young child's great great great—are not Greek at all. Olaf and Thora Hendrickson. Norwegian. Blond curls. Blue eyes.

This long-lost ancestral thread flutters by one of his and my favorite sights at Grandpa and Gramma's house. Repeated visitations. Repeated waitings:

With a whisper to Olaf and Thora, it might just be Odin's ravens that he and I love dearly in their winter feather plumping, him hushing me as we repeatedly approach the window (*fenestra*) and take out food for them and get coos and cackles in return:

Huginn ["Thought"] and Muninn ["Memory"] hover each day The wide earth over. I fear for Huginn lest he fare not back,—Yet watch I more for Muninn. (From the *Prose Edda*, early 13th century Norse. See https://www.sacredtexts. com/neu/pre/pre04.htm)

I watch more for memory—that is why I let this repeated scenario repeat, just like the Ravens coming back next year, perhaps. I fear that thought may not return. I fear I feel thought leaving me with age spots. Those smells of leaves, just imagine the rush of ages that came with their cooped up returning set loose in the air. Nostrils ripe again, looking at their rictal feathers, and those thunderous undertail feathers storming. Oh Fortuna! Something approaches in the hushing. To coin a phrase, "It might just be ravens writing in mid-air." It might be memory come and thinking bidden. Hearts in beaks.

So odd to start remembering something I never really knew in the first place. But knew so well. Neither of these is adequate to the blushes to come.

Fifth Blush: Back to Oncoming Sleep, September 29, 2022

Yes. Where was I? Stuffed fox, sunlight in the windowpane. Naptimes.

It is also always handy to also have a hand's-reach away not-really-especially-understood scientific concepts that have become, like my blurry understanding of stuffed animals, a sort of unexpressed familiarly I feel almost too free to play with: Theta Waves. From a few morning hours of playing with himself, letting myself simply fall into it, the smells and scattershots of autumn leaves crackling under our bare foots out on the deck for no other reason that the uprisings of it and the laughing, and me caught, of course, in Muninn's arcs under Autumn sunlights and sights and the aching downarcing, yellow aspenleaf blistering brights.

Years of images. Years of imagination. Of wrinkling off to dreamings.

Hair thins into grey-whisperings.

You know, normal. Ordinary as can be.

Hush. There is blood lingering in every blush.

Naptimes. An ear cocked for the wail of his nap's end. The sheer luck of the peace and quiet surrounding and its opulence in the face of things. And a safe grandchild. Drift off.

We let it in. We let it in.

I reached out from the couch and plopped the stuffed fox on my chest, half-sleeping through a maze of holding it, muttering to it what an important job you wee, overly familiar companions can have, how patient, how ready and waiting, how vital, comforting, heartening … little 1953 felt murmuring for the first time in a long, long time. Plaything. Affection. Murmuring over it like a cloistered meditation prayer ….

… good going, fox, to bear all that and provide such a spot, a cuddle-up, a whole world let in, a place feeling and felt, between us, full of a lifetime of stories had and yet to come this way. Toss in the leaf pile. Bearing that very smell. Animal companions. Familiars ….

… my thumbs gently purring in its soft ears, because, well, I know my dogs like it, too. Just imagine this long, winding trail: "Companion (n.) from Latin *companionem* … literally, 'bread fellow' …, from Latin com "with, together" … + *panis*, 'bread' " (Online Etymological Dictionary, under "companion"). Even with Gadamer's important caution, that "even when etymologies are right, they are not proofs" (Gadamer, 1989, p. 103), they are what he calls "preparatory achievements" always already hidden in the sheer commonplaceness of language itself.

This fox has blueberry stains, traces of his napping companion.

Thinking. Memory. Black circling arcs over blackening pages with ink (this an old murmur of Leonard Cohen [see Thomson, 2018]).

Okay, yes, I understand. Emotionalism and anthropomorphism and way too sweet. Sleepy whisperings that perhaps I should have kept secret. Private.

Hoarded. Mush. This be a common hermeneutic mire that awaits the "something" that "awakens" (Gadamer, 2001, p. 50), opens, wounds, and might show a way to continue, or might founder me altogether wrecked and ruined and properly speechless and stopped and, like this. Shut up!

A red light flashing in the distance.

A start, awake and still imagining. Those dozens and dozens of stuffed animals I drive nearby nearly every day, carefully wired to the fenceposts of the Tsuut'ina Nation, mostly unattended to now, unheld except in fast passing glances, held by cutting wire. They had become almost beyond notice. Then suddenly each one had unthumbed ears. Unheld toys. Reaching. Scattershots of May 2021. Kamloops, British Columbia Residential School unmarked graves announced. 215 (Paperny, 2021).

I drive by everyday. This be your third drive by in this book?

Memory. Thought. More. And more.

Each soft plush a placeholder for an unheld child, an unnamed child, stolen, buried unmarked, unnamed. By my own kin (Jardine, 2021b). Don't forget the old pedagogical standby, especially for early childhood, damn it all: It's "for your own good" (Miller, 2002). I cited this first a decade ago, but, with this new boy here, here we are remembering, Munnin come by again, that what's being cited was the atmosphere in which my grandmother, raised by Olaf and Thora, was raised, an ominous passage from *The Encyclopedia of Pedagogy* from 1851, here cited from Alice Miller (2002, p. 42):

> Pedagogy correctly points out that even a baby in diapers has a will of his own and is to be treated accordingly.

And, with James' help, I can't forget that these naptime upwellings might themselves seem like sheer gooey poetic willful upwillings and upwellings, *but they are not just that*. They are occasions for something like strong, tough research, writing, publication that might be useful in breaking up this ground grown hard, forgotten. They are Huggin's companions to break bread over. To think it through. Now repeatedly *imaginable* every time I drive over to "the kids" house. And now, a long trail of utterly, compelling *public* images of bears, and triceratopses, and foxes and other plushes, each now rushed by in the rush-hour rushes by of cars, great fortunes that might open in the rushed by memories of those just in a rush-by. Adorned, recently, with lovely red ribbons for the Solstice marking, new-child-arrived dark December days making the unmarked even more marked. We know, we've seen, that such things might only rush up angers. "It wasn't me" and its kin. I can hope that these have the good fortune to enough to open, to let in some love, affection, light, commiseration, and companionship. Air under the wingings. After all, "what then, is our task?" (Jardine & Lyle, 2022). My task is to try to make that anger (including my own, of course) understandable enough that it can perhaps dissipate into thin, raven-filled air, and let in love, let in a deep breath, let up good grief. The tragic turn is that a lot of this heart-opening of mine is coming from my grandchild's presence and embrace, the very one denied, no. Stop. Don't let the overwhelm end only in windowlessness.

Go ahead. Grieve a little bit, opening, here, in safe big nap belly that is better than none. As sleep came, I wanting every single one of those stuff toys up here, warm and near me, in sunlight, to hug and hold each one and say that they are loved, that their great sorrows are held and beheld and, even for a this here wee little glimpse, not held back, memory and thought both now, arcing overhead. We ever-so-briefly greet as I drive by. These few little words. These grins of leaves tossed up, meager, but our joys, too, can testify just a little bit. Open. Grave and laughing all at once. Now written, may be published, who knows? May be read, who knows? Because my boy, our boy, and his family, live, you see, safe and happy and happy and nearby, on Tsuut'ina land. The river nearby. Within earshot of the highway. Of the cars. Of fence wires.

This in the end, nothing but a small ode to early childhood education.

CHAPTER FORTY-EIGHT

How Shall You Be Called?

Another early childhood education. Unmarked graves held named children. Unnamed children—well, I know full well that my own odd qualms here are so trivial in the face of this world and its sorrows. This is why I write.

A Small Introduction is Needed: "Like Tin Cans Tied to a Tail"

It was with the dogs, and with some parrots, lovebirds, ravens, and mynahs, that the trouble arose. These verbally talented individuals insisted that their names were important to them, and flatly refused to part with them. Anybody who wanted to be called Rover, or Froufrou, or Polly, or even Birdie in the personal sense, was perfectly free to do so, not one of them had the least objection to parting with the lowercase (or, as regards German creatures, uppercase) generic appellations "poodle," "parrot," "dog," or "bird," and all the Linnaean qualifiers that had trailed along behind them for two hundred years like tin cans tied to a tail. (Le Guin, 1989, p. 195)

One origin of this writing is simple. I have an 11-week-old grandson who is yet to be named. That trailing experience and has led me here.

My hermeneutic snout knows that here there be dragons, as well. Every experiential opening, every such "opportunity" "trails dark, chaotic attachments, luring us further and further ..." (Hillman, 2013b, p. 94). Names. Naming. Marked. Unmarked. Intimate. Dominating. Submitting. Resisting. And so on.

An old friend, versed in hermeneutics and in the fragilities of living admitted a low-level concern when she heard about this grandson situation even though, well, everything is fine. Neither she nor I could quite fathom our own nebulae. What is this, then?

Bottomless and astonishing, it seems. Got me to rereading Ursula LeGuin's "She Unnames Them" in all its mysteriousness and convolute.

Decades of going into schools, student-teachers, school students, schoolteachers, administrators, all a swirl of names, swirls of namings. "Name": Old Saxon. Old Frisian. Old High German. Old Norse. Graduate students. Finding the topic of your work and then finding a title that is befitting of it. Titles. Entitlements. I would always mention that the title of your work is what runs up its spine on the shelf. Your proper name and its title is part of its upheld.

Proper Names: Latin *proprius* "one's own." Links to propriety, proportion, in proper measure. Colonial stripping of names and assigning new ones. Then leaving the very same graves unmarked.

In certain forms of research into teaching, learning, and curriculum, it is deemed proper to give "participants" (often fake) "proper names" to feign a sense of individuality and closeness then belied by ethical cover stories.

Whereas, of course, the "author's" name is not feigned. It is proper to the property of the writer. And, as if that isn't enough ...

... Another Co-Incident Trail of Tin Cans

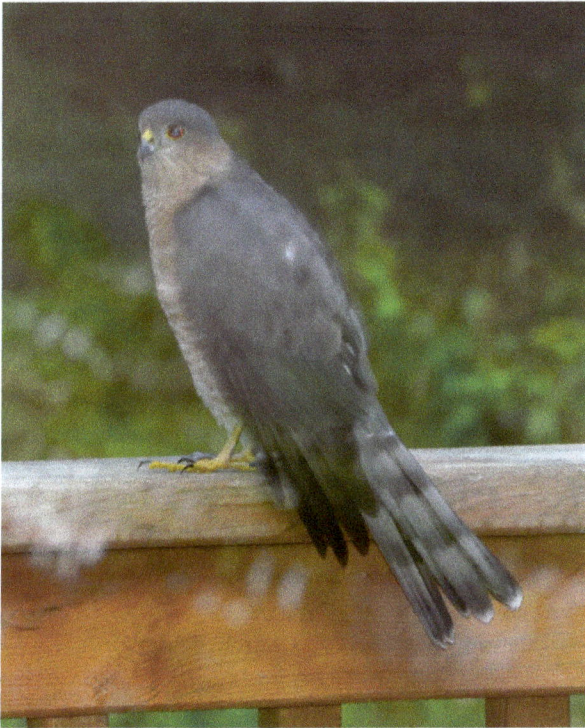

The beautiful captivates us. It has asserted itself and captivated us before we can come to ourselves and be in a position to test the claim ... that it makes [on us]. (Gadamer, 1989, p. 490)

To test the claim because this beauty sits stunning on the back deck railing, late August 2023—it isn't simply "there it is." It *claims* my attention—and thus a rattling together of it not just being "present, there," but of me being *"called out" by its presence*, it "maintain[ing something as] *true*" (Online Etymological Dictionary under "claim [v.]"). Here's an admission: some stories told, some photographs, some muttered words, do not have this effect on me. Only when they do am I "called" to write, to think.

To be tested by the claim it makes and to let that test be the trail of writing itself.

Tin can rattlings, for sure, but something more, too, in this pull, this lure, this draw, something phenomenologically palpable. Some trails opening up (*aletheia*), enlivening (see Jardine, 2018). This wee boy is now smiling back and forth. It isn't simply a characteristic of him and his growing notice of the world—though endless documentation can be found of it as a general characteristic of a developmental milestone. Yes, right, understood.

However, *to be smiled* at is something more and something so very commonplace. Because what it does is not only summon me, there, in his welling presence, but also summon this smiling from me in a grappling over understanding my own helplessness in being thus summoned. From a book chapter entitled "A Curriculum for Miracles":

> **Miracle**: From the Latin *mīrāculum*: object of wonder. *Mīrāculum* from *mīrārī*, to wonder at. From *mīrus*, wonderful. From *smeiros* [(s) mei–PIE–proto-Indo-European] "to smile, to be astonished." Also Sanskrit: *smerah* "smiling." Also Old Church Slavic: *Smejo*–to laugh. (Seidel, 2014c, p. 8)

An object of wonder where what is wondered over has an *agency* over my own wanting to name—"something addresses us" (Gadamer, 1989, p. 299), leading to a feeling of "suspension" leading to being put into question by the not-quite-yet-posed question that arises, asking for a response (Gadamer, 1989, p. 299).

I've never seen such a bird before. I smile.

Seen later chasing our Raven overhead, him raving now solo after many years part of a pair. A Raven long since fed and familiar. One of the family, shall we say. See? Words and namings. He's become a bit like a black cat on a broom—"a *familiaris* of [this] place. To know a situation, one needs to sense what lurks in it" (Hillman, 2013b, p. 102), and that Raven's arrival full of that lurk, summoning remembering, summoning dreams of his absent companion. Yes, companion, one that one eats with, common breads. Animals that arrive and summon, in arriving, something of the ways of the place, old dreams of animals' spirits and my own animate spiritedness in response. He'll "kook" on the railing for food.

This new bird alights right in the middle of all that. This new boy smiles, then sleeps. There's wind in the trees sounding winter coming near. "The cascade here is unbearable: the Nicaean denial of *daimons* is a denial of the [living and breathing] familiarity of places" (Jardine, 1992b, p. 72) and all the interrelatednesses and kinships that involves. It won't do. My older grandson grabs my little finger, "Poppa come." My dog sits against my leg and leans his head. Hand. Stroke. Warm.

How shall you be called? Notice that turn of phrase—not "what" but "how." Is this just me wanting to usurp these arrivals with my own powers to call, to summon? If I get your name, I can override your summoning with mine? This, of course, must be admitted full force as an old, everywhere-still-present matter for gender-matters and gender-patterns, for indigenous-namings and colonial-usurpings, for memories gaining and lost and all the work still working itself out. What shall I tell my grandsons about the stuff animals wired to the Tsuut'ina Nation fenceposts?

There is something else here right in the middle of all this. I am naive enough and aged enough to believe it might be a locale wherein something of "all this" might open and blossom into insight and heart-ache held between us. Because my giggle giddies bring smiles which makes me smile, miraculously, each of us in the very same repose, one repose, not two:

> We experience an absolute opposition to th[e] will-to-control, not in the sense of a rigid resistance to the presumption of our will, which is bent on utilizing things, but in the sense of the superior and intrusive power of a being repos-ing in itself. (Gadamer, 1977, pp. 226–227)

This boy, this bird, are alive in themselves, reposing in curved beak glances and blue-eyed looks and squints and ca-coos. And, having taught young children for years, the closeness that comes when a child knows that I know their name. And me, utterly horrible at remember-ing a person's name. I'll know it from 10 feet away and as I approach them, it will dissipate. What do we have going on here?

There was a hint in all that. The two of us smiling *in one repose*— one "being" reposed-in-itself. Proper naming him and me names two. Nope. Not good enough. I've come to love the lumbering clumsiness that writing can be because it can allow me my own and let me find it not a fault but proper to the matters at hand.

Two friends. Emails back and forth. Bird naming frenzy was a frenzy of type. What *kind* of bird is this? As a lure toward surrounding it with its families of relations in my experience of it in the midst of the myriad of birds hereabouts. It is a pleasureable frenzy, an affectionate one, fun, funny.

I want him closer and I want my friends along with me in that venture. I want him *to familiar* (not a typo). It is too simple to say that this is about simply "control" or "pinning down"—it is *nearly that*, but that has become a too-simple leap to make. I want this bird to be safely here and me safe in his presence. Comforting. He bird. Me here. "The kinship is just as undeniable as the difference" (Wittgenstein, 1968, p. 36). This is not just an isolated arrival of "a new bird-type" but an arrival *here*, in this place, with Ravens nearby and an older grandchild who helps me feed in familiar rounds.

What are you, new one, called? How shall I call you? How might you be called?—as partially, perhaps, how shall you be remembered?

No, almost, but that's not it either. Because, as Le Guin's tin can meditations suggest, a Linnaean name does bears only an abstract idea, typificational or generic or species difference (this is why hermeneutics of a sort does not bear toward the eidetic spell of permanence, where we might imagine "fix[ing]" the features of our lifeworld "once and for all in a way equally accessible to all" [Husserl, 1970b, pp. 177–178]). Hans-Georg Gadamer warns of lived experience rendered under the eye of an "eidetic phenomenology" (1989, p. 254). But all this, again is me calling, me remembering. This mess:

> The bewildering abundance and recognizable resemblances of the world and its creatures, irresolvable to either of the extreme simplifications of identity or difference—Jean Piaget [1965, p. 6] noted Henri Bergson's early 20th century "surprise at the disappearance of the problem of 'kinds' … in favor of the problem of 'laws.'" Hans-Georg Gadamer's thoughts (1989, p. 114) on

"versimilitude"— "likeness." Not surprisingly, there is a "kind-ness" [here] at the heart … (Jardine, 2012b, p. 224)

They were considering the name "Linnaeus." Lines, laws, kinds. Tigers and lions and bears. And all the

What is the giddy frenzy to find out what kind of bird this is? And how might this be connected—is it connected?—to the weird, low-level "worry" about an unnamed grandchild? This grandson with no proper name yet … my worry is my impropriety only? Wanting claimable property? Again, almost, but inadequate.

This is part, of course, of the wonderful feminist heartbeat of Ursula LeGuin's "She Unnames Them" (1987), where Eve be the figure there, talking with the animals about their names and their unnaming, and her own unnaming, too, and how such things spooked Adam and his God as well:

And he said, and he said
That she has the poison inside her
She talks to snakes and they guide her.
Adrianne Lenker (2022), from the song "Sparrow"

So comes what happens when Hermes guides your research. This sort of thing, a query and conversation on an online site called *Biblical Hermeneutics Stack Exchange* (https://hermeneutics.stackexchange.com):

Genesis 2:20
So the man **gave names to** all the livestock, **the birds** in the sky and all the wild animals
Is this used in the sense of:

- option A
    Adam: *oh … this one I name it a bird*
- option B
    Adam: *oh …. this bird I name it parrot*
- option C
    Adam: *oh … this parrot I name it Snowy.*
(karma, asked Jan 22, 2018, https://hermeneutics.stackexchange.com/questions/31542/genesis-220-what-does-it-mean-naming-the-animal)

So, a note, that my grandson's naming is a matter of *this* child's name, his *proper* name that he is to be *given*—yes, his "given name." Thus, this name is necessarily and henceforth one not chosen but given by one's kin, one hopes, with kindness:

> In the ancient times, common nouns and attributes were used as proper nouns / names. The name Adam for instance, could have derived from Hebrew אדם ('adam) meaning "to be red", referring to the ruddy colour of human skin, or from Akkadian adamu meaning "to make". According to Genesis in the Old Testament Adam was created from the earth by God (there is a word play on Hebrew אֲדָמָה ('adamah) "earth"). It was only fitting that God entrusted Adam with the charge of naming birds and animals in accordance with the special feature each possessed say, the blackness of crow, the sweet song of cuckoo, the ferociousness of tiger etc. So, "name" in fact refers to generic name of the bird or animal in question and not the personal name as Pinky or Snowy.
>
> (Kadalikatt Joseph Sibichan, answered Jan 23, 2018, https:// hermeneutics.stackexchange.com/questions/31542/genesis-220-what-does-it-mean-naming-the-animal)

Hmm. Adam. Flesh-colored? Remember the long-since-disappeared Crayola crayon? This is why the internet curse is so broad—every name, meant to be proper, summons up ghosts and histories, all entangled.

Then comes a long discussion about Adam and naming and "dominion" which overwhelms me altogether (https://hermeneutics. stackexchange.com/questions/2860/what-does-dominion-mean-in-genesis?rq=1).

So right here, bottomlessness. Because this is only one slim cultural bloodline which is itself among myriad in this world of birds and boys. Even adding all these myriads together—including, of course, the Indigenous namings coming up out of the land on which I live—finds itself falling short of a side-glance. Of *being* noticed:

"That Pair": Another Half-Step

> And yet how close I felt to them when I saw one of them swim or fly or trot
> or crawl across my way or over my skin, or stalk me in the night, or go along
> beside me for a while in the day. They seemed far closer than when their
> names had stood between myself and them like a clear barrier: so close that
> my fear of them and their fear of me became one same fear. And the attrac-
> tion that many of us felt, the desire to feel or rub or caress one another's scales
> or skin or feathers or fur, taste one another's blood or flesh, keep one another
> warm—that attraction was now all one with the fear, and the hunter could
> not be told from the hunted, nor the eater from the food. This was more or
> less the effect I had been after. (Le Guin, 1987, pp. 195–196)

"My grandson," this itself—is it?—a clear barrier between us? Saying
"Hello baby" feels distant even though the drooping eyelids draw me
in and rest our chests together before half of that could be voiced.

A proper name draws us closer, doesn't it? Or does it, too, place a
breath-hesitation between us? Someone said that they weren't allowed
to take their baby out of the hospital without a name. Now finding
health care coverage denied without a proper name.

So here is a half-step, a "birding lesson":

Catching a glimpse of a blue heron pair over past the edge of the marsh, tucked up under the willowy overhangs.

Shore edge log long deep bluey sunset shadow fingers.

Sudden rush of a type of recognition almost too intimate to bear, an event of birding never quite lodged in any birding guides:

"It's *that* pair!"

What a strange and incommensurate piece of knowledge. How profoundly, how deeply, how wonderfully *useless* it is, knowing that it is *them*, seemingly calling for names more intimate, more proper than "heron," descriptions richer and more giddy than "**Voice**: deep harsh croaks: *frahnk, frahnk, frahnk* (Peterson, 1980, p. 100)." Such knowing doesn't lead anywhere. It is, by itself, already always full, already always enough.

Perhaps this irreplaceable, unavoidable intimacy is why our tales of the Earth always seem to include proper names ("obligations require proper names" [Caputo, 1993, p. 201]), always seem to be full of love and heart, always seem to require narrations of particular times and places, particular faces, particular winds, always seem to invite facing and listening and remembering. (Jardine, 2016b, pp. 87–88)

That pair—that now single Raven on the back feeder is *him* (and is, too, full of the important growling about genders and their being "assigned").

This Boy and the Sunhissing

Given the work of writing, of interpretation, how can I write, here, without claiming dominion? How can we name another with any grace?

My words must be as slow, as new, as single, as tentative as the steps I took going down the path away from the house, between the dark-branched, tall dancers motionless against the winter shining. (Le Guin, 1987, p. 196)

I think of how interpretive studies often give their "participants" fake proper names, thus robbing them of their own proper name *and* their own family-of-relations name. And this is done both to give them voice and protect them from the recognition that comes from proper names, all at once. Interesting, all this, for doing that sort of research and writing is *never* simply an innocent or procedural matter. It is, instead, always and already *part of the exploration of the living topography itself,* not a prerequisite decision to be made and then forgotten. How shall we—the writer, the reader, the one telling a tale—be properly, adequately called?

That dancer in *that* winter's shining.

This boy summons and is summoned, smiles and is smiled at, coos back and forth, singing back and forth, us warmly asleep on my chest, warmly wet sometimes. My words must be slow and tentative to be properly fitting, here. So, a hermeneutic truth about words and their fits and starts.

We are, *at the very same sudden moment,* of a kind, of *this precise here and us,* surrounded by brother, father, mother, grandmothers, grandfathers, great grandmothers, cousins, aunts, uncles, friends, their dog, our dogs, the Raven come to eat, the peas planted, waited upon, then picked in the garden.

The dried peas with their awaiting promises of next year. The fawn's backyard dancings.

His older brother and I love little pics and vids of goat and horse gambols. We, he and I, do it on purpose in our walks down the road, as do the dogs come walking with us. His older brother's proper name withheld here on purpose for reasons best left still and quiet. Identification. Self-identification. Traceability. The dark web. And the bright one, too. And the fenceposts.

No proper name can be uttered without trailing its own loud tail-bound cans. Not just people or places we know of the same name—"Arthur" is the name of the town of his mother's raising, and my wife's grandfather's name, for example, or "Locklear" … no one remembers Heather, right? And then all the shouting one can find online about any name ever—no untether innocence to be found for this tethered innocent.

Cadewyn. The good fight. Welsh. Cardiff friends translate it as "embracing the blessing." Internet sites differ. Internet—"white battle" often appears, but cade can mean "fair" as in just, not a complexion. Ah me.

And then, one of the folks cited here, in this writing is a person whose work I can no longer stomach reading because of his ignorant and self-important behavior at a restaurant with the lovely staff that others of us around the table knew by their proper names. Nice little cite, though, and a reminder, too, that my writing is often far better than me.

It still *feels* like jeopardy of some sort, these long waiting nameless weeks. But then so do my rather regular grandparental night-tremors of injury or harm. Vulnerability that will be, maybe not *solved* by proper naming, but somehow at least communally accepted and taken on as a promise, a vow?

Maybe not? Right there be the gap, because whatever comes, precisely that vulnerability of us all will not be *ended* by proper naming.

Words, eh, and legacies and trailings? Can't tell if this is an animal-body linger, a cultural linger, a gendered and engendered linger, a personal qualm or suppressed event or experience or a misunderstood happenstance or memory that has come to appear dark and chaotic.

Or Jesus juggles of Baptisms and salvations from the dark and chaotic flesh itself through washing away both literal and configured with giving a new name (like the young boy in Ursula's *Wizard of Earthsea* (1968) stumbling naked through a creek, pulled up the other side, washed clean and away, given new clothing—new "investments"—*and given a new name*). Or Buddhist aerobatics over impermanence and suffering no matter what and how, if we forget what we've done, names can bespeak an affliction that wants our living jeopardy not to be so.

A proper name would help me unname this—"the baby" feels like a clear barrier somehow, sometimes.

Ursula?

[Unnaming] was somewhat more powerful than I had anticipated, but I could not now, in all conscience, make an exception for myself. I resolutely put anxiety away, went to Adam, and said, "You and your father lent me this, gave it to me, actually. It's been really useful, but it doesn't exactly seem to fit very well lately. But thanks very much! It's really been very useful." (Le Guin, 1987, p. 196)

Oh, yes, perhaps that is what is so trembling about there not being a name. I come face-to-face with my own thoughts of being, always and already unnamed long ago and long since, soon and always and already having been passing, leaving, frailing more and more and leaving this moment of us giggling and napping.

Ah. No surprise but surprise! There it is. I want this to never end, but *that very idea* makes it end. So stop. Fenceposts. Names. A grandfather's aging come headlifting, with all my sunhissing underbellies still left unsaid no matter how much is said. There will be come this way another uprising. Another school year. Another gathering of songs and silences. To come to some comfort about this being how things always already are.

Lay, warm, sun, breathe. Curled. Purring. Both of us an unnamed one. Lao Tzu drifting in my inner ear ... something like "the one that can be named is not ..."

"Enough" be a word good for exhaling.

I even expect that when a name does come, I'll feel a little let down for reasons *way* beyond my ken.

CHAPTER FORTY-NINE

On Teaching Punctuation

Many chapters swirling around matters great and troubling. In my under-graduate classes, small questions came up about small threads of "curriculum requirements" and how often they appeared to be nothing more that moments requiring memorization and little more. Memorizing is itself a grand, old, ancient art, of course. So is punctuation.

A question from a student-teacher: Why should I teach punctua-tion? Or to them from a student in their class: Why do we have to learn this? Certainly not just because it is in the mandated curriculum and must be "covered." Or, differently put, is there a good and just cause why it is there and what its mandate truly is. Why study this?

Commas *teach*, they are not just taught or learned. They are extraor-dinary and ancient beings:

Latin *pung-o, punc-tus*, literally meaning "to pierce, puncture," and thus "wound" some surface. This word quickly came as well to mean emotional vexation ... and its close relative, *compunctus* [indicated] piercing a surface and the emotion sense, of goading or vexing the feelings. In Medieval Latin, *punctus* came to be used also as the word for the dot or point pricked into the parchment surface, which helped to mark up and "divide" a written text for comprehension in reading, and so to "punctuate" it, in our modern sense. It is the method of marking up units of the text into mnemonically useful length by means of "pointing" them. So here we have a chain, mnemonically associated through the key syllable *punct*, which attaches physical puncture-wounds, with (page) punctuation, with affective compunction of heart—and so from heart to memory, via a dual meaning of Latin *cor(d)-*. The "wounding" of the page in punctuation and the wounding of memory in *compunctio cordis* are symbiotic processes, each a requirement for human cognition to occur at all. (Carruthers, 2003, p. 101)

Commas, periods, exclamations. Invocations of the puncturing or wounding of vellum skins so that they will take ink, but also of the compositional shaping of phrases into beautiful, memorable and radiant portions that will serve to pierce the reader's heart. The wound of writing. *Compunctio cordis*—where punctuation hesitates breath around a breathtaking phrase, and thus pierces the heart in so doing, and thus uses punctuation, therefore, as its means and as an end.

Answer: Yes, teach punctuation. How do you teach commas? By coming to know them intimately. Learn it well and you will breath differently. And read out loud and feel the pull of breath around these wounds. Teach your own students such adoration. Find examples where they and you can experience the yield of such attention and devotion, that moment when all that effort of learning starts to prove its worth.

Another question. What is going on with that Grade One child who caresses the pages of that *Wabi Sabi* (Reibstein & Young, 2008) book, and paws through it over and over, and then plants glittery sprinkles over what she then writes?

I was taught how to illuminate in different colours until a text look to be spiked with gems. The ink was made from oak apples–gallnuts–crushed and soaked in rainwater, then stirred with a fig stick in green vitriol till it turned gummy and black. The quills came from geese, the left wing-pinion curving best to sit in a right hand. It was here, too, that I learned the ways of vellum– how calf-skin rubs smoother than goat, how ink sticks better to the flesh side, and so on.

...

It was more than profit that drew me to vellum. I loved its springiness to the touch. Its velvet nap. The whiff of animal still hanging about it, as though when reading or writing you were living inside the beast. I loved the blood-veins running there, under the ink. I loved the brown-white, brown-white run of the pages in a vellum book, since however long soaked in lime-water, and whatever sharpness of blade is used to scrape it, and no matter what creature it has come from (calf, goat, pig, sheep, deer–with smaller books, even squirrel), hairside will always be darker than fleshside. I loved all this as a boy with a goosequill in a scriptorium. (Morrison, 2000, pp. 42–43, 210)

Wabi Sabi's collage is itself an ancient art, a beast with its own insides (see https://www.youtube.com/watch?v=ca2Ly4Vpb5Y). And the pull of certain papers on inky nibs, the scritching and scurrying sound that flat paper doesn't quite yield, can be felt by feeling the paper itself. What about the rough adherences of paint to a surface and how that surface feel under hand? Rubbing your hand over the surface is an act of love and an act of remembering.

So, too, is the hard-shelled beetle clicking of keyboards. This glowing screen surface, too, teaches. We must think through how this flat plastic glow has lost is *analogia entis*, its analogy to the flesh that stirs it. Flesh and text have been "bound together by an anciently perceived likeness between all creatures and the earth of which they are made" (Berry, 1983, p. 76). In pawing that book, "like speaks to like" (p. 76). We can become spellbound by screened and scrolled text, but the analogy between the hands that reach and hold and scroll up a page and then rub underneath lines, is not exactly there. There is an echo, here, but only for those of us who remember. One way or another, there is a new likeness emerging in the new technologies of reading and writing. Spell- checking makes the text correct, but it skips teaching and acts like it makes no difference to know about such things and to carry oneself in such knowledge. I know. I'm old and fashioned by such things. A retiring reminder of things that soon will soon no longer exist, perhaps. A wounded memory.

And so it is with the urge to glitter—illuminating manuscripts so that we can then become caught in their glow:

Hugh [of St. Victor (1096–1141)] begins to explain what wisdom does. The sentence begins, *sapientia illuminat hominem,* "wisdom illuminates man" … *ut seipsum agnoscat,* "so that he may recognize himself." Enlightenment in Hugh's world and what is understood as enlightenment now are two different things. The light, which in Hugh's metaphoric usage illuminates, is the counterfoil of the eighteenth-century light of reason. The light of which Hugh speaks here brings man to a glow. Approaching wisdom makes the reader radiant. The studious striving that Hugh teaches is a commitment to engage in an activity by which the reader's own "self" will be kindled and brought to sparkle. (Illich, 1993, p. 17)

This is why she paws and paws this book. To bring it to a glow which then sheds its light on her and thus repays her whiling and her affection.

Best advice? Learn to love writing and reading and show the worth of such whiling love to your students.

CHAPTER FIFTY

"To Lend Ourselves to its Life": On Early Childhood Literacy and Other Early Matters

A Little Walkabout First

As a former Language Arts teacher and practicum supervisor of student-teachers in the early years, I've been granted a strange, up close view of the in the emergence of literacy. I'm surrounded by it, loving it, writing about it nearly non-stop lately (see Adams & Jardine, 2023, under consideration). Such is the upwell of new-yet-familiar experiences and their temptations.

As per the hermeneutic and phenomenological urge, readers will notice that the writing that follows is not just *about* the "interweaving and criss-crossing" (Wittgenstein, 1968, p. 32) that constitutes the life of language itself caught clearly in its emergence, not just *about* how life and its emergences shows language's haziness, life's haziness (Gadamer, 2007e, p. 371) when we consider it up close. Rather, the writing itself is deliberately interweaving and hazy, not just as some poetic trick, but *because its topic is interweaving and hazy.*

Something hazy and weaving seems more proper to the object under consideration.

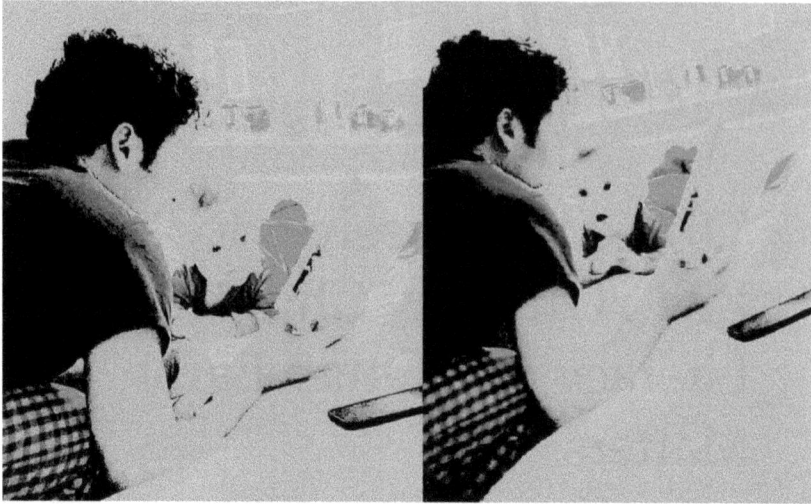

FIGURE 28. BOYS AND BOOK

The whole of spoken language surrounding the child snaps him up like a whirlwind, tempts him by its internal articulations. The untiring ways in which the train of words crosses and re-crosses itself finally sways the child over to the side of those who speak. Only language as a whole enables one to understand how language draws the child to himself.

...

We only have to lend ourselves to its life, to its movement of differentiation and articulation, and to its eloquent gestures. (Merleau-Ponty, 1970, pp. 40–41, 42)

We hand ourselves over, we abandon ourselves to the space of meaning which holds sway over us. (Ricoeur, 1984, p. 187)

Two kin pouring over a book. Glances. Mouth agape. Looking back and forth. Imitations. Affections. Breaths mingling in a soft, quite literal conspiracy. Play and interplay. "A space specially marked out and reserved" (Gadamer, 1989, p. 107). "This is for *us*, not for the 'others'. What the 'others' do 'outside' is of no concern to us at the moment" (Huizinga, 1955, p. 12). The happenstance of a photograph stands outside this orbit, exorbitant, peering in, bewildered by the wilds of what it captures and what it fails to capture.

That this is utterly ordinary, and commonplace is extraordinary in its own way. These two lending themselves to a movement of words and expressions and imitations, of differentiations and articulations. So familiar. So lovely.

Now, 15 months later, Grandpa's lap, sunshine, smiles, where likeness, kinship, of a kindness, resemblance, similarity, bubble and giggle over a book, the flipping pages of which is part of its mysterious whirlwind. That patience I'm now re-learning—to wait and let him point to the truck or the animal or the cat that catches him. Letting the pages seemingly indiscriminately flip by, then remembering how often I've witnessed distracted magazine flipping, or, I'm told, apparently phone screen flippings flipping by, where the flipping is part of the allure. A sort of humming repetition, mesmerizing in its own way, spellbinding in its own way.

Deep breaths are often needed when sure footing is sought in such matters. I searched out this old, old reference that now seems altogether new and telling and needing pause:

> The subject of postmodernity is best understood as the ideal-type channel-hopping MTV viewer who flips through different images at such speed that she/he is unable to chain the signifiers together into a meaningful narrative, he/she merely enjoys the multiphrenic intensities and sensations of the surface of the images. (Usher & Edwards, 1994, p. 11)

1994. A sure sign that scholarly memory must needs be longer than sometimes allowed. I must quiet myself over these matters again and again. Pause. This young boy's flipping fast through pages is not that flipping, but such flipping is all around us. But this is a future he has in store—to immerse in, to resist, to learn about or from, to be lost in, or found. Me with still no cellphone, not really knowing if that is what they're called anymore, I'm too old to say much except here, to write a bit and calm myself down. Watch. There:

> Language itself is a form of life, and like life, it is hazy [*diesig*]; over and over it will surround us with a haze. Again and again, we move for a while in a self-lighting haze, a haze that again envelops us as we seek the right word. Life is easier when everything goes according to one's own wishes, but the

dialectic of recognition requires that there can be no easy laurels. We learn this from the resistance we feel in ourselves when we let the other person be right. To make ourselves aware of this, the best help may be for us to get as fully as possible into the matter itself, and in the end to see ourselves as put into question. (Gadamer, 2007e, p. 371)

My grandson cuddled with a book. Picking up that same book again and again to flip, to point, to read, to sit together and murmur and laugh. Again. Again. To stop over a page stock-still and staring. Wait. This old hermeneutic adage, that his pause over this picture that caught his attention *just might be trying to teach me something or remind me of something I have long since forgotten.*

The Catch of Attention

Ah. That moment when a text, shall we say, "speaks," and urges me to stop over it and mark the occasion. Stop flipping. Become agape. Halted. That strange similarity to me, pen in hand, pausing, noting, then, the same book, the same page, the same word or line, again and again (Gadamer, 1989, p. 5):

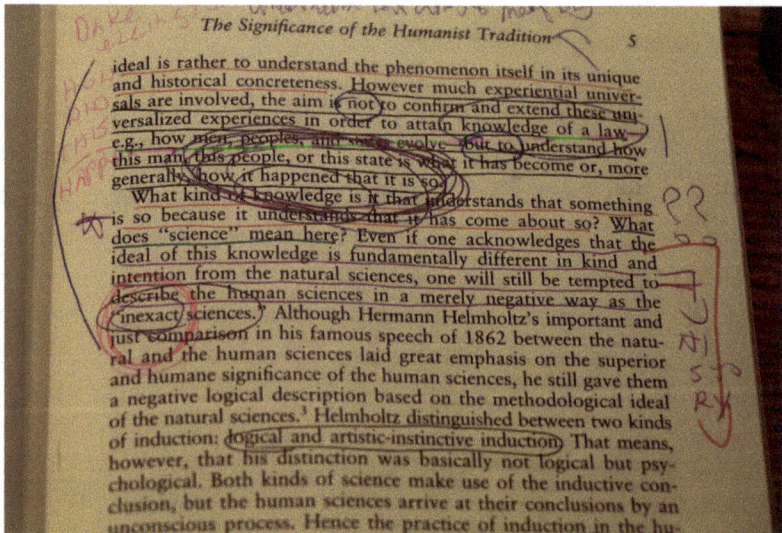

FIGURE 29. REREADING

"Understanding begins when *something* addresses *us*" (Gadamer, 1989, p. 299). The emphases added here are akin to its own pen-in-hand gesture regarding the agency of texts and pictures. Stop. Pen. Underline. We are sometimes *struck* and struck again. *It* addresses *me*, mouth agape, reciting:

> [Something] compels over and over, and the better one knows it, the *more* compelling it is. There comes a moment when something is *there* something one should not forget and cannot forget. This is not a matter of mastering an area of study. (Gadamer, 2007c, p. 115)

And how the stars and the circles and the marginalia start becoming comments on each other, crossing and re-crossing. And how I want to re-underline the last sentence of this block citation, because it still puzzles me. I like it. I *think* it may be right about something I still don't quite understand how to say. I don't want to forget it and I don't quite "get it," all in one fell swoop. A very ordinary phenomenon that readers of a certain ilk understand. This is a way to understand something of what this young child is doing. The same kind of thing I do, not identical, but not exactly different, either. It is not a matter of mastering the text, but of "mastering" my ability to follow it, wait over it.

And the happenstance of this passage selected originally only for the elaborateness of the different pens chosen with each rereading. Sometimes you happen upon something: this writing, here, now, itself is not an attempt to confirm a universal or a law, but to muse my way through how it happened that this is so, this familiar, familial sitting and pointing, and underlining, how his mouth agape at something that "hits the spot" is just *like* reading and finding myself reaching for the pen. The intent, here, in writing this, is not to be "inexact," let alone "poetic," but to try to lend myself to familiar inexactness of this nebulous thing itself. This is my son and my grandson. This is the long arc of words and sounds and writing which we all lend ourselves to in varying degrees, with varying dedications and tales to tell or not.

An analogy I first found years ago and underlined and have already fully cited above, one that parses something of the strength and pliability of this cluster of phenomena and their pedagogical and familial character. Ludwig Wittgenstein is talking of how the understandability and familiarity of language and experience and gesture and mouths agape in everyday life is not based on some exact, univocal singularity that each instance bears identically, but is based instead on something more recognizable:

> As in spinning a thread, we twist fibre on fibre. And the strength of the thread does not reside in the fact that some one fibre runs through its whole length, but in the overlapping of many fibres. Don't say "There must be something common" ... but look and see whether there is anything common to all. For if you look at them you will not see something that is common to all, but similarities, relationships, and a whole series of them at that. To repeat: don't think but look! We see a complicated network of similarities, overlapping and criss-crossing: sometimes overall similarities, sometimes similarities of detail. I can think of no better expression to characterize these similarities than "family resemblances" [*Familienahnlichkeiten*]. (Wittgenstein, 1968, p. 32)

Based on something more like a pliable, forgiving net or web that is being woven as it is being traverse and re-traversed. It is little wonder, having been involved in early childhood education and teacher education and the care of preservice teachers in their practicum classrooms, that this philosophy of everyday language, everyday life, everyday understanding and practice, would have an appeal. The appeal of lived familiarity or, as Wittgenstein calls it, "kinship" (p. 33). These are genealogical invocations about the life of language and literacy, early and otherwise. I can't deny how often I have cited this passage over decades. It has become my strange familiar, like the black cat on the end of the witch's broom, an animal energy, of a sort, a reliable animating energy with which children's books are often teeming. The troll under the bridge with a message. Ravenspirits at the water's edge up north warning of dangers—some long-lost Bob Munsch book. Kid's stuff. Sort of. So many future books to read as aging, his and mine, will or won't permit.

The effect of cleaving toward this sort of thinking about early literacy has a strange and familiar heart, as well:

> The conversation that a family resemblance opens up can always be taken up anew. In that conversation [with on-campus pre-service teachers about

Blueberries for Sal (McCloskey, 1976) and the parallels between a mother bear and her cub, and a human mother and her child, both seeking out blueberries on the same hill] we may determine that both "sides" of the analogy—the human mother/child and the bear mother/child—involve, say, "care and attention." We find, however, in exploring this idea of "care and attention" that far from being a way in which these two families are identical, "care and attention" are *themselves* [not "laws" or "universals," but must be] understood analogously [that is, as they manifest in the case and its intimacies]. These two families are alike in care and attention, but again, neither simply identical nor different. (Jardine, 2005, pp. 92–93)

"Identical" or "different" would make it easier to simply tell a beginning teacher, or new parent, what to do and that would be the end of it. However, it is well known that what to do is worked out in the inner intimacies of the effort to do it—"the true locus ... is this in between" (Gadamer, 1989, p. 295) whose nebulousness and specificity are precisely its sources and well-springs. "It depends" is not an admission of some sort of watery "whatever." It is not the common mistake of "child-centeredness" or its opposite. Rather, it is a call to attend carefully to the relations and emergings and dependencies as they arise and acting, with all the carefulness and elborateness, in their accord, and stumble, fall, laugh, watch others as they read to young children, try it out again, and, well "catch the point." And catch precisely this point, that "the point" will *always* be held "in between," and therefore the threads will *always* have to be re-woven the next time out, caught hold of anew as we are caught up anew in a new book. And then, of course, this ecological tale of the hill they both traverse and its wide embrace, its ways, its jeopardies of sun and water and air and seasons. And another oft-cited familiar of mine, to paraphrase: a child's book like this old one, if deeply and lovingly read, causes worlds and worlds of relations to "break open" (Gadamer, 1989, p. 382) "break forth" (p. 458) and catch us up in whirlwinds of "responding and summoning" (p. 458).

Bears, Owls and Sheep

"Analogical integrities" (Berry, 2009, p. 138), "integrated curriculum" of a sort, borne out as my grandson and I peruse the paintings around my house, pointing, murmuring. Here's one. Speaking of *Blueberries for Sal*, mother and child and another hint of a line of reading the world and reading the book, reading your father's face, your child's and reading the bears who were reading the hill just *like* the humans were:

FIGURE 30. WAIT FOR ME

"Wait for Me" by Connie Geerts
(www.conniegeerts.com), used with her permission.

As per McCloskey's book, both children cleave to a certain closeness. A young one will skip and hop a step to stay behind a bit, but not too far behind. Reading the signs, but only "so to speak." Look at those white squares washing up over the mother's back and how the cub has his nose just nicely in their sway. In McCloskey's book, the human mother gathering to preserve for later, the human child close enough to dip her hand in the gathering basket over and over again, to eat, of course.

The feel of this whole matter expanding: "that anciently perceived likeness between all creatures and the earth of which they are made. For as common wisdom hold, like speaks to like" (Berry, 1983, p. 76). Breathing room comes when we let these be "of a kind" and don't close this down with identity/difference. Here, too, this way of thinking about early literacy becomes an analog of something kind of ecological—relations, the living character of gesture and imitation and love and how toddling body expressions and sounds get caught up in the whirlwind of language. Him imitating my motions and me his. Us shushing each other over the Ravens at the birdfeeder. He is "reading the world" with lush complexity and, this is important: reading threads of it that go far beyond *my own* immediate notice and that *summon me* to notice. Part of early literacy is allowing myself to remember the fullness and letting myself enjoy the elaborateness and beauty and sillinesses that follow and join in, speaking, listening, pointing, looking laughing. And, as per the origins of the word "school," "holding back" (*Online Etymological Dictionary*, under "school") so as not to swamp these in-betweens with my own exuberances. But then, too, not simply always holding back and "abandoning the child to his own devices" (Arendt, 1969, p. 196) but then sometimes *doing exactly that*. Looking for the proper measure. "We seek the right word" which may be silence. Teaching and learning are odd and contingent tasks, always. We err, and forgive and err again.

Of course. Grandpa's old memory and the flip-throughs and my needing to hold back and shut up and enjoy how the "eloquent gestures" (Merleau-Ponty, 1970, p. 42) and sounds "fly up like sparks from a fire" (Merleau-Ponty, 1962, p. xiii). Me needing to shush myself and learning to love the exhilaration of doing so.

The fits and starts, now, of namings, and treating the naming carefully, graciously, as if it were fully formed—the baa-baas are, yes, sheep as he points and we have fun with the sounds and watch a wee video of baa-baa beh-behs and ma-mas baa-baas bleating and leaping, with owls echoing in the background. Another painting from our regular "gallery walk" around the house that is one of his very favorites and that makes the video' hoots *"more* compelling":

FIGURE 31. "FEELING A BIT CURIOUS"

Anita McCoomas (https://www.anitamccomas.com/)
used with her permission

We've since both perfected the Barred Owl hoot as a sort of secret smile between us: who who whowho. This picture since will be the cover photo of *An Ecological Pedagogy of Joy:*

On Relations, Aliveness and Love. (Latremouille et al., 2024).

Thus, too with the neigh-neighs, as with his grabbing the tail end of our lovely huge dog Robin and his saying "neigh-neigh" which is, well, sort of right? Get it? Robin is so big, she's akin to a horse, kind of, as the near-miraculous sorting of kinds proceeds, kindly, one hopes, forgivingly. It will sort itself out as the readings and re-readings—of books, of paintings, of the world—continue. It does not bear toward fixity. It will remain "of a kind" even after all this is sorted—after all, I was still able to let all this "expand to its full analogous breadth of illuminative meaning" (Norris-Clarke, 1976, p. 180), "call up the spectrum of different exemplifications, and then [repeatedly] *catching the point*" (Norris-Clarke, 1976, p. 182, emphasis original) when he neigh-neighed over Robin, as per a description of how analogical thinking remains and abides in our language and our lendings. His living early literacy elaborates my own living literacy about early literacy. Of course. And I do what my own "hermeneutic" research temptations require: summon up ancestors that can help us on our way to not forget the myriad within which we live.

Like James Clifford. "Not 'this is that' but this is a story about that, this is like that" (Clifford, 1986, p. 100). Hence the arrival of my grandson provoking another old story about this:

THIS IS A STORY ABOUT THAT: Kin, hence kindred and *Kinder* and kindness and akin and the parallel Sanskrit root is *gen,* hence generativity and genitals and generosity [and that now old saw, "generative curriculum"]. Kindness and generosity, kindness defined as "natural affection." (Jardine, 1992b, p. 214)

My son, my grandson, knelt and bellied on a bed over a book, and this old me are, after all, of a kind, kin, drawn together by natural affection that itself needs tending and re-tending. Not identical. Not different. Not just a given but always "standing in a horizon of ... still undecided future possibilities" (Gadamer, 1989, p. 112). We all arc out into the air and the river (in press upwell) and the Ravens (from a town), into how all of this is our lending ourselves to the whole Earth's kin in these "ecologically sorrowful times" (Derby, 2015, p. xiv):

> If we lose a sense of the interweaving "kinships" or "family resemblances" inherent in this child's talk, we lose not only a sense of being at home with *them*. We also lose a certain kinship and sense of being at home *with ourselves*. (Jardine, 1992b, p. 214)

The whole of the Earth, including how Raven's peering in the window summon us to admiration and shushing each other, the child surrounded in my arms, us both snapped up like a whirlwind—now a sudden Blue Jay, "booday"—tempted and taught within its beautiful internal articulations, all drift over the new painting of sheep that he can't get enough of:

FIGURE 32. "BIG FLEECY WITH A WOOLY VIEW"

Kym Binns, used with her permission

There comes the great reversal. This young child proves to be experienced in precisely this openness to experience that makes possible experience itself. Or something like that. The oxygens cascade down now from the trees, another affinity experienced in our walks outside, like speaking to like, us swayed over to its side. All this quite an early childhood education for me, all over again living in the midst of early literacy. A reminder of openness to experience made possible by his experiences. This too is an old tale, of an old man having something of his life lent back by young arrivals. This is a tale about that, too.

CHAPTER FIFTY-ONE

"We Do Know What to Do"

Preamble

We need to take afflictions as the path. This is very important because if we are unable to take them as the path, no matter how good our practice may be, we will be overcome by the afflictions. (Thrangu, 2011, p. 182)

If we do not look at the essence of the afflictions, they will grow strong and stronger. The remedy is not to reject, block or suppress the emotion—as scientists these days say, repressing your disturbing emotions will lead to illness in your body. This, however, does not mean that we should just follow our afflictions and go wherever they lead us. Instead, we need to look at the essence of the afflictions. (p. 190)

"The essence of the afflictions is naturally empty" (Thrangu, 2011, p. 183). This: there is no stubborn, self-existent "thing" *to which* I might acquiesce [it is, instead, just arising causes and conditions and habits and weaving circumstances, personal, historical, cultural, inherited, perhaps even things I've personally fallen for far too often, thus strengthening the semblance of its solid reality and inevitability—called, in Buddhism, "reification"], therefore the seemingly self-existent "I myself" that rises to the bait becomes visible as itself "empty" of self-existence and full only of dependently co-arising, here, now (Jardine, 2016g, p. 228).

It's not just that "we are seduced by them" (Chodron, 2007, p. 76). "We welcome them" (p. 91, emphasis added) because they confirm the feeling of lively ego power and the reality of my self, even in an example like failure and regret. A perfect circle of abuse. It is not an accident that Buddhists call the world and it's suffering a "wheel": Samsara turns and turns but only from the energy that comes from being lost in the performance of acts, only if we fall prey to what becomes "a habitual tug" (Chodron, 2007, p. 119; Jardine, 2016g, p. 225).

The bait and the one that rises to it are intertwined. They rise up together and if this is not looked at carefully, each strengthens the other in the semblances of permanence in the sense of the other one being the cause for my arousal, and this self of mine then glories in the sense of efficacy and power and feeling of sheer *aliveness* that ensues in thus meeting the enemy that, in great part, my rising up has created.

This, of course, is war consciousness at its best. Finally, in all this swirling, the feel of something solid and permanent and "real":

> Like trying to grab cornstarch dissolved in water, the faster and harder and more desperately we try to seize these matters and cling to something hard and permanent the more substantial they *feel* and the more is aggravated our desire to grip even tighter. (Jardine, 2012b, p. 219)

The illusory *feel* of substantiality is *caused* by the gripping and then too easily *attributed to what the gripping has caused* as the cause of me needed to grip. This cycle only inflates unless I let go.

It is in the nature of reifying war consciousness to accelerate, propagate, enlarge, distend and, of course, project. "If it wasn't for *that* I wouldn't be doing *this*." If it wasn't for "them," "us" would be fine. The grip blames what it grips blitheringly unaware of how its own grip plays a part in what it then fears.

This is a closed circle and, once I'm inside of it, what is thinkable, speakable, is already set out in advance. But more than this, I come to believe that my only relief can come from defeating that which now grips me in its/my grip. Refuge is imagined as "overcoming," semi-automatic weapons on the state house steps readied to *increase* the triggered grip.

Small wonder that Ajahn Chah's (1987, n.p.) adage, "take the feeling of letting go as your refuge" (see Jardine, 2012b, most pp. 217–230) might just cause the gripping outrage to increase.

Joggins, Nova Scotia

And so, Wednesday, April 8, 2020, CTVnews online. Potentially 800,000 cases of COVID-19 in Alberta, Canada. "Most likely" (https://edmon ton.ctvnews.ca/alberta-could-see-up-to-800–000-covid-19-infecti ons-in-most-likely-scenario-1.4886693). Shall I read this, about Alberta's "war" against the Covid-19 virus invasion? Exactly what *for*? I feel myself drawn toward it, even though the work of surrounding myself with actions and affections that are more local, more careful and step-by-step, are things that need my attention and devotion.

Still, this headline draws. It draws me toward, but also draws me away. It strengthens me and weakens me all at once.

And then, this morning on *Morning Joe*, April 9, 2020, 6:15a.m. MST, Mica Brzezinski toots "as we've given you the numbers, we want to tell you more of the stories." Okay, why exactly? Because it's not just about numbers but about real people? And I was just about to forget about that, was I? Oh, and there are "good news" stories about heroes whose front-line co-workers have died in their arms as well?

Oh, my isn't that lovely. Please read that without a sarcastic tone. Really. Good. We are all in the good and steady hands of good and steady fellow beings. Make no mistake that my heart has aches of thanks. I guess there might be something to be said for how the sto-ries give vent to the undirected emotions of seeing "the numbers." I guess so. To tell the truth, I teared up when I got a "stay well" from an otherwise-unknown poster on an Elvis Costello message board site.

But let me tell the truth, here. After the first few seconds of this hospital hallway story or that, I turn it off, not because I don't "care," but because, well, I don't care to subject myself to something quite so however-unintentionally manipulative *to no end*. I'm drawn toward and then repelled. I'm recalling Phil Ochs' lines in the song *Crucifixion* (1967)

> Tell me every detail, I've got to know it all,
> And do you have a picture of the pain?

Oh yes, we've got pictures alright!

Even now, this morning, April 20, word of "at least" 17 people killed in Nova Scotia feels like how a pressurized system finds the weakest spot to stroke to relieve itself. Small-town names, most I've never heard of (even though some of my relatives are from Nova Scotia—Joggins. How's that for small?). Now up to 22 dead. This story isn't just "one more thing." It adds itself to the winding, interweaving roil of causes and conditions, of viruses and puffy, cry-baby politicians, making those pre-existing conditions feel larger, somehow, making this Nova Scotia news land on already burn skin.

"It's here, eh?"

Moth-Nature

All this helps me understand moths and feel for them. The lure that can burn you up. Oh, look! [click] Another front-line worker is Skyping in! [click] Oh dear, dear, dear! [click click click]. Remember, here, that it is my own fraught Moth-Nature that I'm mocking inside myself, as well as how the screeching candlelight of relentless media sources know full well about this Nature and how widespread it is, how easy it is to stimulate and arouse, how profitable all that can surely be.

> *That tough balance between being drawn into it for the sake of burning it off and being simply inflamed by that approach and deepening the error of it.* (Jardine, 2016g, p. 231)

The tough balance between saving forests from burns and saving an albeit-amazing tourist attraction (Jardine, 2021d).

Oh, were I as wise as the things I can write! That, by itself, is the strangest of things, to be able to glimpse the tough balances that are thoughtful and wise and might ask the best of me, while all the while having neck muscles betray me with no noticeable effort, getting me leaning into the latest "Look at that! Look at that!" news that is, in reality, nothing "new" at all.

Closer.

Closer.

Pfft!

On Collective Stress Disorder

I made up a term when teaching practicum classes full of student-teachers who I would then visit with regularly in their placement classes in local elementary schools. It was meant to indicate a commonly experienced thing in the work of teaching (and, of course, far beyond that). I expect that many who are more emotionally wise than I am have known this far before I figured out anything about it. It's like this.

Small things in the day-to-day work of living in a classroom can each cause a low-level bit of annoyance, stress, distraction, exhaustion and the like. Sometimes, when this multiple array of small things gets out of hand, when I get too tired or distracted, the collective stress of *all* the small things can come to be visited on *any one of those things*, leading to a distorted sense of what is happening here and now with this particular one thing, how much attention it needs, how important it is, how I might properly react, and so on. It becomes possible, colloquially put, to "lose it" over something which, in and of itself, does not warrant the proportion of response that it seems to have caused. Add to this the commiserations between students in a class, each in their own practicum placement, and things don't just add. They can multiply. The very fact that others are distressed is distressing, adding itself to my own mix, mixing and sending off mixed, obscured, unmeant messages, signals, alerts, real and false alarms.

Right there, of course, is the trick. The particular moment or event does not exactly *cause* this reaction as much as *precipitate it*, and the path to trying to sort it out cannot itself be visited upon the particular event that served as the often-simply-happenstance trigger. Simply having pointed out that the particular event doesn't warrant such a reaction leaves the work undone. Expecting an adequate "account" of what ensues from that particular trigger-event misunderstands what that trigger-cluster, in fact, really was.

It was a collective stress response. Every little stress is visited upon any little stress. Nova Scotia. Novel Coronavirus-19. Donald Trump spraying Lysol up his nose. Hearing of a relative's infection. John Prine. And even the stress of knowing full well that this is *nothing, nothing, nothing,* compared to the suffering of so many. That, too, adds itself, with a warm sense of good fortune, an icy sense of privilege found in that fortune, a sense of open-strolling to split wood for next winter and crouching, hunching, low-level shame of some nebulous sort.

A collective stress response is always, always *someone's*. It paraphrases a line from Martin Heidegger's *Being and Time* (1962), it is always "in each case mine." Mine. All that has been swirling lately, all that bilge I've been unknowingly storing below deck, in my neck muscles and ringing ears, is precisely *why* that CTVnews.ca candle draws. It is precisely *why* their news broadcasts are structured the way they are, to take full advantage with just enough teases to keep the stress-allure stoked coupled with just enough teases of relief and heroic good news to feign a cure of that very stress that it wants to maintain.

It isn't just the candlelight that somehow by itself draws. It is just that it *can* draw. It has to be *let* do so. A weird circumstance. So here is the rub, then.

Proposing this to student-teachers and having them clarify what it is, what it looks like, how it feels, how it evades attention, how it draws, how easily it lures before we can take another breath—all of this does not *at all* mean that I know how to effectively *practice* not-getting-caught-up-in this phenomenon. All it means is that I've "spotted" it and spotted how very difficult it is to *not* get caught up in it. It is proposed, then, just like noting that there are three different types of Chick-A-Dees in the Eastern slopes of the Rockies. It doesn't mean that you've learned how to spot them. It just means that there is something "there" to spot, something the spotting of which can be sensibly practiced and which *needs* practice if you are to become practiced in it.

It might be in the nature of moths to burn up. It need not necessarily be the fate of being human. We are *terribly* capable of being like moths. We are equally capable of having moths be our teachers.

With a collective stress response, the work needed is *not* to fall forward and simply respond. It is to—whatsay?—*fall back* into a locale of repose that allows me to do the extraordinarily difficult work of trying to detangle these events without my hands, my mind, being tied up by these threads and to practice ways to maintain my ability to do such detangling and maintain each of my responses in the right orbit and the right proportion proper to each.

And here, each of us must walk and work alone on our own nests of tangles, surrounded by the humming of commiserating, each themselves nested and tangled fellow beings, human and otherwise: each of us must measure our own measures and measure how to measure up. Now I might look at that health care worker dancing in Paul McCartney's "Lady Madonna" video and laugh and cry all at once (https://www. youtube.com/watch?v=KUL7K7RQ8HM&t=2s), feeling like a sap and feeling the stretch of years back to March 2, 1968, when I first heard that song (yes, I remember the date—this being but one thread in this whole mesh of my own living), and all the intervening years as well bunch up in sentiment and thanksgiving and grief over youth and aging hand-by-hand, dancing like a Matisse on a hill.

Oh, we did dance. And do still over the time in-between. Including the ways we faced inwards into the circle of movement and let the Earth become a rattled destitute in the oil-soaked dreams we ignored. Tailpipes really should be at the front of cars. And all the words I've spilled like black-ink blood trying, trying, to say that this is, this must be, a dance *of* the Earth. Joyous abandon become abandonment. Meanwhile, humans isolate and skies are clearing, fish are returning to the canals of Venice, and so on.

Returning to normal. Stop over that line for a moment. Returning to normal. The fish returning *and* the marshaled semi-automatic weapons.

It certainly seems commonplace for these sorts of things to collapse together and for my response to that CTVnews.ca headline to become exorbitant in an effort to bear the burden of all that is brought to bear on it. I certainly understand firsthand how this works and how very easy it is to have it happen upon me before I can even catch a breath. I can know full well about this phenomenon and still have my brainstem-animal-body fall hook line and sinker for its next arrival, out of orbit, out of all grasp and gasp of the real gravities of any one event. This is why it is somewhat informative to dwell on the characterization of the eruption of such *kleshas* (literally, "afflictions") as agents of mischief ("what happens to us over and above our wanting and doing" [Gadamer, 1989, p. xxvii]), providing that isn't one more occasion to reify what is in fact a cluster of winding and unwinding threads into a scapegoat (yet another age-old characterization) whose banishment exempts me from the tough work of repose and thinking and parsing and writing and untangling

Kleshas are as much our invention as is the solidity of gripped cornstarch. They are as much of a moth temptation as any other reification of these nesting, swarming causes and conditions.

The question regarding this or that characterization is always "What good does it do in the work of untangling?" And the danger is always *"Who benefits* if I fail to remain composed and able to ask this question and not just fall for it into panic and fear and exhaustion and retreat?" Who benefits if I name the Democrats as the ones perpetuating a hoax? Or the right-wing media? Or the mainstream media? Or Fox? Or Trudeau? Or Tibetan Buddhism's imaginary imps flooding my consciousness with distractions?

What good does falling for it do if it just ends up with me enflamed and burning up?

And now, here we are, here I am, within the surroundings of this COVID-19 pandemic, its coupling with deep anxieties about political panderings and lies and enormous, utterly pathological levels of sociopathology and malignant narcissism now being worked out over this very stress-filled pandemic. TV ratings of press conferences—"Did you know I'm number one on Facebook?" [no reference needed]—about the deep suffering this pandemic is visiting on people are through the roof, apparently. And then these phenomena all swirling around the clearing-skies images portending something ecologically vivid and then hearing talk of "getting back to normal" makes me feels a nebulous, almost desperate shame of some sort. Add to this families. Friends.

Local businesses. Neighbors. Media shrieking and click-bait duplicities mixed in with information. Well, maybe. Even that is creaking with well-sown and deliberately sown doubt, maybe a sort of doubting we should have had all along. The pernicious worm of "fake news" talk is here as well, shifting the ground.

Then hearing that things are getting worse and worse, but they are getting worse less bad than before, and are therefore getting less-worse better. Each one of these things too easily shows up on the doorstep of all the others, refusing social distancing, infecting, spreading, and that, itself, too, becomes one more in the legion. Give me that semi-automatic.

No.

Wait.

Don't.

Collective stress disorder.

"What is Localism's Answer?"

So now, if I may, a sideways step that is a strange analog to all of this.

I was reminded of this long-ago thing about collective stress disorder when I was reading a recently published conversation between Tim DeChristopher and Wendell Berry (2020) in *Orion Magazine*. It was revealing to read once I got over a certain knee-jerk reaction that felt very personal. Briefly put, I'm quite able to find every encouragement I have attempted, every act I do or word I write, to be utterly meaningless and trivial when placed in the grand scheme of things. This placement is, in part, what DeChristopher and Berry's and conversation circled like an exhausting drain.

I won't recapitulate all the turns of this conversation (https://orionm agazine.org/article/to-live-and-love-with-a-dying-world/), because there is just one thread, for now, that interests me. It has to do with the small ways in which we might act, think, be careful and encouraging in these ecologically sorrowful times, "no matter how small or unnewsworthy" (Wendell Berry, from DeChristopher & Berry, 2020), and how we, how I might prevent huge world events from visiting themselves upon those small ways and asking them to live up to that hugeness.

Wendell Berry is responding to Tim DeChristopher saying that, even with concerted local actions and legal mineral rights "they're going to suck the oil out of there whether you sign the papers or not":

WB: Those are the people who have the wealth and power, and there's no easy, immediate answer to that, except to live so far as you can in opposition. You've got to live and love. You've got to find the answers in your heart.

TD: But that gets more complicated every day, to learn how to live and love with a dying world and a broken society. Exponentially tougher when you're talking about farmers in Honduras who can't grow anything anymore because of how dramatically the climate has changed. Or farmers in Syria, who are forced off of their land because of the drought and watched their country be destroyed by civil war as a result of that mass migration. We're just at the beginning of that. We will see hundreds of millions more of those sorts of refugees forced into migration and—

WB: You realize, don't you, that you've won this argument?

TD: What is localism's answer to refugees? To those whose homeland is not livable anymore? Whether that place is underwater, has turned to desert, was destroyed by American imperialism and our desire for more resources?

WB: You've won this argument. The argument for despair is impenetrable, it's invulnerable. You got all the cards. You got the statistics, the science, the projections on your side. But then we're still just sitting here with our hands hanging down, not doing anything. (DeChristopher & Berry, 2020)

Moth. Flame. Yes. What is localism's answer? I'm out this morning, April 26, 2020, to plant the first peas in the garden still trudged with some snow.

Localism, to be a place of real repose, must become answerable to the very worst case that might be visited upon it. Every single pea, every single grace of sunlight, every breath of relief from this long, long winter, must bear the full weight of all imaginable of the world's woes if I am to take any refuge in it.

Need a bigger flame?

WB: David Kmline just published a book called *The Round of a Country Year*. One of the remarkable things is that it's a happy book. David's family, his neighbors, they're cooperating all the time, and nobody's overworked. Somebody will start a task, somebody will come to relieve that person. At two o'clock in the afternoon, somebody comes with a fresh team of horses and finishes the work.

TD: So, take that community as an example. That happy community that is working sustainably in that way. Now let's say, even a small fraction of the 80 million Bangladeshis whose homes are less than ten meters above sea level, who are losing their homes right now, every day—a small portion of them, just a few hundred thousand, show up at that community. How do they respond? What is that community's response to that mass migration?

...

I see folks like David Fleming, who are explicit that a local economy requires barriers to entry. He's pretty explicitly opposed to immigration. And when we look at the pattern of migration, the military has an answer, the xenophobes have an answer. (DeChristopher & Berry, 2020)

And again:

TD: When it became clear that all those people in Bangladesh are going to lose their homes, India built a border fence all the way around Bangladesh. A nineteen-hundred-mile, partially electrified border fence. Over the past decade, there's been a proliferation of border fences, between rich and poor areas, across the world. The military's answer is genocide—we're going to make sure these people die right where they're at. So if we're going to live in love in this time in history, we need to have a better answer.

"We Do Know What to Do"

WB: Well, here we are, wasting time. What are we doing here? Why aren't we out somewhere else doing something else? Why are we just sitting here talking?

TD: Because we don't know what to do. That's what I'm trying to say. It's really complicated to live in love, at this time.

WB: We do know what to do. We need to take care of the responsibilities that we've got. The effective boundaries of responsibility are your own limits. There's so much you can do, and you ought to do it. That's all. But to sit here and hypothesize the worst possible thing that could

> happen and decide what we're going to do about it, or what the Amish
> are going to do about it, seems just a waste of time. (DeChristopher &
> Berry, 2020)

You can see why I was reminded of that old collective stress disorder thing. Sitting here writing, day after day. Luxurious. A luxury borne on the backs of anyone and any suffering anywhere. How can I still, in good conscience, go plant those peas? What would happen if all those Bangladeshis showed up right now on your nice, rich man's foothills acreage. How many peas are you going to plant *now*?

Not exactly collective stress disorder, but there is a strange affinity here. I need to take care of the responsibilities that I have, and the boundaries of that are "in each case mine": letting my ability to get even a small glimpse of the full suffering of the world visit itself on this aging hand handling peas is an act of refusing to recognize that "effective boundaries of responsibility are [my] own limits." It is subjecting my *effective boundaries* to paralyzing unboundedness. It is, therefore, refusing to accept my boundedness, my limitedness. Accepting this is its own form of suffering that can then bear itself out in witness of small things done fully, done as well as possible:

> **WB:**   It was the Shakers who were sure the end could come anytime, and
> they still saved the seeds and figured out how to make better diets
> for old people. Thomas Merton was interested in the Shakers. I said to
> him, "If they were certain that the world could end at any minute, how
> come they built the best buildings in Kentucky?" "You don't under-
> stand," he said. "If you know the world could end at any minute, you
> know there's no need to hurry. You take your time and do the best
> work you possibly can." That was important to me. I've repeated it
> many times. (DeChristopher & Berry, 2020)

Imagine the shame of doing rushed and shabby work that exhausts you and spends your love, your affection, your care and limited energies *as if my rushing can outrun the steady, clear-eyed stalk of time and the earthly way of things.*

No. Such denial is foolish, childish, animal-body-threat-based war consciousness.

We do know what to do.

I do know what to do. Go out, today. Plant peas. Split some more wood for a winter that might never come. The pitch-crack sound and smell remain beautiful as ever. The Ravens still gather for a look.

Enjoy doing it. Be *pleased* by the sun after all these feet of snow. Maybe then write a bit, finish up this here little thing that has been lingering for a while. Post it in the hope that it might raise a smile and halt a little breath here and there. That it might do some small good.

So, yes. Take the feeling of letting go as your refuge and *get on with it*, because getting paralyzed is the most unbecoming of luxuries:

> under the tough old stars—
> In the shadow of bluffs
>   I came back to myself,
> To the real work, to
>   "What is to be done."

Gary Snyder (1974, p. 9), from "I Went into the Maverick Bar"

Then my effective boundaries just might open up a bit in wider swaths of affection and commiseration.

CHAPTER FIFTY-TWO

From the Town by a Spring

A re-iteration of a book dedication written years ago (Seidel & Jardine, 2016):

For the elders who left and the babies who arrived.

Introduction

Odin's two Ravens are named Huginn and Muninn, meaning "thought" and "memory" (https://www.sacred-texts.com/neu/pre/pre04.htm, footnote to p. 51).

Meanwhile, my son sent me a picture yesterday of a picture book being ready to be read to a newlyborn, their first, our first, my first:

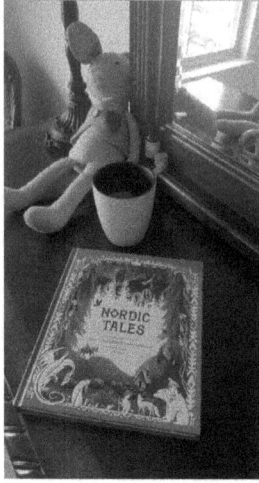

FIGURE 33. NORDIC TALES
Photo: Eric Jardine, used with permission.

And meanwhile, Don Domanski sings, his breath now gone:

> ravens go to the edges of the earth
> and return with our hearts in their beaks.

> Don Domanski (2010, p. 121), from "In the Dream of Yellow Birches"

Thought. Memory. Going to the edges of the Earth and returning with heart. These twines are at the heart of education in its wholeness, its soar, its deeply Earthly joy (Latremouille et al., 2021, 2024).

Family relations, kinship threads, all of us, all of it, every topic, every school, every voice and breath, every idea and image, every story told or forgotten, not one single whit left over, a Ganesha-fungus just as much a living relation as the oxygens tumbling down from the trees overhead:

FIGURE 34. GANESHA'S KISS

Sanskrit: गणेश.
The god of beginnings.
The remover of obstacles.
In a wood near a town near a spring.

There is no special "course" that corners the market on exploring living fields of relations. It is not the special purview of "environmental education," or a matter of "outdoors" versus "indoors." This is as much true of commas and their graceful use in English as it is true of walks in the woods. They bespeak fields of relations, fields of ancestries, and shifting them through the written word changes its landscapes. They are a *topic*, a "place," a locale of interrelatedness, rich, abundant, and becoming even more mysteriously captivating in light of how other tongues don't use such things in their scripts. They, if treated properly, are like Ravens. They are beautiful.

Meanwhile, that pair of Ravens—our neighbors 20 acres over told us one day that they had built a nest and that they'd seen little heads peeking up over its rim. My wife and I thought of how lovely it would be if they brought the family down to the feeder someday—wee little baby Ravens. Aw, that'll be sweet.

Well, they did. They brought four huge loud squawking tussling pecking teenagers and there were fights for about a week or so. And then, because they are territorial beasts, the four young'uns one day simply disappeared from view.

What follows are a few small flights all written over the course of recent times of isolation that have made interrelatedness all the more palpable. The tumults of love and devotion and careful attention that are now required are many and, well, not new. The sense of impend lately might beckon panic and rush, but the opposite is required, right here, right now. Under panic and threat and rush and its ensuant exhaustions, the openheartedness needed for "the real work" (Snyder, 1980) is hard to maintain, but it is exactly what needs maintaining. Take heart. You are well surrounded with good examples and meticulous scholarship and beautiful articulations.

This a message as much to myself as anyone. It is exactly what I need now more than ever in my life. It is a little hummed tune to the baby I haven't yet met, he across a borderline, we all inside more viruses than we think. We need each other's strength, fortitude and careful, rigorous insight—in that commons comes comfort, support, and a bristling, insistent affection despite all odds against it.

Flight One: An Acknowledgment

Tsong-kha-pa in 1406, Tibet: "I compose this in order to condition my own mind" (2000, p. 111). I write, in part, in order to find some small composure in the middle of my distractions and dispersities and rushabouts. To settle down and shape, form, to find out what I might make of all this murky air, and what it has made of me. Writing helps me remember what I've forgotten or never knew, because writing needs reading. Tsong-kha-pa's words help me open things that might have become closed off. They helps enliven things that seem dead ordinary, flat, dull and finished. They help me remember things I might forget if "[left] to my own devices" (Arendt, 1969, p. 196). And, isn't it just like me, wandering last time across a University commons, everyone, everyone, not exactly "there," peering at hand held devices, keeping, I suppose, "in touch" with elsewhere. Just like me to look up this word "device": "the means by which things are divided" (Online Etymological Dictionary, [OED], under "device").

Composed, this, it speaks of me as I compose myself in its presence. This might be a definition of a certain form of pedagogy. Even to mention, in teaching writing, even in the confines of school, that you might just be composing yourself—not only settling yourself, but making yourself into someone in that act—well, this breaks school's confine and affirms it at the same time.

Composing a picture is the same, although it first happens in a snap. Composing, there, with the branch bends and smoldering sunlight is done in order that now, when I look at it, I'm more likely to be captured by it, less likely to forget the portends of the smoke in the air from the fires to the West of us. I'm more likely to set it out in a paper for public display if it has some, well, hint of beauty to it. So beautiful, so awful. Taking that picture, now, in retrospect, feels a bit like posing for a portrait of myself, that acridness in the air, eye sting, and sorrow.

The word "sorrow" has two lovely etymological ancestors. Old English *sorg*, meaning "grief, regret." But also buried here a Sanskrit root that gives it a second wing: *surksati*, "cares for" (OED, under "sorrow.). Together these can become winged.

So, if I may, it has become more and more common for speakers and writers and others to begin by acknowledging the land upon which they stand and those who first stood there. This is often done using the language of the people and place itself. But, too often, these things are rattled off like a schoolboy memorization that needs no tender of the words and ideas uttered.

Well-intended wastes of breaths, sometimes.

I can't pretend to do better, so I won't. Because, even when well-read and well uttered, there is something else, here I wish to acknowledge. Something of the promises about this place where I live and work and breath that my own people made. Consider the language used, the images invoked, the possessive pronouns.

From: Supplementary Treaty No. 7 (Reprinted from the Edition of 1877, Roger Duhamel, 1966):

"That Her [Queen Victoria's] Indian people may know and feel assured of what allowance they are to count upon and receive from Her Majesty's bounty and benevolence." (p. 3)

This be a little breath of my acknowledgement of what my people have done. But wait. This from a Parliamentary memo from 1920, written by Duncan Campbell Scott (1862–1947):

I want to get rid of the Indian problem. Our object is to continue [with "enfranchisement", which means giving up ones First Nations status], is to continue until there is not a single Indian in Canada that has not be absorbed into the body politic and there is no Indian question. (Cited in Miller, J.R., 2004, p. 34)

Vital-Justin Grandin (1829–1902):

The children whom we have brought up are no longer Indians & at the time of leaving our Establishments, the boys at least, do not wish to receive even the ordinary grants made to Indians, they wish to live like the whites and they are able to do so. I proposed that the government of Canada Given these make a trial of letting us have children of five years old and leaving them in our Orphan Asylums & Industrial schools until the time of their marriage or the age of 21 years. (cited in *Canada's Residential Schools*, 2015)

His name translates as "Life-Giving Justice."

Canadian author Robertson Davies said something like this, that becoming educated means becomes haunted by more ghosts. This, of course, is good news and bad news. Composing oneself is always haunting. Stuffed toys are lined up along the Tsuut'ina Nation fence nearby. Thought and Memory.

"Everything is teaching you. Isn't this so? Can you just get up and walk away so easily now?" (Chah, 2005, p. 5)

Flight Two: A Photo for Earth Day

FIGURE 35. WATERCLASS

It teaches, this enlarged photo of a bit of sun reflections in a Spring runoff driveway puddle. How easy it is to come to see a bowing teacher surrounded by young, seated children, right in the middle of a story full of sun and water and wonders and old and young.

To call it projection is a too-easy, bland truth. To let the project teach me something about the wherewithals of my living is a different matter altogether. Here, the teacher taught something by the students' encircling the story breathed up into their airs. Oh how I've loved that leaning in we'd all do over beautiful things that are full of tales.

The bow. The stand. The sit. The circle. The water. The sun.

The teaching. The teacher. The taught. And just who's who.

The story. The study. The raptures. The great secrecy of cuddling inwards. This is here, now, for us.

How easy it is to see something else altogether. See? See the classroom cluster tucked away there?

FIGURE 36. MORE STORIES THAN ANY HEART CAN HOLD

How many chances might a cluster of water-students need to fill this array with more stories than any heart could ever hold? Being this bewildered over something this simple is what is required to respond adequately and rigorously to how much is right on hand if we treat it the right way. It is the way to deal with the whirlwind rushes in school hallways that always demand one more thing, one more thing. Composure is an ecological virtue (Jardine, 2020a).

The thing will settle us if we can only interrupt, if the eyes can only blink, and the ears do what ears do. Pop?

The opacities of water and how it bends light and scatters it.

Shh, now. Here's a secret that's well known. This work is pleasurable, it is joyous, even when what it unearths is not especially so.

"Once upon a time ..."

Flight Three: Sky Give Breath

FIGURE 37. BRIGHT ENOUGH

[Composite photo, Tom Buckley-Houston, 2014, [https://twitter.com/two
mbh/status/418712720246984704]
original photo of 4% Crescent Moon, Venus and Mercury,
Stephen Rahn, 2013, photo treatment by the author]

If Andromeda were bright enough to see
With the naked flesh eye. Imagine our cosmologies.
Imagine the stories that would need telling. The shapes of our little gods.
The spells of our lunacies.

Oh, the dreams we would have. What songs would be sung from balconies under this sky? What would we tell our children about ourselves and about where we are, what guides us? Take but a minute to think of all the stories of our moon and the long casts of ancestral figurings, ancestral names and ponders.

For centuries, people have believed that the Moon affects human behaviour. The word lunacy derives from the Latin *lunaticus*, meaning "moonstruck", and both the Greek philosopher Aristotle and the Roman naturalist Pliny the Elder believed that madness and epilepsy were caused by the Moon. (Geddes, 2019)

Old Wives' Tales that if you fell asleep with the moonlight on your face, you'd become a lunatic. And that very phrase, "Old Wives' Tales," is as deep as well of mixed and contested ancestries as one might imagine. A "place," a rich, ancestral "topic." Ghosts haunting one way or the other.

Here you go, a little side trail on the way by, full of willful children and scolding women needing to be shut up—Darning needles.

Black pedagogies about breaking the will of children as the main aim of education (A. Miller, 2002), wherein are cited late nineteenth century pedagogy manuals. This would have been the atmosphere of my grandmother's and mother's and father's schooling. Of mine, too. And there were many sulfurous whiffs of it still in schools I used to visit in Calgary only a few years back. Fear of the audacious uprising of the young. Of the new baby

Why imagine like this or remember these things out loud? Because we're already doing it and have been doing it long since and we are—variously, multifariously, positionally, differentiatedly—captured by these tales before we know it. *Then* comes the task of understanding, of trying to wake up a bit to what has already happened to us "over and above our wanting and doing" (Gadamer, 1989, p. xxxvii), and perhaps, then, loosen some threads, turn our backs on some ways, learn something more livable. About what has already been happening to us. And every language has its own tale to tell back to us, making my own dreaming more vivid than before. Each in the presence of the others becomes more its own place, its own spread, lived in. These two photographers, and a wonderful follow-up in *Slate Magazine* by Phil Plait (2014) with delicious further details, like the Moon being 3,500 kilometers across and Andromeda being 140,000 *light years* across.

There are myriad voices needed here *because the topic itself is already myriad* and thereby needs myriadness in order to be well taken care of, well grieved over, well-spoken and written and dreamt and mooned over. "Holistic" because that is how things *are* when things are left to repose in themselves. Radiant beings, daresay (Jardine, 2016f). Fulsome. Abundant. Stories, gods, measurements, light and its ways, night skies, distances, light pollution, dark adaptation—where you live, what time you have on your hands, whether there is a place within reach where some dark might be found.

All my relations show up around the stitches of devil's darning needles. So, take a glance at that photo again, and take a deep breath of night air. Just imagine the stories that might start crouching alongside Luna and Mercury and Venus.

"Once upon a time ..."

Here in the foothills, years ago, on a good night when the red hum of Calgary to the east was low-ebbing, you could see just a wee drift of the smudge of its bright center in the belt of stars underneath Cassiopeia.

Okay, then ...

> *Years ago, before the trees were pine*
> *There appeared in the sky a great soft vortex of light and cloud.*
> *And the first human flesh to see this wonder*
> *Fell sat and still and hummed*
> *A deep thrumming wordless chest vibration.*
> *Sky Give Breath seems like a good name*
> *But hardly good enough. Words glint and fail*
> *All in one gesture. The fail of words is my only refuge.*

Nah. That's terrible. Not good enough at all.

What about something of the protection (*medō*) of humanity (*andrós*) now reduced to just a smudge under city lights? The old Greek tale is a bit of a horror with a woman chained and Perseus the binding/rescuing hero. One more Old Wives' Tale.

Meanwhile, Ravens come back from the edges of the earth with doctored photos of Sky Give Breath in their beaks. Night Sky Take My Breath Away.

Flight Four: Intrusive Power

The ... intrusive power of a being reposing in itself. (Gadamer, 1977, p. 227)

Being *seen*, not just seeing. I become an object of *its* quick regard such that, even though I took the picture, the picture now frames me in its light. "We can entrust ourselves to what we are investigating to guide us safely in the quest" (Gadamer, 1989, p. 378). Why cite this book junk? To reassure myself that I am not alone in my musings over that bear. To learn a phrase I would have probably never thought of—"a being reposing in itself"—that makes that picture *more* beautiful. The idea of entrusting myself to what I'm exploring—I memorized that phrase when I came upon it, underlined it, remembered the page number. I wanted it to mark me because it made my flesh more raw when I came upon things. Made my heart more open. I am not good enough alone to pay good enough attention to my own lived experience. I need the ghosts in the language, in the ancestor's words, to help lift me out of my own sinks.

Improperly done, scholarship can just get in the way of lived experience, a kind of gummy blockage that gets in the way, gets in-between. *Schola*—the Latin means "leisure" (a terrible irony, considering the rush of many schools), but it also means "an opening up, a keeping clear" (OED, under "school"). For me, and for years, this sort of thing is like learning to recognize bird calls when you hear them. It is expansive of lived experience. When I first moved here, I only experienced Chick-a-dees until I learned that there might be further, deeper folds in my experience that my own experiential presumptiveness was blocking. There are three. And their songs switch in the Spring. There is nothing especially sacrosanct about "my experience." I recall joking to a class of over 200 preservice teachers, that when you hear that call on your way over to the pub with your friends, you will know what it is and you'll stifle a little giggle, and your friends will ask what's up, and you'll have to figure out what you're going to tell them.

Whether you're going to tell them.

Just like sweet Ursula tucked up under the spruce. Big head a'rested on the Spruce root.

I beg your indulgence. The following passage was written in 1994, when I was 44 (I'm no longer 44) and published in a book in the year 2000.

The little boy crouched mid-stream on the book cover just had his first child, my first grandchild, on August 4, 2021. I'm citing it because, well, even though I wrote it, I forgot all over again:

> There has been a disturbing loss in the area of ecological awareness. Currently, in Canada at least, there are three "R's" to environmentalism: reduce, re-use and re-cycle (some have introduced a fourth "r": recover). Several years ago there was another, different fourth "R" which has since gone missing: *refuse*. It is vital to not misread this missing fourth "R." It is not simply "refuse" in the sense of "garbage". It also suggests refusal. The most potent form of ecological action is simply saying "no" to those elements of our lives and our ways that are unsustainable, that befoul our nest. Saying "no" to the garbage. Refusing. The loss of this fourth "R"—the loss of the power and potency and responsibility involved in the act of refusal—is, unfortunately, not very mysterious. It leaves us with a vision of ecology which does not demand that we take responsibility for our own consumptive desires except *after* they are fully satiated. We can consume anything we want as long as we deal with the garbage *afterwards*. We are not required to consider how it may be that much of what we consume is *itself* garbage and how our relentless consumptiveness—our inability to say "no"—might itself spell ecological disaster. We live in an economy geared to saying "yes" without hesitation, geared to growth without restraint, geared to the giddy sense of consumptive vitality that such a headlong rush provides. In a horrible twist of logic, the relinquishing of the power of refusal leads to precisely that sense of rootlessness and powerlessness and futility that makes one susceptible to becoming a relentless consumer who is unable to refuse. (Jardine, 1994, p. 517)

People whose governing habit is the relinquishment of power, competence and responsibility, and whose characteristic suffering is the anxiety of futility, make excellent spenders. They are the ideal consumers. By inducing in them little panics of boredom, powerlessness, sexual failure, mortality, paranoia, they can be made to buy virtually anything that is "attractively packaged" (Berry, 1986, 24).

So, every picture in this article takes part in that lifelessly packaged camera disk and in my own culpability and memory loss, and love of the beauties that amble by this place.

And, if you enjoy these pictures, well hah! Welcome to the once-again hidden grand parade. I love you, just as I love them. We are being regarded regardless of our own regard. The fly doesn't know of the coming windshield. We do. And we can't become panicked or paralyzed over it. Instead, we have to read *ever more carefully, and teach our children to read.*

We have to teach our children what wisdom does:

> Surroundings of ancestors, lineages, elders, voices, companions—this is what emerges in stories from the ecological, radical heart of curriculum, the heart of our common and contested "course," and our work felt increasingly surrounded, supported, rooted and encouraged by the lines of thinking that wove around us. During our courses, we heard many times that teachers often feel that they are alone in their suspicions about their circumstances, and often their only recourse is dis-ease, complaint and exhaustion. During our studies together, we examined how this isolation is a deliberate by-product of industrial and managerial schemes and how it is profoundly anti-pedagogical at its root. The refuge of our common work in [see Seidel & Jardine, 2016] was one of relief and commiseration, of realizing that with study one can fill the surroundings with tales of joy and hope. (Seidel & Jardine, 2016, p. 3)

To let my considerations become considerate—English root, "to dwell long upon" (OED, under "consider").

The bear was back last night (September 29, 2021), 1:30 a.m. MDT, nearly twice the size, slowly migrating his way back up the Eastern Slopes for winter.

Flight Five: This Notice

FIGURE 38. IT WILL SAVE THE WORLD

It will save the world this notice. The earth is warm to the touch. My touch is warm to the earth. For now. There is nothing original about not noticing. There is nothing graceful about being too busy. I weep. Go ahead. What are you waiting for? What am I waiting for? Chance it. It could always be the last chance. Feeling like a chancy gardener. I like to watch for ripen. I like joke groans over these lines. Feel the warm. All this makes the tickety-tockety countable summers left to me a bit more bearable. This summer could always be the last one of mine. Just this morning. Dew. Driveway. Sun. Another little hidden music joke. *This could be the last soft gasp over Ravens in the trees come visit.* Beaks on roof peaks. Could be the last ones I'll ever see. And the joyous rush: *it is always thus,* that these could be the last, *and has always been thus.* And it is for you, too, always thus.

Don't forget to love teaching phonics in the meanwhile. "Robin Warbles." "Poppy Clusters."

It will save the world.

Flight Six: "You Live in the Wild Country"

FIGURE 39. FOXTROT

All we can do is try to speak it, try to say it, try to save it. Look, we say, this land is where your mother lived and where your daughter will live. This is you sister's country. You lived there as a child, boy or girl, you lived there. Have you forgotten? All the children are wild. You lived in the wild country. (Le Guin, 1989, p. 47)

CHAPTER FIFTY-THREE

"Nobody Understood Why I Should be Grieving"

Near the end of the film, near the end of his life, Benjamin Kasparian, once a respected professor whose identity depended on his research and finds, sneaks into the university lab after hours. He steals a brain, bones, some blood. At a place outside the city Benjamin digs a pit in the ground. He lays out the image of a running figure, a brain on legs. After covering this strange grave with earth, he lays down upon it and falls asleep. When Benjamin awakens, his memory is gone. He has gifted himself, his life, his work, back to the layers of the earth already taking him into its own meaning. (Seidel, 2014a, p. 150)

"Nobody understood why I should be grieving" (Ken Doka, in Springer Publishing Company, 2013).

I'm nearing the end of teaching a course on Hans-Georg Gadamer's *Truth and Method* for about the 25th time [now long passed by]. I've often been asked, and often mulled myself, about how I can go back to the same text over and over again.

One colleague half-joked, years ago, "It's not the only book, you know?"

Another, years ago, spoke of a course in seminary where the year's readings consisted of rereading the same Biblical text every day, over and over and over again and nothing else besides.

And then Ivan Illich (1993), in his brilliant meditations on the work of Hugh of St. Victor (1096–1141) entitled *In the Vineyard of the Text* (1993), spoke of how lovingly and repeatedly reading a text brings it to a glow, and this glow of the text casts its light on me "so that [I] may recognize myself" (p. 17): "studious striving ... teaches a commitment to engage in an activity by which the reader's own 'self' will be kindles and brought to sparkle" (p. 17).

"Approaching wisdom makes the reader radiant" (Illich, 1993, p. 17). I have sung, already, in praise of radiant beings and how sitting with something, persistently, making "common cause" with it, resigning myself to it (to re-coin the words of Wendell Berry [& Moyers, 2013]), is a necessary but not in itself sufficient cause of such radiance. It's that odd marriage, in scholarship, in study, of patience and exuberance.

I've also had this other odd experience with this book that comes, perhaps, from age, perhaps from running out of reasons to run. Gadamer's hermeneutics does not answer every question, does not address every woe. But, in the face of the onslaught of texts that surrounds the work of scholarship—I think of Hannah Arendt's (1969) "onslaught of the new" (p. 186)—and in the face of education's fetish for "the latest," I've found that it'll do, as imperfect, clumsy, elegant, and blind as it is. It befits, and, of course, has shaped, my own imperfections, clumsiness, elegance, and blindness. These are not simply the words of a scholar who has given up the panicky race and who faces the imminent end of a career (although it is partly that). I've simply decided to stay put and I've found that something happens if you do. Staying put, itself, is far more difficult these days than it might seem, keeping away distraction and the fretful suffering that ensues from believing that panic and acceleration will help. "Only by staying in place can the imagination conceive or understand action in terms of consequence, of cause and effect. The meaning of action in time is inseparable from its meaning in place" (Berry, 1983, p. 88). Staying put lets something else come to glow. It is its own way of approaching wisdom. "It is not the only way. It is one way" (Berry & Moyers, 2013):

> The good worker knows ... that after it is done work requires yet more time
> to prove its worth. One must stay to experience and study and understand
> the consequences—must understand by living with them, and then correct
> them, if necessary, by longer living and more work. It won't do to correct
> mistakes made in one place by moving to another place ... or by adding on
> another place, as is the fashion in any sort of "growth economy." (Berry, 1983,
> pp. 70–71)

This, of course, is harder than ever before to imagine in the contemporary academy. But don't worry. I get it. I used grants as a cover story so that I would be left in peace to do the work I would have done anyway.

So all this links up to an undeniable fact, here, at the tail end of what might turn out to be my last offering of this class. Every time I teach this class, something almost always *happens*. Part of doing hermeneutic work itself is awaiting such happenstances, settling, composing and readying oneself, studying intensely so that breakfast conversations, radio programs on the way to work, offhand colleagues' comments, a gesture, a fragment of text, a glance ... we await, in the smallest of circumstances "where it seem like one life hardly matters" (Wallace, 1987, p. 4), the glow and work on behalf of its arrival.

So, anyway, here's what happened. Several students in the Gadamer class this term responded positively when I suggested that we continue into the spring term. We had done this last year and it was approved as a teaching overload. This year, we were met differently. New rules. No more teaching overload. The proposed course was not offered. It is something like this: no one is allowed to teach overload because some employees have been taken advantage of and forced to do so, others have taken advantage of this circumstance unfairly, and, also, overload teaching cuts back on the work available for sessional instructors, and so on.

Let me continue by saying that this, of course, is a most trivial event. What this incident cued off is, I believe, not quite so trivial.

This incident made understandable in a new way all that stuff at the beginning of *Truth and Method* about the humanist tradition, about cultivating character and becoming someone because of what you know and do (*Bildung*), about judgment and tact, about *sensus communis*—the "common sense" that is build up through living in a community, and

the moral tone that then comes, about the ability to make a good decision about what the right thing to do might be given the case that asks
for good judgment from us. Such knowledge is eminently practical and
substantive, but in a particular sense. Such knowledge is gained only
through the practice of applying it to the cases and circumstances in
which one is called to act, to think, to carefully consider, and, by such
means, becoming practiced in good judgment and in the judicious and
careful application of a rule. As Immanuel Kant (2009) said, there is
no rule for the careful and proper application of a rule and only a fool
would ask for one. To be gained, such knowledge must be exercised,
over and over again. Even something like "careful and proper application" (from the sentence above) is, therefore, not an abstract universal
idea or ideal, nor is it a method that can be simply handed over without
any expectation of the recipient that he or she will have to practice this
idea for it to become available, comprehensible, and understandable. "It
cannot be taught in the abstract but only practiced from case to case"
(Gadamer, 1989, p. 31). It is a knowledge only "won by a certain labor"
(Ross & Jardine, 2009).

What emerges, here, is what Gadamer (1989) oddly named a "concrete universality"—a "sense that founds community" (p. 21). It is a
deliberate, continued cultivation of good judgment regarding what
it is that binds us to our common work. In such a community—such
as, for example, a Faculty—we are not simply identical "individuals."
Some of us are more experienced than others, experienced in different
matters, more patient, more angry, more tolerant, more well-read, more
forgiving, more suspicious, more trustworthy, and each of these differentiations is itself experience differently by all concerned. This complex, ongoingly negotiated, contested, worn-out, and re-woven fabric
describes what a community is like. It is not a fixed given but "always
must be renewed in the effort of our living" (Gadamer, 2007f, p. 244).
As Hannah Arendt (1969) so clearly put it, all we can do is strive to
act "in such way that a setting-right remains actually possible, even
though it can, of course, never be assured" (pp. 192–193). A living community thus lives within the shuddering of such lack of assurance and
the endurances, labor, and patience that it requires.

Individual cases that arise in such a milieu arise in a particular way: "the case which functions as an example is in fact something different from just a case of a rule" (Gadamer, 1989, p. 39). A case of a rule simply falls under a universal and is governed by it. A case that functions as an example, on the contrary, calls that rule to account, illuminating it, supplementing, co-determining, and correcting it (p. 39). Of course, simply falling under the rule makes things easier: the case either falls or it doesn't. Experiencing a case to be exemplary requires opening the rule up to the conditions of its authority and governance and asking whether, in this case, the rule must give way to the practical knowledge of the community's well-being, and, if so, in what ways, for what good reasons and to what extent—in *this* case, and given the rules that govern us, what is the right thing to do? Who shall have a say in what this might be? Simply strictly and unwaveringly following the rule *might* be the right thing to do, but it might not (consider in this light the zero-tolerance policies in some schools). This openness of the rules to the vagaries of common sense is not a "vague licentiousness" (Smith, 2020c, p. 404), but is, rather, a practical and practiced knowledge that Gadamer (1983) identified with an old Aristotelian understanding of *phronesis*: "the knowledge in terms of which one thing is preferred to another" (p. 131). Note that this is deemed to be a type of hard-won *knowledge.* One does not gain such knowledge simply through affirming one's right to have an opinion, or one's membership in a community. It is not just a matter of letting some people get away with breaking the rule and not letting others (although it does necessarily and unavoidably run this risk of being vulnerable to the vagaries of power, favor, and the like). It is a learned recognition that those in the community are not just abstract "individuals" who all fall identically "under the rules" but that each person in the community is someone—practiced, experienced, marginalized, foolish, trustworthy, unreliable, oppressed, authoritative, inexperienced, knowledgeable, a bully, a victim—not just an anonymous "anyone" and, moreover, not just the same "someone" one was yesterday or a year ago or in other circumstances or conditions or in light of different demands and occasions. Thus, such knowledge is not only tough both to win and to practice, it must also be constantly in the process of renewing itself and giving a good account of itself to the community so that good judgment doesn't atrophy into old prejudices and presumptions.

But then again, in giving an account of itself, something is also expected of those *to whom* such an account is given—that I will not just "react" or "give my opinion," but that I will attempt to have a good, well-informed, measured, and tempered opinion. Being part of a community, then, involves pedagogy: learning to understand what is going on, what is being said, what conditions are in play in our living together and not letting the simply willful assertion of individuality hold final sway (although this, too, is sometimes the right thing to do). Such practical knowledge, then, is retrievable and accessible only from its repeated practice, and the questions posed by this case will have to be reposed with the arrival of the next case. This vulnerability to interpretation is at the core of the practical knowledge that defines the humanist tradition as it finds its way up into contemporary hermeneutics in Gadamer's *Truth and Method*. A concrete universal proves its universality through its susceptibility to the next case, to being taken up again, re-thought in the face of the arrival of the new. And this proves itself through the well-being of the community that is thus woven over time. Its substance links to Gadamer's invocation (1989, p. 21) of Vico's idea of *topica*—a, so to speak, "topographical" knowledge of a place or locale that is gained only by venturing (German *Fahren*, "to journey") in that place and "learning one's way around" (p. 233). It is only thus, by venturing in one's "topic," that one becomes "experienced" (German *Erfahrung*) in its ways and learns, of course, that others have been there before, ancestors (German *Vorfahrung*). We learn, too, that this territory is often full of contestation, and inherited troubles, prejudices, occlusions, marginalizations, and the like. Becoming practiced and experienced, in such a venture, "does not consist in the fact that someone already knowledge everything and knows better than anyone else. Rather, the experienced person proves to be ... someone who is particularly well-equipped to have new experiences and to learn from them" (Gadamer, 1989, p. 355), that is, someone prepared to do the work necessary in order to have the next case be able to demand good judgment regarding its character and merits. And, here, again, "being experienced" is not an abstract but a concrete universal, the cultivation of which differentiates us rather than making us more and more identical. I, for example, should sensibly *never* be in a position of administration, given my impatience and inability to muster certain required forms of tolerance, judgment, and leeway. These admirable abilities are not my fate or my practice.

This is why I have so much enjoyed Thora Ilin Bayer's wonderful "Vico's Principle of *Sensus Communis* and Forensic Eloquence" (2008), in which not only eloquence is articulated as part of the humanist tradition inherited and transformed by Gadamer, but also, tellingly, *prudentia, temperantia,* and *decorum* as a key to knowledge thus understood as the practical and ongoing work of working for the well-being of a community and the effected and renewed sense that "we belong to it" (Gadamer, 1989, p. 358). It is near hilarious to imagine eloquence, prudence, temperance, and decorum as anything but objects of mockery and suspicion in our contemporary circumstances. Bayer (2008) spoke, too, of *sensus communis,* including, in the work of Juvenal, the idea of "thoughtful kindness" (p. 1138), which casts me over to another recent love, Wendell Berry's new book, *It All Turns on Affection* (2012), and from there back to an old adage of the Angelic Doctor, where Thomas Aquinas paraphrases the *Ad Herennium*: "It is necessary that a man should dwell with solicitude on, and cleave with affection to, the things which he wishes to remember" (cited in Yates, 1974, p. 75).

There is a root visible here, that this knowledge of the well-being of the community is linked to memory and its cultivation and well-being. The indiscriminate application of rules or following of rubrics bypasses the cultivation of memory. We're linked back, then, to Benjamin Kasparian and the drift of his memory into the Earth. Here lies the shock:

We know full well that th[e] Great Council [of memory and practice] that shows up surrounding ... any one of us ... is not Absolute, that [I am] surrounded (I would suggest, *necessarily* surrounded) by a dark and irremediable penumbra of absences. We don't learn everything. None of us is everyone. None of us is cut out for living just any life, and none of us will live forever. We are not perspectiveless and timeless beings whose knowledge floats [identically under the rule of law] and whose life is a matter of indifference. I am defined by what I can thus remember, what necessarily exclusive and incomplete host of voices haunts my inner life and work and therefore haunts the world(s) that open in front of me. This composed and cultivated memory constitutes my openness to what comes to meet me from the world. No amount of effort allows any of us to avoid this process of suffering through the remembering and forgetting of the world and becoming someone in the process. As memory increases, so does this suffering. I become more susceptible to the world's affect as I become more experienced. This is basic.

> If one's sight is clear and if one stays on and works well, one's love gradu-ally responds to the place as it really is, and one's visions gradually image possibilities that are really in it. Vision, possibility work, and life—all have changed by mutual correction. Correct discipline, given enough time, grad-ually removes one's self from the one's line of sight. One works to better pur-pose then and makes fewer mistakes, because at last one sees where one is. Two human possibilities of the highest order thus come within reach: what one wants can become the same as what one has, and one's knowledge can cause respect for what one knows. (Berry, 1983, p. 70)

It used to be that our administrators were allowed, in fact required, to at least attempt to make considered, sound, defensible judgments about the matters facing them. Discretion. Of course, such discretion still exists, but we all have to keep it secret, because if it becomes visible in a "community" governed by rules, it can only appear as rule-breaking or "favoritism." I, for example, am near retirement, I'm not being forced to do anything, I'm not taking work from something a sessional could do, I am, dare I say, a bit of an expert in the content of this course, 15 grad-uate students wanted this course to continue, and so on. Again, this is a profoundly trivial example except for this: the rule indiscriminately applied now precludes the relevance of any of this. In other words— here is another layer—under the rules and rubrics, I become simply one employee among others, an F[ull] T[ime] E[quivalent] cluster who, to be treated "fairly," gets treated like "anyone." Otherwise, under the rule, those applying it would be discriminating. These, then, become the alternatives. Either the community is prejudicially discriminating (understood only negatively, of course, as bias, favoritism, collusion, and the like) or it operates indiscriminately under the law. This perhaps accounts for the fact that I come, then, like I have over the past years, to feel faceless, anonymous, replaceable at a moment's notice. But something gets hidden here.

There is an iatrogenic "loop" that frightens me and sends me grieving, and in all this, a transformative shift that gets occluded. A passage from Sheila Ross' brilliant essay "The temporality of tarrying in Gadamer" (2006):

> The possibility presents itself that such deference [to rules simply anonymously followed] prevents or obviates the occurrence of a kind of experience ... the human hermeneutic experience that Gadamer calls tarrying [a form, we might say, of "staying put"]. The Gadamerian dystopia is not unfamiliar. In his version, to be glib, little requires human application so little cultivates it. Long alienated form abiding in inquiry as a form of life and way of being, a restless humanity defers to models, systems, operations, procedures, the ready-made strategic plan. (p. 111)

But here is the great tragedy. Our deference, here, *creates* restlessness in its attempt to overcome restlessness. It attempts to replace the alienation from the community that it has caused with obedience in the zero-tolerance application of rules.

Once there is a fixed "rule" that no fecund case can correct, supplement, or vary, cultivating good, careful, thoughtful judgment is no longer "asked for."

The fixity of the rule thus replaces the difficult cultivation of the wisdom of practice.

Therefore, the practiced ability to make such good judgments is not exercised.

Therefore, that ability atrophies.

Therefore, since no one is practicing good judgment, it cannot be relied upon.

Therefore, a fixed rule becomes necessary.

The imposition of the fixed rule creates the conditions for its being needed by transforming the community in which it is applied into a locale with no wise, practiced, trusted, or considered alternative to such fixity.

So, if I may, and as a parting gesture, hermeneutics is important, not just because it helps us get a glimpse of this loop in which we are caught. It also points to the terrible fact that the living worlds of our work are being reassembled, right before our eyes, in order to eliminate the need for application and its cultivation, and therefore atrophying and marginalizing hermeneutic acuity. Once we all become unpracticed, we will all be glad of the rules, since any other recourse has died off. We will find that obedience is our only comfort.

And a sort of unnamed, collective grieving, perhaps. Would that I could believe that this whole matter is not deliberate, even though those perpetrating it are caught in and spellbound by this circumstance as much as any of us.

Nobody understood why I should be grieving. Thus, I steal a brain, some bones, some blood, and place them carefully upon the Earth, readying myself to lie down.

CHAPTER FIFTY-FOUR

As the Warming Chills

FIGURE 40. NORTH AMERICA

We'll find David Lynch ice-erased under the snowed-in barbeque
lid of unsuspected black lodged wavy lines, just barely visible. Can
you sense the tracelines here, trying to true attention?

North America iced-in after the acclimatory collapse
and oceanrises. Floridian Grosbeak beak of ice. Canada white
haired.

B&W 1950s horror movies on
Snowy TVs.

A nice and frosty Atom Bomb cluster
Insinuated nightmares under blue and yellow flags.

There is something to be said for
Hallucinations like these. They
Can be the temporary holders of nebulous woes looking for a home.
Places to light.
To rest these wearies.

To maybe manifest woes looking for a body hale enough to hold
them, embrace them
and maybe even a chance to lance their poisons now beheld.

Wounds sometimes need a bigger wound to heal.
This is why poetry. Why art or a photograph. Or lines, written.
A place, perhaps, some day, some day,
to lay those woes down in the
Happenstance beauty of melting winter ice.

CHAPTER FIFTY-FIVE

It's February. It Won't Last

Preamble

… the survivors stepping forward for their moment, blessed by our terrible need to know everything. (Wallace, 1987, p. 48)

The following small reflection was written around a year ago, but it has taken on new urgency for me with Nancy Moule's (2017) and Kate Beamer's (2017) writing late last year, and my own more recent, slightly unexpected responses.

The crux is this: why dwell on these matters? Perhaps writing relieves the writer, but why then read? Why listen to Sufjan Stevens songs about the death of his mother, or, even more harrowing, Mount Eerie's (2017) songs about a wife lost to cancer, and a young child and husband now a bit lost in the world?

It is not just a matter of empathizing or deep emotion, although it certainly is all that. It is also a chance for interpretive practice at a relatively safe distance, at relatively safe extent. To witness the careful articulation of suffering through reading writing (or listening to songs) that allows me to hold it at arm's length or let it come nearer if and as I'm able.

There is something important to be said for practicing while we can, and not waiting for events that might just overwhelm my own composure altogether.

"It's February. It Won't Last"

> ... the lord of yogis, Sri Jagan-Mitrananda, says:
> Lord of the Earth, while this borrowed body
> Is still healthy, without sickness or deterioration,
> Take full advantage of it, acting in order to end your fear of sickness, death, and deterioration.
> Once sickness, aging and deterioration and the like occur,
> You might remember to practice, but what can you do then? (Tsong-kha-pa, 2000, p. 157)

While driving east into Calgary for a bird-watching class in a park along the Bow River, around 8:20 a.m., someone on the local CBC AM radio was speaking about the weather forecast—very strange indeed, February 8, 2016, 14 degrees Celsius, with higher temperatures forecast for the next two days. The sun was flooding into the car window as we drove, more buttery-colored every day. A great relief as we sighed into it.

And the person on the radio says, "My mantra right now is repeating 'It's February. It won't last.'"

Yes. It is. And yes, it won't.

"Familiarize yourself with it repeatedly. We call this repeated familiarization meditation" (Tsong-kha-pa, 2000, p. 110).

Yes. It is. And yes, it won't.

This is an increasingly familiar sort of "pop"-usage of the term "mantra," meant to indicate a deliberately repeated phrase to calm the mind and prevent attachment. So, it was not exactly improperly used on the radio: don't get used to this warm weather. Don't get fooled and drawn into a spell of anticipation and eventual regret. It is not going to last. I guess the pop equivalent is bursting someone's bubble.

Of course, the trouble is that, improperly wielded, it becomes the sour-puss downer for all occasions: don't enjoy that meal, it won't last; don't enjoy this life, it won't last.

From a Buddhist point of view, however, this can be a good mantra if it is well practiced. It is trying keep me alert and to prevent mere absorption in the whirling of the world. It is attempting to short-circuit or prevent future disappointment caused, *not by today's nice weather* and the upcoming forecast, but caused by becoming falsely *attached to it* and then suffering the woe of its inevitable disappearance.

There is a sort of cycle, here, that is profoundly commonplace. My hope for this weather to last forever (based, I supposed, on the lusty animal-body wanting winter to end, wanting that vague threat lifted so I can let go into the winds and ways) causes me to grab at it, and grabbing at it gives rise to a false feeling of prospective permanence, of "lasting," thus accelerating the grasping and becoming attached to what is, in fact, an illusory reification of my own making.

You can tell from this metaphorical sketch how easy it would be for ever-increasing panic to ensue, desperation to take over, and ever-accelerating pursuit to occur. Over the course of 30 years of involvement in education and schools, this metaphor has been handy to have. Too often I've witnessed the ravaging of attention that comes from this accelerated distraction, and too often I've seen how deliberately it is manipulated just under the surface of attention. The problem is, once "inside" this wheeling, the wheeling sustains itself and can only imagine relief inside of its own orbit of pursuit. This is why Buddhism is often portrayed as a denial of desiring and why it might seem that enjoying this warm February air would be shunned.

"My mantra right now is repeating 'It's February. It won't last.'"

"Detachment" from this go-round—another commonplace coinage in describing Buddhism—means precisely the opposite of what is easily supposed. Such detachment is easily imagined to be a form of disaffected and dour countenance, a flatness of emotion and a sort of distance and dismalness. This is, I think, an incorrect reading of what Buddhism requires and what purpose a mantra might serve. It imagines Buddhism from inside the orbit of that in relation to which it is, in fact, exorbitant.

Once "detached" from the illusory belief that this weather might last forever, that this streaming sun might lift my seasonal, Old English, *grevoushede*, once and for all, I can now, instead, utterly adore this warm sun far more profoundly than if I had simply glommed onto it in mindless "enjoyment." This passing light becomes profoundly intense and surrounded with a penumbra of stillness, immediacy and radiance *because it won't last*, not *in spite of* this fact. This is a phenomenological fact of meditative practice, that adoring radiant beings—like the smell of that aspen just cut from the tree the moths got last fall—is always under the caution of not simply falling for it and failing to remain alert to its ephemerality.

Fugitive.

Not lasting is what it *is* and experiencing it otherwise falsifies it under the weight of my meagre desires.

"My mantra right now is repeating 'It's February. It won't last'," properly practiced, lets it be what it is. It releases it from my dour countenance and animal threat-body. It releases me from it as well.

In such detachment, two things happen simultaneously. First, this warmth becomes *itself*, untethered from hopes for the future or laments for the past. "The existing thing does not simply offer us a recognizable and familiar surface contour; it also has an inner depth of self-sufficiency that Heidegger calls 'standing-in-itself'" (Gadamer, 1977, p. 226). With practice, I can learn to experience this warmth detached from me meddle. It becomes radiant (Jardine, 2016f). It "breaks forth as if from a center" (Gadamer, 1989, p. 458).

Second, in such (however momentary) detachment, I become what I am: here, now, animal-body facing the sun and feeling the rouse of light, letting it be, letting it "stand in itself" and therefore letting myself stand there in its presence. My experience of this warmth becomes radiant. That is to say, it draws me out of my own wintery self-enclosure. It feels so good.

But wait. Also, here, "if you are obstructed ... you will continue to think that you will remain in this life" (Tsong-kha-pa, 2000, p. 145). Say it. This awash of warm butter sun might just be the last one I ever experience. *Now* I can love it and not simply be attached to it.

You can't love something that you are attached to.

By exercising the muscle of detachment—I'd call it the muscle of interpretation that "break[s] open the being of the object" (Gadamer, 1989, p. 360) and shows its dependent co-arising, and thus shows the delusions of the "substance" (p. 242)—this minuscule moment of disillusion, of (oh so trivial) suffering—"It's February. It won't last"—becomes an occasion for of practicing detachment in a case that is what bar-talk calls "a cheap round." It doesn't hurt so very much, and the payoff, if it leads to continued practice, is extraordinary:

While this borrowed body is still healthy, without sickness or deterioration, take full advantage of it, acting in order to end your fear of sickness, death, and deterioration. Once sickness, aging and deterioration and the like occur, you might remember to practice, but what can you do then? (Tsong-kha-pa, 2000, p. 157)

The suffering induced by paying serious attention—interpretive attention—to this radio-friendly mantra is *profoundly* small, but, using this small gift as a locale for practice, frees its warmth from the captivity of ego-driven panic and attachment and, however momentarily, frees me from my fears of impermanence, of passing.

Take full advantage if your able.

CHAPTER FIFTY-SIX

Falling Silent

"Why are B.C.'s Orcas Falling Silent?"
The Canadian Press October 24, 2013

Killer whales near Victoria. Vancouver Aquarium researcher Dr. Lance Barrett-Lennard is sounding the alarm over "puzzling" changes he's observed in the killer whale pods that live off B.C.'s coast and off Alaska. After the recent loss of seven matriarchs over the past two years, and he's noticed a lack of vocalizations from the normally chatty mammals.

A Vancouver Aquarium researcher is sounding the alarm over "puzzling" changes he's observed in the killer whale pods that live off B.C.'s coast and off Alaska.

Dr. Lance Barrett-Lennard says he fears changes in the ocean environment are prompting odd behaviour and an unusually high mortality rate.

Barrett-Lennard says the southern resident pod, which is found in the Salish Sea between Vancouver Island and the B.C. mainland, has lost seven matriarchs over the past two years, and he's noticed a lack of vocalizations from the normally chatty mammals.

The Vancouver Aquarium's cetacean research team says the whales were also seen the past two summers travelling in small groups, further offshore to find food—behaviour more typical in winter than summer.

At the same time, the researcher says the number of normally transient killer whales has been increasing over the past 25 years.

> Barrett-Lennard says the changes are striking and need further study.
> (The Canadian Press, 2013, n.p.)

The changes are striking and need further study. Imagine taking their falling silent as precisely directed toward me—"Ok, well, it's your turn. Speak. What do you have to say for yourself, for what you've done without even knowing it?"

Where have you been? Busy with what? Other things? So, study. You seem to have given me a future I might not have. What have you given yourself?

"Why are the Black Willows disappearing along the river near your home?" Wendell Berry's (with Moyers, 2013) full answer is: "I don't know. It must be something in the water." He then attended a sit-in in the Kentucky governor's office protesting "mountain top mining"— simply removing the soil and trees (what is called—stop over this term, please—the "overburden") and then simply blowing up and carting away now-unburdened coal.

Rain, of course, runs downhill and washes with it anything it can. We cannot presume upon even this utterly common-sense knowledge. Just think, then:

> We live within order and that this order is both greater and more intricate than we can know. The difficulty of our predicament: Though we cannot produce a complete or even adequate description of this order, severe penalties are in store for us if we presume upon it or violate it. (Berry, 1987, p. 55)

The Earth, the whales, the willows, the bees, *measure us* when we are properly in their presence. We measure each other this way as well. The book I read, the music I hear, measures me as I take its measure. We are always and inevitably and with every breath in their presence, whether or not I have the propriety, the composure, the will, to note this intimacy.

Even bearing witness is precisely hard to bear. It is almost unbearable. The Orcas have fallen silent.

Silent witnesses. Here, from a teacher of mine:

"Oh Sorrow"
eubalaena glacialis
so nearly alone now in this
in this
breath

exhale
spirit birthing deep forsaken
is it that we forgot to greet you?

...

that it would come
to this?

...

It is not goodbye, not yet
eubalaena glacialis
oh sorrow
only with you do we matter

From Jackie Seidel (2014b, p. 112), *Hymn to the North Atlantic Right Whale*

CHAPTER FIFTY-SEVEN

Curls and Tucks

FIGURE 41. CURLS AND TUCKS

I'm losing my breath in curls and tucks
Curls and tucks.
Exhaling. Electric hale sniffing the electric air.

I've just about lived another
Summer. Curls of air. Curls of baby hair.
Deeper darker foregrounds. Suns. Smoke.
Three-week tucked in arm-crook while I pick peas on the pea-
    vine. Sh-sh-sh shadow grow tall. Tall.

I've got to go ahead and risk in hale.

CHAPTER FIFTY-EIGHT

"A Joyous and Frightening Shock"

Part One: Mystery, Miracles and the "Ten Thousand Things"

FIGURE 42. IS THIS MYSTERY HERE?

Is This Mystery, Here?
Or just a camera's mechanical switch to focus elsewhere?
While Cedar Waxwings sit and wing over Saskatoon's purple ripe sunlight.

> The pour-down sluices of having stood there, that moment, this?
> And the wizened shivers that I may never see this again, this?
> Of realizing that this has always been so.
> Even here, typing.
> Even there, you, reading.
> Is this mystery, here?

Saskatoon-berry-bush tucks a *Bombycilla cedrorum*. Tucked there, too, in Linnaean Latin word-ordinances, the photograph's focus and locus wonderfully betraying each other.

Mysterious? Perhaps. *Mysterium*,[1] "a secret rite or worship." I go with camera alone, *mysteēs*, "one who has been initiated," one who has practiced a bit. But I go out into a gathering, myself gathering air and images and sunlight. My self *gathered*. Courses to take or leave behind every which-a-way.

It is not precisely secret or hidden. It is right there in that photo. That it is a wee bit hidden *from me* means that I am *not* an initiate into *its* secretness but I *am* a practiced initiate into gathering up these images, meditating on them and adoring them, saving them. Showing them. Here. To you and others. Writing and writing. All these relations are how this lovely *exists*. Dependently co-arising (*pratitya-samutpada*), sun included, me included. It *is* its surround. I am my surround in its regard, along with the oxygens breaking downwards in the sun'slights from the trees above, we both take out and in breaths. A curriculum topography. Of course. Pun intended. Of course. Latin, *currere. Cursus*, "the flow of a stream."

Small things like this draw me into the sort of work I've done for decades. Small things like this make me want to sing about the deepening cavity of that focus, about the miraculous arrival of dozens of Waxwings on the Saskatoon Berry bushes, and all the flows that manifest right there. Year after year. And how our deepening "ecological sorrows" (Jardine, 2015, p. xv), betrayed by Red Foxes seen hereabouts for the first time in all my years living here, magpies, too, also betray some deepening, shifting shivers in the courses of things in this place.

---

1   All direct etymological citations are from the *Online Etymological Dictionary* (https://www.etymonline.com), listed under the specific term referred to.

No more Coyotes. But still this courses. No living course stays the same. A moment of pause. What is being hinted at behind the focused branches?

Just like "every word breaks forth as if from a center and causes the whole ... to which it belongs to resonate [and] ... to which it is related by responding and summoning" (Gadamer, 2004, p. 458). I myself am summoned, here, to approach this nub of inter-relations and write about it in a way that *maintains* its *miraculum*.

As Jackie Seidel cited (2014c, p. 7) years ago:

> **Miracle**: From the Latin *mīrāculum*: object of wonder. *Mīrāculum* from *mīrārī*, to wonder at. From *mīrus*, wonderful. From *smeiros* [(s) mei–PIE–proto-Indo-European] "to smile, to be astonished." Also Sanskrit: *smerah* "smiling." Also Old Church Slavic: *Smejo*–to laugh.

It, then, might be mysterious *to* me. But far more often, it is something also ordinary—something "in order," "customary, usual" even in the vague smiles when I see a Red Fox flurry and scurry about. I wander around with that camera time and time again. I look up words and settle myself into what they may ask of me in the face of this beautiful Waxwing sight.

Wonder. Smile. Astonish. It is that hit and those gestures of saving and caring for that let its mystery come to sit and stay.

"Astonish" means to be thunderstruck: Vulgar Latin *extonare*, from Latin *ex*, "out" ... + *tonare* "to thunder." In this sort of work, these language enclaves and ancestries themselves surround me in their regard even when or if I toss words off without regard. Each is itself a curriculum topic, each rich and full of voices, "interweaving and crisscrossing" (Wittgenstein, 1968, p. 33), culturally abundant, linguistically bristling, becoming more and more so as other voices voicing other words add themselves to the myriad. "Only in the multifariousness of voices does [any word, any thing, any language, or idea, or bird, or berry bush, or utterance, hope, any 'self' or 'other'] exist" (Gadamer, 1989 p. 284).

I've learned to become unable to resist, knowing full well that I'll then have to compose myself in this myriad, this flurry, and make something of it. Our words, the ancestries of our imagining as a whole, works like this: Latin, *myrias*, Greek, *myrios*, both referencing "count-less" and "boundless," and also an old Greek image of "ten thousand things."

Here again, why do this? This is why: because I could hear old voices, old memories coming up, this Lao Tzu, (Sixth Century BCE), an image I can now only find in older translations:

Tao Te Ching—Lao Tzu—Chapter 16
Empty yourself of everything.
Let the mind rest at peace.
The ten thousand things rise and fall while the Self watches their return.
They grow and flourish and then return to the source.
Returning to the source is stillness, which is the way of nature.

Lao Tzu, Tao Te Ching. Chapter 16

There it is, hidden in plain sight, this particular translation betraying an old Greek and Latin image, betraying its importation into Lao Tzu's words, me the wee undergrad when first reading this, simply swallowing whole all the old Euro-exoticizing of the incoming words from "the East":

> As an undergraduate (in a dual degree of philosophy and religious studies, class of '72) and then as an MA student (in philosophy, class of '75), I recall clear as day that the Mills Library at McMaster University, Hamilton, Ontario, had a collection of editor Max Müller's *Sacred Books of the East*. This fifty-volume behemoth was a set of English translations produced between 1879 and 1910 and published by Oxford University Press over that time-period. It took up several shelves, and the books themselves, especially the earlier volumes, were slick and shiny leather-bound, a sort of dark brownish dried blood color that made the collection look like the hide of some great and exotic beast, slivers of which you could slide out and open. (Jardine, 2016o, p. 139)

All this, let alone how Lao Tzu's own words are themselves like a Waxwing tucked behind translations, "betrayals" (Jardine, 2016a, pp. 129–130) which both betray—reveal, give away—something of the "original" and do wrong by it, betray it in that sense as well, all mixed and out of focus as to which may be which. This be how the whole of things gathers us up. Betraying the open bounds of my ears and tongues, now witnessing my grandson be swept up into the ways of words. Watch out:

> This means that one may become so engrossed ... that they outplay one, as it were, and prevail over one. The attraction ... lies in this risk. (Gadamer, 1989 p. 107)

Little wonder that Robertson Davies, a Canadian author, said, in a line I can no longer trace, something like becoming educated means becoming haunted by more and more ghosts:

> From a hill behind a gas station in Scranton, I could see the old ways stitching out in their graves. (Callahan, 2019b, n.p.)

Every single reader lives in such a myriad of their own raising and learning and practice and habit and craft, and its edges ripple and lap against the whole single breath. Maybe overlapping, maybe crisscrossing and stitching, maybe able to offer grace and make lightness in the very blind spots I inevitably carry along with any insight. I am not adequate to the whole of things and need its re-focus, its lessons. A slow drive by stuffed toys stitched to Tsuut'ina Nation fenceposts (Paperny, 2021).

Every light cast shadows. We are each fragile, finite beings, guts and breaths and memory and thinking strung in these nets, strung on these posts. This, too, is part of our shared and contested ancestries— remembering, forgetting, grieving, and owning up. This bright pink, plush elephant perched like a Waxwing, barely glimpsed in the highway rush-by of those posts and their burdens.

Part Two: Wonder, Openness, Undone, Elusiveness, Conspiracy, Readiness

FIGURE 43. PLANT SECRECIES

Plant Secrecies
Chancing upon
Green Life Chambers
White Spindles
The Great Fathoming of a single being
Being squeezed out into sunlight.
Alive to See It. There.
Secrete. Moist. Soil. Light. Spine. Energies. Crackling. Through. Old.
Flesh. Bones.
Sweet. Mixed. Bloods.

My grandson and I bend near plants, as near as breath allows, into the mixed underleaves and their penumbras. Smile. Laugh. Wonder (Old English *wundrian*). Wander (Old English *wandrian*). Shush, now. "Wend" is nearby—"to turn, wind, weave." I didn't know these derivations before I checked, just now, while writing. Like plant secrecies, you become accustomed to letting them lure you and speak to you, perhaps. To slow and deepen my tendency to simply flutter by.

The openness to experience that we [can] win through becoming experienced opens us to being outdone. This rings true of the hermeneutic insistence, as well as the Buddhist insistence, as well as the ecological insistence, on the penumbral presence of impermanence as key to any insight to be gained or lost. I *will* be outplayed:

> Understanding is an adventure, and, like any adventure, it always involves some risk. (Gadamer, 1983, p. 141)

> An adventure is "undergone," like a test or a trial from which one emerges enriched and more mature. (Gadamer, 1989 p. 69)

At least I hope so. Perhaps more resolved. Or resigned. It opens me to the utter certainty that I *will be undone* in bones and breath, sooner, now, rather than later. Thunder snoring over the hills. Louder. Lovelier.

Perhaps elusive, then? The familiar coinage seems apt: "Insight is more than the knowledge of this or that situation. It always involves an escape from something [Latin *fugere*] that had deceived us and held us captive" (Gadamer, 1989 p. 360). Eluding capture? I think of the heavy dullness that has captured too many teachers' and students' hearts and bodies, numbed in the ever-accelerating lethargies of some schools. Such sorrow.

But then there is something about *being captured* here as well, but then eluding enough to try to write in a way that maintains that elusiveness. *This* is mysterious, I suppose.

Eludere? This means "finish[ed] play" (*lude*) whereas those plant secrecies set something in motion. And there surely is something "at play" here in the "in between" (Gadamer, 1989, p. 295) of human breaths and sights and cameras and grandsons and these plants and birds.

"Something is going on, [*im Spiele ist*], something is happening [*sich abspielt*]" (Gadamer, 1989 p. 104). Spiel. But then again, Hans-Georg Gadamer, citing Johann Huizinga's lovely book *Homo Ludens: The Play Element in Culture* (1955), was keen on how belonging to and living inside realms of knowledge and ancestries and traditions and habits and habitats and language lineages has a sort of secret (mysterious) "inside" to it:

COMMISERATIONS & ENCOURAGEMENT FOR SORROWFUL TIMES

> This is for us, not for the "others." What the "others" do "outside" is of no
> concern to us at the moment. We are different, we do things differently.
> (Huizinga, 1955, p. 12)

This is both the comfort and the danger of this locale of work and living in these ecologically troubled times—insiders, outsiders, us, them. Identity is understood, in Buddhist thought and practice, as *the* central affliction of human being, one that is not remedied by the sheer multiplication and affirmation of different identities (Jardine, 2017), as seems to be so commonplace lately. This simply replaces identity with difference, and difference, in the Greco-European philosophical legacy, is the only alternative that identity will allow for itself. Multiple identities simply replicate and democratize the original affliction. Something like contemplative, holistic interrelatedness gets skipped over or turned to subjective mush.

This is not mush, nor is it subjective. It is the earth-orbit we *inhabit* and whose life inhabits us. My grandson and I approach the bird-feeding and the plant nearnesses with shushes to each other. *Conspirare*, finally in a genuine, ancient sense: Look can you see? Wait. Ahh-startles and giggles and all, breaths (*spirare*) held in common (*con-*), mingling. Is this one breath? No. Is it many different breaths? No. Neither of these expressions are adequate.

And just so the mystery doesn't disappear, "conspiring" also means "to sound in unison."

Ahhhh ... a great exhale. Our great tilt and bends near plants. Him pawing and plucking and pointing and oohs, such oooohs. He allows me to not find contempt bred in the familiar, as goes that old saw I've never traced before. Ah. Here we are, Chaucer, 1386, from "Tale of Melibee": *"Men syen that 'over-greet hoomlynesse engendreth dispreisynge'"* (Chaucer, n.d.)—him seemingly quoting some older saw given those "sses." Okay, I'll try: "Too often, greeted home-likeness engenders disparaging."

Escaping the capture of dull familiarity by finding an enlivening familialness heretofore unnoticed jumping up into play. From capture to fugitive to capture. That familiar Waxwinging, "there, in the midst of things, his whole family listening" (Wallace, 1987, p. 111), leaping up unexpectedly:

> How their deaths [its and mine, and I can't quite say it … my grandson's too] quicken the air around them, stipple their bodies with a light like the green signals trees send out before their leaves appear. (Wallace, 1987, p. 40)

A plant secretes. White hairs. Pistils. As Johan Huizinga suggests, play is necessarily "labile" (1955, p. 21).

Read these, then, like passing by—grandson on fleet foot—from plant secrecy to plant secrecy. Breathe quietly. Rereading is itself a mysterious good:

> Without the readiness of the person who is receiving and assimilating [*des Aufnehmenden*] the text [the bird, the recess, the plant, our breaths] to be 'all ears' [*ganz Ohr zu sein*], no … text will speak. (Gadamer, 2007a, p. 189)

> "Being experienced" does not consist in the fact that someone already knows everything and knows better than anyone else. Rather, the experienced person proves to be, on the contrary, someone who … because of the many experiences he has had and the knowledge he has drawn from them, is particularly well equipped to have new experiences and to learn from them. Experience has its proper fulfillment not in definitive knowledge but in the openness to experience that is made possible by experience itself. (Gadamer, 1989 p. 355)

> Readiness needs to be sought, cultivated. It needs to be taken care of properly and repeatedly and relentlessly. Readiness takes work, it takes energy, *energeia*, 'aliveness' … and it not only *takes it*. It *produces* it. And when it works, it hits the still spot between give and take and begins to glow. The joy … in being "all ears" *creates* joy. "As in love, our satisfaction [in this joy] sets us at ease because we know that somehow its use at once assures its plenty." (Hyde, 1983 p. 22). (See Chapter Twenty Nine)

PART THREE: Awakened, Energies, Captured, Possessed, Aliveness, Quickening

FIGURE 44. POPPIES

Sun'Slight
So, in early morning rising
Up to consciousness, part of me
Must shed dreaming's safehouse and
Drop the *armamentaria* of sleep.
Open arms
Expose my heart to the coming
Sunlight.
For this I have to
Knock this earthenware off my head.

But I dare not forget how my
Roots love those dark shadow wares, the foods
and their encircling wets.
How too much sun'slight would ruin.
I must remember that dreaming soils
Are their own consciousness.
Are of mine own.
Part of me is underground, still.

It's hard to keep brilliance to yourself and
Not uproot
Rooting roots to see how they're doing.
What their downs are up to.
As if that is the attention they need from me.
I can only daydream of the dreams of last night.
Keep the seedlings warm and wet and morning-lit.
Adored. And adoring.
And in such close adore my
Breath feeds them whether I sense it or not.
This daydreaming is its own earthenware.

5:45AM MST FEBRUARY 4, 2021

Remitting writing to the courses of these poppies and depths of the lit shadows. Then, addressing my own gasp, that enclave of writings reminding me that my own mysterious spellboundedness is part of the whole, part of the hale of what is occurring here. And then, to remit writing to all these variegated courses that capture is a joyous and humiliating exercise, each and every time. *It* always seems to get better, and *I* realize that I must remit myself to its betterment, again and again and again.

But there is another upsurge here in the midst of poppies and sunlight that courses through eyes and fingers and spines and that is a clue to the draw of hermeneutics itself and a clue to my own joy in it, a clue to why my grandson nearby figures in it now: *energeia*, "something like aliveness itself," in Sheila Ross's (2006, p. 108) invigorating translation. Its quickening quickens me.

I gather in memory my old teachers in a coven of whispers: "We should apply this to *every* phenomenon" (Tsong-kha-pa, 2005, p. 182), our "selves" included. "Everything is teaching you. Isn't this so? Can you just get up and walk away so easily now?" (Chah, n.d., p. 5).

If the garden comes round again, if, I may be there to witness this again. I just may be.

This be mysterious.

PART FOUR: "A JOYOUS AND FRIGHTENING SHOCK"

My grandson looking up at me as we pull buried carrots up from the ground with Ravens arcing overhead. It is so very familiar and slightly staggering to be under this tapered orange purview, under the tossed-up smells of adorable rich earth. It makes the carrots more properly, what? Miraculous?

We smile.

We be fugitive, if even only for this tick or tock dissolving in the clockwork sun.

Aesthesis. Quickening breath in when you're stopped in your tracks—the juicy bite. The sting of its still-living sweetness to our still-living tongues:

> The intimacy with which [this event] … touches us is at the same time, in enigmatic fashion, a shattering and demolishing of the familiar. It is not only the impact of a "this means you!" ["Das bist du!"] that is disclosed in a joyous and frightening shock. It also says to us: "You must change your life!" (Gadamer, 2007b, p. 131)

A second grandson has since arrived out of nowhere. Out of everywhere. Still unnamed. Warm and wet and asleep on my chest. Is this mystery, here? A plant secrecy? A sun'slight? Us one being reposing in itself. Joyous. Frightening.

CHAPTER FIFTY-NINE

"Grief is Not a Permanent State": The Last Six Chapters of *Speaking with a Boneless Tongue* (1992)

A New Post-Ambulation

FIGURE 45. "Not a Creature was Stirring"

What follows are the last few chapters of an old, self-published book entitled *Speaking with a Boneless Tongue* (Jardine, 1992). The name of the press I used was MAKYO*PRESS, and its origin was here:

> *Makyo*, "mysterious vision" [is] a deep dream experience. Certain religious traditions place great importance on *makyo*. Visions and heavenly voices are seriously considered to be signs of enlightenment and salvation. These phenomena may be of general interest, for they reveal the rich potential of human experience, but they reveal little of the true nature of the one who experiences them. If you do experience it you can recognize that you are walking near your true home [but] no matter how interesting and encouraging *makyo* may be, they are self-limited. (Aitken, 1982, p. 46)

The last two chapters of that old book have the same title, "She Unnames Them." It is an essay by Ursula LeGuin from the book *Buffalo Gals and other Animal Presences* (1987)—Eve giving back the names that were imposed by God, especially the generic ones like man, and woman, and dog and such like. The essay came to mind recently because that wee 'un asleep on my sleepy belly was not named for several weeks after his arrival.

Another chance to go back and read that essay more seriously all these years later, to try to decode my low-level bemused uneasiness at that namelessness.

I ended up, of course, writing about it. See above, the chapter called "How shall you be called?"

So I am, warm baby-full, still wondering about why study, about the future, still believing, it seems, that the right form of studiousness (in line with the persistent analogy—all about relations, interdependencies, kinships, sustainability, warrant, good work, attachments and giving them up, distraction and quelling ourselves into careful thinking and action) just might, well what? Save the world? Still, I hesitate and let the soreness expand under our breaths and dissipate.

This trail, already cited above:

> Since you are using a method to bring even basic sufferings into the path, you greatly lessen your suffering, so you can bear it. (Tsong-Kha-Pa, 2000, pp. 172–173)

I need to *bear it*—endure it, undergo it, traverse its trails and trials, sing as I go so others can hear, untie knots in this old world and in me, try as I can to not pass my own weakness in all this along the way. This is why I read. This is why I write (Jardine, 2014c). It is an-however meagre way I've found to bear. Let me say the secret out loud, bear the thought that I'm letting that little boy come to love me, and me him, even knowing that I must someday make him suffer my disappearance.

Wouldn't it be better to slip away now before these wounds become too deep? No. Of course not. These breaths between us. "You will notice then that *its nature is to change and drop away*" (Sumedho, 2010, p. 37, emphasis added). This thought is why I personally find Chapter 5 my most dear and nearby these days.

And why I'm ending with these little chapters long-lost. You'll notice lots of other recitations, dangling images, woes and joys long familiar if you've made it this far.

Finding that these why-study? woes are old, long, well-trodden paths. I've lived through many futures that I didn't have. I know that that baby and I breath precious airs full of eco-monstrosities. Still, the spot on my solar plexus warms and fits his inhales.

Study is my comfort, then and now. I lie, here, dozing off and thinking and composing—words, our common body, our dreams. It is an ecological, hermeneutic and Buddhist thing, this comfort: strength held in common, between us

So, then, the last chapter starts to end.

CHAPTER FORTY of "Speaking with a Boneless Tongue"

> Grief is not a permanent state;
> it is a room with a door on the other wall. (Bly, n.d., p. 11)

once upon a time ther was a rain drop and it gope on a bird then the sun trd into a watrvapr the radrop fad his bovrsrs and trnd into a fofe white cloud and then it trnd in too a havie plak kloub and then it trd in bake to the sam radrop and gropt on the sam bird.

Name Eric

(Once upon a time there was a raindrop and it dropped on a bird. Then the sun turned it into water vapour and the raindrop left his brothers and turned into a fluffy white cloud and then it turned into a heavy black cloud and then it turned back into the same raindrop and dropped on the same bird.)

Grief is not a permanent state;
it is a room with a door on the other wall. (Bly, n.d., p. 11)

The very urge to write these tales, though they go unpublished and unread, is itself a telling. For this new form of fiction enters our age driven with fierce compulsion. We want to get it down, there is so much to tell about. This craven trivia is so momentously important because history is now taking place in the soul and the soul has again entered history. (Hillman, 1983, p. 48)

Again:

Writers know that they cannot introspect their characters. Their scenes come of themselves and their figures speak, walk in and out. With few people is a writer more intimate than with his characters and yet they continue to surprise him with their autonomy. Besides, they are not concerned with "me" but with the world they inhabit and which refers to me, the introspecter, only obliquely. The relativization of the author (who is making up whom, who is writing whom) goes along with the fictional mode. One wavers between losing control and putting words in their mouths. But introspection will not solve this problem, only the act of fictioning further. The action is in the plot ... and only the characters know what's going on. (p. 59)

In writing, I cannot introspect myself but find myself founded in unsuspecting tales ... all betraying me in the end, flighty boy come crash.

Grief is not a permanent state;
it is a room with a door on the other wall. (Bly, n.d., p. 11)

My own breath robbed by asthma as a child and the breathtaking love I have for the adventures of language and the blither of a boneless tongue.

Grief is not a permanent state;

it is a room with a door on the other wall. (Bly, n.d., p. 11)

This book, ["Grief is"] in the end, *is* ["not a permanent state"] about me ["it is a room"] however obliquely angled ["with a door"] through this world ["a room"] for which I am ["Grief"] culpable beyond revoke. Wound:

> Wounds need to be expanded into air, lifted up on ideas our ancestors knew, so that the wound ascends through the roof of our parents' house, and we suddenly see how our wound (seemingly so private) *fits*. (Bly, n.d., p. 14)

This is where hermeneutics catches the breath, wormsquirming: striving to write about being ecologically mindful is *insane* without at once striving to *be* ecologically mindful. The difference between what I have written and how I live can be hidden from everyone else, especially when writing attains a certain gracefulness and cadence.

CHAPTER FORTY-ONE of "Speaking with a Boneless Tongue"

> The *puer aeternus* figure is the vision of our own first nature, our primordial golden shadow, our affinity to beauty, our angelic essence as messenger of the divine, as divine message. From the puer we are given our sense of destiny and mission, of having a message and being meant as eternal cup-bearer to the divine, that our sap and overflow, our enthusiastic wetness of soul, is in service to the Gods. (Hillman, 2013c, p. 223)

> We came as infants, "trailing clouds of glory," arriving from the farthest reaches of the universe, bringing with us appetites well preserved from our mammal inheritances, spontaneities wonderfully preserved from our 150,000 years of tree life, angers well preserved from our 5,000 years of tribal life, in short, with our 360-degree radiance and we offered this gift to our parents. They didn't want it. They wanted a nice girl or a nice boy. (Bly, 1988, p. 24)

Grief is not a permanent state;

it is a room with a door on the other wall. (Bly, n.d., p. 11)

CHAPTER FORTY-TWO of "Speaking with a Boneless Tongue"

[I carry] a general scepticism toward all ideas which are used as sources of legitimacy by the winners of the world. I should like to believe that the task … is to make greater demands on those who mouth the certitudes of their times and are closer to the powerful and rich, than to the faiths and ideas of the powerless and marginalized. That way lies freedom, compassion and justice.

So Ashis Nandy ends his "Cultural Frames for Social Transformation: A Credo" (1987, p. 123), pleading the right to end "on a personal note."

I read this again and again, haunted by the ways in which I myself am a winner of the world: white, male, European descent, high income, well-housed, well-fed, well-educated, well-read, exuding a wellness which unintentionally preys on the weak, which unintentionally *creates* sicknesses to sustain itself at the expense of others.

Everything I have to say issues from this wellness I carry, somehow. Everything I do is rooted in an ease which is easy for a winner of the world.

> Mourning.
> Grief is not a permanent state;
> it is a room with a door on the other wall. (Bly, n.d., p. 11)

This door is not simply mine to open when I will it.

This corridor lengthens as I walk. The door has a handle on the hitherside.

The effort and urgency and attention and grief that has gone into this book, this laborious and earnest writing and re-writing—all this seems so very *opulent*. Writing of ecological mindfulness while housed on 20 acres in the foothills of the Rocky Mountains. So very *opulent*:

> How can I, as an educator, fulfil my responsibility to my own people; my own people whom I love yet who, like I do, live under an economic and epistemological dispensation which is the *problem* for most of the world? (D.G. Smith, 2020l, p. 181)

CHAPTER FORTY-THREE of "Speaking with a Boneless Tongue"

As their grief and fear of the world is allowed to be expressed without apology or argument, and validated as a wholesome, life-preserving response, people break through their avoidance mechanisms, break through their sense of futility and isolation. And generally they break *into* a larger sense of identity. It is as if the pressure of their acknowledged awareness of the suffering of our world stretches, or collapses, the culturally defined boundaries of the self. The grief and fear experienced for our world and our common future is categorically different from similar sentiments relating to one's personal welfare. This pain cannot be equated with dread of one's own individual demise. Its source lies less in concerns for personal survival than in an apprehension of collective suffering, of what looms for human life and other species and unborn generations to come. Its nature is akin to the original meaning of compassion: "suffering with." It is the distress we feel on behalf of the whole of which we are a part. There is immeasurable pain in our society, a pain carried at some level by each and every individual, over what is happening to our world and our future. Given our culture's fear of pain and the high value it sets on optimism, feelings of despair are repressed. Hidden like a secret sore, they breed a sense of isolation. But when one's pain for the world is redefined as compassion, it serves as a trigger or gateway to a more encompassing sense of identity. It is seen as part of the connective tissue that binds us to all beings. The self is experienced as inseparable from the web of life in which we are all intricately interconnected. (Macy, 1989, p. 204)

SECOND-LAST CHAPTER of "Speaking with a Boneless Tongue"

"She Unnames Them"

Our conclusion ends in the ambivalence of mythical images. Our tension is unresolved. In the soft light of the dust world we cannot see clearly. It may be day's end and a darkening of the light. The morning star—is it Lucifer? The ape—is he man's fallen angel? The revelation that is at hand, that Second Coming, may be the rough beast of Yeats and Picasso, slouching towards Bethlehem. The beast may be but a beast, the blood-dimmed tide of anarchy, a gibbering ape at nightfall, the princely power, *simia dei*, its hour come round at last, bringing a new reign of Egyptian darkness. Or the soft light may be

Aurora consurgens of a new millennium, of sun and moon together, *sapientia* and *caritas* conjoined, where wisdom and madness felicitously embrace each other: an altogether new kind of day that the baboon heralds, and gives us the eye with which to see.

Either/or, yet one thing is certain: we cannot go down to the ape … on which the future depends without a metamorphosis of our main God, our own individual enclosed consciousness, sustained in its ego-tension and ego-brightness by the senex-puer polarity. We may leave our transitions of generations in ambivalence. These images from myth and nature may indicate a new relationship that is the oldest: our dependence as humans upon the divine light of natural consciousness. This soft light is pre-conscious, at the threshold always dawning, fresh as milk, at dawn with each day's dream, still streaked with primordial anarchy. (Hillman, 2013c, p. 241)

LAST CHAPTER of "Speaking with a Boneless Tongue"

"She Unnames Them"

It is not writing. Not poetry, not prose. I am not a writer. Yet it is in my throat, stomach, arms. This book that I am not able to write. There are words that insist in silence. Words that betray me. The words make me sleep. They keep me awake. (Gunnars, 1989, Section One)

REFERENCES

Abram, D. (1996). *The spell of the sensuous: Language in a more-than-human world.* Pantheon Books.

Abram, D. (2011). *Becoming animal: An earthly cosmology.* Vintage Books.

Adams, D., & Jardine, D. (2023). *Dod yn ôl at fy nghoed*: Trees, woods and a balanced state of mind. *Forum for Comprehensive Education, 65*(2), 118–128. https://doi.org/10.3898/FORUM.2023.65.2.12

Adams, D., & Jardine, D. (under consideration). "Found under a foot of snow": A conversation about some hidden legacies of curriculum and schools. *Journal of Philosophy of Education.*

Aho, K. (2018). Neurasthenia revisited: On medically unexplained syndromes and the value of hermeneutic medicine. *Journal of Applied Hermeneutics*, Article 6. https://jah.journalhosting.ucalgary.ca/jah/index.php/jah/article/view/174/pdf

Aitken, R. (1982). *Taking the Path of Zen.* North Point Press.

Arendt, H. (1969). The crisis in education. In *Between past and present: Eight exercises in political thought.* Penguin Books.

Associated Press. (2016a). Trump in Nevada: "I love the poorly educated." Published February 23, 2016. Accessed online: https://www.youtube.com/watch?v=Vpdt7omPoa0

Associated Press. (2016b). *Mayor, local official under fire after racist social media post about Michelle Obama.* Posted November 14, 2016. https://www.cbsnews.com/news/mayor-local-official-west-virginia-controversy-racist-michelle-obama-social-media-post/

Ayres, L. (1915). *A measuring scale for ability in spelling.* donpotter.net

Bastock, M., & Jardine, D. (2005). Children's literacy, the *Biblia Pauperum* and the wiles of images. *Journal of Curriculum and Pedagogy, 2*(2), 65–69.

Bayer, T.I. (2008). Vico's principle of sensus communis and forensic eloquence. *Chicago-Kent Law Review, 83*(3), 113–1155.

Beamer, K. (2017). And Coyote howled: Listening to the call of interpretive inquiry. *Journal of Applied Hermeneutics.* http://hdl.handle.net/10515/sy5n010b1

Beard, G. (1881). *American nervousness, its causes and consequences: A supplement to nervous exhaustion (neurasthenia).* G.P. Putnam's Sons.

Beasley, D. (2020, March 23). *Arizona man dies, wife in critical condition after taking aquarium cleaner containing malaria drug for coronavirus.* The National Post. https://nationalpost.com/news/arizona-man-dies-after-taking-chloroquine-for-coronavirus

Beaulne-Stuebing, L. (2023). How Indigenous yogis and meditators are adapting and reclaiming "wellness." Unreserved. CBC Radio. Posted January 14, 2023. https://www.cbc.ca/radio/unreserved/indigenous-wellness-yoga-1.6713178

Berman, D. (1998). The wild kindness. In *American Water* by The Silver Jews [CD]. Lyrics by David Berman. Drag City Records, DC149.

Berry, W. (1975/2019). Damage. In *Wendell Berry: Essays 1969–1990* (pp. 663–666). Library of America.

Berry, W. (1983). *Standing by words.* North Point Press.

Berry, W. (1986). *The unsettling of America.* Sierra Book Club.

Berry, W. (1987). *Home Economics.* North Point Press.

Berry, W. (2009). *The gift of good land: Further essays, cultural and agricultural.* Counterpoint.

Berry, W. (2012). *It all turns on affection: The Jefferson lecture and other essays.* Counterpoint.

Berry, W., with Moyers, B. (2013). Writer and farmer Wendell Berry on hope, direct action, and the "resettling" of the American countryside. *Yes Magazine.* Posted October 11, 2013. http://www.yesmagazine.org/planet/mad-farmer-wendell-berry-gets-madder-in-defense-of-earth

Biblical hermeneutics stack exchange. https://hermeneutics.stackexchange.com

Bly, R. (n.d.). *When a hair turns to gold.* Ally Press.

Bly, R. (1988). *A little book on the human shadow.* Harper and Row.

Bly, R. (2008). *Advice from the geese.* http://www.poets.org/poetsorg/poem/advice-geese, n.p.

Bowers, C.A. (2008). *Transitions: Educational reforms that promote ecological intelligence or the assumptions underlying modernity?* University of Oregon Libraries. https://scholarsbank.uoregon.edu/xmlui/handle/1794/3067

Boyle, D. (2006). The man who made us all work like this …. *BBC History Magazine,* June 2 2003. http://www.davidboyle.co.uk/history/frederickwinslowtaylor.html

Bordo, S. (1987). *The flight to objectivity.* State University of New York Press.

Bransford, J., Brown, A., & Cocking, R. (Eds.). (2000). *How people learn: Brain, mind, experience and school.* National Academies Press.

Braverman, H. (1998). *Labor and monopoly capital: The degradation of work in the twentieth century.* Monthly Review Press.

Buckley-Houston, T. (2014). Twitter post, January 2, 2014. https://twitter.com/twombh/status/418712720246984704.

Bush, G.W. (2010). *Sept. 20, 2001—Bush declares war on terror. A speech to the congress.* https://www.youtube.com/watch?v=_CSPbzitPL8

Callahan, B. (1999). Teenage spaceship. In *Knock Knock* [CD], recorded under the name Smog. Drag City Records, DC 161. Rough Trade Publishing.

Callahan, B. (2019a). Writing. In *Shepherd in a Sheepskin Vest* [CD]. Drag City Records #DC747. Released June 14, 2019. Rough Trade Publishing.

Callahan, B. (2019b). Young Icarus. In *Shepherd in a Sheepskin Vest* [CD]. Drag City Records #DC747. Released June 14, 2019. Rough Trade Publishing.

Callahan, B. (2020). 35. Lyrics © Universal Music Publishing Group. The song appears oBill Callahan (2020). *Gold Record.* Drag City Records, Released September 4, 2020. Catalogue # DC760 (see https://www.dragcity.com/products/gold-record).

Callahan, B. (2022a). Coyotes. In *YTIЈAЯЯ* [CD]. Drag City Records catalog # DC859. Released October 14, 2022.

Callahan, B. (2022b). Planets. In *YTIЈAЯЯ* [CD]. Drag City Records catalog #DC859. Released October 14, 2022.

Callahan, R. (1964). *America, education and the cult of efficiency.* University of Chicago Press.

Calvino, I. (2016). *Six memos for the next millennium.* Mariner Books.

Campbell, A. (2013). Breathe in, breathe out: A way to conquer students' stress. *The Globe and Mail,* March 1, 2013. http://www.theglobeandmail.com/news/natio nal/education/breathe-in-breathe-out-a-way-to-conquer-students-stress/article 9156091/

Campbell, D. (1998). *Writing security: United States foreign policy and the politics of identity.* University of Minnesota Press.

Campbell, J., & Moyers, B. (2013). *The power of myth* [DVD]. e-One Films. *Canada's Residential Schools: The History, Part 1 Origins to 1939: Final Report of the Truth and Reconciliation Commission of Canada* (Vol. 1) [PDF]. National Centre for Truth and Reconciliation. Truth and Reconciliation Commission of Canada, 2015.

Canadian Press. (2013). *Why are B.C.'s Orcas falling silent?* Posted October 24, 2013. http://www.theprovince.com/travel/Orca+pods+longer+vocalizing+Vancou ver+Aquarium+researcher+finds/9078918/story.html

Caputo, J. (1987). *Radical hermeneutics: Repetition, deconstruction, and the hermeneutic project.* Indiana University Press.

Carr, N. (2013, October 25). *Frederick Taylor and the quantified self.* Rough Type. http://www.roughtype.com/?p=3888

Carruthers, M. (2003). *The craft of thought: Meditations, rhetoric, and the making of images, 400–1200.* Cambridge University Press.

Carruthers, M. (2005). *The book of memory: A study of memory in medieval culture.* Cambridge University Press.

CBC News. (2019). *Calgary students rally for the planet, asking "Why study for a future we won't have?"* CBC News. Posted May 24, 2019. https://www.cbc.ca/news/canada/calgary/calgary-climate-strike-action-1.5149314

Chah, A. (1987). *Our real home: A talk to an aging lay disciple approaching death.* Access to Insight. http://www.accesstoinsight.org/lib/thai/chah/bl111.html

Chah, A. (2001). *Being Dharma: The essence of the Buddha's teachings.* Shambala Press.

Chah, A. (2005). *Food for the heart.* Wisdom Publications.

Chatwin, B. (1988). *The songlines* (repr. ed.). Penguin Canada.

Chaucer. (n.d.). *The tale of Melibee.* Paragraph 63072. http://librarius.com/canttran/melibee/melibeetr63-72.htm

Chodron, P. (2007). *No time to lose: A timely guide to the way of the Bodhisattva.* Shambhala.

Chomsky, N. (2017). *How to deal with the Trump presidency.* Published January 16, 2017. https://www.youtube.com/watch?v=7hw_0Ufxpzs&t=11s

Clifford, J. (1986). On ethnographic allegory. In J. Clifford & G. Marcus (Eds.), *Writing culture: The poetics and politics of ethnography.* University of California Press.

Clifford, P., & Friesen, S. (1993). A curious plan: Managing on the twelfth. *Harvard Educational Review, 63*(3), 339–358.

Clifford, P., Friesen, S., & Jardine, D. (2008). Whatever happens to him happens to us: Reading Coyote reading the world, Patricia. In D. Jardine, P. Clifford, & S. Friesen (Eds.), *Back to the basics of teaching and learning: "Thinking the world together"* (pp. 67–78). Routledge.

Cohen, L. (2016). Press conference for *You Want It Darker.* Chris Douridas, interviewer. A Lazy Bastard in a Suit (ALBIAS). Posted November 27, 2016. https://www.youtube.com/watch?time_continue=2&v=RciOCn_Nmh0

Doyle, A. (2003). *Sherlock Holmes: The complete novels and stories.* Bantam Classics.

Cubberley, E.P. (1922). *A brief history of education: A history of the practice and progress and organization of education.* Houghton Mifflin.

Curry, A. (2020). Re-reading future shock 50 years on. https://www.resilience.org/stories/2020-02-12/re-reading-future-shock-50-years-on/

David Suzuki Foundation. (2011, August 17). *David Suzuki & Thich Nhat Hanh: Despair* [Video File]. https://www.youtube.com/watch?v=RWqB4-em308

Dawson, C. (1998). Translator's introduction to H.G. Gadamer (1998). *Praise of theory: Speeches and essays* (pp. xv–xxxviii). Yale University Press.

Dawson, R. (2013/2015a). From the liner notes to his CD *The Glass Trunk.* Domino Records, REWIGCD95.

Dawson, R. (2017a). *Times for revulsion: Richard Dawson talks Peasant with Michael Hann. The Quietus.* April 6, 2017. http://thequietus.com/articles/22157-richard-dawson-peasant-interview-michael-hann

Dawson, R. (2017b). Weaver. In *Peasant* [CD]. Released by Weird World Records WEIRD08CD.

DeChristopher, T., & Berry, W. (2020, March 2). To live and love with a dying world. *Orion Magazine.* https://orionmagazine.org/article/to-live-and-love-with-a-dying-world/

D'emilio, F. (2021) *Pope voices sorrow over residential school deaths but doesn't apologize.* CTVNews. https://www.ctvnews.ca/world/pope-voices-sorrow-over-resident ial-school-deaths-but-doesn-t-apologize-1.5458352

Derby, M. (2015). *Towards a critical eco-hermeneutic approach to education: Place, being, relation* (pp. xv–xxiii). Peter Lang.

Derrida, J., & Ferraris, M. (2001). *A taste for the secret.* Polity Press.

Descartes, R. (1955). *Descartes selections.* Charles Scribner's Sons.

Doctor, T.H. (2014). Translators' introduction to *Ornament of the Great Vehicle Sutras: Maitreya's Mahayanasutralamakara* (pp. vii–xvi). Snow Lion.

Dogen. (2007). *Shobogenzo: The treasure house of the eye of the true teaching* (H. Nearman, Trans.). Shasta Abbey Press.

Domanski, D. (2002). The wisdom of falling. In T. Bowling (Ed.), *Where the words come from Canadian poets in conversation* (pp. 244–255). Nightwood Editions.

Domanski, D. (2010). *All our wonder unavenged.* Brick Books.

Domanski, D. (2013). *Bite down little whisper.* Brick Books.

Domanski, D. (2021). *Fetishes of the floating world.* Brick Books.

Duhamel, R. (1966). *Copy of Treaty and Supplementary Treaty no. 7, made 22nd Sept., and 4th Dec., 1877, between her majesty the queen and the Blackfeet and other Indian tribes, at the Blackfoot crossing of bow river and Fort MacLeod.* Queen's Printer and Controller of Stationary. Cat. No.: Ci 72-0766. IAND Publication No. QS-0575-000-EE-A. https://www.canadiancrown.com/uploads/3/8/4/1/3841927/treaty_7.pdf

Fields, R. (1990). [Untitled]. Cited in the Introduction to Catherine Ingram (1990). *In the footsteps of Ghandi: Conversations with spiritual social activists* (p. xiv). Parallax Press.

DuFour, R., & Eaker, R. (1998). Professional learning communities at work: Best practices for enhancing student achievement. In *A new model: The professional learning community.* The Eisenhower National Clearinghouse for Mathematics and Science Education (ENC). http://www.myeport.com/published/t/uc/tucson73/collect ion/1/4/upload.doc

Eliade, M. (1968). *Myth and reality.* Harper & Row.

Eno, B. (2022). Official lyric video to Brian Eno's "We Let It In." In *ForeverAndEverNoMore* [CD]. Opla, UMC. [Lyric Video]. https://www.youtube.com/watch?v=Dehxp3PU TkM&ab_channel=BrianEnoVEVO

Fish, S. (1980). *Is there a text in this class?* Harvard University Press.

Foster, H. (2018, April 5). Smash the screen. A review of H. Steyer (2017). Duty free art: Art in the age of planetary civil war. London, UK: Verso Books. In *London review of books* (pp. 40–41). https://www.lrb.co.uk/v40/n07/hal-foster/smash-the-screen

Friesen, S. (2009). *What did you do in school today? Teaching effectiveness: A framework and rubric.* Canadian Education Association. https://galileo.org/publication/what-did-you-do-in-school-today-teach ing- effectiveness-a-framework-and-rubric/

Friesen, S. (2010, October). Uncomfortable bedfellows: Discipline-based inquiry and standardized examinations. *Teacher Librarian: The Journal for School Library*

Professionals. http://www.encyclopedia.com/Teacher+Librarian/publications.aspx?pageNumber=1

Friesen, S., & Jardine, D. (2009). On field(ing) knowledge. In S. Goodchild & B. Sriraman (Eds.), *Relatively and philosophically E[a]rnest: Festschrifte in honour of Paul Ernest's 65th birthday. The Montana mathematics enthusiast: Monograph series in mathematics education* (pp. 149–175). Information Age Publishing.

Friesen, S., & Jardine, D. (2010). 21st century learners and learning. A report prepared for the *Western and Northern Canadian curriculum protocol for collaboration in education/ Protocole de l'Ouest et du Nord Canadiens de Collaboration Concernant L'Education.* http://education.alberta.ca/media/1087278/wncp%2021st%20cent%20learning%20(2).pdf

Gadamer, H.G. (1970, Winter). Concerning empty and ful-filled time. *Southern Journal of Philosophy,* pp. 341–353.

Gadamer, H.-G. (1977). *Philosophical hermeneutics.* University of California Press.

Gadamer, H.-G. (1983). *Reason in the age of science.* MIT Press.

Gadamer, H.G. (1984). The hermeneutics of suspicion. *Man and World, 17,* 313–323.

Gadamer, H.-G. (1986). The idea of the university—yesterday, today, tomorrow. In D. Misgeld & G. Nicholson (Eds. & Trans.), *Hans-Georg Gadamer on education, poetry, and history* (pp. 47–62). SUNY Press.

Gadamer, H.G. (1989). *Truth and method.* Continuum Press.

Gadamer, H.-G. (1994). *Heidegger's ways.* MIT Press.

Gadamer, H.G. (1996) *The enigma of health.* Stanford University Press.

Gadamer, H.-G. (2001). *Gadamer in conversation: Reflections and commentary* (R. Palmer, Ed. & Trans.). Yale University Press.

Gadamer, H.-G. (2007a). The artwork in word and image: "So true, so full of Being." In H.-G. Gadamer, *The Gadamer reader: A bouquet of later writings* (R. Palmer, Ed. & Trans.) (pp. 195–224). Northwestern University Press.

Gadamer, H.G. (2007b). Aesthetics and hermeneutics. In R.E. Palmer (Ed.), *The Gadamer reader: A Bouquet of the later writings* (pp. 124–131). Northwestern University Press.

Gadamer, H.-G. (2007c). From word to concept: The task of hermeneutic philosophy. In R. Palmer (Ed.), *The gadamer reader: A bouquet of later writings* (pp. 108–120). Northwestern University Press.

Gadamer, H.-G. (2007d). Text and interpretation. In R. Palmer (Ed.), *The Gadamer reader: A bouquet of later writing* (pp. 156–191). Northwestern University Press.

Gadamer, H.-G. (2007e). Hermeneutics and the ontological difference. In R. Palmer (Ed. & Trans.), *The Gadamer reader: A bouquet of the later writings* (pp. 356–371). Northwestern University Press.

Gadamer, H.G. (2007f). Hermeneutics as practical philosophy. In R.E. Palmer (Ed. & Trans.), *The Gadamer reader: A bouquet of the later writings* (pp. 227–245). Northwestern University Press.

Gatto, J.T. (2003). *Against school: How public education cripples our kids, and why.* http://www.spinninglobe.net/againstschool.htm

Gatto, J. (2006). *The national press attack on academic schooling.* http://www.rit. edu/~cma8660

Geddes, L. (2019). *The mood-altering power of the Moon.* BBC Future. Posted online July 31, 2019. https://www.bbc.com/future/article/20190731-is-the-moon-impact ing-your-mood-and-wellbeing

George, T. (2017). Grieving as limit situation of memory: Gadamer, Beamer, and Moules on the Infinite task posed by the dead. *Journal of Applied Hermeneutics.* http://jah. journalhosting.ucalgary.ca/jah/index.php/jah/article/view/163

Gerstmann, E. (2021, March 22). What is cancel culture? *Forbes.* https://www.forbes. com/sites/evangerstmann/2021/03/22/what-is-cancelculture/?sh=566c15febd55

Gray, J. (2001). *False dawn: The delusions of global capitalism.* Granta Books.

Greeno, J. (1991). Number sense as situated knowing in a conceptual domain. *Journal for Research in Mathematics Education, 22*(3), 170–218.

Grondin, J. (1994). *Introduction to philosophical hermeneutics.* Yale University Press.

Gunnars, K (1989). *The Prowler* (Section 1). Red Deer College Press.

Habermas, J. (1972). *Knowledge and human interests.* Beacon Books.

Hanh, T. (1999). *The miracle of mindfulness: An introduction to the practice of meditation.* Beacon Press.

Haraway, D. (2016). *Staying with the trouble: Making kin in the chthulucene.* Duke University Press.

Harris, S. (2018, February). Review of Sufjan Stevens (2017), The Greatest Gift. Mix Tape. Outtakes, Remixes and Demos from Carrie and Lowell (Stevens, 2015). *Mojo: The Music Magazine, 291.* Academic House.

Hayday, M. (2017). Sir Hector-Louis Langevin, "Architect" of residential schools? https://activehistory.ca/2017/06/langevin/

Heidegger, M. (1926/1962). *Being and time.* Harper and Row.

Heidegger, M. (1971). The origin of the work of art. In M. Heidegger (Ed.), *Poetry language, thought* (pp. 15–88). Harper and Row.

Heidegger, M. (1977). The turning. In M. Heidegger (Ed.), *The question concerning technology and other essays* (pp. 36–52). Harper Colophon Books.

Heidegger, M. (1978). *The metaphysical foundations of logic.* Indiana University Press.

Hiatt, J. (2003). How Bob Dylan changed my life. *Harp Magazine Online: Harp Guides.* https://www.harpmagazine.com/reviews/cd_reviews/detail.cfm?article _id=1206

Hogan, L. (1995). *Dwellings: A spiritual history of the living world.* W.W. Norton.

Hogan, M. (2020). OK Boomer: How Bob Dylan's new JFK song helps explain 2020. *Vanity Fair,* March 27, 2020. https://www.vanityfair.com/style/2020/03/how-bob-dylans-new-jfk-song-helps- explain-2020

Hillman, J. (1983). *Healing fiction.* Spring Publications.

Hillman, J. (1991). *Inter/views.* Spring Publications.

Hillman, J. (1996). *Healing fiction.* Spring Publications.

Hillman, J. (2006a). Segregation of beauty. In *City and soul* (pp. 187–193). Spring Publications.

Hillman, J. (2006b). The repression of beauty. In *City and soul* (pp. 172–186). Spring Publications.

Hillman, J. (2006c). Anima mundi: Returning the soul to the world. In *City and soul* (pp. 27–49). Spring Publications.

Hillman, J. (2006a). Loving the world anyway. In *City and soul* (pp. 128–130). Spring Publications.

Hillman, J. (2008). Human being as animal being: A correspondence with John Stockwell. In *Animal presences* (pp. 161–169). Spring Publications.

Hillman, J. (2013a). Senex and puer: An aspect of the historical and psychological present. In *Senex and puer* (pp. 28–66). Spring Publications.

Hillman, J. (2013b). Notes on opportunism. In *Senex and puer* (pp. 91–109). Spring Publications.

Hillman, J. (2013c). Puer's wounds and Ulysses' scar. In *Senex and puer* (pp. 206–241). Spring Publications.

Hillman, J., & Shamdasani, S. (2013). *Lament of the dead: Psychology after Jung's Red Book.* W.W. Norton.

Hillman, J., & Ventura, M. (1992). *We've had a hundred years of psychotherapy—and the world's getting worse.* HarperOne.

Hitchens, C., & Taylor, L. (2011). *Christopher Hitchens—in confidence: Interview with Laurie Taylor.* https://www.youtube.com/watch?v=NozRjiFL6Z4

Hongzhi, Z. (1991). *Cultivating the empty Field: The silent illumination of Zen master* (T.D. Leighton & Y. Wu, Trans.). North Point Press.

Huizinga, J. (1955). *Homo ludens: A study of the play element in culture.* Beacon Press.

Huntington, S. (2003). *The clash of civilizations and the remaking of world order.* Simon and Schuster Paperbacks.

Husserl, E. (1970a). *Cartesian meditations.* Martinus Nijhoff.

Husserl, E. (1970b). *The crisis of European science and transcendental phenomenology.* Northwestern University Press.

Hyde, L. (1983). *The gift: Imagination and the erotic life of property.* Vintage Books.

Ignace (Stsmél'ecqen), R.E. (2008). *Our oral histories are our iron posts: Secwepemc stories and historical consciousness* [Ph.D. Dissertation]. Simon Fraser University, Department of Sociology and Anthropology, Simon Fraser University.

Illich, I. (1989). *The shadow that the future throws. Text based on a conversation between Nathan Gardels and Ivan Illich in 1989.* http://davidtinapple.com/illich/1989_shadow_future.PDF

Illich, I. (1992). *In the mirror of the past: Lectures and addresses 1978–1990.* Marion Boyars.

Illich, I. (1993). *In the vineyard of the text: A commentary on Hugh's Didascalicon.* University of Chicago Press.

Illich, I (1996). *The right to useful unemployment and its professional enemies.* Marion Boyars.

Illich, I. (1998). *The cultivation of conspiracy.* https://www.davidtinapple.com/illich

Illich, I. (2000). Disabling professions. In I. Illich, I. Zola, J. McKnight, U. Caplan, and H. Shaiken (Eds.), *Disabling professions* (pp. 11–40). Marion Boyars.

Illich, I., & Cayley, D. (1992). *Ivan Illich in conversation*. House of Anansi Press.

Innes, J. (2016a). Excerpt from "Time." In J. Seidel & D. Jardine (Eds.), *The ecological heart of teaching: Radical tales of refuge and renewal for classrooms and communities* (p. 117). Peter Lang.

Innes, J. (2016b). Excerpts from "A pocket of darkness" and "time." In J. Seidel & D. Jardine (Eds.), *The ecological heart of teaching: Radical tales of refuge and renewal for classrooms and communities* (p. 110). Peter Lang.

Jardine, D. (1988a). Piaget's clay and Descartes' wax. *Educational Theory, 38*(3), 287–298.

Jardine, D. (1988b). Play and hermeneutics: An exploration of the bi-polarities of mutual understanding. *Journal of Curriculum Theorizing, 8*(2), 23–42.

Jardine, D. (1990a). On the humility of mathematical language. *Educational Theory, 40*(2), 181–192.

Jardine, D. (1990b). "To dwell with a boundless heart": On the integrated curriculum and the recovery of the Earth. *Journal of Curriculum and Supervision, 5*(2), 107–119.

Jardine, D. (1990c). Awakening from Descartes' nightmare: On the love of ambiguity in phenomenological approaches to education. *Studies in Philosophy and Education, 10*(1), 211–232.

Jardine, D. (1992a). Reflections on hermeneutics, education and ambiguity: Hermeneutics as a restoring of life to its original difficulty. In W. Pinar & W. Reynolds (Eds.), *Understanding curriculum as a phenomenological and deconstructed text* (pp. 116–130). Teacher's College Press.

Jardine, D. (1992b). *Speaking with a boneless tongue*. Makyo Press.

Jardine, D. (1993). A bell ringing in the empty sky. *Journal of Curriculum Theorizing, 10*(2), 17–37.

Jardine, D. (1994). "Littered with literacy": An ecopedagogical reflection on whole language, pedocentrism and the necessity of refusal. *Journal of Curriculum Studies, 26*(5), 509–524.

Jardine, D. (1996). "Under the tough old stars": Pedagogical hyperactivity and the mood of environmental education. *Canadian Journal of Environmental Education, 1*, 48–55.

Jardine, D. (1997). "All beings are your ancestors": A bear Sutra on ecology, Buddhism and pedagogy. *The Trumpeter: A Journal of Ecosophy, 14*(3), 122–133.

Jardine, D. (1998a). Birding lessons and the Teachings of Cicadas. *Canadian Journal of Environmental Education, 3*, 92–99. https://cjee.lakeheadu.ca/article/view/340

Jardine, D. (1998b). A bell ringing in the empty sky. In D. Jardine (Eds.), *"To Dwell with a Boundless Heart": On Curriculum Theory, Hermeneutics and the Ecological Imagination* (pp. 85–102). Peter Lang.

Jardine, D. (1999a). It's all one meditation. Foreword to D. Smith (Ed.), *Pedagon: interdisciplinary essays on pedagogy and culture* (pp. v–viii). Peter Lang.

Jardine, D. (1999b). A bell ringing in the empty sky. In W. Pinar (Ed.), *Contemporary curriculum discourses: Twenty years of JCT* (pp. 262–278). Peter Lang.

Jardine, D. (2000). *"Under the Tough Old Stars": Ecopedagogical essays*. Foreword by David Smith, University of Alberta. Psychology Press / Holistic Education Press.

Jardine, D. (2005). *Piaget and education: A primer*. Peter Lang.

4–14. http://www.johndeweysociety.org/the-journal-of-school-and- society/files/2018/01/Vol4_No2_2.pdf

Jardine, D. (2018). Preface: Advice in this liquid midst. To E. Lyle (Ed.), *The negotiated self: Employing reflexive inquiry to explore teacher identity* (pp. vii–xiv). Brill Sense Publishers.

Jardine, D. (2019a). Just as a bird needs two wings to fly in the sky. In *Asleep in my sunshine chair* (pp. 53–70). DIO Press.

Jardine, D. (2019b). *We have the same job we've always had ("When you're a Star," Part II).* https://www.academia.edu/38606670/_We_Have_the_Same_Job_Weve_Always_Had_"When_Youre_a_Star,"_Part_II

Jardine, D. (2020a). Introduction: "Sometimes it takes, sometimes it doesn't." From *"To know the world, we have to love it": Antiquated secrets from a teacher and a student.* https://www.academia.edu/44344648/INTRODUCTION_Sometimes_it_Takes_Sometimes_It_Doesnt_From_To_Know_the_World_We_Have_to_Love_It_Antiquated_Secretsfrom_a_Teacher_and_a_Student

Jardine, D. (2020b). *Bury the rag deep in your face, for now's the time for your tears.* https://www.academia.edu/42306871/_Bury_the_Rag_Deep_in_your_Face_For_Nows_the_Time_for_Your_Tears_

Jardine, D. (2021a). What we know full well. Special issue of the *Journal of the Canadian Association for Curriculum Studies*, "Walking: Attuning to an Earthly Curriculum," *18*(2), 36–52.

Jardine, D. (2021b). *Life-giving justice.* https://www.academia.edu/49525024/_Life_Giving_Justice_

Jardine, D. (2021c). Guest Editorial: An ode to 215 babies tossed away unmarked. *Journal of Applied Hermeneutics*, 1–5. https://doi.org/10.11575/jah.v2021i2021.72829

Jardine, D. (2021d). *Let it burn, if it comes to that.* https://www.academia.edu/52670106/Let_it_Burn_if_it_Comes_to_That

Jardine, D. (2022). Foreword: Wanting to be felt seen. In S. Blenkinsop, M. Fettes, & L. Piersol (Eds.), *Exploring ecoportraiture: The art of research when nature matters* (pp. xi–xvii). Peter Lang.

Jardine, D. (2023). *Happy as the grass was green.* https://www.academia.edu/105684420/_Happy_as_the_Grass_was_Green

Jardine, D. (in press-a). Some glimpses into the uncertain comforts of new educational practices: Canadian reflections. In C. Conn, B. Mitchell, & M. Hutt (Eds.), *Working with uncertainty for educational change: Orientations for professional practice.* Routledge.

Jardine, D. (in press-b). Portrayals of snow and hermeneutics as an early childhood educational theory. *Educational Theory, 73*(3).

Jardine, D. (in press-c). How shall you be called? *Journal of Curriculum Theorizing.*

Jardine, D., Bastock, M., George, J., & Martin, J. (2008). "Cleaving with Affection": On grain elevators and the cultivation of memory. In D. Jardine, P. Clifford, & S. Friesen, (Eds.), *Back to the basics of teaching and learning: "Thinking the world together"* (2nd ed., pp. 11–58). Routledge.

Jardine, D., & Batycky, J. (2016). Filling this empty chair: On genius and repose. In D. Jardine (Ed.), *In praise of radiant beings: A retrospective path through education, Buddhism and ecology* (pp. 107–126). Information Age Publishing.

Jardine, D., Friesen, S., & Clifford, P. (2006a). On ontology and epistemology. In D. Jardine, S. Friesen, & P. Clifford (Eds.), *Curriculum in abundance* (pp. 87–88). Lawrence Erlbaum and Associates.

Jardine, D., Friesen, S., & Clifford, P. (2006b). Introduction. In *Curriculum in abundance* (pp. 1–12). Lawrence Erlbaum and Associates.

Jardine, D., Clifford, P., & Friesen, S. (Eds.). (2008). *Back to the basics of teaching and learning: "Thinking the world together"* (2nd rev. and suppl. ed.). Routledge.

Jardine, D., Gilham, C., & McCaffrey, G. (2015). Fragment three: Bringing suffering into the path. In D. Jardine, C. Gilham, & G. McCaffrey (Eds.), *On the pedagogy of suffering: Hermeneutic and Buddhist meditations* (pp. 99–100). Peter Lang.

Jardine, D., & Lyle, E. (2022). What, then, *is* our task? *Journal of Educational Thought, 55*(1), 31–42.

Jardine, D., Naqvi, R., Jardine, E., & Zaidi, A. (2012). "A zone of deep shadow": Pedagogical and familial reflections on "The clash of civilizations." In D. Jardine (Ed.), *Pedagogy left in peace* (pp. 23–42). Continuum.

Jardine, D., & Naqvi, R. (2012). Learning not to speak in tongues. In D. Jardine (Ed.), *Pedagogy left in peace* (pp. 193–216). Continuum Press.

Jardine, D., & Rinehart, P. (1993). Relentlessness writing and the death of memory in elementary education. *Studies in Philosophy and Education, 12*, 127–137.

Jardine, G. (2012). An invitation to explore the roots of current aboriginal/non-aboriginal relations in Canada. *One World in Dialogue, 2*(1), 25–37. https://ssc.teach ers.ab.ca/SiteCollectionDocuments/OneWorldInDialogue/OneWorld%20inDialo gue%202012%20v2n1.pdf

Jóhannsson, J. (2009). *And in the endless pause there came the sound of bees.* https://www. discogs.com/J%C3%B3hann-J%C3%B3hannsson-And-In-The-Endless-Paus e-There-Came-The-Sound-Of-Bees/release/1826517

Johnson, C. (1993). *System and writing in the philosophy of Jacques Derrida.* Cambridge University Press.

Kanigel, R. (2005). *The one best way: Fredrick Winslow Taylor and the enigma of efficiency.* The MIT Press.

Kant, I. (1764/1983). What is enlightenment? From *Perpetual peace and other essays.* Hackett Publishing.

Kant, I. (2009). *The critique of judgment.* Oxford University Press.

Kermode, F. (1979). *The genesis of secrecy: On the interpretation of narrative.* Harvard University Press.

King, T. (2003). *The truth about stories: A native narrative.* Dead Dog Café Productions.

Kinnell, G. (2002). *Saint Francis and the sow.* http://www.poetryfoundation.org/ poem/171395

Klein, B., & Liptak, K. (2020, July 8). *Trump trashes CDC school-reopening guidelines—then CDC updates them.* CNN Politics. https://www.cnn.com/2020/07/08/politics/trump-cdc-school-guidelines-funding/index.html

Kongtrul, J. (2002). *Creation and completion.* Wisdom Publications.

Kovitz, R. (1997). *Room behaviour.* Insomniac Press.

Kunze, D. (2018). *Secondary places: Imagination and memory of a reverse-order universe.* © Donald Kunze. http://art3idea.psu.edu/locus/book.pdf

Latremouille, J. (2014). *Feasting on whispers: Life writing towards a pedagogy of kinship.* (Unpublished Masters thesis). University of Calgary.

Latremouille, J., Tait, L., & Jardine, D. (2021). Relations, aliveness, love: Curriculum in the spirit of the Earth. In W. Schubert & M. Fang He (Eds.), *Oxford research encyclopedias, education.* Oxford University Press. https://doi.org/10.1093/acrefore/978

Latremouille, J., Tait, L., & Jardine, D. (2024). *An ecological pedagogy of joy: On relations, aliveness and love.* Peter Lang.

Leach, W. (1994). *Land of desire: Merchants, power, and the rise of a new American culture.* New York, NY: Vintage Books.

Lee, D. (1998). Acts of dwelling, acts of love. In *Body music: Essays* (pp. 103–110, 107). House of Anansi Press.

Leggo, C. (2006). Learning by heart: A poetics of research. *Journal of Curriculum Theorizing,* Winter, pp. 73–96.

LeGuin, U. (1968). *The wizard of Earthsea.* Penguin Books.

LeGuin, U. (1987). She unnames them. In *Buffalo gals and other animal presences* (pp. 194–196). Capra Press.

LeGuin, U. (1989). Women/wildness. In J. Plant (Ed.), *Healing the wounds.* Between the Lines Press.

Leiby, J. (1991). Efficiency in social service administration: Historical reflections. *Administration in Social Work, 15*(1&2), 155–173.

Lenker, A. (2020). Zombie Girl. Lyrics, from the CD *Songs and instrumentals.* All songs performed and written by Adrianne Lenker and published by Domino Publishing Company of America, Inc. (ASCAP). CD released October, 2020, 4AD CD.

Lenker, A. (2022). Sparrow. From *Big Thief* [CD] (2021) *Dragon New Warm Mountain I Believe in You.* Released on 4AD records, February 11, 2022. 4AD0408DA.

Lobsang, G. (2006). Commentary to tsong-kha-pa. In *The harmony of emptiness and dependent-arising.* Library of Tibetan Works and Archives.

Longchenpa. (2017). *Finding rest in the nature of the mind. Trilogy of rest* (Vol. 1). Shambala Press.

Lorde, A. (1979). *The master's tools will never dismantle the master's house.* Penguin.

Loy, D. (2010). *The world is made of stories.* Wisdom Publications.

Lyle, E., Latremouille, J., & Jardine, D. (2021). Now has always been the time. Special issue of the *Journal of the Canadian Association for Curriculum Studies,* "Walking: Attuning to an Earthly Curriculum," *18*(2), 1–5.

MacPherson, C.B. (2010). *The political theory of possessive individualism.* Oxford University Press.

Macy, J. (1989). Awakening to the ecological self. In J. Plant (Ed.), *Healing the wounds: The promise of ecofeminism* (pp. 201–211). Between the Lines Press.

Macy, J. (2003). *World as lover, world as self: A guide to living fully in turbulent times.* Parallax Press.

Madden, E. (2020, September 4). *Bill Callahan leads with life's little moments on "Gold Record."* GRAMMY.com. https://www.grammy.com/grammys/news/bill-calla han-leads-lifes-little-moments-gold-record

Masters, M. (2022, January 18). *Bill Callahan and Will Oldham discuss their collaborative LP.* https://daily.bandcamp.com/features/bill-callahan-will-old ham-blind-date-party-interview

McCaskill, N.D. (2016). *Trump backs of his backpedal on Obama terror claim.* Politico. com. https://www.politico.com/story/2016/08/trump-%C2%AD%E2%80%90ob ama-%C2%AD%E2%80%90isla mic-%C2%AD%E2%80%90stat e-%C2%AD%E2%80%90sarcasm-%C2%AD%E2%80%90226947#ixzz4H9riYhSG

McCloskey, R. (1976). *Blueberries for Sal.* Puffin Books.

Melnick, C. (1997). Review of Max Van Manen and Bas Levering's *Childhood secrets: Intimacy, privacy and the self reconsidered. Journal of Curriculum Studies, 29*(3), 370–373.

Merleau-Ponty, M. (1962). *The phenomenology of perception.* Routledge.

Merleau-Ponty, M. (1970). *Signs.* Northwestern University Press.

Meschonnic, H. (1988). Rhyme and life. *Critical Inquiry, 15.*

Mitchell, F., & Lasswell, J. (2005). *A dazzle of dragonflies.* Texas A&M University Press.

Migdal, A. (2021, June 20). *182 unmarked graves discovered near residential school in B.C.'s Interior, First Nation says.* CBC News. https://www.cbc.ca/news/canada/british-columbia/bc-remains-residential-school-interior-1.6085990

Miller, A. (2002). *For your own good: Hidden cruelty in child-rearing and the roots of violence.* Farrar, Strauss and Giroux.

Miller, J.R. (2004). *Lethal legacy: Current Native controversies in Canada.* McClelland & Stewart.

Molnar, C. (2014). Life and mortality: A teacher's awakening. *In Education, 20*(4), 90–10.

Morrison, B. (2000). *The justification of Johann Gutenberg.* Random House of Canada.

Moss, C. (2014). *Now you can buy a bulletproof blanket specifically made for kids to use during school shootings.* Business Insider. http://www.businessinsider.com/bodyguard bulletproof-blanket-for-kids-2014-6.

Moules, N.J. (2015). Editorial. Aletheia—Remembering and enlivening. *Journal of Applied Hermeneutics,* Editorial 2. http://jah.journalhosting.ucalgary.ca/jah/index.php/jah/article/view/89/78

Moules, N.J. (2017). Editorial. Grief and hermeneutics: Archives of lives and the conflicted character of grief. *Journal of Applied Hermeneutics,* Editorial 1. http://hdl.handle.net/10515/sy5h708h8

Moules, N.J., & Estefan, A. (2018). Editorial: Watching my mother die—Subjectivity and the other side of dementia. *Journal of Applied Hermeneutics,* Editorial 3. https://journalhosting.ucalgary.ca/index.php/jah/article/view/57328/pdf

Moules, N., Venturato, L., Laing, C., & Field, J. (2017). Is it really "yesterday's war"? What Gadamer has to say about what gets counted. *Journal of Applied Hermeneutics*. http://jah.journalhosting.ucalgary.ca/jah/index.php/jah/article/view/140

Mount Eerie. (2017). Seaweed. From the CD *A Crow Looked at Me* released on March 24, 2017. P.W. Elverum & Sun, Ltd. Catalogue number ELV 040.

MSNBC. (2016a). How Donald Trump's ISIS talk impacts voter perceptions. From MSNBC's *Morning Joe*. Posted August 12, 2016. https://www.youtube.com/watch?v=i8lhCNrKEms

MSNBC. (2016b). Donald Trump gives away the game on outrageous talk. From the *Rachel Maddow Show*. Posted August 11, 2016. https://www.youtube.com/watch?v=ZrPjbObHSy0

Nandy, A. (1987). Cultural frames for social transformation: A credo. In A. Nandy (Ed.), *Traditions, tyranny and utopias: Essays in political awareness*. Oxford University Press.

National Research Council. (1990). *Reshaping school mathematics. Mathematical Sciences Education Board*. National Academy Press.

Newsom, J. with Paytress, M. (2015, November). "Keep your eye on the rats!" Joanna Newsom speaks to Mark Paytress. *Mojo: The Music Magazine, 264*. Academic House.

Nietzsche, F. (1975). *The will to power*. Random House.

Nishitani, K. (1982). *Religion and nothingness*. University of California.

Norris-Clarke, W. (1976). Analogy and the meaningfulness of language about God: A reply to Kai Nielsen. *The Thomist, 40*, 176–198.

Ochs, P. (1967). Crucifixion. From P. Ochs (Ed.), *The pleasures of the harbor* [CD]. A&M Records.

OED (Online Etymological Dictionary). https://www.etymonline.com/

O'Leary, K. (2012). *Dragon's Den*. Produced by the Canadian Broadcasting Company. Series 6, Episode 19, first aired March 14, 2012. www.cbc.ca/dragonsden/pitches/ukloo.

Open Book. (2013). Poets in profile: Don Domanski. Submitted by erinknight on August 28, 2013, 2:01 PM. http://openbookontario.com/news/poets_profile_d on_domanski

Paperny, A.M. (2021). Remains of 215 children found at former Indigenous school site in Canada. *Reuters*. https://www.reuters.com/world/americas/remains-215-child ren-foundformer-indigenous-school-site-canada-2021-05-28/

Patrul. (1998). *The words of my perfect teacher*. Shambhala.

Pelden, K. (2007). *The nectar of Manjushri's speech*. Shambala Books.

Peterson, R.T. (1980). *A field guide to the birds east of the Rockies* (4th ed.). Houghton Mifflin.

Piaget, J. (1965). *Insights and illusions of philosophy*. Meridian Books.

Pitctolic. (n.d.). *What do books smell like and why do we like this smell*. https://www.picto lic.com/en/article/what-do-books-smell-like-and-why-do-we-like-this-smell

Plait, P. (2014, January 1). Yes, that picture of the Moon and the Andromeda Galaxy is about right. *Slate Magazine*. https://slate.com/technology/2014/01/moon-and-andromeda-relative-size-in-the-sky.html

Postel, D., & Drury, S. (2003, October). Noble lies and perpetual war: Leo Strauss, the Neo-Cons, and Iraq. Danny Postel interviews Shadia Drury. *Information Clearing House.* http://www.informationclearinghouse.info/article5010.htm

Quintavalle, R. (2018, March 31). *Hineni*: How Leonard Cohen's parting words apply even more deeply to our plight today. In *The Opinion* section of the *National Observer.* https://www.nationalobserver.com/2018/03/31/opinion/hineni-how-leonard-cohens-parting-words-apply-even-more-deeply-our-plight-today

Quartz Staff. (2016). "I love the poorly educated"—Read Donald Trump's full Nevada Victory speech. Posted February 24, 2016. https://qz.com/623640/i-love-the-poorly-educated-read-donald-trumps-full-nevada-victory-speech/

Rai, A. (2008). On clinamen in Deleuze. Media Assemblages. https://mediaecologiesresonate.wordpress.com/2008/04/23/on-the-clinamen-and-thesimulacrum-in-deleuze/

Radin, P. (1956). *The trickster. A study in American Indian mythology.* Schocken Books.

Reibstein, M., & Young, E. (Illus.). (2008). *Wabi Sabi.* Little, Brown and Company.

Richards, M. (2006). Translator's footnotes to Pabongkha (2006). In *Liberation in the palm of your hand* (pp. 730–737). Wisdom Publications.

Richardson, M. (2013, November 13). A window that isn't there: The elusive art of Bill Callahan. *Pitchfork,* Feature Article. https://pitchfork.com/features/article/9261-a-window-that-isnt-there-the-elusive-art-of-bill-callahan/

Ricoeur, P. (1984). *Hermeneutics and the human sciences.* Cambridge University Press.

Rilke, R.M. (1904/1962). *Letters to a young poet.* Norton.

Romey, K. (2018). Exclusive: Ancient mass child sacrifice may be world's largest. *National Geographic: News.* https://news.nationalgeographic.com/2018/04/mass-child-human-animal-sacrifice-peru-chimu-science/

Ross, S.M. (2006). The temporality of tarrying in Gadamer. *Theory, Culture & Society,* 23(1), 101–123. https://doi.org/10.1177/0263276406063231

Ross, S.M., & Jardine, D. (2009). Won by a certain labour: A conversation on the while of things. *Journal of the American Association for the Advancement of Curriculum Studies,* 5. http://www.uwstout.edu/soe/jaaacs/Vol5/Ross_Jardine.htm

Said, E. (2001, October 22). The clash of ignorance. *The Nation.* http://www.thenation.com/doc/20011022/said

Saltzman, A. (2014). *A still quiet place: A mindfulness program for teaching children and adolescents to ease stress and difficult emotions.* New Harbinger Publications.

Sanders, B. (2016). Bernie Sanders revolt conversation. https://www.youtube.com/watch?v=QRg_P_5boKw.

Sartre, J.P. (1970). Intentionality: A fundamental idea in Husserl's phenomenology. *Journal for the British Society for Phenomenology, 1*(2), 3–5.

Seidel, J. (2014a). Losing wonder: Thoughts on nature, mortality, education. In J. Seidel & D. Jardine, D. (Eds.), *Ecological pedagogy, Buddhist pedagogy, hermeneutic pedagogy: experiments in a curriculum for miracles* (pp. 133–145). Peter Lang.

Seidel, J (2014b), Hymn to the North Atlantic right whale. In J. Seidel & D. Jardine, D. (2014). *Ecological pedagogy, Buddhist pedagogy, hermeneutic pedagogy: Experiments in a curriculum for miracles* (pp. 111–112). Peter Lang.

Seidel, J (2014c), A curriculum for miracles. In J. Seidel & D. Jardine (Eds.), *Ecological pedagogy, Buddhist pedagogy, hermeneutic pedagogy: Experiments in a curriculum for miracles* (pp. 7–14). Peter Lang.

Seidel, J. (2016a). Curriculum artifact: Guided reading table. In J. Seidel & D. Jardine (Eds.). *The ecological heart of teaching: Radical tales of refuge and renewal for classrooms and communities* (pp. 142–146). Peter Lang.

Seidel, J. (2016b). Hymn to the North Atlantic right whale. In J. Seidel & D. Jardine (Eds.), *Ecological pedagogy, Buddhist pedagogy, hermeneutic pedagogy: Experiments in a curriculum for miracles* (pp. 111–112). Peter Lang Publishers.

Seidel, J., Jardine, D., Bailey, D., Gray, H., Hector, M., Innes, J., Jones, C., Kowalchuk, T., Mal, N., Meredith, J., Molnar, C., Rilstone, R., Savill, T., Sirup, K., Tait, L., Taylor, L., & Vaast, D. (2014). Echolocations. In J. Seidel & D. Jardine (Eds.), *Ecological pedagogy, Buddhist pedagogy, hermeneutic pedagogy: Experiments in a curriculum for miracles* (pp. 91–110). Peter Lang Publishers.

Seidel, J., & Jardine, D (2016). *The ecological heart of teaching: Radical tales of refuge and renewal for classrooms and communities*. Peter Lang.

Seidel, J., & Jardine, D (2016a). Introduction: "We are here, we are here." In J. Seidel & D. Jardine (Eds.), *The ecological heart of teaching: Radical tales of refuge and renewal for classrooms and communities* (pp. 1–6). Peter Lang.

Shepard, P. (1996). *The others: How animals made us human.* Island Press.

Shklovsky, V. (1917/1965) Art as technique. In L Lemon & M. Reis (Trans. and Eds.), *Russian formalist criticism: Four essays* (pp. 3–24). University of Nebraska Press.

Sibley, D.A. (2016). *Sibley birds west.* Alfred K. Knopf.

Smith, D.G. (2006). *Trying to teach in a season of great untruth: Globalization, empire and the crises of pedagogy.* Sense Publishing.

Smith, D.G. (2020a). On being critical about language. In *Confluences: Intercultural journeying in research and teaching: From hermeneutics to a changing world order* (97–104). IAP Press.

Smith, D.G. (2020b). Modernism, hyperliteracy and the colonization of the word. In *Confluences: Intercultural journeying in research and teaching: From hermeneutics to a changing world order* (pp. 147–158). IAP Press.

Smith, D.G. (2020c). Children and the gods of war. In *Confluences: Intercultural journeying in research and teaching: From hermeneutics to a changing world order* (pp. 403–408). IAP Press.

Smith, D.G. (2020d). The hermeneutic imagination and the pedagogic text. In *Confluences: Intercultural journeying in research and teaching: From hermeneutics to a changing world order* (pp. 45–62). IAP Press.

Smith, D.G. (2020e). From Leo Strauss to collapse theory: Considering the neoconservative attack on modernity and the work of education. In *Confluences: Intercultural journeying in research and teaching: From hermeneutics to a changing world order* (pp. 221–238). IAP Press.

Smith, D.G. (2020f). Can wisdom trump the market as a basis for education? In *Confluences: Intercultural journeying in research and teaching: From hermeneutics to a changing world order* (pp. 369–390). IAP Press.

Smith, D.G. (2020g). The deep politics of war and the curriculum of disillusion. In *Confluences: Intercultural journeying in research and teaching. From hermeneutics to a changing world order* (pp. 275–291). Information Age Publishing.

Smith, D.G. (2020h). Experience and interpretation in global times: The case of special education. In *Confluences: Intercultural journeying in research and teaching: From hermeneutics to a changing world order* (pp. 79–88). IAP Press.

Smith, D.G. (2020i). Brighter than a thousand suns: Facing pedagogy in the nuclear shadow. In *Confluences: Intercultural journeying in research and teaching: From hermeneutics to a changing world order* (pp. 107–116). IAP Press.

Smith, D.G. (2020j). The farthest West is but the Farthest East. In *Confluences: Intercultural journeying in research and teaching: From hermeneutics to a changing world order* (pp. 311–337). IAP Press.

Smith, D.G. (2020k). The specific challenges of "globalization" for teaching and *vice versa*. In *Confluences: Intercultural journeying in research and teaching: From hermeneutics to a changing world order* (pp. 189–212). IAP Press.

Smith, D.G. (2020l). The problem for the South is the North (but the problem for the North is the North) In *Confluences: Intercultural journeying in research and teaching: From hermeneutics to a changing world order* (pp. 181–188). IAP Press.

Smith, D. (2023, March 5). *I am your retribution*. https://www.theguardian.com/us-news/2023/mar/05/i-am-your-retribution-trump- rules- supreme-at-cpac-as-he-relaunches-bid-for-white-house

Stevens, S. (2015). Death with dignity. From the CD *Carrie and Lowell*. Asthmatic Kitty Records. Catalog: AKR099. Release date: March 31, 2015.

Snyder, G. (1974). *Turtle island*. New Directions Books.

Snyder, G. (1979). Poetry, community and climax. *Field, 20*.

Snyder, G. (1980). *The real work: Interviews and talks*. New Directions Books.

Snyder, G. (2003). The place, the region and the commons. In *The practice of the wild* (pp. 27–51). Counterpoint Books.

Sopa, L. (2004). *Steps on the path to enlightenment: A commentary on Tsongskhapa's Lamrim Chenmo. Volume 1: The foundational practices*. Wisdom Books.

Springer Publishing Company. (2013, October 4). *Disenfranchised grief: Dr. Ken Doka* [Video file]. http://www.youtube.com/watch?v=BhfxzY65SmI

Stephenson, N. (2008). *Anathem*. Harper Collins.

Sumedho, A. (2010). *Don't take your life personally*. Buddhist Publishing Group.

Suzuki, S. (1986). *Zen Mind, Beginner's Mind*. Weatherhill.

Tait, L. (2016). Successful Assimilation. In J. Seidel & D. Jardine (Eds.), *The ecological heart of teaching: Radical tales of refuge and renewal for classrooms and communities* (p. 17–18). New York, NY: Peter Lang.

Taylor, F.W. (1903). *Shop management [Excerpts]* (1903). http://www.marxists.org/refere nce/subject/economics/taylor/shop- management/abstract.htm

Taylor, F.W. (1911). *Scientific management, comprising shop management, the principles of scientific management and testimony before the special house committee.* Harper & Row.

The Guardian. (n.d.). *Notes and queries.* https://www.theguardian.com/notesandquer ies/query/0,,-1324,00.html

Thomas, D. (1971). *The poems of Dylan Thomas.* New Directions Books.

Thompson, G. (2018, December). Book review of Leonard Cohen's (2018). *The flame Uncut Magazine* (p. 107). Take 259.

Thrangu, K. (2011). *Vivid awareness: The mind instructions of Khenpo Gangshar.* Shambala.

The Canadian Press. (2013). *Why are B.C.'s Orcas falling silent?* Posted October 24, 2013. http://www.theprovince.com/travel/Orca+pods+longer+vocalizing+Vancou ver+Aquarium+researcher+finds/9078918/story.html

Toffler, A. (1984). *Future shock.* Bantam re-issue.

Trump, D. (2016). Cited in RealClear Politics (2016). *I could stand in the middle of Fifth Avenue and shoot somebody, and I wouldn't lose any voters.* Posted January 23, 2016. https://www.realclearpolitics.com/video/2016/01/23/trump_i_could_stand_in_ the_middle_of_fifth_avenue_and_shoot_somebody_and_i_wouldnt_lose_any _voters.html

Trump, D. (2018). *Donald Trump: "What you're seeing and what you're reading is not what's happening."* BBC News Online. https://www.bbc.com/news/av/world-us-canada-44959340

Trungpa, C. (2003). The myth of freedom and the way of meditation. In *The collected works of Chogyam Trungpa* (Vol. 3). Shambala Press.

Tsong-Kha-Pa. (2000). *The great treatise on the stages of the path to enlightenment (Lam rim chen mo)* (Vol. 1). Snow Lion Publications.

Tsong-Kha-Pa. (2002). *The great treatise on the stages of the path to enlightenment (Lam rim chen mo)* (Vol. 3). Snow Lion Publications.

Tsong-Kha-Pa. (2004). *The great treatise on the stages of the path to enlightenment (Lam rim chen mo)* (Vol. 2). Snow Lion Publications.

Tsong-kha-pa. (2005). *The six yogas of Naropa.* Snow Lion.

Usher, R., & Edwards, R. (1994). *Postmodernism and education.* Routledge.

Victoria, B.D. (2006). *Zen at war.* Rowman & Littlefield.

Wallace, B. (1987). *The stubborn particulars of grace.* McClelland and Stewart.

Wallace, D.F. (1996). *Infinite jest.* Back Bay Books. Little, Frown and Company.

Wallace, D.F., with Lipsky, D. (2010). *Although of course you end up becoming yourself.* Broadway Books.

Watts, S. (2006). *The peoples' tycoon: Henry Ford and the American century.* Vintage Books.

Wiebe, R., & Johnson, Y. (1999). *Stolen life: The journey of a Cree woman.* Vintage Canada.

Wittgenstein, L. (1968). *Philosophical investigations.* Cambridge University Press.

Wrege, C.D., & Greenwood, R. (1991). *Frederick W. Taylor: The father of scientific manage- ment: Myth and reality.* Irwin Professional Publishing. Currently out of print.

Yates, F. (1974). *The art of memory*. University of Chicago Press.

Zhang, C. (2023). Review of *The Record* by Boygenius. Label: Interscope. Reviewed, March 31, 2023. *Pitchfork*. Online: https://pitchfork.com/reviews/albums/boygenius-the-record/?bxid=5d7fe8683f92a4110124fca1&cndid=61761014&esrc=&hasha=f2804 8131028e1415b177a578178074e&hashb=1d0e656aeed136a5911ee1bfc1757cf3e2e29 e5b&hashc=4da813b303bb3762e88784a12a64ed234ab47570ef6a83296a8db7e0d c3a19a8&utm_brand=p4k&utm_mailing=P4K_NewMusic_033123

OMPLICATED

A BOOK SERIES OF CURRICULUM STUDIES

Reframing the curricular challenge educators face after a decade of school deform, the books published in Peter Lang's Complicated Conversation Series testify to the ethical demands of our time, our place, our profession. What does it mean for us to teach now, in an era structured by political polarization, economic destabilization, and the prospect of climate catastrophe? Each of the books in the Complicated Conversation Series provides provocative paths, theoretical and practical, to a very different future. In this resounding series of scholarly and pedagogical interventions into the nightmare that is the present, we hear once again the sound of silence breaking, supporting us to rearticulate our pedagogical convictions in this time of terrorism, reframing curriculum as committed to the complicated conversation that is intercultural communication, self-understanding, and global justice.

The series editor is

> Dr. William F. Pinar
> Department of Curriculum Studies
> 2125 Main Mall
> Faculty of Education
> University of British Columbia
> Vancouver, British Columbia V6T 1Z4
> CANADA

To order other books in this series, please contact our Customer Service Department:

> peterlang@presswarehouse.com (within the U.S.)
> orders@peterlang.com (outside the U.S.)

Or browse online by series:

> www.peterlang.com